W9-BZC-028

DEFIANT COURAGE:

Norway's Longest WWII Escape

A True Story

Astrid Karlsen Scott and Dr. Tore Haug

Nordic Spirit Productions, Inc.
Olympia, Washington

Published by:
Nordic Spirit Productions, Inc.
P.O. Box 11043
Olympia, WA 98508-1043
1-800-618-0013
E-mail: nordicspirit@olywa.net

Copyright © 2000 Astrid Karlsen Scott and Dr. Tore Haug.
All rights reserved.

No portion of this book may be reproduced or used in any form, or by any
means, without prior written permission from the publisher.

First printing October 2000
Second printing September 2001

10 9 8 7 6 5 4 3

Printed in the United States of America

Scott, Astrid Karlsen and Haug, Dr. Tore
Defiant Courage: Norway's Longest WWII Escape
Includes bibliographical references.
ISBN 0-9634339-8-9

Disclaimer:
This book is intended to be an historical account of Jan Baalsrud's escape
from the Gestapo, and of the courage of the people who helped him.

The authors and Nordic Spirit Productions, Inc. have made every effort to ensure
that this book is as complete and factual as possible, and have neither
responsibility nor liability to any person or entity with respect to any loss or
damage caused, or alleged to be caused, directly or indirectly by the information
in this book. Any person not wishing to be bound by the above may return this
book to the publisher for a full refund.

Printed in the United States of America by:
Publishers Press
P.O. Box 27408
Salt Lake City, UT 84127-0408
1-800-456-6600

WITH LOVE
TO OUR FAMILIES:

Melvin McCabe Scott, Jr.
Susan, Eric, John
and their families

Wenche Haug
Carolin

CONTENTS

ACKNOWLEDGMENTS

The material in this book has been gathered from the following sources:

Jan Baalsrud's benefactors and the many others who were directly drawn into the happenings in 1943 reconstructed the dramatic events in minute detail.

Historians, authors and journalists shared with us their well-researched knowledge.

Jan Baalsrud's own report, written accounts from benefactors now deceased, and documents from the German war archives aided our search for the truth.

Nils Ivar Baalsrud, Jan Baalsrud's brother, lifelong friend and confidant, helped us understand Jan better. As a leader of the Jan Baalsrud Foundation for many years, Nils generously shared the information gathered by the foundation.

We also express our sincere gratitude to the following sources:

Karlsøy *kommune* and the International Sons of Norway for their grants in support of this work.

Christine Hansen, our editor. Your eye for accuracy and detail brought clarity to our words and your love for the people in this story helped to create a book which is a pleasure to read. Your dedication of long hours to meet the deadline is gratefully acknowledged.

Jan-Barman Jensen, District Manager for Braathen Airlines in Troms, we appreciate your generosity in obtaining complimentary flights to help us with our research.

Erland Rian, *Destination Tromsø,* we gratefully acknowledge your help with accommodations and transportation. Your interest in our work in its beginning stages was an inspiration.

Thank you, Holger Raste, reporter and authority on the Baalsrud story, for taking us in hand and guiding us in many of Jan's footsteps. You generously shared your innumerable articles about Jan Baalsrud and his benefactors with us; your information is liberally sprinkled throughout this book.

Author and research-historian Kjell Fjørtoft, we are grateful that you met with us repeatedly and answered our many questions. Your research and early articles on the Baalsrud story are responsible for much of the information included in the chapter, "The Fate of the Brattholm Men," as well as other information in the book.

Ragnar Ulstein, historian and author, many thanks for your time spent with us and wisdom shared.

Torleif Lyngstad, historian, you were a major contributor in helping us to understand the happenings regarding the Baalsrud affair in and around Kåfjord. Thank you for the hours spent with us.

Tore Hauge, author of *"De brente våre hjem,"* thank you for your interest and help.

Edvin Wikan, Tromsø policeman, thank you for sharing your personal knowledge and pictures.

Our appreciation goes to the Idrupsen family, our steady guides who recounted in detail the evidence of the dreadful day, March 30, 1943. Our thanks to Dagmar, Olaug (Idrupsen) Hågensen, Halvor and Idrup Idrupsen.

Peder Nilsen, your modest and tender spirit made the events at Løvli and Tyttebærvika and your involvement come alive for us.

Alvin Larsen, in 1943, you helped carry a wounded soldier up the Revdal mountains on a sled. Since 1995, you helped "carry" the story, as our enthusiastic confidant and guide from Furuflaten. We thank you for the countless hours of your time spent guiding us through Furuflaten.

Asbjørn Dalhaug, your unending enthusiasm for Jan Baalsrud and his benefactors helped us clear up details we had struggled with, and guided us into Lyngsdalen where Jan suffered the avalanche.

Peder Isaksen, your methodical description has helped to reveal the efforts the Manndalen people made to rescue Jan. You introduced us to the courage of the Manndalen people, and for that we are grateful. We have enjoyed many an hour in your home, sitting around a groaning table of delicacies prepared by your loving wife, Eliva.

We thank you, cousins Arvid and Viggo Heika from Kopparelv, who played in the snow as Jan peeked around your century-old farm building. You described for us Jan's visit to Kopparelv, an event discussed many times in your families.

At 92, Signe Hansen, you still remember the day Jan came over the mountains to your home in Karanes, as clearly as if it was yesterday, and his handsome smile. We appreciate your help.

Pete Taylor, many thanks for the innumerable hours you freely gave to this project.

Leif Erik Iversen, we are deeply indebted to you for your many pictures and for your help, chauffeuring, and guiding, for opening your home to us on several occasions, and for going the many extra miles.

Arvid Grønnslett, we thank you for unnumbered hours spent on our behalf and we are grateful for your guidance during the Baalsrud mountain-touring.

Annika Gustafson, your delicious meals and comfortable accommodations eased the physical strain of intense research.

Thorleif Henriksen, your deep interest and help with this project is greatly appreciated.

Else Aas, dear friend, thank you for your continual support of every project promoting Norway.

Jack Fjeldstad, we appreciate your generosity. Your friendship with Jan and your portrayal of him in the movie, *"Ni Liv,"* gave you insight into Jan's character, which you shared with us.

Jaye Compton, we thank you for the many long hours spent on a tight deadline to complete the final typesetting and prepare this manuscript for printing.

Thank you to all of you, too many to mention, who have for years sustained us with your faith and interest in this project, and for your willingness to help where needed.

We are profoundly thankful for our mates, Wenche Haug and Melvin Scott, Jr.; as you both know, this book would not exist had it not been for your support, encouragement and patience during the years we spent researching and writing.

We sincerely thank all of you as we share this piece of Norwegian history. Our lives have been enriched as we have been inspired by the courage and selflessness of Jan and his benefactors.

Tusen takk,
Astrid Karlsen Scott & Tore Haug

ịntroduction

We traveled to the Troms District in northern Norway to walk in Jan Baalsrud's footsteps and to meet with his benefactors who helped him escape from the Gestapo in the spring of 1943. We were educated! And we discovered that what we knew from earlier times about Jan's escape and those who helped him was much deficient, often inaccurate, and frequently fictitious.

Peder Isaksen, one of Jan's benefactors from Manndalen, expressed his feelings to the newspaper *Tromsø* in 1987. He said he had a deep wish that one day a book would come out that would tell the truth about what had happened in Manndalen in 1943 with regard to the Baalsrud affair. Peder continues, "Little or nothing has been told of what happened here, (in Manndalen) and what has been told is wrong. I am especially indignant over how badly the Samis have been portrayed."

We, the authors, have been received with the greatest kindness, and were given preferential treatment by all we associated with in the Troms District. Jan's benefactors from 1943, together with others who were indirectly involved and were drawn into the Baalsrud happenings, have reconstructed, explained, drawn maps and shared the dramatic details of those dangerous days in minute detail to us. Historians and reporters have generously shared their records and their knowledge.

Our research includes Jan Baalsrud's own report, documents from German war archives, reports, letters, interviews, and, from Jan's benefactors who have passed on, accounts which were previously unknown. All these things have helped us to put the facts in their proper places and given us a profound understanding of what took place.

It has taken five years and many trips to the Troms District to gather all the data. We hired a helicopter to fly us into the inaccessible areas (for most of us in the winter) of the Arctic Mountains where Jan trudged alone, wounded and hunted in freezing, stormy weather. We hired motorboats and crews to track down information and to understand the distances involved. And we hiked many a mile, visiting the Baalsrud cave in Skaidijonni and the Gentleman stone in the Revdal Mountains, and into Lyngsdalen where Jan was caught in the avalanche. We climbed precipitous mountains in our attempt to understand every fraction of this story. What you will read in this book will be new to many of you, but nothing is dramatized or fictitious. The story is filled with its own drama - it does not need any embellishments. All the details included are as we learned of them from the participants. Every boulder and small islet has been searched out, described and can be found on the maps we have included. Cross-checking of our sources, weather reports from the actual days in 1943 and the helpers' explanations have untied many a knot.

Even after all this, we struggled with some of the major happenings for five years. The reason is that the sources did not agree. Then, as we neared the end of our journey, small details led us in the right direction. Suddenly the puzzle pieces fit. Important, unexplained riddles were finally revealed to us.

The events of this story are all true; however, in the chapter "A Tragic Decision," we changed identifying names and relationships of people involved with the merchant in Bromnes so as not to bring unhappiness to their families.

Much of the dialogue presented in this book is actual conversation as recalled by the participants. Other conversation is based on the recollections of people still living. Where dialogue had to be re-created, we held fast to the facts.

Our foremost motive has been to honor not only Jan's courage, and that of the men of *Brattholm*, but also that of his selfless helpers, and to give an accurate and complete account of the whole Baalsrud affair. We believe we have accomplished this by searching out the many helpers who had never been mentioned before, either in books or films. Many of his helpers have passed on without being honored for their contributions. For them, our efforts are too late, but their self-sacrifice, toil and bold courage will continue to shine brightly for all of us.

The women's and the Samis' offerings have also been close to our hearts. The Baalsrud story would not be complete without mentioning the Sami brothers' contribution; Nils and Per Siri and Aslak and Per Thomas Baal are given a central place. The same goes for Hjalmar Steinnes and John Olav Ballovarre from Kåfjord and the brothers Leif and Rolf Bjørn in Birtavärre.

Jan's 11 friends from *M/K Brattholm* suffered a fate seldom brought to the forefront. We have written about their torment in our book, and though the horror of it might not suit itself to print, we have included it. By showing a glimpse of what they suffered for Norway, we hope to honor them.

When we first started to collect the background material for this book, we had no idea what a task we faced. It would have been an impossible undertaking without the willingness of all we approached. In our efforts to get to the truth, our innumerable questions, phone calls, letters and frequent interviews with many were always received with the greatest of courtesy and openness. Because of the help given us, the story of Jan Baalsrud and his benefactors will be an inspiration of selflessness and courage for many years to come. Our deepest thanks.

Astrid Karlsen Scott   Dr. Tore Haug
Olympia, Washington   Jessheim, Norway

German soldiers march down Karl Johan's gate,
Oslo's main street.

German attack against Norway last night. Norway at war with Germany.

Frightening newspaper headlines tell of the German invasion on Norway, April 9, 1940.

Reichskommissar Terboven and
Minister President Quisling arrive at Akershus Castle.

At Anchor in Scalloway

March 22, 1943: "Well men, we are on our way home at last." Sigurd Eskeland, a tall slender man, broke the silence while with his fingers he made a small clearing on the train compartment's fogged up window.

"*Jaja,* and this time we are not leaving before we drive the devils out!" another chimed in. "If the Germans only knew what we have in store for them!" Jan Baalsrud flashed his handsome smile and with blue-gray eyes blazing, drew a finger across his throat.

"*Ja,* think about it. Our efforts might bring the war to a standstill in the north. That thought excites me!" The third man, Per Blindheim, straightened up and leaned toward his comrades. "Believe me – I'm eager to play a small part in liberating Norway."

The Norwegians returned to silence, each absorbed in his own thoughts, unaware of the train's rocking motion. The train sped from London through Scotland's lower Grampian Mountains en route to Aberdeen. Strong winds from the Atlantic Ocean brought dark clouds sloshing heavy rains against the windows, blurring their view of the Scottish Highlands.

The men were returning from a furlough in London. They had been selected for an extremely dangerous and top secret commando operation in northern Norway, in the Troms District. Though many military men felt this particular mission was suicidal, the saboteurs were anxious to be on their way.

March 23, 1943: A small fishing vessel took the Norwegians from Aberdeen to Scalloway in the Shetland Islands, a cluster of small islands off the northern tip of the Scottish coast, 210 miles west of southern Norway.

During World War II, the Norwegian Resistance used the Shetland Islands as a base. They ferried refugees from Norway to Shetland in small fishing vessels and returned with supplies and trained resistance fighters.

Scalloway Harbor where <u>Brattholm</u> *lay anchored.*

Several boats bobbed at the quay in Scalloway including a 62-foot Norwegian fishing cutter, *M/K Brattholm*. The Norwegians spent the final day preparing for their upcoming journey, double-checking the ammunition, explosives and the other provisions and loading them into *Brattholm*'s hull. In the early evening they were joined by the team's fourth saboteur, radiotelegrapher Gabriel Salvesen, who arrived by plane from London.

March 24, 1943: Evening shadows veiled *Brattholm* as she set forth from the quay heading for occupied Norway. Aboard, in addition to the four saboteurs and the seven-man crew, was Erik Reichelt, a man of vital importance to the operation codenamed *Martin*.

In the fall of 1942, Erik Reichelt had been sent as a courier to the Troms District by Consul Nielsen, chief of the S.O.E. branch at the British legation in Stockholm. Reichelt's assignment was to find men loyal to Norway and to get to know them and the Troms District. Reichelt was also to track down patriots willing to help saboteurs who would arrive later by boat. Reichelt had familiarized himself with the district and had come to know the resistance leaders in the area. The plan was that he would return to the Shetland Islands with the crew after he helped the saboteurs get established, and in contact with the incorruptible men in the Northland.

Brattholm's route across the north Atlantic, one of the most treacherous waterways in the world, was toward Senja, a large island 35 miles due south of the city of Tromsø, in northern Norway.

Brattholm, on her first voyage across the Atlantic, had left Norwegian waters under daring circumstances; her return passage, unquestionably, would be even more dramatic. A first-rate boat, she was heavily armed and well supplied with the best navigation equipment for crossing the high seas. Her beam was 18 feet, four inches wide and she had a nine-foot draw. A two-cylinder 60 horsepower Wichman motor enabled *Brattholm* to cruise at seven to eight knots.

Brattholm's skipper Sverre Odd Kvernhellen was much admired by the crew. Years of operating vessels in the Norwegian Sea and several Atlantic crossings had made Kvernhellen an exceptional navigator.

Machine guns hid in large fishing barrels on *Brattholm's* deck, a camouflage to prove they were peaceful fishermen should they be approached by the enemy. Eight tons of dynamite, explosives, a hand radio transmitter, survival kits and other provisions filled *Brattholm's* hull. All were necessary requirements for survival in the Arctic and had been carefully planned and chosen. She rode heavy in the water.

"If there is anyone who still wonders why this war is being fought – let him look to Norway.

If there is anyone who has any delusions that this war could have been averted – let him look to Norway.

And, if there is anyone who doubts of the democratic will to win, again I say, let him look to Norway."

**— Franklin D. Roosevelt, President
of the United States of America,
September 16, 1942**

M/K BRATTHOLM

September 3, 1940: Leonard Larsen and his grandfather were enjoying a balmy Saturday evening on their Remøy Island farm when a man appeared. The stranger carried an unusual phonograph, and, without a word of explanation, started it up, but no sound emerged. In a heavy German accent, the man asked Leonard many questions. Leonard realized the conversation was being recorded and he became wary.

For the past several months, Leonard and his friend Alfred Remøy had worked for the Norwegian underground. The two young men and their friends Fritjof Remøy, John Remøy, Julius Remøy, Johan Remøy,

M/K Brattholm docked in Ålesund, Norway.

and Lars Sævik, had helped many refugees escape occupied Norway across the Atlantic. All young bachelors, the men helped English and French soldiers as well as Norwegians.

After the stranger left, Leonard sought out Alfred Remøy and some of the other men who had helped the refugees. The mysterious man had been busy with his phonograph all across Remøy Island and the young men realized their peril.

"We must get away from Norway," Alfred urged. "If there is no room for us on any other fishing vessels, I will steal *Brattholm*." Alfred shared ownership of *M/K Brattholm* with two brothers, Petter and Arthur Sævik.

"It's pretty risky to take the vessel across the Atlantic," worried Leonard. "And it will be quite a blow to Petter and Arthur."

"*Ja*, but our lives are at stake," Alfred said. "This is war! If you men want to come along, we sail!"

The young men decided to make their escape while they could. A few nights later, as the dark autumn night blanketed the Norwegian coast and fear of the Nazis haunted every dwelling, *M/K Brattholm* lay moored near the Sæviks' home.

Taking care to muffle the sound of their oars, the seven resistance workers rowed a small boat toward *M/K Brattholm*. They had thoroughly planned their escape, but their nerves grew taut when the rowboat gently bumped up against *Brattholm*. In tense silence they attached a hawser to the fishing vessel and loosened the moorings.

They pulled the cutter 150 meters across the inlet to Skotholmen Islet.

The two strongest men pulled on each set of oars with all their might to get the 72-foot *Brattholm* to slide along the pier.

Oil was stored in barrels and tanks on Skotholmen. The young men broke into one of the tanks and filled *Brattholm's* bunker with fuel and lifted additional oil barrels onto *Brattholm's* deck.

Another small dinghy, this one with an outboard motor, came forth from the darkness. A friend had agreed to tow *Brattholm* further out to sea. When the men felt sure that *Brattholm* could not be heard from the shore, they started her engine. By 5 a.m., the cutter was on the open sea.

A few hours later, Petter and Arthur Sævik were shaken when they discovered *Brattholm* missing.

"Arthur, *Brattholm* is gone!" Petter shrieked, looking through the window. "Call the police! The thieves can't have gone far. Have the police hunt them down!"

The woman who received the incoming call at the telephone exchange was an aunt of one of the young men aboard *Brattholm*.

"Unfortunately, there is no answer at the police station. I tried several times, but they must be out on a call. Please try later."

The aunt owned a small grocery store and she had helped the runaways with food for their voyage. She knew who had stolen the Sæviks' boat and she was determined to give them as long a head start as possible.

Furious, the Sævik brothers called back later, and finally reached the police. But *Brattholm* was now far out to sea, heading north. While planning the getaway, the young men expected that the theft would be reported immediately and they decided to set a course straight north, and later, northwest toward Iceland. That decision spared their discovery by German patrol planes sent out once the hijacking had been reported. The Germans assumed the runaways were heading west for the Shetland Islands, the destination point for most boats escaping from Norway.

The men aboard *Brattholm* heard the planes, but the thick Atlantic fog cloaked them in safety. The weather worsened with a heavy wind and high seas. The men moved the heavy oil barrels below deck to stop their constant rolling and to stabilize the vessel. *Brattholm* struggled against the storm. A beam tore loose and slammed into Fritjof's back. He was badly hurt and the men considered turning back to get him to a doctor, but Fritjof refused and they continued ahead.

The men's and *Brattholm's* relentless struggle ended when they reached Rejkjavik, Iceland's capital, five days later. They were welcomed by both Norwegian and English authorities, who had received advance notice of their arrival. The young men had planned to earn a living by fishing while in Iceland, but instead the boat was taken over by Nortraship and rented out to the British Navy Sea Transport. On November 18, the resistance workers were ordered to sail to Seydesfjord, on Iceland's east coast. For two years, the cutter carried English troops and supplies to and from the outposts in the Icelandic fjords.

In November 1942, *Brattholm* was recalled to Reykjavik. She and her crew were ordered to the Shetland Islands. Two armed whaleboats escorted them to Lerwich, in the Shetland Islands, without mishap. *Brattholm* was put into secret service between the Shetland Islands and Norway against the Germans. The seven Norwegian underground workers were sent on to London where some ended up in the Norwegian Merchant Marine and others in the Navy.

the convoys

February 2, 1942: A gruesome battle over Stalingrad in the Soviet Union took place between the Germans and the Russians. Germany lost the battle against the Russians but not before leaving the city in ashes. It would have been an impossible victory for the Soviet Union without the huge weapon supplies delivered from the United States and England.

When Denmark was attacked and invaded by the German Army in 1940, England occupied Iceland with the consensus of her people. Iceland was strategically located in the North Atlantic.

Convoys to the Soviet Union with war materials and other provisions were sent from the West via Iceland, the shortest and the safest route at the time. They sailed through the Arctic Ocean a few hundred nautical miles above the North Cape, the northern tip of Norway, and on to Murmansk and Archangel in the Soviet Union.

The plan worked well, with most ships bearing the desperately needed materials reaching their destination. The convoys only lost one ship, but after the first few months, the situation changed drastically.

Arctic pack ice forced the convoys within 300 nautical miles of the Norwegian coast.

To pinpoint the convoys' position, German reconnaissance planes were sent out from Bardufoss Airport in the Troms District, as well as seaplanes from Skatøyra seaplane-harbor close to the city of Tromsø, in the same district.

As summer had returned and the midnight sun did not set, it was easy for the German pilots to detect the convoys. The information from these sorties was forwarded to the German High Command.

Convoys were sent from the west via Iceland with war-materials. They sailed to Murmansk and Archangel in the Soviet Union through the Arctic Ocean above the northern tip of Norway.

June 27, 1942: Convoy P.Q.17 left Iceland for Archangel with 34 ships. German spy planes spotted them, and soon the German bombers and U-boats were on their way. They sank 23 ships and several hundred men went down.

Due to the terrible loss of lives and ships, the convoys were briefly halted. This caused large weapon supplies to accumulate in the West. In this serious situation the Allies had to find a way to stop German planes from flying out of northern Norway.

Early in the War, England had established an organization, Special Operations Executive (S.O.E.). Its purpose was to organize secret operations in countries occupied by the Germans. The Norwegian branch of the S.O.E. and the British had, for some time, planned sabotage activities against the German reconnaissance operations originating from the northern Norwegian airports. The military strategists felt these efforts, along with Russian participation in the defense of the convoys and strengthening Allied escorts, would make it reasonably safe for the convoys to resume.

The four saboteurs' assigned work placed them at the heart of the war. The importance of the men's success was beyond measure. A successful outcome of their actions could possibly shorten the war - though their lives were at risk.

Their most daring assignments, and crucial to the mission's success, was to detonate the air tower at Bardufoss Airport located 50 miles southeast of the city of Tromsø and to sink the seaplanes at the seaplane harbor in Tromsø. Jan Baalsrud, an expert swimmer, was charged with the perilous responsibility of affixing the explosives to the seaplanes' pontoons beneath the water.

The expedition leaders in England had high hopes for, and much confidence in, the operation planned so carefully in top secret meetings.

Martin Linge

the Linge company

When Hitler's war machine brutally attacked Norway on April 9, 1940, in reality, the battle was over within two months. But not everyone gave up. Many Norwegian youths wished to continue the fight; they had not capitulated morally. They wanted another chance against their powerful enemy. An inner moral strength, idealism, eagerness to fight and a deep love and patriotism for their country kept them going and were the motives behind their optimism.

After a while, many a Norwegian youth had to escape from Norway, and some were able to work their way over to England.

There they contacted the Norwegian division of S.O.E., where they received a short period of training before they were sent back to Norway on secret missions as early as the summer of 1940.

One man, Captain Martin Linge, participated in the battle at Åndalsnes. He was wounded, and came to England in September 1940. This idealistic man refused to give up the fight for Norway until she was liberated. He realized that the Germans were vulnerable, and that they could be thwarted as long as the right method was chosen.

He understood that specially trained Norwegian commando soldiers, who knew the Norwegian nature, climate, geography and the Norwegian temperament, could cause havoc for the enemy. Soon, Martin Linge was given the responsibility for representing the Norwegian Government in S.O.E. An office was established in London, and from there, Norwegian fugitives who arrived in London were recruited for these well-planned assignments. Linge personally selected the men.

In March of 1941, British forces together with Norwegian soldiers from England carried out a raid against Svolvær in Stamsund in the Lofoten Islands in northern Norway. Linge led the Norwegian soldiers. The raid was successful; they did not lose one man.

Because of the success, they made the decision to further develop a Norwegian military company, about 200 men. In the end, the whole company was transferred to the Scottish Highlands, a place which was chosen with great care. The terrain was excellent for the type of training necessary for commando soldiers. The group was divided between three buildings, Glenmore Lodge, Forest Lodge and Drumintoul Lodge. Company Linge was given their own division within the Norwegian High Command in July 1941.

Company Linge participated in two separate raids against occupied Norway during Christmas of 1941, one raid against Reine in Lofoten and the other against Måløy. Again Captain Linge led the Norwegian forces. The Germans fought bravely, but in the end had to fall back. Captain Linge ran in front leading his men, and he reached his goal, but was felled by a bullet.

The Company had lost a great leader, and it was a heavy loss. But new leaders took over, and the assignments never stopped. That same year, plans were laid for sabotage work to begin along the Norwegian coast to be carried out by the Linge men.

fEARLESS mEN

The four saboteurs were members of the Linge Company, a group of selected Norwegian men who were part of the Special Operations Executive, S.O.E., and who received sabotage training in Scotland. They all lived for the opportunity to return to Norway to fight the Germans.

The Linge men were chosen for the special sabotage services because of their abilities. They were men from all walks of life, farmers and office workers, students and fishermen. For some, it was their first contact with the military. Others were veterans from the Winter War in Finland and in Norway.

Lieutenant Sigurd Eskeland was chosen as the *Brattholm* expedition's leader. Sigurd's slender build masked his physical strength. His wisdom and maturity qualified him for the job. He was 41 years old, born in Gjerstad by Risør in southern Norway.

Though several years senior to most of the men in Company Linge, Sigurd participated in the same training as the younger men without showing any sign of fatigue or lack of will.

Lt. Sigurd Eskeland

Aboard *Brattholm* he was the only man who knew the whole story and all the demanding tasks assigned the saboteurs once they reached Norway.

As a young man, he'd served for a time as a postal official in northern Norway. While there, he made many friends among the stalwart Norwegians in the Troms District and had become familiar with the city of Tromsø and the geography of the surrounding islands.

Later, Sigurd immigrated to Argentina where he became a successful mink farmer. Not long after he had established a comfortable future in Argentina, Germany attacked Norway. The news of the April 9, 1940 attack caused him great anguish. He left the comforts of his

home and set out for Europe, arriving in England in May of 1941.

Second in command was 25-year-old Second Lieutenant Jan Baalsrud. He grew up in the city-center of Oslo, Norway's capital. Jan attended ILA School. When he was sixteen years old, his mother perished in a car accident. The oldest of three siblings, Jan shared with his father the responsibility for taking care of his 12-year-old brother, Nils Ivar, and his eight-year-old sister, Bitten, fell to him.

2nd Lt. Jan Baalsrud

Jan enjoyed sports - soccer was his favorite. He was a rough-and-ready guy with a tender heart and a high tolerance for pain.

Coal-black hair and dark brows framed Jan's resolute blue-gray eyes. Strikingly good-looking with an athletic build, he was 182 cm tall. In 1938, following a stint in the military, he traveled to Hannover, Germany where he studied cartography at Wetzlar. In 1939, he received his certificate for apprenticeship as a land surveyor and instrument maker.

Two days before the Germans invaded Norway, Jan returned home from Junior Officer School in Fredrikstad. On April 9, he reported for service in the Norwegian Army. Later he saw combat at Østfold, south of Oslo near the Swedish border. His unit put up a gallant fight, but the Germans outmaneuvered and outnumbered them with their superior strength and war materials. Soon the Norwegians were surrounded.

Jan escaped to Sweden. Here, almost chaotic conditions existed because of the great influx of escapees coming across the borders. He was interned in Gothenberg; however, his former commander came to his defense and within three weeks he was freed.

The Swedes wanted to make use of his talent as an instrument maker, but Jan wanted to use his energies to help Norway. The Norwegian Embassy in Stockholm advised him to contact the British Embassy, who recruited him as a secret agent. In that capacity he made three trips to Norway from Sweden. During the hours of darkness Jan slipped across the border, and hid during the days. When able, he visited Gardemoen Airport and made rough drawings of the German fortifications and their ongoing construction, which he forwarded to England.

On Jan's third return trip to Sweden, the Swedish police arrested him. Tried in a Stockholm court, Jan was charged with espionage for a foreign country against a foreign country, and received a six-month jail term. After three months he was transferred to Varmland where his cellmate was the son of a ship owner. While in prison, his cellmate learned he had inherited a great deal of money from an aunt. The prison officials' attitudes changed toward the rich ship owner and his friend, and soon they were set free. They were ordered out of Sweden – a difficult situation for Jan, who was condemned to die by the Germans in Norway, and now had but two weeks to leave Sweden.

A few years earlier Madam Kollantay, a close friend of Stalin, had served as the Russian Ambassador to Norway. While serving in that position, she had become a warm friend of the Norwegian people. Presently she was the Russian Ambassador to Sweden, and she learned of Jan Baalsrud's plight. She arranged a visa for him enabling him to travel to Leningrad in the Soviet Union and continue on to Odessa on the Black Sea.

From Odessa, Jan traveled via Turkey on to Bombay, India. During his two-month stay in Bombay he met another Norwegian fugitive, Per Blindheim, and the two young men developed a deep friendship.

They traveled on to Aden, Mozambique, Durban, Cape Town, Brazil, Trinidad, the USA and Canada, and eventually London. In the spring of 1942, their six-month long journey ended when they arrived in Scotland and joined the Linge Company.

Sergeant Per Revold Blindheim came from Ålesund, and was the same age as Jan. Per was the son of a master baker who owned a bakery located at Kirkegaten 8 in Ålesund, and he learned much of the trade from his father. Per finished middle school and business school and then followed in his father's footsteps, training as a baker.

When the Soviet Union launched an unprovoked attack on Finland on November 30, 1939, Per was angered at the injustice and volunteered to fight with Finland. At the war's end on March 8, 1940 Per returned home. Within weeks, his homeland was at war. He was mobilized into the Norwegian Army and fought at the battles of Romsdalen and Gudbrandsdalen Valleys.

Sgt. Per Blindheim

Subsequent to Norway's capitulation, Per worked in an office in Ålesund, and later in Tromsø. Near the end of 1942 he escaped to Sweden with the hope of reaching England. Like Jan Baalsrud, he traveled nearly the world around to get there.

Per wanted a second chance to fight off the Nazi grip. He was an outdoorsman, and a loyal friend with a happy outlook, strong and yet compassionate. Without hesitation, Per fought for what to him was priceless, Norway's freedom.

The fourth saboteur, Sergeant Gabriel Salvesen, came from Farsund. He was among the many patriotic youths who raged against the Nazi occupation of Norway and had determined to fight against the tyranny. Like

Sgt. Gabriel Salvesen

many other Norwegians, he escaped Norway and sailed across the Atlantic in a fishing vessel. He arrived in England in August 1941.

The following spring he joined the Linge Company.

Salvesen was an experienced seafarer with great technical insight. He excelled in all his training, and became an excellent wireless telegrapher. Within the Linge Company he was highly respected by his leaders and teammates. It came as no surprise when he was one of the four men chosen to participate in the perilous top secret mission to northern Norway. His mastery of wireless telegraphy was vital to the establishment of a radio communication system between occupied northern Norway and England.

Strong of mind and will, the four saboteurs were well trained for their mission, having spent months in England and Scotland preparing for this assignment. They'd learned every weapon skill and military drill known. The men climbed ropes up precipitous mountains and ran for hours through obstacle courses in difficult terrain. When near exhaustion, they swam raging rivers. They learned compass and map reading, and learned to deviate from true north because of the Earth's magnetic field. They studied Morse code and became proficient at receiving long messages by signals and lamps.

Quick to learn about fuses, detonators and explosives, they were given actual assignments to plan and execute, demolishing railways, oil refineries, and large construction sites. As the saboteurs gained confidence, their assignments grew in difficulty.

Highly qualified, with unique talents and strengths, these saboteurs from Company Linge, the Norwegian branch of the British Special Operation Executive (S.O.E.,) were among the best men Norway had to offer in the fight against Hitler.

Upon their arrival in Norway, their first task was to find a safe hiding place ashore for the explosives and the other provisions. The most daring assignment of their mission was to detonate the air tower at the Bardufoss Airport in the district of Troms. In addition they were to destroy German communication lines, disrupt anything they could, and blow up ferries. They were to slow down and halt, if possible, German troop movements. Lastly, they would organize and train small units of Norwegians in all types of sabotage work.

The expedition leaders at the headquarters in London had chosen early spring for this mission to increase the chances of the saboteurs' survival in the Arctic. The North Atlantic was frequently calmer at this time of the year, which made navigation easier for a small boat.

With the four saboteurs aboard *Brattholm* was another man, 25-year-old mate Erik Reichelt, from Kragerø. Erik had important work to perform once they landed in Norway. He was graduated from Middle school and Mate school. In 1941 Erik married Kari Rønning in Tønsberg. They had one child.

Since the beginning of the war, Erik had been heavily involved in intelligence work and in the transport of fugitives in Tønsberg and the Oslo area. He left Norway in 1942 but returned several times on secret missions.

His father, Captain Gerhard Reichelt, lost his life on December 21, 1941 when his ship, *D/S Annovare,* was torpedoed in the Atlantic Ocean. His brother, Borti, was shot in 1944.

CROSSING THE ATLANTIC

March 24, 1943: *Brattholm* made good headway as she left the Shetland Islands heading northeast toward the Norwegian coast. The weather was pleasant and the seas calm. Some five hours after they had left Scalloway, with more than 200 miles to go, the engine acted up. It coughed, muttered, and sputtered until it gave out. The boat floated with the current, rolling and bobbing sideways on the swells. The cook turned green with seasickness from the motion and he retired below deck.

The rest of the men worked feverishly on the motor, their skipper joining in, but to no avail. The hours dragged on. It seemed an impossible task. Every test known was made. They continued work for the better part of the day, drifting helplessly in the North Atlantic. Eight hours after the motor stopped, they found the cause: a small metal piece in the oil conduit had stopped the flow of fuel to the motor. The piece was removed and the motor started easily.

Following the mishap, the motor functioned smoothly. With its steady thumping, and a speed of seven knots, the men sailed on.

The cook stayed below for most of the crossing, unable to attend to his duties. Per took over the cooking. His experience in his father's bakery in Ålesund made the men happy with the change - his cooking was a vast improvement over the food the cook had served.

March 26, 1943: The day dawned with a light cloud-cover and with some blue patches shining through. It looked to be another day with fairly good weather, and it gave the men more time to ensure the equipment was in top condition, to mentally contemplate their training in Scotland and to

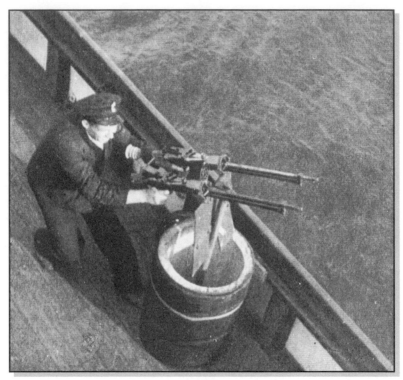

Machine guns were concealed in fishing barrels.

rehearse their challenge ahead. Each man aboard *Brattholm* knew his assignment and was busy throughout the voyage.

Three German planes broke the calm productivity. One, a large four-engine bomber, flew low, heading straight for them.

"Action stations!" shouted captain Kvernhellen.

The men rushed to their positions by the fishing barrels with the concealed machine guns. The bomber circled the vessel a couple of times, and then, to everyone's surprise, turned and disappeared over the horizon. On other days the men spotted two warships. Since they paid *Brattholm* no mind, her crew assumed they were allies.

March 28, 1943: The Norwegians expected to reach their home waters this day. All peered toward the east, but Norway still hid on the horizon. The Germans kept close control of the Norwegian coastline. As *Brattholm* neared the coast, her passengers expected a German patrol to emerge at any moment. The saboteurs had to be prepared for all eventualities; hand grenades were readied and preparations to demolish *Brattholm,* should it be necessary, were taken. Under no circumstances could *Brattholm* be confiscated with all her papers, maps, ammunition and other provisions aboard.

A vague outline of the Norwegian coast came into view in the late afternoon. A deeply personal experience for these young men, the sight of their homeland brought a shine to their eyes. A cry went up, *"Alt for Norge,"* All for Norway!

"We're home at last!"

"Jaja, we'll give what it takes!"

"Nothing can stop us now."

"We'll make the Germans wish they had never come." The lively conversation broke loose in the midst of back slapping, hand clasping and hugs.

"Jaja. Now it is our turn!"

All were forced to leave Norway because of the war. Their lives had turned to chaos. Some had lost friends and family, but now they were back with a vengeance. Several of them had journeyed around the world before they landed in England and signed up with the Linge Company. Now the circle was complete: the Norwegian coast was close at hand.

Brattholm reached the Norwegian fishing limits and sailed within its boundary. German patrol planes paid no attention to the innocent looking cutter, shielding eight tons of explosives in her hull and plowing her way northward. The men, however, took note of the many German planes flying above them. All headed northward, no doubt toward the Arctic Ocean in search of the Allied convoys headed for Russia.

Salvesen looked up toward the sky. "We will soon put a stop to that!"

March 29, 1943: *Brattholm* and her twelve men arrived safely at their goal, the majestic island of Senja some 320 miles above the Arctic Circle. Occasionally, the prevailing winds enclose the island in a veil of low-hanging clouds; at other times fog completely blocks her beauty. But today, Norway's second largest island stood proud and tall. Linked together, a chain of boldfaced jagged granite mountains ranging from 200 to some 1800 feet high constituted Senja. Granite walls surrounded the island's narrow strips of land while the ocean skirted the frontage of the clustered, quaint homes. Small boats of every variety crowded the docks, some secured to the buoys. This was Norway! It felt good to be home.

The instructions were, when they reached Senja, to draw as near the mouth of Malangenfjord as possible. From there, Lieutenant Eskeland and Reichelt were to take the cutter's small boat and row up Malangenfjord 18 miles to Tromsø. The plan was thwarted when a German patrol boat shooed *Brattholm* away from the entrance to the fjord (the Germans did not wish to be disturbed during their pursuit of a Norwegian suspected of illegally listening to a radio). Eskeland and Captain Kvernhellen decided to go further north rather than risk contact. Happy to leave unscathed, the men were puzzled at the presence of the patrol boat. They had not been forewarned to expect any German patrols in this particular area, although information from northern Norway to England was scarcer than that from southern Norway.

As they journeyed north, Captain Kvernhellen and Eskeland pored over the maps. Archipelagos break up the sea-lanes in the Troms District and underwater boulders made it a treacherous journey.

They cruised north, now more than 300 miles above the Arctic Circle, on the outer side of Kvaløya Island; this area is called Sagaland, with many traces of the Viking period.

Some 32 miles north of Tromsø, *Brattholm* made her way between Sør Fugløy (Bird Island) and Sandøy Island. The blue-black cliffs of Fugløy heave themselves more than 1500 feet straight up from the water's surface, providing a home for more than 50 species of birds.

The vessel passed through Grøtøy Sound. With Grøtøy Island to the north, *Brattholm* swung around the tip of Rebbenes Island, past the headland of Toftefjordnes, and sailed on into a landlocked fjord on the north side of Rebbenes – the peaceful Toftefjord.

Around 4 p.m., *Brattholm* anchored safely off a small rockbound island, a calm undisturbed place. The islands protected *Brattholm* from open view. Here in the innermost area, the fjord was less than 2000 feet wide. When Captain Kvernhellen stopped the engine, a hush fell over the men. Arctic peace filled them with serenity. High mountain ridges, their ascent scattered with the dwarfed Arctic birches and other deciduous bushes and large boulders, shielded them to the south, east, and west. To the north where the fjord emptied out into the open sea, numerous small islands gave good coverage.

They had found the perfect hiding place.

1) Where _Brattholm_ was anchored. 2) Toftefjordnes. 3) Grøtøya Island. 4) Arctic Ocean.

i won't tell a soul

March 30, 1943: The map had not shown any buildings, so the men were surprised to discover a modest yellow cottage with a small barn partially hidden on the east side of the fjord. Soon after they secured the fishing vessel, Eskeland and Kvernhellen lowered *Brattholm's* motor dinghy and rowed to the shore to investigate.

They pulled the dinghy up among the rocks then trudged through the deep snow to the solitary cottage.

From the window, Haldis Idrupsen saw the two men approach her house. Her children saw them too and became curious. Haldis tensed. She was home alone with four of her five children, ranging in age from seven to seventeen. Her husband Hans was away at the Lofoten fishing grounds, with their oldest son Idrup. Lofoten, a 40-mile stretch of islands, lies 125 miles south of Toftefjord and is the richest cod-fishing field in the world. The two were not expected home for several weeks.

Haldis opened the door and greeted the strangers. The men told their fabricated story.

"Hallo. I'm Eskeland, this is my partner Kvernhellen."

Haldis nodded. "What are you doing in these parts?" She was still a little nervous.

"We are fishermen and have had a bit of bad luck - motor trouble."

"We need to get to Tromsø to buy some spare parts," Kvernhellen broke in.

Haldis caught a glimpse of a uniform collar protruding out from underneath one of the men's coveralls and wondered if the men were genuine. They seemed to be in earnest though and she dismissed it.

The men wore Navy uniforms underneath their coveralls. The uniforms were issued to them before leaving the Shetland Islands for Norway. It was the hope of the English authorities that it would serve as a protection to them in case of capture.

"My husband is away fishing. I am afraid there is no one here who can help you."

Peder, her seventeen-year-old son, watched closely and listened intently to their story. He had been surprised when the fishing cutter with the Norwegian split flag flying high came in from the sea. But maybe it was not surprising considering that down the fjord a bit there was a fish-processing plant. He and the other children were used to seeing

Haldis Idrupsen

Idrupsen home in Toftefjord.

countless fishing vessels come and go. There seemed to be something unique, almost mystical, about this large fishing vessel anchored in sight of their home.

"You wouldn't know of anyone who could give us a lift to Tromsø, would you?" Eskeland queried Haldis.

"I know of two half-brothers on Grøtøy Island," Peter interrupted. "Since you are new to this district, I'll be happy to guide you over there."

"Thanks, but we're exhausted and worn out from the long hours of fishing the last few days. Think we'll turn in first."

They began to leave. Eskeland turned abruptly. "You don't have a telephone do you?"

"No. I wish we did, but such luxuries are not available in Toftefjord," laughed Haldis.

"It's so peaceful around here. Are you the only family in this area?"

"Oh no. Families are scattered around the islands. The nearest one is only about a mile away."

Eskeland raised his cap and nodded.

"So long then."

"Thanks for your help," Kvernhellen smiled and also started to leave, but he turned back to Haldis. "Oh, have you seen many Germans around here?"

"No, we haven't seen a German soldier in Toftefjord since the war began three years ago," Haldis answered.

"May they stay away the rest of the war. Thanks again." Eskeland concluded the conversation. He and Kvernhellen started for the boat.

"Ha det bra," take care of yourselves, called Haldis.

The men were happy with the information they had learned, especially that the nearest neighbor lived about a mile or so away, and that the family did not have a telephone.

On leaving the Shetland Islands, the plan had been to contact a person in southern Troms, known to be quite reliable, and in whom the expedition leaders in England had great faith. Even so, when in their attempt to dock on the island of Senja they were forced out to sea by the German patrol boat, they had chosen Toftefjord because of its remote location, and the convenience of being fairly close to several other trustworthy contacts.

The next person they hoped to reach after their frustrated attempt at Senja was a merchant in Mikkelvik, a few miles from where they had anchored. Subsequent to their visit with the merchant, they intended to visit underground leaders Kaare Moursund and Tore Knudsen in Tromsø.

After the visit with the Idrupsens, Eskeland felt compelled to get the provisions hidden ashore and to be on their way. Under the cover of darkness, Eskeland, Kvernhellen and Blindheim took leave of the other men and set out into the fjord in their small boat. Second Lieutenant Baalsrud was left in charge of *Brattholm* and her men.

The boat chugged along on its three-mile-long journey out of Toftefjord into Vargsundet Sound and around the top of the island until it reached the sparsely populated area of Mikkelvik on Ringvassøy Island. The men looked up the merchant; his name was Peder Nilsen, but due to the late hour he had retired. Nilsen was a fur merchant and the young man who worked for him and who opened the door explained that there was another merchant in Bromnes, and that it was possibly him they were looking for. He had a Mikkelvik mailing address but his shop was in Bromnes. Returning to their boat, they continued on a northwesterly course toward Bromnes on Rebbenes Island.

On the southeast end of Rebbenes, one of the many smaller islands encircling the larger Ringvassøy Island, lay the tiny hamlet of Bromnes with a few closely built houses, and one general store, resembling a *fiskebu,* a fishermen's shelter. A couple of fishing dories lay moored at the dock, and the three *Brattholm* men engaged the men aboard in conversation.

"Getting ready to go out?"

"*Ja,* we're just about ready."

"We hear there is plenty of herring this season."

"That depends on how soon one gets to the fishing grounds. And if the weather holds."

Eskeland recounted his fabricated story. "We have had problems with our motor on this fishing trip. Somehow we've got to get to Tromsø for a spare part."

"That's quite a ways."

"What are the chances that you could give one of our men a lift to Tromsø to get help? We'll pay you well."

"No, I'm afraid not. We want to get to the fishing grounds while the herring is still plentiful," said one.

"I have a good friend," said Pål Olsen. "He runs the general store here in Bromnes. He could possibly be of help with transport, seeing that he owns his own boat."

Pål Olsen and Karl Johnsen, skipper of one of the boats, offered to take them to the friend's home, just a short walking distance away, close to the water. The house, like most homes in this area, was an unpretentious wood house—in this case a joint home/store combination. The general store supplied the islanders, as much as possible under the difficult wartime conditions, with many of their needs.

It was close to midnight when the proprietor was awakened from his sleep. He seemed befuddled by all the men waiting at his door at this unusual hour. Pål introduced the three *Brattholm* men who repeated the story they'd told the fishermen earlier. "Could you help us get to Tromsø to pick up a spare part for the failing motor?" The proprietor shook his head; he was in the middle of taking inventory of all the livestock on Rebbenes, and this task would keep him too busy to make the 60-mile round trip to Tromsø by boat.

Eskeland knew the area well from his service as a postal official in the Troms District before the war. He had reliable information about the trustworthiness of the merchant of Bromnes, Anaton Pedersen, a man highly respected by all the islanders. Besides, there was only one merchant in the hamlet of Bromnes. But Anaton had passed away months earlier, and the news of his death was unknown to the saboteurs. The *Brattholm* men suggested they talk privately with the proprietor in the adjoining room.

"We're the men from England. We have a hull full of explosives, radio equipment and provisions. We were told you were willing and able to get men to help store such things."

The proprietor's eyes just widened. He looked at all three men, one at a time, and then nervously backed away, running trembling fingers through his disheveled hair. "What do you mean?" He asked, his voice cracking.

"We'll pay you well. 5000 *kroner.* And we'll throw in some white flour and tobacco."

"It's just a small thank you for your help." Kvernhellen smiled cheerily.

"We know flour and tobacco are in short supply and it's our way to help make life a little more pleasant for those of you who risk so much by aiding us," added Eskeland.

As the men talked, the proprietor's demeanor darkened and he became extremely anxious. Rubbing his hands together, he paced back and forth in the tight quarters, weighing the odds in his mind. Should he be caught in the act, or reported by one of the Nazi sympathizers who seemed to have eyes and ears everywhere, it would mean sure death for him and possibly his wife. The Gestapo's lack of mercy on those who aided the "enemy" was well known to all Norwegians.

Haakon Sørensen

"No, no. No!" He shook his head. "I can't help you! I have too many responsibilities."

As the conversation continued, the *Brattholm* men learned that the man with whom they were conversing was not the man they had come to see, Anaton Pedersen. In his stead was his assistant, Haakon Sørensen, a 38-year-old married man without any children. He took over as proprietor since Anaton's children were too young to take on the responsibility of running the store.

By the time Eskeland realized his mistake, that Haakon was not the man they had come to see, and that the man they had expected to see was dead, it was already too late.

"Check out Jernberg Kristiansen, and his half brother, Sedolf Andreassen on Grøtøy Island." Haakon appeared worried. "I'm sure Kristiansen will be happy to help you with transport to Tromsø." He made an attempt to sound encouraging.

"We've not had this conversation, you understand?" Eskeland stared at Haakon. "Don't breathe a word or it might mean trouble."

"Oh, I won't tell a soul. What good could come of that?" Haakon sighed with relief when the men prepared to go.

The unfortunate incident added further doubt and gloom to the men's spirits; the pressure to get the explosives safely ashore was mounting.

A TRAGIC DECISION

Bromnes, March 30, 1943: Haakon Sørensen crawled back in bed a little after 1 a.m. His mind in turmoil, he was unable to sleep. He rehashed every word he had exchanged with the three mysterious men. "Who were they really? Were they Norwegian saboteurs as they claimed, or German provocateurs?" He tossed and turned.

Within the hour he tensed at another knock on the door. It was his friends returning. Pål and Karl had become a little suspicious and came to inquire what had happened. Haakon's wife also got up and joined them.

Extremely disturbed, Haakon forgot all about his promise and poured out all that Eskeland had told him.

He begged for advice on how to handle the situation. "What am I to do? Do you believe the story they told me about coming from England?" His friends just listened.

"If they really came from England, it would be a terrible misdeed to report them," Pål said.

"What about all the ammunition they brought? Are they telling the truth? How am I to know?" Haakon was at a loss for what to do.

"I smell a rat here. Maybe you should call the sheriff," his friend suggested.

"What if they are who they say they are, Norwegians fighting the Germans?" The merchant did not even hear his friend's suggestion, and rattled on in his agitated state. "If they are Norwegians, a telephone call to the sheriff would be disastrous!"

"*Ja,* but what if they are German provocateurs? Don't be an idiot, Haakon. Make the call!" prodded Pål.

Haakon glanced at his wife. "If I don't call and they were Germans sent to test us, we will both be imprisoned or shot." His friend urged him again to make the call and then he and Karl left. Haakon felt defeated. No matter which choice he made, he would be condemned.

Sleep escaped the merchant for the duration of the night. "Don't be an idiot Haakon!" reverberated through his mind. The visit from the *Brattholm* men bewildered him and he lay awake weighing his options. By the time the morning sunrays brightened the mountain ridges, he had made his decision.

The Bromnes store is in the building to the left. Haakon Sørensen made the call to Sheriff Hoel from Anaton Pederson's house on top of the hill.

The Sørensens did not have a telephone. Haakon threw on his pants, yesterday's shirt and added his heavy jacket. As he hurried up to the Pedersens' large white house on top of the hill, the wind was bitter cold.

When the Pedersens' door opened, Haakon was shivering – but not from the cold. The Pedersens were accustomed to Haakon using their phone. He was glad when the kitchen door closed and he was left alone in the hallway with the wooden wall phone. He hesitated. Still arguing with himself, he finally grabbed the earpiece. His hand jerked violently and the phone leaped from his hand. He had not realized how frightened he was. As the mouthpiece bounced off the wall, Haakon scrambled to grab it. He held it tightly in his left hand and with his right he cranked up the phone. Upon hearing the exchange operator's cheerful greeting, Haakon requested the sheriff; she told him it would just be a moment. It was a dreadfully long moment for Haakon.

The first ring! He rapidly drummed his fingers on the telephone writing rack, waiting for Sheriff Hoel on Karlsøy Island to pick up the telephone.

"Hello."

"Uh - uh, Sheriff Hoel?"

"*Jaja*, good morning!"

"This is merchant Sørensen at Bromnes."

"*Ja*, Sørensen, I recognize your voice." A painful silence followed.

"What can I do for you, Haakon?"

"I was away inventorying the cattle further in on the island yesterday."

"Yes, yes?"

"Well, something happened last night that I feel I should tell you about."

"Yes?"

The merchant spilled out every detail, all that he had learned from the three mysterious *Brattholm* men the night before. He told the sheriff of the fishing vessel docked at Toftefjord, and how the men aboard were in need of assistance to take a man to Tromsø for a badly needed spare part. He also volunteered that before they visited him they had already been to Mikkelvik.

"I will check into it. Thanks for the call." The telephone clicked.

Sheriff Hoel

In 1941 Sheriff Hoel joined the *National Samling,* (NS), National Unification Party, a political party founded in Norway in 1933 to support the Nazi movement. He joined as a result of a directive that had gone out from the ministry. All government workers had been warned that unless they joined NS, their jobs would be terminated. The cost of joining was 76 *kroner*, approximately $10 by today's exchange. In 1943 Sheriff Hoel had held the position as sheriff of Karlsøy municipality for 17 years. He was 56 years old.

Haakon Sørensen's early morning phone call and the story of the three men and their fishing cutter puzzled Hoel. He wondered why they would offer 5000 *kroner* for a 30-mile boat ride to Tromsø to pick up a spare part. Though he wasn't a Nazi, Hoel was terrified of the reprisal the

Edwin Wikan

Germans would inflict on him for not doing his job as sheriff. He immediately called the police station in Tromsø.

Police officers Edwin Wikan and Einar Kjeldsen were on watch that evening between March 30 - 31, 1943. It was early morning when Sheriff Hoel came on the line. He instructed Wikan to call the Gestapo and to let him know the results.

Edwin Wikan was a police officer who refused to conform to Nazi orders. He tried to sabotage the call from Sheriff Hoel by not sending the message out. He hoped that by doing so, should the men in Toftefjord be patriots, they would have time to get away.

Some two hours later Hoel called back, and wanted to know what was happening. Police Officer Wikan took the call and said it had been delayed because of another important case that had come up, but that they soon would be able to call the Gestapo. He was asked to report the incident to the German Security Police at once, and he realized that this time there was no way around it - he had to call police president Fiane and relate what Hoel had reported.

At that point, Wikan did not know it, but Hoel himself had already called Hagen in the Norwegian State Police and Grau in the Gestapo Security Police.

Hagen, a friend of Hoel's, warned him to handle the happenings at Rebbenes Island with care, because German provocateurs might be the instigators. He suggested Hoel take the sheriff's boat out to Toftefjord for a closer look at the situation. Before leaving, Sheriff Hoel called merchant

Nilsen in Mikkelvik and asked him to be on the lookout for further developments.

Next, Sheriff Hoel called his assistant Valdemar Figenchau, who lived at Vannskammen and asked him to take the boat ride out to Rebbenes Island. No sooner had Hoel hung up the phone than Merchant Nilsen from Mikkelvik called and confirmed that an unknown vessel was docked in Toftefjord. Hoel then rescinded the command that sheriff assistant Figenchau go out to Rebbenes.

Karl Grau, Jr., a German translator, said the Gestapo would dispatch a boat with about 20 or 30 men aboard and that Hoel himself was to be on board to pilot them.

Obersturmbandführer Stage was in charge of the operation. He sent the largest and fastest boat available in Tromsø, a high-speed minesweeper from five minesweeper flotillas. Aboard were Adwehr soldiers, sailors and Gestapo folk (SIPO). Grau was also aboard and they picked up Sheriff Hoel en route.

Police station in Tromso where Edwin Wikan worked.

"ANYONE WHO...

4.   PURSUES PROPAGANDA ACTIVITIES
FOR AN ENEMY COUNTRY OR OTHERWISE
REPRESENTS, OR OBTAINS OR SPREADS
INFORMATION OR OTHER THINGS WHICH
ARE DETRIMENTAL TO GERMAN INTERESTS,
OR

5.   LISTEN TO ANYONE OTHER THAN
GERMAN OR GERMAN CONTROLLED OR
STATIONARY RADIO TRANSMITTERS, OR...
....
WILL BE PUNISHED BY DEATH....
....

> Oslo, October 12, 1942
> Reichskommissar Für die
> besetzten norwegischen
> Gebiete Terboven."

BAttLe in toftefjoro

March 30, 1943: Jan and the crew were anxious for the others to return. The relief on their faces was apparent when, shortly after midnight, the silhouette of the dinghy emerged from the shadows. Eskeland, Kvernhellen and Blindheim told the men aboard *Brattholm* about the disappointing conversation with the merchant Haakon Sørensen.

Together they discussed the many variables that could occur because of this twist in their plans. In the end, the decision was made to look up the fishermen recommended by the merchant. Soon after, Eskeland, Kvernhellen and Blindheim pushed off in their little dinghy and set out of the fjord northward toward Grøtøy Island.

They were glad for the cover of darkness and that only a moderate wind was blowing, though it was piercing. On arrival at Grøtøy, after introducing themselves and explaining their mission, Jernberg Kristiansen and his half-brother, Sedolf Andreassen, warmly welcomed the men. Eskeland did not mention that they had come from the Shetland Islands. Rather, he told them they had brought a fishing vessel up from southern Norway loaded with provisions of various kinds: explosives, weapons, ammunition and food. They were in desperate need of assistance to get the goods hidden ashore.

Happy to help with the mission, Jernberg and Sedolf immediately offered their assistance. They knew of a safe hiding place on the west side of Toftefjordnes, just under two miles from where *Brattholm* was docked, and they agreed to come and guide the cutter. The brothers arranged to meet them in Toftefjord the following day at 4 p.m.

They shook hands; both fishermen were elated to play a small part in helping to free Norway.

After their all-night excursion, the three men arrived, exhausted, back at the fishing vessel around eight in the morning. The weather was still holding, and they felt satisfied and somewhat encouraged with the help offered them by the half-brothers. All the same, an uneasy feeling tugged at Eskeland. He was not at all sure he could trust the merchant at Bromnes, who had promised to keep silent. They had to be prepared for all eventualities.

While Eskeland and the others searched for help, Jan examined the ammunition and weapons, making sure all things were in order. Charges with one-minute and seven-minute fuses were prepared. The intent was that the seven-minute fuse would ignite the eight tons of provisions, and the one-minute fuse was to be used in case of a surprise attack should they have to abandon the fishing vessel.

They placed the lists of people to contact with matches and a gasoline bottle. In case of an emergency, whoever was closest was to pour the gasoline over the papers and set a match to them.

As time passed, the men felt more at ease, and concluded that if the merchant had reported them, the Germans would have had plenty of time to have come from Tromsø by now. All twelve men were aboard, and they began thinking in terms of relaxing. The men from Grøtøy were expected at 4 p.m. and the *Brattholm* men had made all necessary preparations to have the provisions brought ashore at Toftefjordnes.

At noon they heard the monotonous drone of planes in the distance. Since they were far away, no precautions were taken. Now and then they heard a few shots fired at the approach to the fjord. The *Brattholm* men assumed they were German patrol planes carrying out their assignments. (Later, it was learned the Germans had been patrolling the entrance to the fjord to prevent *Brattholm* from leaving, should she attempt to do so. The shootings the men heard were warnings to fishing vessels to force them back into the fjord.)

The saboteurs looked forward to 4 p.m. when they could rid the boat of all evidence and see the crew safely on their way back to the Shetland

Islands. The saboteurs were eager to finish their mission. They went below to take a well-earned rest. Sleep came easy to the weary men.

A short while later their peace was shattered.

"Germans! The Germans are here!" The shrill sound of the lookout's cry rang out on the deck; it bounced from bow to stern and penetrated the very guts of the fishing vessel. The men jumped from their berths. All signs of fatigue vanished. Their well-trained minds and bodies responded immediately to the alert. Was this not what they had trained for?

In the tight quarters below, they crashed into each other as they grabbed for their boots and hand weapons. They scrambled up the steep, narrow ladder, through the hatch, and onto the deck. Jan, on the way up, grabbed a Sten gun and his pistol. He bolted through the hatch onto the deck in time to see the top of the mast of a German warship above the rocky ledges of the islet. The thumping motor became noisier as the ship steadily approached them from behind the rock-bound isle, their protection from discovery. The ship cut off all possibilities of retreat.

Half of the fishing vessel was hidden by the elevated part of the isle where they had anchored. The distance from the Germans had narrowed to some 400 feet, and when *Brattholm* became fully visible to the warship, the Germans fired. *Brattholm*'s machine guns were dismantled, but the men instantly saw they could not win this fight taking the warship with frontal attack. *Brattholm* had to be blown up.

The deck was in total turmoil as the men tried to avoid the line of fire while carrying out their duties.

"Men! Abandon ship!" Kvernhellen yelled to the crew. "Leave all codes and compromising papers behind." The seven-man crew swiftly lowered one of the rowboats and jumped in one by one.

"Row!"

"It's too risky! They'll kill us!" Priceless moments were lost because the cook felt it too chancy to row away from *Brattholm*. The men switched back and forth and another of the crew took to the oars. They pushed away from the vessel and rowed rapidly toward the west side of the fjord, warning shots flying over their heads and the soldiers in fast pursuit.

The saboteurs stayed behind to wrap up their assignments. Eskeland and Blindheim scrambled down into the hold, lit the seven-minute fuse, and placed the radio equipment on top of the charge. Salvesen and Baalsrud poured the gasoline on the name list and lit it. Erik Reichelt held the second rowboat up close against *Brattholm* on the far side from the Germans, where they could not see him. He was to wait there until the other four had finished their work aboard the boat.

The warship rapidly neared *Brattholm*. Eskeland yelled at Jan to shoot at them with whatever he had. Jan aimed at the bridge and opened fire with his Sten gun. His gun was a mere toy against the Germans' powerful cannons, but it had the effect they hoped for. The warship momentarily stopped, which gave the four men an opportunity to almost complete their duties before it once more continued toward *Brattholm*.

The warship's intense fire persisted as the saboteurs finished their work. Most of the shots whistled above their heads and rammed into the mountain on the other side of the fjord. As soon as their tasks were completed, all four crouched and darted toward the rowboat. They vaulted over the railing and down into the boat Reichelt held waiting. Eskeland misjudged and splashed into the water; the others hauled him in.

Brattholm was deserted. The sputtering fuse and its small vapor of smoke were the only movements on deck. The men stayed low in the rowboat in *Brattholm's* shadow. The few short minutes they sat there and clung to the side of the boat felt like infinity. Across the fjord, the crew who had escaped in the first rowboat had reached the rocky beach on the west side of the fjord, only 500 feet away. Two of them were standing in the boat with their hands in the air; three others were ashore and in the process of giving up. One man, rendered incapacitated, probably shot, was sprawled across a rock a little further in; it looked to be the machinist. Captain Kvernhellen was the only one who had managed to head for cover.

Eskeland stared intently at his watch until the fuse had been burning five and a half minutes. To the second, the five had to push away from *Brattholm*. With all their strength, they rowed rapidly, taking advantage of *Brattholm*'s cover. It was only seconds before they became visible to the Germans a short distance away. Nothing but a little water separated them from the warship.

The moment they were seen, the Germans fired. At the same time, they lowered two rowboats with four soldiers in each. Both boats were rowed at high speed toward the west side of the fjord. The four Lingemen and Reichelt also rowed hard, heading for the east side of the beach.

The warship pulled up close to *Brattholm*. At the same moment, the seven-minute fuse went off. The men heard a muffled sound, and realized, to their horror, that it had failed. Only a small fire was burning. The Germans also had heard the noise, and saw the flames, and knew the danger brewing. In spite of the narrow and shallow strait, the Germans quickly reversed the warship and maneuvered a short distance away from the fishing cutter, all the while continuing the vigorous firing towards the little rowboat on its way to the shore.

Machine gun bullets whipped up the water around them, and the rowboat's wooden planks shattered, sending splinters flying through the air. The men heard the bullets slam into the rowboat on one side, boring themselves out the other. Amidst the panic, they shouted frantically to each other "Row on! Keep rowing!"

Blindheim, in a somewhat subdued, melancholy voice, turned to his friend Jan and said, "*Jaja* Jan, we were given a few good years together."

The boat had received too many hits. As if by a miracle, none of the men were hit. Tree-white splinters protruded all around the gaping holes left by the bullets and the water gushed in. It engulfed their feet and in the moment's bewilderment, left them paralyzed, unable to move.

The saboteurs came ashore. The German route is reflected by the broken line.
The Gestapos discovered Jan in the ravine indicated by the arrow. Jan shot the Gestapo officer at the X.

εχ Plosιoη

March 30, 1943: A thunderous boom filled the fjord. People from neighboring islands stopped their labors and turned toward Rebbenes Island as the roar reached them. The men in the sinking dory were hurled backwards and thrown on top of each other.

The eight tons of explosives in *Brattholm's* hull had ignited. Voluminous masses of water surrounding the cutter were thrust aside, and a huge forty-foot crater formed at the bottom of the fjord. Seconds later, the water plunged into the hole and out gushed a colossal tidal wave that rolled on to the shore. *Brattholm's* masts were broken into short stubs, and whirled through the air like matchsticks. Pieces of engine, wheelhouse, lantern glass, metal and hatch covers flew over the five men. Burning oil barrels cut through the air, like torches and with big thuds, crashed into granite boulders far up the mountainside behind them.

In an instant, *Brattholm* was extinct. At the time the sea enclosed *Brattholm's* debris, a document case fell out of the sky and splashed onto the water's surface. It bobbed along on the huge waves like a life jacket. Aboard the *Schnell* boat an officer signaled to some soldiers to lower a rowboat. With shrill screams and frenzied gestures he pointed toward the document case. The rowboat splashed into the waves and moments later, their lucky discovery was brought back to the ship.

The bullet-ridden dory began sinking beneath the five men. Their only choice was to swim. At the moment Jan delivered himself to the glacial waters, the sock and rubber boot on his right foot got caught in the splintered boat and went down with the dinghy.

The frozen waters instantly permeated their uniforms and underclothes. The piercing cold jolted their flesh while the ice floes barred them from the shore. In their efforts to thrust floes aside with their bare hands, the ice forced the men backwards away from the shoreline. It was quicker to swim around the ice than it was to pass through it.

The hundred yards or so to the rocky seaside seemed so far. No one thought of surrendering, but the frigid water sapped their strength. Bullets crashed near them, cracking the ice; a miracle was needed.

A rowboat with four German soldiers worked its way around to the head of the fjord on the west side; simultaneously they kept a close eye on the five men swimming. The Germans' plan was to cut them off before they reached the rock-bound shore.

Baalsrud, Salvesen, Blindheim and Reichelt reached the bank followed by Eskeland a few feet back. All were utterly spent. Jan mustered his strength and crawled up the steep slope by the waterfront. He managed to crouch on a hillock behind a rock some yards higher up. Jan's right foot was bare, and yet the hardened snow did not appear to be any colder than the water. His uniform, heavy with saltwater, soon become rigid and creaked each time he moved; he was being encased in ice.

The rock was his only refuge from the dangers around him. He struggled to get in a position where he could look down toward his friends without being discovered by the Germans. All of them still lay exhausted by the water's edge. Per Blindheim dragged himself toward a rock, but a bullet penetrated the back of his head and he fell backwards halfway into the water. Dead. A sickening feeling engulfed Jan as he watched his good friend killed. Repeatedly he called for his other friends to follow him. Stillness was his only answer.

The warship continued its bombardment. The bullets rammed into the snow and the hillside down by the water. The German soldiers landed, but dared not stay too close to the edge for fear of being hit. Rather, they scrambled up the hillside away from where Jan was hiding. The snow up the slope was deeper than the snow down by the shoreline. With each laborious step the soldiers sank deeply, hampering their chase. Jan watched their movement between the gnarled black and white trunks of the dwarfed birch trees. He saw no way of escaping.

The saboteurs came ashore where author Tore Haug is sitting.

When Toftefjord is calm, part of <u>M/K Brattholm's</u> twisted skeleton is visible on the bottom.

As fate would have it, the Germans suddenly noticed where he crouched. Tumbling down the hill towards him, they opened fire 150 feet away. Surprisingly, they ran past him towards the Idrupsens' house further down on the eastside, then towards the water's edge, blocking him from using that way as an escape route. To the left Jan now had four pursuers, behind him the warship and the water, and to the right, a path which led straight toward the Germans who had subjugated the crew. Momentarily Jan thought maybe the cold would win out. He felt as if the bitter chill would take his life. Only a few feet from him lay his dead friends.

Jan, a good sportsman and in top physical condition, had become a commando soldier through his training with the Linge Company in the Scottish Highlands. He let his instincts take over at the right moments. His overwhelming desire to live crushed the possibility of surrendering. Jan's iron will triumphed over the frigid Arctic, his exhaustion and bare foot, and the test of wits between him and his chasers. In a dire situation such as this, most men might sink into the deep snow, bow their heads, and plead for mercy. But like his Viking ancestors, admired for their bravery, fighting spirit, and extraordinary courage, Jan determined to take up the fight against the insurmountable odds. He had to act. Stooped over, almost to a crawling position, he bolted forward into the snow.

The four German soldiers who scrambled down the hillside had crossed a long deep furrow behind the hillock where Jan was hiding. In doing so, they disappeared from Jan's sight. He was not sure where they would come out, but he grabbed his only chance of escaping, and dashed straight toward the mountainside. Jan ran away from the water's edge, and headed for the Germans' newly made tracks; he crossed them, and pressed on directly toward a shallow ravine which swept upwards from the fjord, and which he had noticed between the birch trunks while he was observing the soldiers' movements.

This ravine was a little to the left of his hiding place and toward the Idrupsens' house, where the four Germans had disappeared over the ridge. Jan reasoned that in the ravine ahead, he would be hidden from the ship's barrage of death, and could possibly reach the top of the mountain that way. The four soldiers were still out of sight and he pushed onward.

Rushing through the deep snow, the Germans discovered him. Most likely they had intended to creep toward Jan at the water's edge and subdue him where he had hidden behind the rock. Astonished to see him 120 feet behind them on the way up the steep incline, they quickly turned and rushed toward him, demanding that he stop and surrender. Jan kept running. Filled with Viking spirit, no thought of relinquishing the fight ever entered his mind. Summoning his last strength, he tumbled through the deep snow. When Jan reached the ravine, he began clawing his way up the nearly vertical mountain, but the powdery snow had no favorites. Using the heavily intertwined underbrush, Jan pulled himself up a few feet, only to slip backwards and start anew. Jan's struggle weakened him, but he refused to give up. Only a few feet away, and yet so far, a large rock jutted out above him. With his indomitable will, he determined he *would* make it! Exerting all his strength, Jan threw himself behind the stone and pulled out his pistol.

The energy and vigor he had enjoyed earlier in the day had deserted him. The chill Arctic air hurt to inhale and he was cold, so very cold. Two choices were left open to him: he could continue the useless climb and die, or he could stay and fight. Jan cocked his pistol.

"*Halt! Halt! Ubergeben!*" Stop! Stop! Surrender! The Germans, hastening ever closer, called out for him to stop. The shots from their guns churned the snow around Jan like a foaming river.

Swiftly he popped his head out from behind the rock, aimed at the soldiers, and pulled the trigger. Nothing happened. He pulled the trigger again, and again and again. The pistol that had been at his side during the swim remained silent, crammed full of ice. The shouts from the German soldiers grew louder as they approached Jan's hiding place. With fingers blue and clumsy from cold, he feverishly dislodged the magazine and removed the first two cartridges.

Should the pistol not work this time, his life would end. Anew he swiftly popped his head out and fired. Relieved, Jan heard the pistol go off. The nearest soldier, a lieutenant in Gestapo uniform, received two hits. His arms shot heavenward and he fell backward into the snow. The soldier following him was wounded, but not mortally. The last two soldiers turned around in panic. They alternately ran and rolled down the steep slope toward the water and disappeared from sight.

COURAGE THAT DEFIED DEATH

March 30, 1943: The snow clung to Jan's frozen uniform. Teeth chattering uncontrollably, Jan shivered in the merciless cold. He struggled with cramped, frozen fingers to force the pistol back in his pocket.

As the echoes of the final shots dissipated into the mountains, he took comfort in the sudden respite from the guns, and momentarily felt safe. An eerie stillness settled over the mountain slope broken only by Jan's breathing and movements.

From his vantage point behind the protruding rock he scanned the mountainside all the way up to the plateau nearly 200 feet above his head. It would be a strenuous climb. All the same, he had already climbed more than 100 feet. Compared with the view below, the snow above him was untouched, and spread itself like a huge, soft white blanket, beckoning him upward. The snow below was a patchwork of footprints, scattered spots of crimson blood and one dead Gestapo officer.

The ravine was Jan's only hope. Beginning in the marshes down by the fjord, the ravine cut deeply into the mountainside all the way up to the plateau. Here in the lower part of the ravine, he was concealed from the warship.

From across the fjord Jan heard screams, some quiet, others more piercing and sharp. There did not seem to be any complete sentences or clear instructions issued, just short yells. Between the shouts were long periods of quiet. During those moments, a tense stillness returned to the ravine on the mountainside. Jan knew what was taking place on the other side of the fjord: the yells were from his *Brattholm* friends, caught and mishandled by the Gestapo.

The arrow points to the mountain crest that shielded Jan from the warship.

Each shout reminded him of the urgent need to climb. Every muscle tensed as he struggled upward. Jan fought for a foothold. His frozen foot was an encumbrance but he grasped for small rocks, shrubs or birch tree trunks to cling to. He inched his way upward, continually slipping and sliding backward and starting all over again. The only thought in his mind was "climb!"

At the upper part of the ravine, the steep precipice on the south side no longer provided protection from the warship. Jan feared the moment he came into the Germans' view, their bullets would penetrate his body and he would roll down this mountain he had fought so hard to conquer. Memories flashed through his mind. He saw his former peaceful life: the family gatherings, his parents, and the hikes in the mountains with his father and younger brother Nils Ivar, his dear sister Bitten. In split seconds he relived the preparations for this mission, and he saw his friends, the men of *Brattholm.* Fear gripped him; he felt totally alone and unnerved. Yet, Jan possessed a natural determination; it unlocked his will. Jan's resolve to live surged up from deep within him and mingled with his iron will. He knew his chances were slim, but giving up and sacrificing himself to the Germans' baseness would accomplish nothing. He kept climbing.

The Germans sighted him and the guns roared out. The bullets lashed the snow into white waves that frothed around him. Pain. The snow turned red. Jan coiled up. A bullet had torn off the bottom part of his large right toe. "Will the next bullet end my life? I'm so close to the top. I must try." The cold snow and the freezing temperature prevented the wound from bleeding heavily. All the same, Jan's injury was extremely painful and made it almost impossible to climb. He managed to drag himself uphill a few more feet. He could hardly see in the stirred-up snow but crawling and scratching, he reached the plateau. The whole way up he fully expected that one last bullet would end it all.

The texture of the snow on the plateau was coarse. The sharp grains of the crusty snow felt like a grater scratching against his wound. He limped doubled over for a few steps, slipped and fell, pulled himself up again, then clawed and scratched his way inland and out of sight of the Germans. At last their bullets could not reach him anymore.

Enervated, Jan sank into a pile, and for a few seconds, lay still, gasping for breath. For the first time since he'd defended himself against and shot the Gestapo lieutenant, he could rest. Once more he noticed the fjord's silence. After lingering a few moments, he mustered strength and courage to crawl back to the brink of the mountain to see what was happening. With bated breath he looked down upon the blue-gray Toftefjord below. The German warship was quite visible. The deck was a scurry of activity.

Jan spotted his friends – the four men who had swum with him and the crew on the opposite side of the fjord. None of them were moving and he presumed they were all dead. He also spotted some of the widely-spread debris from *Brattholm*. German soldiers swarmed about; some had gone ashore on some of the smaller islets. "How could it all have gone so wrong?"

Jan scrutinized his chances, and was left feeling desperate. On this arctic mountain plateau with nothing but snowclad mountains and freezing water as far as he could see, loneliness and fear gnawed at him. He was in a place totally unknown to him. He was comforted by his knowledge of cartography, his good sense of direction and his memory. Seemingly he had lost his friends. He yearned to help them but he was powerless. The

Germans would surely follow in his tracks soon. His wet clothes had long since frozen to ice and for the most part, his large toe on the bare foot was gone. Though death seemed imminent, he determined he would fight until the last pittance of strength left him. His courage defied death.

Jan knew he had to keep as warm as possible. He flapped his arms and limped about. Somehow he had to escape this forsaken place. On the east side of the mountain plateau, the snow was shallower; in places there were only patches. He tried to leap from one bare plot to the other as much as possible. In this way he hoped to baffle the Germans if they came up to the plateau hunting him. Sometimes he walked backwards in the snow to confuse his pursuers further.

For a long time Jan continued toward the southwest part of Rebbenes Island. He reached the periphery of the mountain. There were too many houses below to attempt that direction. Later people down in Leirstrand reported they had seen a man up on the mountain ridge. They had heard the roar from Toftefjord and they were on the lookout, but they puzzled over this stranger who disappeared seconds after he had appeared.

Jan turned eastward. He was unable to reckon time anymore but he had reached the end of the plateau and looked down on the little settlement of Bromnes. He looked over the scattered rooftops and yearned for help. Because of its nearness to Toftefjord, Jan realized this would be one of the first places the Germans would search.

The craggy, treacherous descent toward the shore was strenuous. Jan hung on to the scattered underbrush where it was not covered by snow. Clinging to jagged, protruding rocks, he slowly worked his way down toward the beach. He ended up some 300 feet from the little dock in Bromnes where the three men had come in to seek help the night before.

Jan was aware that the Germans would soon catch him unless he could find a way to fool them. Once he reached the shore, instead of going toward Bromnes and the built-up part of the village, he turned in the opposite direction and went northward. He went away from the people. Desperate, hungry, and suffering, Jan almost turned back toward Bromnes. He knew he'd find comfort in the village. In place of satisfying his urgent needs, he let his instinct rule and forced himself to take the opposite direction.

Along the shoreline there was no snow, which eliminated his worry of leaving tracks. There was a wide belt of slippery, icy seaweed that hid the sharp uneven beach rocks. It was nearly impossible to move forward. Jan slid in every direction and fell every-which-way each time he tried. It took all his concentration and progress was slow. He continued northward. A few feet on the inside of the seaweed, he found it wasn't slippery, but there were huge craggy rocks, boulders and clefts which he had to pass through or over.

Jan hurried as fast he was able; his only hope was to get away before the Germans arrived on top of the ridge. In his wild escape it was difficult to see where he was treading. Sometimes his wounded foot hit upon sharp rocks, which smarted. He was grateful when his foot hit even surfaces. The blood had begun to seep out again. With his life at stake he would not let pain stop him.

After he had crossed the Småtrollneset he continued northward some distance. About 30 feet from the shore he spotted a small islet, about nine feet high and 45 feet wide. Maybe his pursuers would not see him if he was on the islet. To cross the wide belt of seaweed, Jan had to crawl. Even then he slipped and fell sideways, his arms and legs shooting out in every direction. Seaweed and rocks hit his stomach and hips, but there wasn't time to be careful. Jan repeatedly turned to search for Germans on the mountain ridge. He knew he was a sitting

The craggy, treacherous descent down to Bromnes.

*Jan waded out to the little island (indicated
by an arrow) when the tide was low.*

duck for them. He reached the water and waded in. His Navy uniform
filled with ice water once more. Soon he had to swim again.

For some time Jan had felt he was close to freezing to death. Should
he die here in the Arctic, his family would never know. For the rest of their
lives they would wonder what had happened to him. He did not want to
cause them that pain. It was the love of his family and his refusal to die by
himself that forced him to suffer this added cold. His body quivered and
his muscles stopped responding. His consciousness had slipped into a
strange emptiness filled only with a bizarre scenario of horror, pain,
aloneness, grief and utter despair. Yet he pushed himself forward. He did
not know where he was, nor where he wanted to go. But the calm voice
within always prompted him to go further, someplace away from the
nightmare he was living.

VÅRØYA ISLAND

March 30, 1943: Small waves coursed around the islet as Jan grasped the wet beach rocks. Iced up and slippery, Jan attempted to hold on but lost his grip and slid backwards into the water. Moving to the left a few feet, it was easier and he was able to get a foothold.

Jan dragged himself up onto the islet and lay exhausted on his back. His uniform, soaked, was heavy and he hoped some of the water would run off before it froze. Jan's clothes soon creaked ominously anyway.

On top of the islet was a square deep hole. Jan exerted all his efforts to pull himself out of the water up over the edge and let himself fall in the hollow with a thump. He believed the Germans would reach the mountain ridges of Rebbenes shortly, but he hoped his enemy would not look for him on the islet.

His right foot was nearly numb. Covered with frozen blood and grime, part of the foot had turned a corpse white. A slow trickle of blood oozed out. His running, climbing and swerving had effectively kept the wound gaping. The pain had subsided somewhat, but he was aware that he had frostbite.

Jan sat up and tugged at his only boot. Full of water, it gurgled when he pulled and adhered to his foot. Wrenching on the boot sapped his stamina, but at last the boot gave way. The wet sock came off with the boot. He jerked it out and wrung it as best he could. With trembling fingers, Jan stretched the neck of the sock and bunched it up with his thumbs and fingers all the way down to the tip of the toe. It amazed him that such a simple thing could take so long a time and require such concentration.

With infinite care he pulled it over his wounded toe, grimacing when it stuck to the wound or other rough parts of his foot. Once on, the sock felt comforting, almost warm. He slipped his bare left foot back into the soaked boot. Having both feet covered, though sparsely and wet, gave him solace.

Numbness brought on by the freezing cold gradually crept through his body. It was almost overwhelming. For two hours Jan tried to stay active. He lay on his back in the hollow and flapped his arms, but it was not enough. He crawled out and rolled back and forth on the 45-foot islet, keeping a steady eye on the mountain ridges across the fjord. He wondered if it really mattered. He felt sure if he stopped to rest, death would result. Though he feared the Germans, they were no longer his worst enemy. The bitter, all-encompassing cold was.

In the late afternoon he had clung to the rock for two hours when he heard voices and he saw several flashlights in the dim light. The Germans had arrived and they were hunting him. They searched carefully behind each rock and boulder and they signaled each other. Jan crawled back down in the hollow feeling confident they would never find him there. He watched the soldiers: they were rather unsystematic, almost as if they were frightened. After all, one Gestapo officer was dead and another wounded, and they were not sure they were safe.

Jan's second swim was to the rock indicated by an arrow —
his third swim was to Vårøya Island on the left.

Slowly they moved back over the grassy, rocky hillside, their voices became distant until he couldn't hear them any more nor see their flashlights. It became evident to Jan that the Germans knew he was alive. They still thought him to be on Rebbenes Island and were determined to hunt him down.

He had to get away from this little islet. It was too close to Rebbenes. Another 150 feet away he noticed a smaller rock about ten or 15 feet across and it only protruded above the water about three feet from what he could see. He waded into the water. The bottom here was even and at first it reached only up to his waist. But as he waded toward the rock, the bottom slanted sharply downward and Jan had to swim once again.

Frozen through, Jan pulled himself up on the outside of the rock. He was further away from the Germans here and felt safer. As long as he was lying down, no one could see him.

Jan had swum out to the little rock when the tide was out. Now he noticed the tide was returning. He continually had to crawl higher up on the rock. Soon only the top was visible above the water's surface. The rock would soon be covered completely and Jan had to take to the icy waters for the third time.

He only had two possibilities—he could return to Rebbenes where the Germans were or continue further out in a northerly direction towards the next island. Jan estimated the distance to be around 300 feet. The current looked strong but he knew he was a good swimmer. On the other hand, Rebbenes was much closer and maybe the Germans had given up hunting him by now. He reasoned he could work his way south toward the hamlet of Bromnes as soon as his pursuers had left Rebbenes.

He began to swim back toward the little round island. The strong current helped push him along.

He was about half way back to Rebbenes when he again heard German voices up in the hillside. Though dusk was approaching, he realized that to return to Rebbenes would be to sign his own death warrant. Jan turned. Now he was fighting the current, much stronger than he had realized. He hoped to find the rock he had left earlier, but the water completely covered it. Jan needed to rest and he was freezing, but he could not find the rock.

His only hope now was to reach the larger island, Vårøya. Jan believed it was the island straight ahead, if he remembered the map right. If he was unable to reach it, the current would force him down to Bromnes and toward Ringvassøy Island, which would mean certain death. He would rather drown than fall into German hands.

As he realized how slowly he was moving, he tried to swim faster and harder, but his strokes became shorter and quicker. He was surrounded with black water; the current churned around him and formed large eddies which floated past him in the opposite direction. In spite of Jan's expert swimming ability, he was in the midst of his life's most grueling scuffle. He was about 25 feet from shore when his strength gave out. His muscles refused to function; they were stiff and they would not obey his strong mind. "Is this is how it will all end?" he asked himself.

Jan became aware that he was still alive when his whole body went into spasms as he lay partially in the water with the upper part of his body over a low rock. He did not remember how he got there. The spasms seized him and the unbearable pain forced him to move up into a crawling position. He moaned and twisted and moved as fast as he could. Finally he forced himself to limp along and after a while, the spasms weakened. Jan flopped back down on the uneven rocks, but was only able to stay down for a couple of minutes. The cold was getting the upper hand. He forced himself to move again.

Jan clutched the long dried up, ice-covered grasses and painstakingly pulled himself up again. Vårøya Island was one of the smaller islands, midpoint in the sound between Rebbenes Island and Hersøya Island further east. Vårøya's low rolling hills were bare of trees and most other vegetation, and were uninhabited. The terrain was low, reaching only a height of about 150 feet. Jan hid himself in the hollows to stay out of the Germans' sight. Though water streamed off his weary body, it wasn't long before his uniform stiffened again as it froze.

Jan forced his mind to concentrate, to think, and lay new plans. He ended up toward the east side of the island. Here he discovered yet another bay and another island toward the east. This surprised him. From his vantage point on the mountain plateau of Rebbenes Island it all looked

*Vårøya Island. Arrow shows where Jan was picked up
by Olaug and Dina.*

like one large island. This bay was about 450 feet across, and he again noticed a strong current. The island ahead was much larger than the one he was on. In a cove he saw a compact two-story wooden house built on a slope and surrounded by a small field, not too far from the water's edge. He remembered he had seen this house from the plateau in Rebbenes.

While he was taking it all in, a small rowboat came from the south on its way into the sound. Two people were aboard. Jan tensed. Coming from the south as it was, the boat surely could not be Germans looking for him. Yet Jan felt safest hiding. The boat glided past through Vargsundet Sound.

Jan's situation had deteriorated and seemed utterly irreversible. His hope of finding some help here on the island had been dashed. There was nothing for any human being here. Darkness was slowly but steadily moving in. Alone here on this island at the mouth of the Arctic Ocean, without any hope of warmth or shelter, it would be impossible to withstand the cold for many more hours. In spite of all the suffering he had experienced in the hours since the Germans overwhelmed them in Toftefjord, Jan knew what

he had to do. He had to leave this island also - but how? Only frigid water
with a strong current surrounded him.

In the oncoming dusk, across the water, the Germans' torches flickered
back and forth, signaling each other. He wondered how much longer they
would hunt him tonight – or did they even realize one man had escaped?
While watching them, he felt the temperature drop by several degrees.
Time was running out.

Jan limped back and forth as best he could. He looked toward the
newly-discovered island and the house. The current looked swift, but he
had no choice. Warm rays of light cast their glow on the snow beneath the
little windows and smoke had been visible from the chimney before the
twilight shadows blocked the view. How comforting it would be to be dry
and warm again. He had to act now! Slowly he crept over icy, slippery
rocks and headed straight for the water's edge.

Suddenly Jan became aware of children playing close to the house,
and he momentarily stopped and watched them. They were veiled in mist
but their voices reached him. Yes! It was children's voices. Deep emotion
gripped him as he heard their playful sounds. A new thought formed in his
mind. Maybe it would work?

He had to be careful not to be seen or heard on Rebbenes Island
behind him.

"Ho, ho. Ho, ho!"

"Ho, ho. Ho, ho!"

One of the children heard him. She grabbed the arm of another. The
playing stopped. All the children turned and looked toward him, or was
he imagining? It was getting so dark it was difficult to see. But then the
most delightful sounds reached him.

"Ho-ho, Ho-ho!"

It was nearly seven in the evening. Olaug and her cousin Dina thought
it was Peder, Olaug's brother who had returned from fishing, though they
did not quite understand why he was over on Vårøya Island. They left the
other children, jumped into the rowboat, and headed out to pick him up.

"Peder!" they called as they neared the island.

"Ho -ho," came the answer.

They had almost reached the shore before they discovered that it was not Peder. The girls began to turn the boat around. They relaxed a little when the man spoke Norwegian.

"Come back! I am not dangerous." The stranger spoke with a southern dialect. They rowed to the shore and picked him up.

Jan did not know it was possible to be so cold for this long and still live. His whole body shook violently as he crawled in the boat. His body began to cramp again and he massaged his arms and legs while the girls started to row. Jan took out his pistol and said, "Remember, if we are discovered before we reach the shore, it was I who forced you to row me across." He patted his pistol and the teenage girls understood.

From left, Olaug Idrupsen, Dina Pedersen, and Dagmar Idrupsen

*"I venture to say no war
can be long carried on
against the will of the people."*

— **Edmund Berke**

the Gestapo brings terror

March 30, 1943: Amidst the fresh and transparent purity of the Arctic solitude on this idyllic spring afternoon in late March, the two youngest Idrupsen children, without knowing, used the splendor of the day to its fullest. They frolicked in the deep snow outside their home in Toftefjord. The fun the rosy-cheeked siblings shared eclipsed the chill of the wind brought in from the frigid iced-up fjord.

The peaceful surroundings were disturbed only by the delighted squeals coming from seven-year old Halvor and his 12-year old sister Dagmar. Inside, close to the kitchen's cozy-warm black wood stove, big sister Olaug was helping her mother with the dinner dishes; it gave them a chance to visit without interruptions from the younger children.

The previous day, two men from the fishing vessel *Brattholm*, still anchored by the solitary island in the narrow fjord, had been ashore and visited them. *Brattholm* added to the tranquility of the day as it rolled in the gentle whitecaps. Chunks of broken off ice floated close up to the boat.

The children playing on the lower hillside could easily see the movements on the deck and found it exciting to have this large fishing vessel so close at hand, and all to themselves.

"Halvor, would it not be fun if the men returned and let us visit them on the boat?"

"I am first," Halvor demanded.

Suddenly the humming of an engine from the fjord behind the headland reached the children. They leaped for joy; it was a boat and obviously it had to be Papa and their brother Idrup, the children believed, returning from the fishing grounds early. Papa always, on his return from his trips, brought a surprise package for the children, which made his returns even more exciting.

The boat came into view, but it was not Papa's. Rather, it was a huge, dark and threatening boat unknown to the children, outfitted with bulky cannons, and soldiers with rifles on the deck. Dagmar supposed something was terribly wrong. The murky boat and the soldiers with their pointed rifles gave her an ominous feeling. She called for Halvor to come, grabbed his wrist and the two darted towards the house. She tore the kitchen door open, and they rushed in to the safety of their family.

"Did you see your papa?" her mother asked, peering through the tiny kitchen window panes without really looking, at the same time pointing out at an angle toward the mouth of the fjord.

"But Mama, can't you see?" Dagmar's frightened eyes and gestures startled her.

The mother looked and saw - a German warship! She suddenly understood the connection between the fishing vessel and the warship and froze in place. She hardly had time to react before the shooting began.

The Idrupsens fled up the hillside behind their home.

"They're going to kill everyone!" the mother cried out in horror.

The family heard the cracking guns and shouts from terror-stricken men aboard the fishing vessel. Whining projectiles flew about. Haldis made a quick decision; they were leaving their home.

Swiftly they grabbed only the most necessary clothes to ward off the cold. The children clustered about her as she fumbled to lock the door behind them. The family scattered and rushed, struggling up the craggy snow- covered hillside behind their house. Upward they climbed toward the plateau.

The Idrupsens had only reached about halfway up the slope when a deafening explosion rolled over them coming from the fjord; the mountains, unable to hold the noise, sent it back out again over the fjord. The leafless birches all around them and up the other mountainsides encircling the fjord laid down flat as if a strong hurricane was blowing grass and lanky stemmed flowers that could not withstand the force. Burning oil barrels flew through the air like tiny toys, landing up in the mountain outcrops. Black smoke rose from where the fishing vessel had been anchored. It was gone! Several rowboats were in the water. Yells and shooting vibrated around the fjord that had stood undisturbed for thousands of years but now, in a flash, had been transformed into a burning combat zone. War had come to their tranquil Toftefjord.

Halvor and Dagmar ran in front up the hillside. Olaug stayed back a little, and waited for her mother, fraught with fear and exhaustion. Once the roar eased and the echo silenced, they still heard thuds of wreckage fall to the earth. All the way up on the plateau some of the pieces fell.

Haldis was breathless. Coming to a standstill, she sank down on a rock almost hysterical.

"They have no consideration for others," she cried. "We might as well give up, we're all going to die!" Dagmar ran back down to her mother, trying with Olaug, to comfort her as best a 12-year old could. They steadied her between them and brought her, still sobbing now and then, up to the plateau.

On the plateau, it was nearly flat and there were only patches of snow. They were able to hurry along. The family headed for the steep slope on the east side of Rebbenes. Across the Vargsund Sound, on the island of Hersøy, they had family. Aunt Anna Pedersen and her children lived there in a dark green wooden house.

From the water's edge, they could see Aunt Anna's house on the other island. They jumped about, shouted, and waved their arms in hopes that somebody on Hersøy, a half mile away, would notice.

Home with Anna Pedersen were her three children Ingvald, Ragnar and Dina. Her husband Hans, like most of the men around these islands, was away fishing in the Lofoten Islands. Anna and her family had heard the explosion and were extremely anxious to know how their family on Ringvassøy was. They kept looking out across the sound, hoping that somehow Haldis and the children would come into view. Joy surged through them when they did see their family waving from the other shore. Ragnar and Ingvald quickly ran down to the dock, scrambled into the rowboat and rowed to pick them up.

Between sobs, Haldis and the children told of the happenings in Toftefjord. Anna Pedersen sickened as the story unfolded. Such horror was not known here among these peaceful islands. Though they were aware a war was raging in their country, up to now they had mostly been left untouched by it. Ingvald became anxious to get the whole story and rowed over to Bromnes to learn about the happenings of the last few days. He tied his boat to the dock in Bromnes. There he learned the fishermen aboard *Brattholm* had been betrayed by the merchant in Bromnes and reported to the sheriff at Karlsøy. Ivanna Pedersen, Anaton Pedersen's widow, the man the saboteurs were supposed to have met up with, was furious. She said that had she known that these men would be informed on, she would have cut the telephone wire for Haakon Sørensen.

The two women sat by the little kitchen table and over a cup of coffee spoke of the events that had just happened. They both felt comforted being together. Suddenly their lives had turned about, changing from serenity to fear and insecurity. If only their husbands had been home they could have drawn from their strength. Anna's son, Ingvald, was still away at Bromnes, while the other cousins played together outside.

"It's amazing how children are able to regain their composure so quickly," sighed Anna.

They kept a lookout for Peder, Haldis' son. He had been fishing, supposedly close to Rebbenes, when the fighting began in Toftefjord. No one knew where he could be found.

A SICKENING FEAR

March 30, 1943: Small fishing vessels dotted Grøtsund Sound just outside of Toftefjord. Peder Idrupsen, Haldis' son, was on one of them. The fishermen enjoyed the peaceful afternoon until two approaching German fighter planes and a bomber shattered the tranquility. Warning shots were fired at the fishermen at the mouth of the sound, driving them back into the fjord. Then the planes turned, headed into the inner fjord, and swooped down close to Peder. His nose filled with the exhaust and hurriedly he pulled his lines in and started rowing homeward. The planes flew away.

When Peder reached the outcrop between Andammen Island and Toftefjord, he heard a loud, steady drone coming from the direction of Bårdset Sound among the outer islands. A German Schnell-boat headed for Toftefjord! He felt sure there was a connection between the fishermen anchored close to his home and the warship. Soon shooting began and shortly afterwards, a deafening explosion. The racket echoed across the water and black smoke billowed skyward. It settled over Godstrandtinden Peak in the distance.

Peder Idrupsen

Concerned about his family, Peder rapidly rowed homeward. But a young girl from the only family living at Toftefjordnes came running down to the edge of the water, and screamed "Don't go any further!"

Peder set ashore. Borrowing binoculars, he ran to the nearest hilltop.

All he could see in Toftefjord was the warship. *Brattholm* was gone! Several rowboats were in the fjord and it looked like the Germans had taken prisoners and were bringing them aboard the Schnell-boat. The fishing cutter had vanished. Peder stood and watched the warship leave Toftefjord.

Soon after, he rowed home. Toftefjord and the beach, even the tree branches were littered with *Brattholm*'s wreckage. Myriads of cigarettes floated among the debris along the shoreline. Peder pulled his rowboat up on the rocky beach and sprinted toward his little home. On the way he saw several razors, pieces of wood and iron rods. All the windows were blown out in both his home and the nearby barn where the animals bleated their terror. The front door to the house was locked! They had never locked the door before. Peder ran around the house to the back. The back door was open, swinging on its hinges.

Rushing into the house, Peder called for his family.

"Mother! Olaug! I'm home! I'm home!" No answer. The only sound was the wind, still chill under winter's grasp, rustling the curtains through the broken windows. The kitchen was in disarray and leftover dinner was scattered among broken dishes on the counter and the floor and kitchen chairs were turned over.

Panic gripped Peder. "Where are my siblings and mother? Have the Germans taken them prisoner?"

Everything had happened so quickly. There was no time to think or reason; he did not know where to turn. "Maybe they had been able to escape? But where can I find them?"

He pondered these questions as he walked among the wreckage scattered across their beach lot. The fjord was still filled with floating rubble. Now Peder noticed that even the surrounding mountains held scattered debris.

A man came skiing down the mountainside, a friend from Leirstrand who was concerned about the family's well being. Peder did not know what had happened to them but he had decided to row out to his aunt Anna Pedersen on Hersøy Island. The friend accompanied him.

A WARM WELCOME ON HERSØY ISLAND

Hersøy, March 30, 1943: Jan helped the girls secure the boat. "You're so wet and cold. You've got to come home with us!" Dina pointed to the house Jan had seen from Vårøya Island. "That's my home."

Anna Pedersen and Haldis Idrupsen were horrified when they saw who the girls brought home.

There were no questions. The women immediately knew where this man had come from. Like mothers know so well to do, they saw a need and went to work. A kettle of water was put on the stove to heat. Off came Jan's navy uniform and the underwear. On went warm wool undergarments belonging to Anna's husband. While Haldis rinsed Jan's clothes out in water to get rid of the salt, Anna stoked the range with wood the children had brought. Soon the little kitchen heated

Anna Pedersen

up until it was nearly impossible to remain inside. The women massaged Jan's arms and legs to start circulation, and then they cleaned and bandaged his foot.

The women gave Jan a blanket to wrap around himself and hung his clothes to dry over the range. Jan recovered quickly and a spirited conversation ensued. He explained the fate of his comrades and the subsequent events. Children and adults listened horror-struck. The event

Anna Pedersen's home on Hersøy.

could not be hidden from the children; they had heard the explosion and their cousins' and aunt Haldis' explanation.

All found Jan's good disposition following such a disaster amazing. He was able to both tease and laugh, and showed no sign of fear. "I'll be back in London celebrating in two weeks," he joked. His upbeat mood was a completely natural occurrence. Known as psychological euphoria, it sometimes happens after a devastating experience such as Jan had suffered. But Jan felt the weight of the tragedy as well.

His main concern was for this caring family. He told them exactly what to say when the Germans came searching. Jan had no doubt they would come around, because of the Pedersens' vicinity to Toftefjord. "And remember, I threatened you with my pistol to do as I commanded," Jan said as he pointed to the pistol lying close by him on the kitchen table.

Anna's son Ingvald returned from his row-trip to Bromnes. He gave the details of what he had learned and Jan understood why the Germans had launched the surprise attack against *Brattholm.*

Jan planned to leave as soon as his clothes dried. He had to protect this beautiful family even if they had no thought for themselves. Two of the older girls stood watch outside. Should someone approach they were to come in and give warning. Two boats arrived and docked. The girls ran in to warn Jan and he rushed outside and hid behind some large boulders. The first boat held friends of the family wanting to know if the Pedersen family was all right after the huge explosion. The second boat held Peder Idrupsen and his friend.

Peder left the man in the boat while he went to check on his aunt and her family. On the way up to his aunt's house, his cousin Ingvald ran to meet him.

"Who is the man in the boat?"

"Just a friend from Leirstrand."

"Hurry! Take him away. We have one of the escapees from *Brattholm* here!"

Just then Peder saw Jan pop his head out behind one of the rocks. Peder hurried back to the dock.

"Thank goodness Mother and all the others are here. They are just fine. I'll take you back to Leirstrand." Peder untied the boat stepped in and rowed off.

Once Jan was back inside, Anna found him a pair of socks and an old seaman's boot that fit his wounded right foot. Jan kept the military boot; it would not be as slippery.

He discussed with Ingvald and Ragnar how to best continue his escape. They decided that Ingvald would row Jan the nearly two miles to Mikkelvik on Ringvassøy Island. The family sketched out a map for him and gave him information about people they knew along the chosen route. They told Jan who was trustworthy, where the Nazis lived, and the built-up areas he should avoid. Jan memorized the map and burned it. Around 1 a.m. he left with Ingvald.

"Tusen, tusen takk," thousands and thousands of thanks. "No words can express my deep gratitude for all you have done for me. I promise you, I'll never be caught. You have nothing to worry about."

"Be careful, Jan. Remember who to stay away from."

"So long."

Ingvald and Jan slipped down to the dock and set out into the fjord in silence. There was no place to hide out on the open water. The thump of the oars echoed across the channel. This late in the year, even at the hour they had chosen, the Arctic night was only murky gray when the sky was fairly clear as it was tonight. If the Germans were still out hunting an escapee, their chances of success were good this evening.

Toftefjord, March 31, 1943: In the wee hours of the morning, Haldis Idrupsen and her children left for home shortly after Ingvald left with Jan. Haldis was appalled at the sight of her home. With all the windows broken, the cottage was ice cold and in total chaos. Their home was wrecked, but under the circumstances they had so much to be grateful for. They still had each other.

The night was a sleepless and uncomfortable one for the Idrupsen family. Early in the morning they heard a large boat. They woke each other and rushed to the glassless windows.

"German soldiers! They are returning!"

The terror-stricken children began to cry. The horrors of yesterday were still too vivid in their innocent minds. They watched the soldiers lower a small skiff and approach the house. Soon they banged on the door with a gun butt.

"*Guten morgen!*"

"Come in." Haldis replied. Her offer was rejected – the family was ordered outside. Peder placed himself close to his mother to protect her. The Germans had brought a translator and began their interrogation. They wanted to know all the family knew.

"Are you aware that one man from *Brattholm* escaped?

"No."

"When is the next boat from England expected in Toftefjord?"

"We don't know anything," answered Haldis.

"I don't know of any boats. Don't you think *one* is more than enough?" interrupted Peder. The officer in charge gave him an icy stare. He left no doubt that such a rash remark was received with disdain. Haldis nudged her son. Both shuddered unnoticed.

The soldiers searched the house and the barn. Behind the door in the cow barn Haldis' husband Hans kept his rifle and a shotgun. The soldiers did not discover it.

The family breathed a sigh of relief when the Germans returned to the warship.

Peder was frightened at the thought of their return. The following day he took his father's guns, rowed far out into the fjord, and threw them overboard. They could not take any chances.

CROMSØ HAPPENINGS

The Norwegian Navy had worked to build up intelligence services along the coast in northern Norway as early as the summer of 1940. Editor Oscar Larsen in the newspaper *Tromsø* had heard rumors about this. He realized the importance of building an intelligence service before the Gestapo was able to infiltrate the population.

One day in the late summer of 1940, Larsen gathered several prominent persons in Tromsø to a secret meeting in his home. Eight men were present including Larsen, editorial secretary Tor Knudsen and department head Kaare Moursund. The men discussed how to build a resistance group and what they could do.

Knudsen and Moursund became two of the most actively involved people in building up the resistance movement. Before long, they had organized several smaller resistance groups throughout the Troms District. Knudsen and Moursund were responsible for collecting funds for needed activities, including the printing and distribution of underground newspapers, the installation of clandestine radio transmitters, and the establishment of lines of communication in the Tromsø region.

In the spring of 1941 a radio transmitter was opened in the attic of the office building of the *Tromsø* newspaper. Telegrapher Egil Lindberg attended the station. Later it was moved to the attic at Tromsø Merchant Bank. The bank was located about 20 feet from the Gestapo headquarters in Bankgaten 13. The problem was that the street lamps flickered each time the telegraph keys clicked. The transmitter was again moved, this time to the tower at the Tromsø Hospital.

One evening in the late fall of 1942, a man rang Kaare Moursund's doorbell. The man introduced himself as Erik Reichelt. He said he had just arrived from London. Moursund's wife and medical student Sverre Sandmo were present at the time, and Tor Knudsen had dropped in for a cup of coffee.

Reichelt was originally from the Skien district, and he had come to Tromsø to gather information. He was interested in what the people in the area felt about the occupation authorities, and what the mood was among the Norwegians in the Troms District. He was particularly interested in learning about the mine fields in Kvalsund, Langsund and Malangen. These were the most important gateways to Tromsø. Moursund promised Reichelt he'd contact the pilots aboard the local boats to learn more about the mine fields. The discussions lasted about two hours before everyone went his own way. Reichelt never mentioned a word about the planned *Brattholm* expedition that would arrive only four months later.

FATE OF THE BRATTHOLM MEN

Tromsø, March 30, 1943: Per Blindheim was killed at Toftefjord. Skipper Kvernhellen had been able to hide for some time, but was eventually captured before the warship sailed out of the fjord.

When the *Schnell* boat arrived in Toftefjord and the shooting battle began, Sheriff Hoel had become quite disturbed and retired below deck. He was still aboard as the warship made its way up the fjord to the Tromsø docks with the men captured from the ill-fated mission in Toftefjord.

The city of Tromsø lies three hundred and fifty miles north of the Arctic Circle; heavy snows of several feet cover the city during winter each year. Tromsø is sometimes called the capital of northern Norway; it is also known as the Gateway to the Arctic.

Today, seagulls squawked and played in the air beneath the somber clouds, then hung suspended as if this was an ordinary day. A few nervous but curious people watched from a distance as the Schnell boat docked, and the longshoremen, noticing something unusual happening, paused in their work.

Two ambulances slowly rolled down the cobblestone streets and stopped on the dock. Near the ambulances, a German Gestapo officer stepped out from a black car adorned with swastika flags flying from short poles mounted on each front fender. Dressed in mossy green vestment, officer's cap with black brim and the German eagle, a double-breasted long wool coat, shiny black high boots and leather gloves, he paced back and forth. Stopping at intervals, he tapped the leather gloves in his right hand over his left wrist, carefully watching the happenings.

A few German soldiers carried two stretchers up the lowered gangplank. They returned with Eskeland and Reichelt fastened to each stretcher with heavy straps. The instant the doors of the waiting ambulances slammed shut with the stretchers and their cargo, they sped off to St. Elizabeth's Hospital. The Gestapo officer rushed back to his car and ordered the driver to follow them.

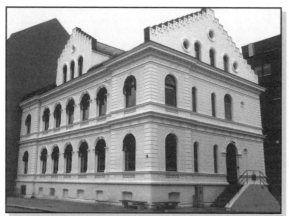

Gestapo Headquarters in Tromsø.

Eight disheveled prisoners chained together and under heavy guard appeared at the head of the gangplank. Ordered down to the dock, they were loaded into the waiting canvas-covered truck and taken to Gestapo headquarters at Bankgaten 13. Gestapo agents were waiting for them.

Numerous Gestapo agents worked at the headquarters in Tromsø. Men and women imprisoned by the Gestapo agonized about their upcoming treatment, knowing full well the Gestapo's lack of pity for prisoners. Before interrogation, they rehearsed the answers to the assumed questions in their mind, and could but hope they would be believed.

Two of the Gestapo agents at the headquarters were more feared and detested than all the rest. One, a short, slight man named Kneiser, was known to be extremely cunning in his interrogation of the prisoners, constantly laying shrewd traps.

The other Gestapo agent's name was Adam Schmidt. A man of a totally different sort, stocky and only about five feet tall, Schmidt's lopsided flat face was framed by thick dark blond hair. Some said his face reminded them of a flounder. He was an uncouth boor who took pleasure in torturing prisoners. No method was too grisly for Schmidt, the most hated of all Gestapo agents in Tromsø.

The men from *Brattholm* were interrogated individually. Crewmember Sjur Trovåg was the first. Three grim-looking agents were stationed around the room. Schmidt, with his crooked false smile, bid him welcome as he strutted around his desk and pointed for him to sit down in the chair held out for him. Schmidt offered Sjur some candy. The Norwegian shook his head. Schmidt's face turned red; with his eyes flashing, he clenched his fist and lunged out toward Sjur, jamming his fist into his face. The young man flew backward out of the chair and slammed into the wall behind him. The three other Gestapos in the room pounced on him, kicking and beating until Sjur was nearly unconscious. They grabbed him by his arms and legs and dragged him through the door and down the narrow steps into the dingy basement. Unbolting the cell door they threw him like a potato sack into the over-crowded cell that held most of the other *Brattholm* men. No one mistook the Gestapo's intent; they wanted the other men to know what was in store for them upstairs. Sjur's swollen face and hoarse moaning filled his cellmates with dread.

St. Elizabeth's Hospital, March 30, 1943: Followed by the Gestapo car, the two ambulances delivered Erik Reichelt and Sigurd Eskeland to St. Elizabeth's Hospital. Sigurd had been shot in the thigh. Erik, with grenade fragments in his stomach and a broken finger, was so seriously ill that his doctor, a courageous man, refused Gestapo agent Adam Schmidt and his cohorts permission to interrogate him. Schmidt and his men left in a huff, but made it very plain they would return soon, no matter how sick Reichelt was. The wounded saboteurs were placed on the second floor of the hospital and soldiers with automatic weapons were stationed in front of their rooms.

The Gestapo had knowledge of Erik Reichelt's contacts with the resistance leaders on his earlier trips to Tromsø. Because of this, his treatment was more vicious than what the other *Brattholm* men received. The Gestapo agents put him through barbarous torture hoping he would reveal secrets to them.

Tromsø, March 31, 1943: The day following the battle in Toftefjord, Haakon Sørensen and Sheriff Hoel were summoned to appear at Gestapo Headquarters in Tromsø. They gave a complete report and Sørensen also explained that the men from *Brattholm* were referred to the two half-brothers at Grøtøy. These two were quickly arrested and brought to Gestapo Headquarters.

After Sørensen and Sheriff Hoel explained the happenings to the Gestapo, they were told they were to stay until the following day. The Gestapo summoned them once again. As a reward for work well done, each one was given a large crate of food, 30 packages of cigarettes, cured sausages, coffee, butter and ten bottles of hard liquor. In addition, Sheriff Hoel received 500 *kroner* and Sørensen was rewarded with 5000 *kroner.*

Sørensen felt uneasy about taking the gifts. He was told that refusal would be understood as a demonstration. He took the gifts.

Both men returned to Sheriff Hoel's home on Karlsøy after leaving the Gestapo headquarters. Sørensen remained until the following day because the weather was too stormy to return to Bromnes. In the evening they tasted some of the liquor.

St. Elizabeth Hospital, Tromsø, April 1, 1943: Schmidt and his men returned to the hospital. A terrified hush filled the hospital corridors as personnel and guards were rushed off the floor. The Gestapo interrogated Sigurd in the bathroom, but Erik, too ill to be moved, was interrogated in bed. A short, suspense-filled time passed, then Erik's spine-chilling screams pierced through bone and marrow of all who heard them. He had nothing to tell the Gestapo despite their inhumane torture.

Reichelt's heart-wrenching outcry and suffering meant nothing to Schmidt and his agents as they tormented him for several hours without compassion. They had only one mission: gathering information. Since the Germans had for some time been convinced that the Allied invasion would happen in northern Norway, Adam Schmidt believed that the *Brattholm* men might hold the key that would unlock some of the enemy's ambitions. Therefore, no punishment was too brutal or too drawn out - no sacrifice too exacting to get the information he desired.

When the Gestapo agents left the hospital, the nurses rushed to Erik's side. They found him, lying on bed linens soaked with blood. His face was swollen and misshapen. He had received several blows to his face and thick needles had been forced underneath his fingernails, leaving deep bloody grooves that had turned purplish-black.

Erik was in a daze, and no doubt realized that his life was coming to a close. Turning to one of the nurses, he whispered, "please send greetings to everyone at home."

Tromsø, Evening, April 1, 1943: Moursund and Knudsen, the resistance leaders Reichelt had met with a few months earlier in Tromsø, were rounded up in their homes. Schmidt and Kneiser interrogated both. The two prisoners had agreed beforehand, to concede to the Germans all the information they knew they already had, if they were taken prisoner. Moursund and Knudsen knew everything and everyone involved with the resistance movement in Tromsø and the surrounding area. Their hope was to pacify the Germans so as to escape torture and not be forced to reveal other secret information that would put many other lives at stake. Most likely the Gestapo agents became perplexed over their responsiveness because the men were not tortured.

Tromsø, April 2, 1943: Early in the morning, 20 Norwegian prisoners who were incarcerated at Krøkkebærsletta, a German internment camp in Tromsø, were summoned for a special assignment. They were ferried across Tromsøy Sound, herded into a canvas-covered truck and driven to the Gestapo headquarters in downtown Tromsø. Ordered inside, they each were given a long-handled shovel. Led back outside, they were rounded up and pushed back into the truck, which set off for the Njord factory on the outer edge of Tromsø.

As the truck came to an abrupt stop, the prisoners were ordered out. Soldiers with machine guns stood ready. The officer yelled for them to head in the direction of the rifle range at Grønnåsen, several hundred yards away. Dressed in rags, the prisoners sank into the wet snow and labored to advance uphill lifting, and sometimes dragging, their spades along with them.

Situated on a steep hill, the rifle range was covered in part by marshland with numerous dwarfed deciduous trees, mainly birch. From here, one could view Tromsøy Sound and the lofty mountain ranges across the fjord. At the foot of the mountains in Tromsdalen Valley, the closely-built wooden homes came into view among the evergreens and the white snow. It was a majestic panorama, but not one the prisoners paid attention to.

The twenty prisoners struggled to keep their composure. When ordered to dig a large grave, to a man they thought it was for them. The strong tried in their way to encourage the weaker.

"Don't worry, they have no reason to kill us."

"And if they do, let's not give them the satisfaction of seeing our fear."

"If they kill us, I guess that's our fate," another chimed in.

When told that the grave had to fit eight bodies, the prisoners were both bewildered and relieved. One prisoner then recalled a conversation overheard when the spades were handed out.

"*Hei*, I remember hearing some talk about eight men from the fishing vessel *Brattholm* at the Gestapo headquarters," he said just loud enough for the other prisoners to hear.

"But those men were in the service. They wouldn't execute them."

"Oh, wouldn't they? When did the Gestapo ever follow the laws of society?"

"I pity those men. *Må Gud bevare dem,*" may God protect them, a rough, trembling voice added.

"*Ruhe!*" Silence! A Gestapo officer cocked his gun and came closer.

The strenuous work of digging the large grave continued in silence. The deep snow was shoveled away to enable them to break up the heavy marsh soil. The frost lay shallow because of the heavy snow, and yet it took real strength to hack with their spades at the intertwined roots. The Gestapo and their loaded machine guns made the prisoners uneasy. One could never be too sure of what would set the soldiers off. The prisoners' conversation had made them more alert.

Once the gaping hole had been readied, the prisoners removed the snow from one edge of the grave. The Gestapo wanted it cleared twenty-five feet back to where the executioners would stand to give them a full view of the edge of the grave. The soldiers did some trial shooting and found all to be satisfactory. The shots unnerved several of the younger prisoners. Some tensed, others grabbed hold of a comrade's arm, while others who turned pale had to be steadied by their buddies.

"Take it easy, we'll be all right!" encouraged an emaciated, tall prisoner.

Earlier in the day the Gestapo had instructed the men that they were to remain until after the execution to cover up the corpses. Instead, when the grave had been dug in the late afternoon, the Gestapo hustled them down the hill and back into the truck that had brought them to Grønnåsen. The temperate April spring day sent sporadic rays of sunshine through the back of the truck. Nearing the center, the streets filled with run-off from the melted snows and brief sun breaks warmed the day.

When they reached Skippergata in downtown Tromsø, another truck with a tarpaulin cover fastened to the iron frame covering the truck bed approached. The eight Brattholm men and their executioners sat inside. Silence fell over the prisoners who had been forced to dig their graves.

Earlier in the day the eight *Brattholm* prisoners had been brought up from the basement in Bankgaten 13, Gestapo headquarters. Police officer Edvin Wikan watched, heavy-hearted, a short distance away. Gestapo soldiers ordered the cluster of men into the waiting truck. Wikan had watched such happenings before and surmised something dreadful was about to take place, though he did not know what. The prisoners were chained together two by two, some with cow chains, and others with thick cords.

The *Brattholm* men had been ordered to walk barefoot. At the last moment the Gestapo changed their directives. The truck with the prisoners would be parked a good distance away from the rifle range, and most likely they would encounter passersby on the long walk. The Gestapo did not want to appear cruel. The prisoners' wrists were linked together, the right arm of one to the left of the next. Because of the torture inflicted on them during the last 48 hours, some had difficulty walking. Their comrades helped them along.

It was nearing 8 p.m. by the time the prisoners began their walk to the rifle range. The soldiers threw their capes over the prisoners so the chains would not be visible to other pedestrians. Harassed and fatigued by their treatment, the prisoners trudged through the spring thaw. They carried their private burdens heroically. All knew death was imminent. What they did not know was what had befallen their other four friends. They would have gloried in knowing that one had escaped, Jan Baalsrud.

At the Tromsø rifle range, the Gestapo ordered the *Brattholm* men lined up in a row with their backs to the open grave. One Gestapo officer felt they moved too slowly.

"*Schnell! Schnell!*" Quick! Quick!, he pushed a prisoner with his rifle butt.

Some twenty-five feet in front of them the executioners lined up and readied their rifles. They took aim and fired a few rounds. The cracking shots resounded several times among the nearby hills.

Ordered by the Gestapo to be present, Sheriff Hoel observed the execution. As the sheriff watched his countrymen fall, he agonized over the telephone call he'd made only a couple of days earlier — the call which took so many lives.

Most of the men were shot in the abdomen and doubled up with pain as the bullets hit their mark. Those who fell pulled the others down with them, chained together as they were. Those who did not fall down into the grave were kicked over the edge, dead or not. The agony remained on their frozen faces as they laid helter skelter in the large black cavity prepared for them in the marshes. A load of Russian prisoners was brought in to cover their tortured bodies with the black soil.

The *Brattholm* men gave all for Norway and freedom. All had eagerly returned to Norway to take part in her fight for freedom. There were no flower-strewn caskets or platted wreaths or garlands for these young men. Instead, their sacrifice was dignified and majestic. There had been no whimpering or self-pity among them. They had chosen their work, and they knew the odds. To them a free Norway was worth even life itself, and in the end that is what they gave.

St. Elizabeth Hospital, Tromsø, April 2, 1943: By mid-morning the day following his arrest, Moursund was yanked from his cell and taken by car down the hilly snow-covered streets of Tromsø. All too fast, the colorful, individually constructed wooden row homes, some still with snow piled high in front, passed by them as the car sped up and down the winding streets. The sound of the tire chains hitting the car frame brought back many happy wintertime memories to Moursund. White-clad, snow-bedecked mountains surrounded the city he loved.

The black car he rode in turned a corner and rumbled down Strandgaten. Moursund's blood chilled. They were heading down the cobblestone street leading to the Tromsø hospital, where a transmitter had been installed in the hospital's tower. Moursund assumed the Germans had located it. To his amazement, the car did not stop, but continued some distance and turned in to St. Elizabeth Hospital. When he was ushered from the car up the cement steps leading to the hospital, bewilderment swept over him like a sudden wind gust. He could not have known Kneiser was setting one of his shrewd traps. The Gestapo led Moursund down pale green hospital corridors into a dimly lit small room of the same color. The room held only one bed.

Kneiser pushed Moursund forward and he was brought face to face with the patient in the bed. The man had an extremely deformed face and a deathlike pallor, making it difficult to tell his age. The patient, it was obvious, had been through a harrowing experience. He just lay there and moaned. Moursund wondered why he was brought here. To be shown what was in store for him and Knudsen? The patient's face seemed to lighten as if he recognized Moursund. His cheekbones were a dark bluish-green, and he had difficulty seeing through his swollen eyelids. His slurred speech made it difficult for Moursund to understand his words.

Abruptly, as Moursund scrutinized the man, he came to the ghastly realization that he knew this beaten, mishandled being. Four months had passed since he last saw his face, but this had to be him. It was Erik Reichelt!

Reichelt tried to speak but could not be understood. He was offered some water through a straw, and he tried again. He motioned to Moursund to come closer to him. Kneiser moved in at the same time. The swollen lips began to move as Reichelt exerted all his efforts to share these last important words with his friend.

"It was not I who betrayed you, Kaare," he groaned and closed his swollen eyes.

Kneiser's trap had worked. He now had the proof that Reichelt and Moursund knew each other. Moursund was taken back to prison. Reichelt died the following day, April 3, 1943.

Tromsø, April 5, 1943: The Gestapo tortured a prisoner at their headquarters in Bankgaten 13, a prisoner who had illegally listened to a radio transmission from London. He had received blows to the face and kicks to the groin from the man with the flounder face. He ended up in one of the cells in the basement. The cell door suddenly was kicked open, and two men were tossed on the dirt floor and the cell door slammed shut. The new prisoners were half-brothers Jernberg Kristiansen and Sedolf Andreassen who had offered to hide *Brattholm*'s provisions. Haakon Sørensen gave their names to the *Brattholm* men and then to the Gestapo.

A few minutes passed and their cellar door flung open with a clang once again. The soldiers cocked their machine guns and pointed them straight at the two, as if they were going to shoot. The half brothers struggled to their feet as best they could and huddled together in their corner. The other prisoner grew angry at such inhumane treatment, and he pulled at the half-brothers' clothes in his effort to calm these bewildered men.

"If they shoot you men, they will have to kill all of us," he shouted.

The soldiers grabbed the door and pulled it shut behind them. These two resolute fishermen had been torn away from their peaceful existence and thrown into the lion's den. They endured bestial torture and several hours of interrogation. Following Schmidt's treatment, all they revealed was that they had been offered 3000 *kroner* and some coffee in return for helping the men of *Brattholm*.

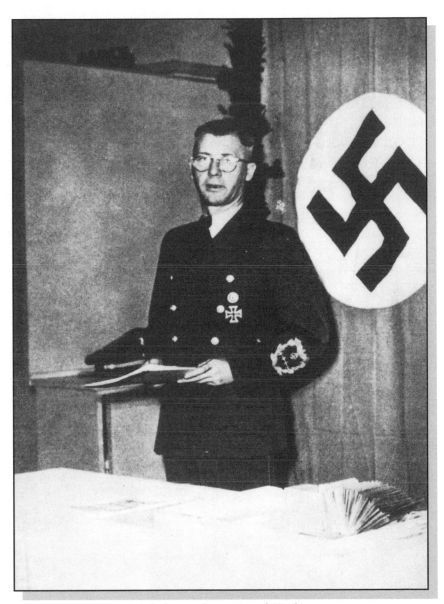

Reichskommissar Josef Terboven

On May 8, 1945, the war ended and Norway was liberated. The Gestapo officers in Tromsø were taken prisoner, and in the late summer of 1945, they were ordered to Grønnåsen Rifle Range to unearth the executed *Brattholm* men. When they neared the victims as they dug, the Gestapo officers were forced to lay down their shovels and use their bare hands so as not to damage the bodies. Before the Norwegians were placed in their caskets, they were cleaned by the Gestapos.

Left: Graves are opened.

Right: The Gestapo was ordered to excavate the graves.

Left: A view of the mass graves.

Left: Two men linked together with cow chains.

Right: Their suffering was still evident.

Left: The bodies are removed by the Gestapo.

Right: The bodies were washed and readied, and placed in their caskets by the Gestapo.

FALLEN
Per Blindheim, Ålesund, Norway
Killed at Toftefjord, March 30, 1943.

EXECUTED AT TROMSØ RIFLE RANGE APRIL 1, 1943
Bjørn Norman Bolstad, Solbergfoss pr. Askim, Norway

Gabriel Salvesen, Farsund, Norway

Magnus Johan Kvalvik, Husøy i Solund, Norway

Sverre Odd Kvernhellen, Husøy i Solund, Norway

Harald Peter Ratvik, Borgund pr.Ålesund, Norway

Frithjof M. Haugland, Norway

Sjur Ludvigsen Trovaag, Kalgras i Ytre Sogn, Norway

Alfred A. Vik, Øystesø, Kvam i Hordaland, Norway

DIED AT ST. ELIZABETH'S HOSPITAL
FROM GUNSHOT WOUNDS AND TORTURE
Sigurd Eskeland, Risør, Norway

Erik Reichelt, Tønsberg, Norway

A Triumphant Find

Toftefjord, March 30, 1943: The attack on *Brattholm* in Toftefjord was an extraordinary coup for the Germans. That is why they rewarded the informers with both food and spirits. In addition, the killing of one of the commandos, Per Blindheim, and the capture of ten prisoners made the triumph especially sweet.

Brattholm's explosion tossed wreckage in every direction. The only thing remaining intact was the attaché case with the top-secret material. The attaché case was the one thing the saboteurs were to keep out of German hands at all costs. When the Germans saw it splash undamaged back down into the fjord, they quickly lowered a small rowboat off the warship and rowed out to recover it from the water. At that time even the Germans did not know how very successful their assault had been.

From the German Archives we learned that the attaché case contained numerous documents with secret information. The Germans had the *Brattholm* documents translated and scrutinized thoroughly. Analyses and reports were sent to several sources within two days. In addition to the recovered attaché case, the Gestapo interrogated and tortured eight of the *Brattholm* prisoners at the Gestapo headquarters in Tromsø. Two others were wounded and had been admitted to St. Elizabeth Hospital. They were also tortured. The Gestapo used every method available in their efforts to understand all that was happening around them.

Tromsø, April 1, 1943: A report was sent out. The exact translation follows:

"SECRET COMMANDO WORK."

From GENERAL COMMANDER IN TROMSØ TO A.O.K.Ic:
"Evaluation of sabotage-fishing vessel in Toftesund, Toftefjord Sound:

12 men were aboard, all Norwegian under the leadership of Lieutenant Eskeland from Risør, (southern Norway), among them five seamen, all had a six-month training at sabotage school, including training as paratroopers.

Additionally four fishing vessels headed south from Tromsø in the direction of Bergen, among them were probably the fishing vessel *Trondheim* that was discovered empty in Trondheimsfjord March 22.

All the fishing vessels came from Shetland.

Assignment: To build up sabotage organizations that would take actions against military bases, battery positions, billets, chief of staff quarters, and bridges. Following a three months period of accomplishments, executing-on-command, and at the same time carrying out planned sabotage activities.

Arrangement to stockpile the sabotage supplies were made.

A few addresses of Norwegians willing to offer assistance were found. In that connection necessary steps are being taken.

Ten maps with military bases were noted. Five planned military camps with transcript or photos will follow via air with the quartermaster. Evaluation has already begun. Further information show planned arson, sabotage actions, silent executions and the use of chemicals to attain temperature fluctuations. The Gestapo's initiatives will continue. Much more information is likely.

Preliminary information also to be found at Bds. and Ast.

Own interpretation: A full scale invasion in Norway is not likely within the next three months, thereafter waves of sabotage actions, and attacks are possible."

General Commander LXXI.X.K.
Ic nr. 69/43 g. Kdos.

The Germans feared a surprise full-scale invasion in northern Norway. They had obtained the names and addresses of Kaare Moursund and Tor Knudsen, the resistance leaders in Tromsø. Moursund and Knudsen were picked up in their homes during the evening of April 1. Erik Reichelt was tortured the following afternoon, proving he spoke the truth when he groaned, "It was not I that betrayed you, Kaare."

The same sender in the German General Commando squad sent an additional report to the same addressee:

"Evaluation sabotage vessel, Toftesund:
26 maps confiscated and eleven situation reports, whereof five have sketched outlines, nine maps from Geographical Section Staff Nr. 4090 1: 00000, conveying Norwegian county charts 1:200000. Primarily maps of established territory reported, and some summary maps of Sweden, the latter probably because of the escape routes to Sweden.

General Commander LKKI.A.K.
Ic Nr. 148/43 III. Ang.

Tromsø, April 6, 1943: A third report was sent out:

"SECRET"
"To the leader of the Air Force North/East."
"Concerning sabotage vessel Toftesund."
Conf.: Tlf.-conversation Captain Treppe/Lieutenant Colonel
Langbein v.6.4

1: Following a report from a Norwegian an enemy vessel
was seized by own minesweeper in Toftefjord 30.3 around
5 p.m. As it neared, the vessel was blown up. The crew
was seized, and overpowered following a shooting battle.

Of the 12 men, two killed, ten taken prisoner, of which two
were wounded.

2: The Norwegian Navy sent the vessel out from Scalloway.
Armaments two machine guns, two machine guns hidden
in barrel, in addition four machine guns, six machine pistols,
four cases of egg-hand grenades, 1000 kilos explosives,
one small hand radio-transmitter. The leader aboard the
vessel was a Norwegian Lieutenant.

3: The purpose was to build an organization for sabotage
actions against military bases, battery positions, military staff
and troop quarters, and bridges. The Administration was in
London.

Build up of the organization over a 2-3 month period.
Stockpiling the sabotage material was planned. The seized
maps presumably showed the operation territory for the
troops between Porsanger and Narvik. In this area certain
sketches showed diverse German Military bases and road
and railway junctions on the mainland, Vesterålen and
Lofoten Islands. Four other vessels with saboteurs aboard
are supposed to land between Tromsø and Bergen."

The General Commander stated that ten men were taken prisoners, two of these were wounded, Reichelt and Eskeland. They knew that there had been 12 men aboard *Brattholm*, and that one was dead, Per Blindheim. They were not quite sure of the last man, was he dead or had he been able to escape? After all, this man had killed a German officer up in the ravine.

In another document, the Germans presented another version of the twelfth man:

> "General Commander LXXI.A.K.A.
> Dept. Ic Ax: BV/2
> Nr.143/43 Secret."
> "Conc. Sabotage vessel Toftesund."
> To the Army High Command Norway/Ic
> Oslo.
>
> "—The escape of the crew from the fishing vessel was prevented by machine gun fire and hand rifles. One man was killed, one man seriously wounded and another man more lightly wounded. One member was killed in the explosion. The Gestapo took prisoners all together ten Norwegians, among them two wounded—"
>
> "—The mine sweeper brought the survivors back to Tromsø, and were taken into custody by the Gestapo. Another search on 31 March did not reveal any additional enemy positions and contacts between the Norwegians on the islands of Rebbenesøy and Hersøy and the saboteurs.—"

According to this report, the twelfth man had blown himself up together with *Brattholm*. And Per Blindheim was dead. The ten survivors were brought to Tromsø, and with this explanation the German High Command had been able to account for all the men aboard *Brattholm*.

The Germans took the information revealed from the attaché case quite seriously. From another report we read:

"SECRET."
To Admiral of the Polar Coast **(?)**
Chief of the Air Force Lofoten
Commander Airfield Territory Moen
1: Concerning the Sabotage vessel Toftesund:
Establishment of five vessels between Tromsø and Bergen to build comprehensive sabotage groups under the direction of the best possibly educated men, modern equipment and large quantities of explosives and hand grenades. Administrated from England. The saboteurs are seeking to make contacts with willing Norwegians patriots.

The enemy has the most accurate information about the military units in Storsteinnes, Setermoen, Finsnes, Kvernmones, Harstad, from Bardufoss Airport extremely good documents regarding their own work.

Continuous vigilance, critical evaluation of sabotage defense, all military quarters, stations and important communication centers and continual education of the troops concerning sabotage Io Nr. 143/43 geh.II. Dangers and sabotage defense is necessary."

Commanding Officer in the Polar Territory.

che helpful miouife

Mikkelvik, early morning, March 31, 1943: A small rowboat moved quietly toward the glazed, frost-covered rocks by the water's edge at Mikkelvik on Ringvassøy Island.

"That house over there in the middle of the field is where the Jensens live." Ingvald pointed to the wooden house. "I'll introduce you to the Jensen family," offered the 17-year old.

"Thanks, but no. I'll be just fine."

"It'll just take a minute. We know them well."

"No! You have risked too much on my behalf already." Jan was firm. "I do not want anyone to see you with me. Row back home and comfort your mother and family. They need you," he directed.

Jacoba Jensen's home in Mikkelvik.

The discussion ended; Jan climbed out of the boat. The men shook hands and said their goodbyes. Ingvald rowed homeward and Jan headed straight for the house some 200 feet from the shore. In the darkness the house stood out like a large boulder; no bushes or trees surrounded it, and Jan hoped he could get inside unseen.

The women on Hersøy Island had told Jan that Jacoba Jensen, the midwife on Ringvassøy, lived in that little house. They felt sure her husband Alfred could give him a lift to Tromsø. Because of the birthing mothers on the second floor, Jan hesitated to disturb the household in the middle of the night. His choices were few though, as his life was at stake.

Jan half-limped up to the entrance door rather optimistically. When Jacoba Jensen, the midwife, opened the door at that hour of the night he was somewhat taken aback. He explained his untimely arrival. Disappointment showed on Jan's face when he learned that Jensen had left for Tromsø a few hours earlier with his boat, *Vesle Tor.*

Jacoba opened the door wide, stepped aside and bid him enter. She tried to make up for his dashed hopes and showed him the same warmth and friendliness the women on Hersøy had earlier. The first floor of the little home had only a kitchen and living room. Jan was ushered toward the small wooden kitchen table, which soon was set with food Jacoba had on hand. He was hungry and the food comforted him.

Jacoba had a couple of women upstairs ready to give birth but this didn't stop her from wanting to help this brave patriot.

"Stay until my husband returns tomorrow."

"Nei, nei, it is too risky."

"I have an idea. We can dress you up as a birthing mother, and tie a scarf around your head."

"No, no this is foolishness," Jan chuckled.

"Being a midwife, I'll come along and care for you," Jacoba offered. "The Germans will not suspect a thing."

"I will not hear of it! You have already done so much. It's too dangerous for you and your family, and the birthing women upstairs."

"At least stay the night and rest up after your ordeal," she coaxed him.

"I cannot take advantage of your kindness. The Gestapo could flock in anytime. The worst scenario would be that I might have to kill myself. I cannot inflict such a drama on you women."

Jacoba waved her hand as if to say, "Nonsense." She realized she could not change Jan's mind. The midwife offered suggestions on where he could safely go, and who to avoid.

"A thousand thanks for all your help," Jan reached his hand out and shook hers firmly. He left without telling her in which direction he was heading.

Upstairs on the second floor, in addition to the birthing mothers, slept the Jensen's 14-year old daughter, Gunnvor. She awoke when she heard her mother talking with a man down in the kitchen. "Strange," she thought. "With Dad out of town. Could it be?... No! I don't believe it!"

She crawled out of bed and laid her ear to the floor. But the voices were muffled and she could not make out what they said. The next morning Gunnvor decided to get the story straight.

"Mother, who visited with you last night?"

"Oh that. It was only Søren from Fagerfjord. He just wanted to know if Dad was going to make a trip to Tromsø, because he wanted to come along."

That was all her mother would say and Gunnvor did not have the courage to ask any more questions. When her father came home the next day and her mother hustled him into the living room and closed the door, she was really puzzled. This was very unusual.

Gunnvor was unable to forget the incident, and when her brother Oddmund came home, she took him aside and told him about the mysterious visit. He understood the gravity of it all.

"You are to shut up about this," he cautioned her sternly. "If this should get out we might lose both father and mother."

Not another word was mentioned about this incident in the Jensen house until Norway's Liberation on May 8, 1945; then Jacoba Jensen told her daughter the whole story.

Outside in the darkness Jan's feelings tugged at him. Once more, without a moment's hesitation, he had been received with abundant kindness. The honorable woman who had helped him never expressed any fear for her own safety, though she knew it meant her death if she was discovered. Across the sound he saw the outline of Rebbenes Island where he had left his other newfound friends. He could only wish them the best.

Jan headed west, though his plan was to go east. His training in

Scotland had taught him, and his own instinct was, to mislead. If someone was on the way to a barn, or watched from a window somewhere, he wanted them to see a stranger walking toward the west.

After several hundred meters he made a sharp turn southward and disappeared between some small round knolls. He then changed direction anew, toward the east. His chosen path took him around the few houses in Mikkelvik. Jan then headed for the water, and followed the rocky beach toward Fagerfjord. He stopped at a house at the end of the fjord, which Jacoba had suggested he do.

Engenes, March 31, 1943: About seven in the morning, Jan arrived at Engenes farm, home of Nelle and Leonhard Johansen, siblings. A friendly pair, the brother and sister welcomed him. Jan told them his story, the same story he had related to the midwife, without revealing any names. After a nice meal, they prepared a comfortable bed for him with several sheepskins in the summer-barn. Jan's concern was always for his helpers first and he had refused to sleep in the house.

Worn from hours of limping and trudging through deep snow and climbing over slippery rocks, Jan gratefully accepted their offerings, but not before he warned them about the Germans. He instructed them on what to say should the Germans come asking questions. Jan fell into a deep sleep that lasted the whole day through and into the late afternoon.

Around 7 p.m. Jan was again on his way, this time to a small hamlet called Karanes. In spite of his wounded foot, he felt refreshed and confident. He chuckled as he looked down on his feet with one rubber boot and one seaman's boot. He had studied and memorized maps of the area and felt sure, even with his footwear, he could scale the mountain that loomed ahead of him.

The mountain abruptly rose and was awkward to climb. Several times he thought he had reached the top only to discover another precipitous climb ahead, more difficult and higher than the last. In the distance, yet another wall rose up before him. Jan fought his way upward, making detours to reach the next cliff. The knitted Selbu mittens given to him by Ingvald were soaked, his fingers frozen. The snow was unduly deep and he sank to his waist often. When he fought to get out, his rubber boot filled with snow and with each step the snow packed itself firmly around his freezing legs. Sometimes the rubber boot came off and Jan turned it upside down and shook it to empty it of the snow.

Toward midnight the Arctic darkness deepened. Yet he could still make out the contour of ridges and gaps of precipices. Some four hours into the climb the ashen-gray clouds merged above. Large fluffy snowflakes began falling. Suddenly the wind increased and the snowfall thickened. Within minutes Jan was in the midst of a gale. In the darkness the wind tore at him and whipped the blinding snow around him, lashing his face and making it impossible to see but a few feet ahead. He pushed upward but soon realized it was futile to continue. Jan knew the fickleness of the Arctic winters; he had to get back to lower ground.

On his way up he had caught sight of a small sheepcote built on a hillside; he needed to reach it. The descent was agonizing and slow but as he neared the empty shed, his distress faded. The wind blew the slat door from his hands and he breathlessly stumbled in and brushed himself off. Farm implements lay scattered around the floor between the piles of hay. Jan gathered enough hay to make a mattress. The wet snowstorm left him soaked and frozen. Ice bits clung to his hair and eyebrows making them frosty white. He removed his boots packed with snow and massaged his feet and legs, trying to bring feeling back into them.

The cracks in the timber along the walls blew the snow straight through, filling corners and other areas with snow, but at least he had cover overhead. Inadequate as it was, Jan was grateful for this shelter from the raging storm. It did shield him from the powerful wind gusts and snow squalls. He buried himself deep into the hay but the night was a cold and sleepless one.

April 1, 1943: The following morning at 6:00 the storm ceased as abruptly as it had begun. Jan left his little shelter and took up his battle with the mountain afresh. Within a few hours a penetrating wind with a thick obscuring mist overshadowed him. The visibility diminished, but this time Jan felt it imperative to reach his goal if he was to survive. Every step he forced himself to take gave him a sense of victory. After several hours, the storm subsided, but heavy storm clouds hovered over him. He reached the ridge of the mountain plateau and far below he saw Veggefjord. (*Vegg* means wall, an appropriate name for this fjord bordered on two sides by mountains jutting straight up from the water.) As soon as he descended the steep mountain, Jan found that he next needed to traverse a white-shrouded marshland covered with shrubs and dwarfed birch trees. The marshland led to a cove at the head of the fjord; after crossing the rocky beach, Jan needed only to climb up the mountain wall on the other side; then he should be able to see Karanes close-up.

The Norwegian soldier expected the large rocks along the beach to be easier to cross than plodding through the deep snow in the marshland, but he found them to be cumbersome and slippery. When he came to the end of the beach where the mountain met the water, he realized the impossibility of scaling it. Should he slip, he would end up in the fjord. Instead, Jan turned inland several dozen yards where the mountains were not quite as treacherous. The snow was deeper, but there was less chance of falling. Once on top, Jan headed back toward Karanes. Thirteen hours he had struggled against the elements, but when he reached the tip of this mountain plateau looking down on the small forest below the tree line, he saw that it bordered a field running down to the shore. Toward the bottom of the field stood the house he had been longing to reach. He was in Karanes. Before him the silver-gray Dåfjord stretched long and wide and at the head laid the little village of Dåfjord, his next goal.

Caught up in his own struggle, Jan did not know that the storm he had been grappling with was the same storm which detained merchant Sørensen from Bromnes at Sheriff Hoel's home following their visit with the Gestapo in Tromsø.

KARANES

Karanes, April 1-2, 1943: Karanes protrudes at the end of the northeast point of Ringvassøy Island, between Veggefjord and Dåfjord. The Hansens were the only people living at Karanes, accessible only by boat. Eighteen miles in a northeast direction lay the island of Vanna. Past Vanna was the Arctic Ocean.

Jan worked his way down the mountainside and through the forest, arriving at the farm of Ragnhild and Morten Hansen around one in the afternoon. In the clearing he spotted a young girl playing by herself in the snow. The little house he had noticed from the plateau looked warm and inviting. At the lower end of the sloped field was a small barn. A little boathouse stood near the breakwater where a rowboat lay tied up.

"Hello, little lady. I came to see your parents. Are they home?"

"*Ja da.* Come with me."

Ragnhild Hansen opened the door as they approached. Working at the kitchen sink, she had seen Jan coming down from the mountains and watched him greet Margareth, their daughter.

Unexpected visitors seldom came to isolated Karanes, and if they did, they always came by sea. Ragnhild wondered who this man was, handsome and terribly frozen.

"Please come in," she said as she stepped back for Jan to enter. "My husband is just firing up the wood stove. Sit down." Ragnhild offered him a chair close to the fire.

Morten Hansen looked a little surprised at their guest, but he was friendly and made Jan feel welcome.

Veggefjord. Jan came down the mountains on the left, crossed the field, climbed up over the mountain ridge on the other side, and continued down to Karanes.

At first the Hansens had a difficult time believing Jan because he refused to tell them where he had come from. Jan's earnest appeal for help won them over. The Hansens found him easy to talk to and were convinced when the commando revealed his Norwegian Navy uniform and pulled his boot off to show them his wounded foot. Shocked at his condition, they never pressed him for further information. The couple was convinced the stranger was telling the truth, and they were filled with amazement and admiration for him. They realized how much he had suffered, both emotionally and physically, and that he had to be totally spent.

The news of Toftefjord had preceded Jan. The Hansens believed his story in spite of the account that all the men of *Brattholm* had been killed. Seeing his sad condition, they offered to share all they had. If they worried about the Germans and the personal risk they were taking, they never let Jan know. Their concern was for this brave Norwegian soldier and how best they could help him to safety.

Jan was calm, but always on guard with his pistol nearby. He was anxious to get away from Ringvassøy Island as quickly as possible and on to Sweden.

The Hansens cleaned and bandaged Jan's wounded foot. They hung his clothes to dry on a line over the wood stove, and they shared with him the best food they had. Both Ragnhild and Morten enjoyed visiting with Jan and hearing his stories of England and his travels. Jan appreciated their kindness.

"I'm eager to see a map of the Troms District. Do you happen to have one?" asked Jan.

"I'm sorry, but we only have a local map. Let me show you your next best bet."

From a kitchen drawer across the room Morten pulled out a map and spread it out on the kitchen table. He brought a piece of notepaper and drew another map which he thought would be of help. Morten's plan was to row Jan to Dåfjord the following day, after he had rested. Jan asked some questions about the map and studied it intently. After a while he tore it up and burned it. "I keep it all up here," Jan said, pointing to his head.

"You're quite a guy," commented Morten. "You seem calm, yet I notice you are always on guard."

"I've got to be; one never knows when the Germans will show." Jan patted his pistol.

"Jan, we'd like for you to stay through the night. I'll make up a bed for you," offered Ragnhild.

"A thousand thanks, but that is too risky for you. Would you mind if I slept in the barn?"

"All right then," Morten said. "Mama, we'll have to make him a comfortable bed of hay."

Before retiring, Jan planned a possible escape route. Even in this remote area, he did not feel safe from the Germans. If they sent a patrol plane, it would be easy to follow his tracks in the snow; they were wide and deep and would lead straight to this house. There was no way to know if the Germans were still searching for him, but they were known to pop up in the strangest places at any hour of the day or night. Jan was not only grateful to the people who had been so generous and willing to sacrifice all for him, he was concerned for their safety; and always, with that concern, was the guilt of leaving his comrades behind.

Later that evening, after retiring and relaxing in his comfortable bed of hay Jan realized how exhausted he was. The last two evenings had not afforded him sound sleep. Fighting his way twelve miles through deep snow over wild mountain plateaus in dreadful storms had robbed him of his strength. He fell into a restless sleep but did not awaken fully until late the next day.

Karanes, April 2, 1943: Jan rested and visited with the Hansens during the remainder of the day until early evening. Though the stabbing pains running through his legs concerned him, Jan still felt good. Being with people and having someone to talk with minimized his discomfort.

During the day the Hansens left Jan alone for a while with their two girls, Margareth and Gerd, while they rowed out to sea to set the long line. "Hopefully the fish will take the bite today," said Morten as he and his wife made ready to leave.

Jan worried when they left. He asked the Hansens' daughters how far it was to a telephone; Jan was concerned the Hansens might report him. He needn't have worried. The Hansens were solid patriotic people and they never said a word about Jan to anyone until after the war.

"In Bjørnskar there lives a man, Einar Sørensen. He is one dependable Norwegian. I know him well. I've been fishing with him several times. You need to go to him, Jan," said Morten just before he was ready to leave.

"Do you think he'd able to help get me closer to Sweden?" Jan questioned.

"He'll not only be able to, but he'll be glad to help. He's probably your best bet to get to the mainland."

"Thanks. I'll not tell him who sent me."

Jan's Karanes visit was encouraging, but he felt pressed to hurry onward; there still were so many miles to cover. Straight south, another eight and a half miles into Dåfjord Sound, lay the sleepy village of Dåfjordbotn, his next goal. From the Hansens' window earlier in the day Jan observed the forested mountains rising to the rear of the village with homes scattered up the slopes. As the day wore on, it started snowing and soon turned to heavy snowdrifts. The north wind roared and stirred up the sea. Huge waves pounded the coast and made it impossible for Morten to take Jan to Dåfjord.

It was close to 8 p.m. when Jan said goodbye to the Hansens.

Thirty-five miles away at Grønnåsen Rifle Range in Tromsø, precisely at 8 p.m., machine gun volleys ripped through the air. Linked together with cow chains, eight courageous freedom-loving men plunged headlong into a dark, dug out marshy tract. Jan's duty was to reach freedom and to tell their story of courage.

Jan worked his way uphill through the snowbound field into the bordering forest. He continued onward into the mountains so as to be hidden from possible onlookers. The Arctic spring added several minutes of light daily and he felt it too chancy to begin his trek on the beach. Jan didn't know it, but the Hansens stood in the window and watched him until the snowdrifts enveloped him and he vanished from their sight.

The wounded commando pressed forward. Enmeshed in his private emotional struggles and physical exertions against the elements, he was spared the knowledge of the fate of his friends from *Brattholm*.

The snow eased after a few hours and Jan headed south toward the rockbound shore. He would make better time there; the snow dwindled along the waters' edge.

Often the steep mountainsides plunged headlong into the sea. Not realizing how steep it was, Jan started his climb, only to be forced back down by the jagged impenetrable masses. His appreciation grew for the many tough weeklong mountain hikes he had endured in Scotland with a heavy backpack. His endurance level had increased, and he was convinced of his own ability to survive this ordeal. He tackled his way back down, and forced a path further inland. Back up on the mountain plateau, Jan worked his way around seemingly impassable places. Repeatedly his crossing took him up, down, forward, and back up again. The pain in his legs haunted him. Exhaustion came sooner this time than it had on his first hike after he had left the sheepcote. The Norwegian's iron will enabled him to push his body through more hours of struggle. Just after five in the morning Jan reached the village of Dåfjordbotn.

ÐÅFJORÐ

April 3, 1943: Jan quickly found the little yellow house bordering the river, just like the Hansen family in Karanes had told him. It stood where the river cascaded over the rocky hillside and flowed straight down into the inlet. It was the only house pressed up against the hillside. But it was too early to wake up strangers. He dug himself down into the snow and lay quietly waiting for smoke to rise from the brick chimney. The forceful north wind blew in a northwesterly direction. Jan waited patiently.

The house was bitter cold after the long freezing night. Artur Olsen, up first this morning, wrapped his robe around him snugly and went downstairs to stoke up the wood stove on the first floor. Sleepily he reached over for the aluminum coffee kettle, added the substitute coffee grains, the only kind available during the war, and water. With the lid lifter he removed the center griddle plate and placed the kettle over the heat. It always took time before the warmth spread through the house and it was reassuring to know a cup of coffee was brewing.

Upstairs Harald, six years old, and his elder brother slept in a separate room from their parents. The young boys liked taking their time getting up, always waiting until after the wood stove had been fired up. The cozy warm down covers kept them warm while the floor remained very cold. Unusual for Harald, this morning he awoke to the sound of his father stoking the wood stove on the first floor. The sound of the crackling fire clearly reached him upstairs.

Harald's morning thoughts were interrupted by a knock on the front door downstairs. The outer-door creaked as his father opened it and Harald heard a stranger's voice. He nudged his brother, and both became quite curious; the suspense made it impossible to stay in bed. They hurriedly dressed and went down to see who this stranger was.

Jan found that convincing Artur Olsen to help was not an easy task. The man was quite nervous and reserved. He had already heard rumors about an escapee from the *Brattholm* disaster. He also knew that the State Police was hunting people with illegal radios, and this he connected with the frozen man on his doorstep. What if he was a German provocateur?

Olsen finally took pity on Jan because of the freezing weather, and though still uncertain as to the stranger's identity, he invited him in.

"You can't stay long, but you need to come out of this weather for awhile."

"Choice weather for me," Jan smiled and kicked the snow off his boots. "My tracks are covered."

Unsure of what to believe, Olsen took a chance. "You can rest here for a couple of hours." He nodded for Jan to move closer to the stove. The crackling wood stove brought Jan's body temperature back up, and his clothes began to steam dry as he snuggled close to the stove. Olsen got his wife Jermine up, and she soon served him coffee and good food.

Jan's optimistic outlook impressed the Olsens. He rubbed his hand over his pistol and told them, "The Germans will never catch me, dead or alive."

Artur liked Jan. He began to believe his story and felt more at ease with him. He shared what he had heard about the Toftefjord incident. "There was a rumor among the people that one man had escaped. But since we did not hear any more, we thought the man had succumbed. Besides, we did not believe anyone could make it in this frigid weather."

"Well, now you know they can."

"We also heard that the rest of the men were either killed in Toftefjord or taken prisoner and brought to Tromsø."

Jan leaned forward. He became edgy.

"Do you have any news of what happened to the men in Tromsø?"

Artur hesitated as he studied Jan's face. "I did hear that those who were captured were taken to Tromsø and…and executed." It seemed cruel to pass such news on to this man who had already been through so much.

Jan's demeanor fell. "I can't help but wonder what went wrong? It is a question I ask myself over and over again."

Olsen changed the conversation to less weighty topics. He drew Jan a map. Jan memorized this map also. While Olsen and Jan were visiting around the coffee table, the boys had to leave for school and their parents said they were not to mention this visit to anyone. Some provisions for Jan's lunch were prepared, and the boys gathered that he would also soon leave. When the boys returned that afternoon, the stranger was gone.

"Boys," Olsen said on their return, "I want to share with you the soldier's last words to me. They were, 'I have not been here. And you, forget that I have been here.' We must heed his wishes. It might make the difference between life and death for all of us. We will never speak of this incident again." Olsen's stern warning not to tell a soul was heeded. The family never mentioned a word about the soldier until after the war.

Again, Jan chose a mountain path hoping to reach Bjørnskar on the south end of Langsund Sound. Accessible by boat, Bjørnskar, nineteen miles south, was in a good location. Maybe he could find someone willing to take him further. He was totally dependent on the willingness of his countrymen to assist him, yet he was acutely disturbed, because to help him they risked life itself.

Langsund divides Ringvassøy Island from Reinøy Island toward the east. Reinøy lies in the main passageway toward Tromsø. On the south promontory of Reinøy Island lies Finnkroken, a heavily fortified German battery installation in the Troms District. Straight west across the fjord on the opposite side of Langsund lies Bjørnskar on the island of Ringvassøy.

Jan wanted to avoid Hansnes and the heavily populated coastal areas of Langsund. It was too risky to walk the shoreline in daylight through populated areas. Germans were stationed all around and the danger of being caught was imminent. He felt safest in the mountains.

Leaving the Olsens' home in Dåfjord, Jan climbed straight up the hillside along the river. When he reached the top of the elongated hill, he turned around in the direction of the cold, steel gray fjord for one last look. The haze partially hid the fjord from his view. Jan then headed for and followed the river path in toward the source, Solvatnet Lake. The snow on these vast mountain plateaus was deeper than he had experienced up to now. He felt like the wet, white mountain masses stood ready to swallow him up. With each step he fell in up to his knees. Often he sank in up to his waist and armpits. He struggled to free himself from the snow's vise-like grip. And when he was able to free his leg, time and again, his one slippery rubber boot would be left in the snow, and he had to dive for it. Step by step, hour after hour, by pure will, Jan forced himself onward against the strong wind and mist that surrounded him. The boots hurt him, and his toes throbbed.

Four days had passed since Jan fled barefoot through the snow around Toftefjord. He knew frostbite had already caused serious damage. Nothing could stop the process once begun. Jan remembered learning about the dangers of frostbite and gangrene from his scouting days. Surely this could not turn out that bad. Jan was uneasy but refused to let fear get the upper hand.

He forced himself onward.

From Solvatnet Lake, Jan set his course over Grønnliskaret Pass, around Soltindene Summit, and down towards Langsundet Sound on the south side. Suddenly the fog evaporated and gave him a glance of the fjord far below. He saw a few scattered houses. It encouraged him onward. His skirmish with the mountains had lasted 28 hours except for the two hours rest he had enjoyed at Dåfjordbotn.

From the fateful moment Jan crawled ashore at Toftefjord, he had put behind him nearly fifty miles on foot. Not very far during normal circumstances perhaps, but Jan had forced his way through long distances in treacherous conditions. Up steep mountains he'd gone, across deserted, frozen tundra and slippery rock-strewn beaches while suffering excruciating pain. His footwear and clothing were inappropriate for Arctic weather conditions. Both his feet had frostbite, and his right foot had a gunshot wound. Hostile weather, fear and loneliness added to his difficulties. No one could help or comfort him nor tell him if he was heading in the right direction. The heaviest burden Jan carried was not knowing the fate of his

Solvatnet Lake. In the background is Soltindaksla Mountain.

friends from *Brattholm*. It gnawed at him continually. "Had they really been executed? Maybe it was just a rumor." His instincts and education, his iron will and ability to endure pain had helped him through. Even so, the soldier nearing Langsund was a wounded man, mentally broken, and close to physical collapse.

DOWN FROM THE MOUNTAINS

April 3, 1943: Jan's first goal in his journey toward freedom was to reach Bjørnskar, but Artur Olsen had suggested he look up Håkon Heika at Kopparelv by Langsund Sound. From the outer ridges of the mountain plateau, Jan looked down upon the few scattered houses by the fjord down below but was unsure if it was Kopparelv or Bjørnskar. The mountainside sloped steeply at first, and ended in a slanted field toward the fjord.

Jan felt good about the tempo he had been able to keep most of the way from Dåfjordbotn, even throughout his six hour struggle against the deep snow and thick fog. In the course of the day he had put more than nine miles behind him. It was three in the afternoon when Jan moved down through the field with the few dwarfed Arctic birches and crawled through the wire fence put up to contain the cattle in their summertime pastures. He didn't realize he was just above the Heika family farm in Kopparelv.

Kopparelv lies on the rainy side of Langsund Sound, skirting the beach. Håkon and his brother Marineus Heika shared the homestead but lived in opposite ends of the house from each other. Both were married, Håkon to Magna, and Marineus to Alida.

As Jan worked his way through the deep snow close to the dilapidated, century-old log outbuilding, he stopped briefly and looked around the farm. He saw two young boys frolic in the snow in the farmyard. The two cousins Arvid and Viggo stopped and watched him closely at first.

From time to time the Heika family had visitors from Skogsfjord, several miles away. The children called in to the adults that they had a

Cousins Arvid and Viggo Heika with author Astrid Karlsen Scott in front of the old outbuilding. The Heikas played here as children in 1943 and greeted Jan upon his arrival from Dåfjord.

visitor from there and then turned to their play. Jan stood there hesitating for a moment, and the boys realized this was a stranger. He looked worn and exhausted, and his clothes were soaked up to his waist; his hair tousled and frosty white. This time the kids ran all the way up to the kitchen window and shouted, "There's a stranger here."

Magna Heika went out to meet Jan, who asked to speak to the man of the house. There was something urgent about his request and she realized this was not just a casual visit. She thought it best to get him indoors before some neighbor caught sight of him.

For Jan, this home was like all the other places he had been. He was showered with kindness and courtesy and concern for his welfare. The table was soon set and his wet clothes removed and placed around the wood stove to dry. Jan wiped his pistol carefully, patted it, and placed it near him on the table. Magna helped remove his boots and wet socks and was astonished to see his feet and legs. She massaged them, applied some healing salve, and bandaged his wounded foot as well as possible. Jan was able to relax and regain his strength. He enjoyed these kind people.

The Heika family was amazed that Jan was so well informed about their little settlement. He knew exactly who the Nazis were and where they lived. They noticed Jan always kept the pistol close by; even when he drank coffee it was next to him on the table.

"I am quite eager to reach the mainland as quickly as possible," Jan explained.

No matter where Jan was, he was continually planning his next trek, where to go and how best to get there. As with one voice, those he had visited recommended that Jan seek a man named Einar Sørensen in Bjørnskar. Håkon Heika and his wife Magna also spoke very highly of this man.

"Einar Sørensen in Bjørnskar is your best bet to help get you to the mainland," said Håkon. "He is a courageous and dependable man."

"*Åja,* there is no one better in this area. You must go to him," urged Magna.

"I have heard many good things about Einar. I need to reach him quickly," said Jan.

"He lives about seven miles from here. The only way to reach him is to walk along the beach. There are no roads."

"The beach will be a lot easier than the mountains," replied Jan.

In their efforts to win the war, the Germans infiltrated and made close contact with several Norwegians in the Troms District. Abwehr, a German spy organization, hired about two hundred of them outright. The secret to Abwehr's success was that they gave each agent a cover name. Many operated so unobtrusively that even their family and neighbors had no idea of their involvement with the enemy. These spies were diligent and were a great help to the Germans. One of the key assignments for some of them on the outermost islands was to keep a close watch on all ship traffic in the ocean and to faithfully report all sightings of boats and convoys to the German Headquarters in Tromsø. This was an easy task, because many were fishermen and no suspicion was attached to them when their fishing vessels sailed out. They were equipped with two-way radios the Germans had given them and taught them to operate.

One such agent was paid 1000 *kroner* (about one hundred and fifteen dollars today) a month during busy periods when his fishing vessel was in service; in less busy seasons he was paid 800 *kroner* per month. It was a goodly sum of additional income for a young man fighting poverty in the Northland in the 1940's. This agent's reason for joining was the promise that his father's fishing vessel would not be confiscated.

This dangerous man lived less than a mile from the Heika family. Being a close neighbor, he knew them well and often dropped in on them unannounced. Kopparelv was sparsely populated and the few homes were spread out. All the same, people knew each other and were always ready to help when a need arose. Abwehr recruited this spy in February of 1942. Even though Abwehr spies worked in secret, knowledge, or at least suspicions of this spy's involvement with the enemy had come to light, and most everyone in the area was afraid of him. The word had quickly spread and a warning to beware of this man was sent out.

To their horror, the Heika family and Jan saw him walking briskly toward the house. Jan leaped to his feet, bolted up the staircase to the second floor and closed the door. The spy had been in Tromsø and the Germans had assigned him the task of inquiring round about in the hamlets and villages about anyone or anything suspicious.

Håkon opened the door. "Well, come on in."

"Thanks. I'm here to invite you to come along with me to collect driftwood around the islands." Large free-floating logs, known as driftwood, were occasionally gathered and used as building materials. The Abwehr spy used this activity as a cover to go ashore and talk to people.

"Oh I don't know. I have a lot of responsibilities right now. I'll pass," said Håkon.

"What do you mean you'll pass? I'm amazed at you, Håkon. There's good money in collecting driftwood as you know!"

"I know, but I've other things going."

"What's the matter with you? This isn't like you, Håkon," said the spy.

"Sorry. I told you this isn't a good time for me."

"Listen here. I don't appreciate being turned down. You'll come or else. This is war and you know things just happen. You know what I mean?" Håkon was not quite sure what the spy meant, but with a family, he didn't want to take any chances.

"Well, I guess I'll have to do my work later. I didn't realize how important it was to you that I'd come along." Håkon said he would come along whatever day he needed him.

Later the spy sent a report to the German headquarters in Tromsø with information he had gathered about the *Brattholm* affair. He made his co-workers on the wood-collecting jaunt, including Håkon Heika, sign the report. The spy expressed afterwards that he felt the Heikas had acted strange on that particular visit, but was unable to ascertain what caused this.

When the spy finally left the Heika family, they were concerned, and didn't know what to do about Jan. When he was brought down, it was all too clear to the Heikas and to Jan that he had to escape while he still had the chance.

Again Jan had been spared disaster. All were relieved that the second floor ceiling had not creaked while the informer was present, and that the children never said a word, nor made a slip about Jan's presence in the house. It was also a godsend that the spy left in the direction he had come without milling about the farm. He could have discovered Jan's tracks leading down from the mountains.

Jan spent a few more hours with the Heika family.

"We know you're anxious to leave Jan, but you have to wait until the snowdrifts start up again before you continue on to Bjørnskar," Marineus, Håkon's brother explained. "I will walk with you down to the beach," he offered.

"See, what happens here in this sector of Langsund, is that the snowdrifts, at this time of the year, begin instantly as if dropped from the sky." Håkon clarified. "The snow will only last ten or twenty minutes, then the horizon will suddenly clear, only to start up again within a short while." The Langsund Sound was fairly narrow around Kopparelv.

"Should someone across the fjord be looking out a window with binoculars, questions could arise about the strange man who left the Heika home with Marinius and headed down toward the beach," Magna laughed. "And soon the telephone wires would heat up."

In isolated areas like these, any exception to the daily routine raises the curiosity level, and particularly so during wartime. The questions might be innocent, without malice, but in the end they would have the same devastating result. Jan's flight would be in the open, and it would only be a matter of time until the Germans learned of it.

"As soon as you notice the snowdrift clearing, drop down and curl up behind a rock if possible, or prostrate yourself flat on the beach and do not move a muscle until the snow starts up again," warned Håkon.

"You've all been so wonderful. I hope you'll be safe. Many, many thanks."

"We wish you God's speed."

With a few sandwiches in his pockets, and directions on how to reach Bjørneskar, Jan was ready to leave the comforts and the warmth of the Heika family.

"Now is the time, Jan. Let's hurry! These snowdrifts will cover us." Marinius had watched for the weather change through the window. The men set off down toward the beach.

BJØRNSKAR

April 3, 1943: Jan felt energized when he left the Heika house. Twilight and the driving snow gave him and Marinius Heika good cover on their way to the shore.

"Here we are. Just follow the water's edge and you will reach Bjørnskar before too many hours," said Marinius.

"Many thousands of thanks, I…"

"Nonsense. No problem, we were happy to help. Hurry while you have the snow cover, Jan. And all good luck to you." Marinius enfolded Jan's hand in his and shook it warmly.

"All good to you and yours, and again a thousand thanks." Jan turned toward Bjørnskar.

The weather, as Håkon had warned, changed between thick snowdrifts and sudden cessations. He took care to lie down quiet as soon as the thick snow let up, hoping to blend in with the rocks. The episode with the spy at the Heika home made him aware of how vulnerable he was. He was willing to take his time to get to Bjørnskar because he knew carelessness would carry a high price. Soon it would be dark and the seven miles along the shoreline to Bjørnskar seemed an easy undertaking compared with traversing the deep snow up and down mountainsides and over plateaus. The snowdrifts and large rocks were probably the best possible camouflage he could have until total darkness set in.

The southern end of the Langsund coastline where Bjørnskar was located, like Dåfjordbotn, had no connecting roads. Jan hurried along as far and fast as feasible while the snow showers hid him. The rubber boots were perilous on the large slippery rocks and boulders and he limped around them when he could. By the water's edge the snow was sparse, so he stayed as close to the water as possible; then again, sometimes the water licked the rocks far inland, making it impossible.

There were no homes along the stretch to Bjørnskar. Because Langsund was heavily mined, there was no traffic on the fjord except for the smaller boats that could maneuver inside the minefields close to the shoreline. Jan's chances of being discovered here in the dark were slim.

Jan had been fleeing four days. The exertions he suffered consumed the physical strength he had regained while resting in the Heika home. In spite of the generous help and rest granted him by all the strangers along the way, his strength ebbed quickly. Despite the nuisance of the rocks, the going was easier down here by the water, but his ability to keep a steady straightforward course had vanished. His arms and legs lacked vigor. Jan's feet moved ahead but his arms hung limp by his side, except when he steadied himself on a large rock. His tracks were those of someone intoxicated, wavering from side to side, but he counted each step as a victory. Jan's whole body ached, his feet the worst. In spite of it all, the word "impossible" was not part of Jan's vocabulary. He didn't know how to give in. In the past he had cheated death more than a few times, and now to reach Bjørnskar was just a question of enduring a few more hours. All he needed to do was to put one foot in front of the other, and not give in to the weight of the anxiety or the pain. In fact, walking seemed almost automatic by now; it had become a habit.

He had been told that there were no houses between Kopparelv and Bjørnskar. Bjørnskar consisted only of three houses belonging to the same family. In the southernmost house lived Bernhard Sørensen and his wife. Close by in the middle house lived his son, Einar Sørensen, and his family. Einar was the man so many had suggested that Jan should contact.

It was near nine in the evening on an unusually dark night for this time of the year. For some time Jan had kept his eyes open for three houses. Jubilation surged through him when he saw a small light coming from a house in the distance as he came around a bend on the shore. The remainder of the way was made quicker and easier with the hope of warmth and friendly people close by. A German patrol boat was stationed just inside

The Sørensen's home in Bjørnskar.

of Sjurnes, less than a mile from Bjørnskar. Jan tempered his excitement with caution.

Nearing the house, Jan made out the silhouettes of a man, a woman, and two young boys sitting around the kitchen table close to the window. He did not know Einar Sørensen and his family were discussing the gruesome tragedy in Toftefjord four days earlier. Einar related to his wife Elna and his two boys what he had heard during his visit to Tromsø. "The rumors are flying. People believe that one man did escape the Gestapo's claws."

"Then it will not be long before he will come visiting us," Mrs. Sørensen firmly resolved.

She was used to her husband's generosity toward escapees and his reputation among the underground. That moment, all noticed a dark shadow below the kitchen window. Einar took a closer look and saw a fatigued and somewhat wobbly form steadying itself by the south house-corner. The form stopped a few feet back from the steps leading to the kitchen door, and peeked through a window. Einar turned to his family and looked somewhat astounded.

The Sørensen family. From left, Odd, Elna, Ragnhild, Einar and Svein in 1950.

The four of them looked at each other and all thought, "He is here already!" Einar hurried to open the door and went out into the cold to meet the stranger, who asked for Einar Sørensen.

Jan was ushered into the warm kitchen, where he again told his story, that he had come from Toftefjord and as far as he knew he was the only survivor from the skirmish with the Germans and the warship.

"My situation is desperate. I need to escape across the border to Sweden as soon as possible."

Einar did not feel comfortable with Jan's story; it was difficult to believe that a wounded, hunted man could have survived the Arctic weather conditions for four days not knowing the area, and not properly outfitted.

"Tell me, if you can, how did you find Bjørnskar? And how did you know we were here? Who sent you?" Einar had to know.

It was obvious to Jan, from the many people who spoke highly of Einar, that he was a respected and trustworthy fellow. Jan knew he would be in a despairing position if he was turned down. He tried a bluff. "The reputation of your good deeds has reached London."

"You mean they arrived in London?" Sørensen asked, surprised. His answer revealed that he had helped others escape.

"I can't tell you for sure if those you helped reached London, or Sweden, but at least the report of your efforts has reached London." Jan felt a twinge of guilt for leading this good man on.

Subsequent to Jan's explanation, Einar was satisfied; it was not a question of him being willing to help, but rather how he could best help Jan get out of the difficulties that he was in. His wife was not so easily convinced. She wanted more answers and continued her questioning.

"Tell us how many other homes have you visited?"

"None."

"Who were the people you saw?"

"Yours is the first home I have stopped at."

"Who gave our names to you?" Elna ignored Jan's answers and kept pressing. Jan became a little irritated at this lady and somewhat indignant at her repeated questioning.

"Listen here. How many ways do I have to repeat the same answer? I've told you yours is the only home I have visited."

Jan firmly denied ever having been any other place. During his saboteur training with the Linge Company in Scotland it was strongly impressed upon the men never to reveal the name of anyone who had helped.

Elna backed down. "I'm sorry. We just have to be sure. You understand, don't you?"

"I understand and appreciate your concern. And I realize you have to be careful. I am also grateful you invited me in out of the weather."

Following the settling of this little controversy, all three enjoyed and were open toward one another. The Sørensens had Jan remove his wet clothes and hung them to dry, and they gladly shared with him what food they had available. Under such soothing conditions, Jan soon relaxed a bit and felt his body slowly recovering.

Considering his traumatic, demanding last few days, Einar noticed that this man was in incredibly good condition. However, he had a difficult time understanding how he had been able to survive the trek across the untamed mountains in the middle of the arctic winter storms with a wounded foot and no skis. Einar had great admiration for such a man, his courage and fortitude. Jan lightly dismissed it by saying, "I had good training in Scotland; I was in good shape, and I am the right age."

He took out his pistol, polished it and stroked it; a grateful smile brushed his face. "This gun saved my life when I shot the Gestapo chasing me up the ravine in Toftefjord."

At first, they did not talk much about the battle in Toftefjord. Instead they concentrated on the possibility of getting Jan to Sweden. He felt bad that he still did not know the true fate of the men from *Brattholm.*

"I just returned from Tromsø earlier today," said Einar.

"What can you tell me?" Jan leaned forward attentively.

"The people were in shock. Rumors were flying as the story of the battle in Toftefjord got out. The tragedy was on everyone's lips."

"What did the people know? Or was it just rumors that they'd heard?"

"It was rather chilling," Einar continued. "When the evening sky darkened they all stayed inside and pulled the blinds. They were frightened, and in spite of that, they could talk of nothing else. Terror spread of what reprisals the Germans would mete out on the populace. There was special concern for the resistance men and whether the movement would be unraveled. Everyone's nerves were raw."

"And the Germans? What did they do?"

"Oh…that was the astonishing part! It was not only the Norwegians who were scared; the Germans were unnerved as well. The Gestapo headquarters was buzzing and the German soldiers were called on an immediate alert. Throughout the city they were marching through the streets with loaded guns, breaking into homes, pushing people around, questioning and arresting some and hauling them into the patrol wagons. Patrol cars, with screeching sirens, sped off to the Gestapo headquarters with them. Many Germans wondered if the *Brattholm* affair would be the beginning of the suspected Allied invasion."

"And what did you learn about the *Brattholm* men?"

"The way I heard the story," Einar continued, "was that a fishing cutter had anchored in Toftefjord and that the boat had had trouble with its motor. But there were no fishermen aboard, only saboteurs from England."

"How did the Germans find us?"

"The story was that a merchant at Bromnes had betrayed the saboteurs. The Gestapo was called and a German warship, a *Schnell* boat, launched the surprise attack against them. The cutter had been blown up, and the remaining crew imprisoned."

Jan was totally absorbed in Einar's report. "And my comrades? What did you hear about my comrades?"

Einar hesitated, but he realized he couldn't keep anything from Jan. "It was believed that most of them were shot on the spot. Nonetheless when the warship returned to Tromsø the people had noticed that the Gestapo had three prisoners, two of them seriously wounded. The third man seemed older than the rest."

"That must have been Eskeland," Jan interrupted.

"It was also said," Einar was loath to pass on this piece of news, "that two of them were shot the following day, but that a third one was still alive either in the hospital or imprisoned."

Jan was helpless against the depression that settled over him when he learned the fate of his friends. The realization set in that he was indeed the only survivor. Guilt swept over him that he had been unable to help his comrades. It also occurred to him that the two contacts in Tromsø, Moursund and Knudsen, the underground leaders, had to be forewarned.

"This is a messy situation, Einar. With one, or possibly more of the *Brattholm* men still alive, there is no doubt the Gestapo will torture the men. It's obvious that in time, one or more will break," said Jan.

"It's humanly impossible not to," agreed Einar.

"We have to warn Moursund and Knudsen somehow. I would like to go and warn them myself." Jan was in earnest.

"That's unthinkable! You'll be arrested and executed."

"Einar, do you dare take the risk? It is a lot to ask."

"You know our identification cards are always checked going in and out of the city. And I have just come back," Einar was thoughtful. "The Germans have the uncanny ability to keep track of everyone and everything going on around them. Moreover, gas rationing is on and Tromsø is some 20 miles away."

"It's too much," Jan reflected. "It was a terrible thing of me to have asked."

"Give me some time, I'll find a way."

"Please be extremely cautious. You know the possibility remains that Knudsen and Moursund might already have been rounded up, or they at least might be shadowed."

"Yes. All things considered, Jan, it might not be safe to keep you here overnight."

Jan and Einar sat at the kitchen table and discussed Jan's continued flight.

"If we can get you to the mainland on the other side of Grøtsundet Sound, you will be closer to Sweden without risking your life going into Tromsø," said Einar. Both men were aware that Jan's flight was extremely dangerous both for his helpers and for himself.

They decided to leave around two in the morning, the darkest time of the night. Einar would take Jan across the fjord in his rowboat. Jan would be set ashore close to some friends of Einar's, a family where he knew Jan could safely get some rest.

Jan left his code name with the Sørensens in case he didn't reach his destination alive. The code was MARTIN 3. Elna wrote it down on the back of their kitchen calendar in the right hand corner, a simple square piece of cardboard. In the center of the front, a smaller block of 365 pieces of white paper was glued. Bold black numbers were printed in the center of the white paper, one for each day of the year. Holidays and Sundays were easy to distinguish and those numbers were printed in red. Each day a numbered piece of paper was torn off. On the back of the Sørensen calendar it now said, "MARTIN 3." Maybe this was not the safest place if the house was raided. In any case, they all hoped that Jan would reach Sweden in safety, eliminating the need to give his code name to the Norwegian authorities in the future.

EINAR AND BERNHARD

Einar needed someone to come with him to take Jan across the fjord. The choice was between his stoic, seventy-six year old father and his oldest son, Odd. Just fourteen years old, Einar's son was a good lad and strong; moreover he was anxious to come along and help his father. In truth, both Einar's sons would have liked to help.

There was a good chance that no one would return. Should this be their lot, his wife would lose both a husband and her oldest son, and Einar felt that was too much to ask of a woman. He chose his father Bernhard.

Bernhard had worked hard all his life and had even rowed the 125 miles to the Lofoten fishing grounds on occasion. He was still strong and vigorous despite his years. And, with his heart full of hatred for the Germans, he would relish the opportunity to snatch Jan away from under their noses. Einar went next door and discussed it with his father, who readily accepted the challenge. He and his father worked out the details of how to transport Jan further.

The Sørensens outfitted Jan with dry clothes. Jan wore the civilian clothes underneath his Navy uniform. Should the Germans be lucky enough to catch him, he wanted them to know he was a soldier above all, nothing but a Norwegian soldier.

Elna prepared some traditional open-face sandwiches for Jan, the only kind Norwegians made, with a little cured meat. She placed a small square piece of wax paper between each slice of bread, and then wrapped them all securely in a separate piece of wax paper. Jan put several of these packages in his pockets. He had learned how tough it was to be hungry in the mountains, but a knapsack he did not want to carry.

At long last, Jan's one military boot and the one sea boot were retired for real ski boots. The Sørensens even had a pair of skis with bindings that fit. The boots were quite snug for Jan's feet, but at least he could wear one pair of dry socks with them, and Jan felt it was quite an improvement over the rubber boots.

The old unmatched boots had been with Jan in so many places they had become part of his own pain and struggles. They reminded him so much of the generous ladies who had first given them to him, Haldis and Anna at Hersøy Island. He was reminded of the snowstorms, and of being numbed by cold, pain and frostbite. When he changed his boots at Einar's, Jan felt like he was leaving two friends behind.

Southeast of Bjørnskar across Grøtsundet Sound was the little settlement of Snarby, almost seven miles across the water. Jan had to get off Ringvassøy Island if he was to make any serious progress toward Sweden. On the southernmost point of Reinøy Island, on clear days, they could see Finnkroken from Bjørnskar. From here the powerful searchlights of the German batteries constantly skimmed the waves. A few hundred meters out from Finnkroken lay Finnøya and Nipøya Islands; between them was a narrow sound. This was Sørensen's route to Snarby.

There were three main gateways for ships to sail into the city of Tromsø. Kvalsundet Sound on the west side of Ringvassøy Island, Langesund Sound on the east, which was loaded with mines, and the third entrance, Grøtsundet Sound, which was guarded by a German patrol boat which went shuttle-wise back and forth twenty-four hours a day. It went as far north as Grøtnesodden and to the battery installations at Lattervika on the north side of the Ullsfjord. In the south, the patrol boat turned between the battery installations at Tønnes and the estuary at Kvalsundet Sound. From here it was open sea to Tromsø. Most ships or small boats on their way to Tromsø for the first time were ordered to stop for control at the battery installations at Tønnes.

It was unusual that boats were stopped, however, unless they arrived at unusual times or came from unusual directions. In that case, they would have to be prepared to stop. A rowboat on its way from Bjørnskar to

Snarby in the early morning hours was definitely unusual as far as distance and time of day went. The challenge was to cross the wide fjord without being discovered by the patrol boat.

The route the patrol boat took southward gave them a little more time than the northern route. The Sørensens' plan was to cross the fjord to Finnøya and Nipøya Island, lie in hiding on the northern end of Nipøya, wait for the boat to pass them on its southern route, then start out again across Grøtsundet Sound toward Snarby.

A thick fog surrounded them when they left. The men were a little concerned about the unstable weather conditions. The wind blew a strong gale and they were surrounded by a thick whiteout. The Sørensens knew the rough seas would increase as they went further south, where the prevailing winds came screaming down the shipping lanes from the Arctic Ocean. There was a limit as to what a small rowboat with three men aboard could handle, but on the other hand, the Sørensen men were used to rough seas and wind, and they knew the seas had to be quite high before the rowboat would capsize. The thick snow reduced their visibility, so much so that all land vanished from sight, but they had learned to navigate by the directions of the waves. The blinding snow, though limiting, was also a good camouflage from the patrol boat.

The patrol boat chugged past Nipøya and the three men watched intently as the lanterns disappeared in the soupy gray-white mixture of heavy fog and snow. As soon as the boat vanished in the darkness, they started out on the remaining four miles across Grøtsundet Sound. With the wind to their back, they made good headway. Though Jan had rested, he did not have much strength left. He was still very tired, so much so that he was grateful when they did not ask him to row. If they had, he was sure they would have had a hard time believing he was a Navy man.

Often when the men dipped the oars into the white-capped waves and pulled them out again they were splashed with seawater, but beyond that, they reached the other shore safely without any major mishaps.

With warm handshakes and well wishes, Jan was put ashore just north of the headland at Lyngnes. From there it was only a few hundred yards to the nearest farm. The Sørensen men, Jan learned later, had an extremely tough return trip. They fought a roaring northwesterly headwind and did

Jan was brought ashore just north of Lyngneset.

not arrive home until the morning hours. Luckily no one had seen Jan, no one discovered that the men had been rowing most of the night – and no one knew they returned with one less man.

The family at Bjørnskar had outfitted Jan for the next segment of his escape. In spite of the difficult times, with shortages of commodities and food, a generous spirit of selflessness and compassion characterized all the people he met in the Troms District of northern Norway. They offered all they had to the wounded soldier, a stranger in need. At the same moment they placed their own lives and those of their families in danger. Jan was deeply touched by this. He knew and understood only too clearly what they had offered. The Germans had tacked copies of a public notice on telephone poles and bulletin boards across Norway with an unmistakable message. The notice read:

"ANYONE CAUGHT HELPING THE ENEMY WILL BE SHOT!"

To the Germans, the "enemy" was anyone involved in opposing the Germans. Jan knew this, and it was this knowledge that continually made him shrink from placing more people in harm's way. Desperation forced him to seek help, but he was careful never to reveal where he came from or where he was going. He could never, on purpose, remember the names of any of his helpers when he was asked.

Einar kept Jan's boots hidden in the boathouse. One day, several weeks after Jan had left, the district doctor came by boat. His boat was rather large and he called for Einar to row out to meet him.

"These are for you to replace the ones you gave away," said the doctor, who winked at his friend as he handed him the package.

"I don't understand," said Einar.

"You will. I hope you'll get a chance to enjoy them."

Einar was astonished when he opened the package and beheld a new pair of ski boots. He didn't ask questions, but shook the doctor's hand warmly. Einar was still shaking his head when he left his boat.

*"Be convinced that
to be happy means to be free
and that to be free means to be brave.
Therefore do not take lightly
the perils of war."*

— **Thucydides**

Løvli

April 4, 1943: The rugged Sørensen men rowed away as Jan picked up the skis and poles and placed them on his shoulder. He continued a few yards along the sandy beach. The Sørensens had pointed out the house where Jan should seek help. Directly ahead about 300 feet from the beach lay the houses belonging to the Løvli farm, owned by Alfred and Anatona Lockertsen. They had a grown daughter and a 12 year-old foster son, Alvin, who had come to live with them a year earlier.

Today was Sunday. Alfred and his wife's bedroom was a small side room on the first floor, close to the front entryway. The walls were not heavily insulated and Alfred awakened to a noise in the anteroom. It was inky-black, and he rolled over and glanced at the green-lighted figures on the alarm clock. Four in the morning! No one ever came visiting at this hour of the night, and especially not at this time of the year. A visitor now could only mean someone was in grave need of help or it was the Gestapo! Alfred reasoned the Gestapo would have made more of an uproar. Rolling out of bed, he dressed hastily and went to open the door. A dark-headed, frozen stranger faced him.

Jan greeted Mr. Lockertsen and at the same time apologized for the early hour. His presence, tall and handsome with the skis and poles at his side, exacted Alfred's close attention. He had come out of nowhere, and it was still night. When Jan explained to Alfred that he had escaped from the Germans following a battle in Toftefjord, Alfred just shook his head. He had a difficult time believing this man was who he said he was. Alfred had also heard about the happenings at the mouth of the fjord. The story he had heard was to a great extent similar to that of Einar's at Bjørnskar, but not quite. It was Alfred's understanding that all twelve men from *Brattholm* were taken as prisoners and executed. This caused him to be quite skeptical and cautious about Jan's story. If what Alfred had been told earlier was the truth and all twelve men had been caught and executed, then who was this man standing before him in the doorway? Was he a charlatan or was he telling the truth? Was he a bona fide Norwegian commando soldier or was he a provocateur, sent to trap him? His searching eyes observed the stranger was clean-shaven, but his cheeks and nose had a deep ruddy hue making him appear windblown and frozen. Alfred wanted to believe, but he was not persuaded that Jan was telling him the truth. On the other hand, he concluded that if he was telling the truth, he desperately needed his help. Jan was invited in, and was told to lie down on the large sheepskin in front of the kitchen stove to get some rest. Lockertsen wanted to steal a couple of more hours of sleep before getting up, but sleep escaped him; he lay on his bed staring up at the dark ceiling, pondering and being anxious.

The man lying on his kitchen floor, was he an escapee or something else? Lockertsen was mystified. If he did not report him, the entanglement with this man might have ill-fated consequences.

Around 6:30 a.m. Lockertsen moved quietly into the kitchen to start the morning fire in the wood stove. He liked to heat the kitchen before he did his barn chores and enjoyed the welcoming warmth of his home when coming in from the coldness outside. He had scarcely poked his head in the kitchen door when Jan flung himself about to a half kneeling position while at the same time grabbing his pistol and pointed it point blank at Alfred. In that moment Alfred was convinced Jan was no provocateur. This was the action of a desperate man.

Jan had been without sound sleep for 48 hours. Worn to a frazzle, he reacted like a wounded, frightened animal. The ruthless ordeals of the last four days were forcing their way to the surface. He had been half asleep drifting between consciousness and slumber when Alfred stuck his head in the door. Any slight unexpected movement put Jan on guard.

Alvin, the foster son, was sleeping in the room directly above the kitchen, known as the north-room. He woke up at 8 a.m., when Anatona started the milk separator that stood in the hall at the bottom of the steps. Merging with the reverberation of the separator were two male voices coming from the kitchen. Effortlessly he distinguished his foster father's deep resonant voice with its enthusiastic Nordland's dialect, but to whom did the other voice belong? It was a gentler voice, and more careful. Alvin knew straight away, since he was from the South, that the other man did not have a Nordland's dialect at all, but that the stranger spoke with a distinct Southern tongue. He was amused listening to the two men; they spoke with entirely diverse dialects, yet they understood each other perfectly it seemed. Yes, the other man definitely had to be from Southern Norway.

Snarby was a rather deserted, almost forsaken, place north of Tromsø. There was neither road nor telephone communication out here, and Alvin could not remember that a stranger had ever dropped in like this. "So who was this man from Southern Norway? Why did he come in the early morning hours? How had he found them? Who had sent him?" He had so many questions.

Alvin started down the attic stairs but was met half way by his foster mother. Her face was sober.

"Who is that man in the kitchen?" asked Alvin.

"Oh that is just Astrid's boyfriend. He came to surprise her."

"At this hour of the morning? You are just kidding me?"

Anatona could see Alvin's doubts. "All right young man, I'll tell you the truth. But you breathe a word to anyone, and we are all dead! He is a Norwegian commando soldier, the only escapee from the battle in Toftefjord."

"Wow! Why did he come here? How long will he stay?" Alvin found this exciting.

"I am afraid I can't answer any of your questions. You must understand that we can't talk about this, not even to your best friend. It might mean the soldier's and our lives if word gets out. Do you promise not to tell anyone?"

Alvin thought for a long time. Though he was young, he grasped the severity of the situation. Should the Germans come, there were no possibilities of escape and the adults would be shot. The women would probably also be shot or sent to a concentration camp.

Alvin looked into Anatona's unyielding eyes and knew this was serious business. He feebly reassured himself that the Germans probably would extend mercy to him because of his young age and because he really did not belong to the family.

"What is your answer, Alvin? You must not reveal this secret to any other human being. Do you promise?"

"Yes. You have my word," vowed Alvin.

On Sunday afternoons, Alvin's friends from neighboring farms came over to play with him. Today was different.

"You must keep your friends away from the farm today. You go to one of their homes."

Alvin understood and did as he was told.

Intent on continuing his escape, Jan hoped to leave Løvli farm within a short period of time. The fear that innocent people would be harmed or sent off to a concentration camp because of him was ever in his mind, and it made him uneasy.

"It means a lot to me to be on the mainland at last," Jan said happily. "I'm impatient to put my new skis on and begin to climb these forested mountains. I want to head eastward en route to Sweden."

"Jan, you don't have any conception of what the terrain is like out there. It is not a good idea," said a skeptical Alfred. "I'll find you a better alternative." The older man produced a map and spread it out on the table. "Look Jan, this is Løvli farm." He pointed on the map. "Right here, at the outermost part of a huge peninsula, there are miles of steep, precarious Alpine mountain terrain, beginning just to the back of the farm with cavernous clefts. There are no natural paths for a skier to follow. And the weather is unpredictable. Masses of loose, deep snow, and nowhere you can seek help or shelter from the storms."

Jan listened intently, following Alfred's finger on the map.

"The southern part of the peninsula tapers to a narrow neck of land where the German watch posts are strategically stationed," Alfred continued. "On either side of the peninsula, the fjords cut deeply through to the innermost part of the region. If you attempt that route, Jan, it'll all end tragically for you."

Jan relaxed somewhat with this new information. The Lockertsens wanted him to have some rest before he continued onward and showed him up to an attic room, with a window toward Grøtsundet Sound, where he could get some sleep. This room belonged to the Lockertsen's married daughter and son-in-law, but both she and her husband were away. The husband was fishing in Lofoten, and the daughter was in the hospital. From the Cape Cod window in the attic Jan had a splendid view of Grøtsundet Sound, which unfolded before him like a rich blue carpet. He sank down on the bed, and watched as a German patrol boat, probably the same boat that the Sørensens and he had outsmarted the night before, moved unmenacingly past.

The wintry weather had been cold and nasty for some time, but today it had dawned with a bright Northland sun and azure skies. The view from the attic window blessed Jan with peaceful moments while reclining on the bed, though the burden when recollecting the fate of his friends was a hurtful memory he was unable to erase.

Sunday dinner at the Lockertsen's home was always at 12:30 p.m. sharp, and this day was no exception. Jan had been invited to join them. He savored every bite. Jan couldn't remember the last time he enjoyed food to this degree and such a large, warm meal.

The Lockertsens had locked the outer entrance door, just to be sure of no surprises today. Jan looked handsome dressed in his Navy uniform with the Norwegian flag on his shoulder, the pistol by his side. The German patrol boat was returning and everyone thought it came conspicuously near, but

The Lockertson Family

it glided past on its way northward.

Save for the patrol boat and Jan, the afternoon was like any other Sunday at Løvli farm. Every now and then it was difficult to remember the war was raging all around, yet in this home, this afternoon was peaceful and consoling, almost serene.

Astrid, the Lockertsen's younger daughter, had done her best to care for Jan's wounded foot. She washed it with tender care, and applied salve and a new bandage. Her experience in such things was minimal, and she worried that with its appalling coloring, the foot was infected. The nearest doctor was in Tromsø, three hours away by motorboat. The Lockertsens had a boat, but there was no way they could bring a doctor to Løvli farm without someone prying and wanting to know why, not to mention the risk of being stopped by the Germans.

Jan returned upstairs and fell into bed following dinner. Although the Lockertsens had made him extremely comfortable, his mind was ever rehashing the harrowing experiences of the last few days. When sleep finally came, he slept well for a few hours.

At this time of the year, Alfred was busy setting fish nets out in Ullsfjorden. They were set at the innermost part of Jøvika Cove in the Kjosenfjord. To get there, he had to row northeast toward Grøtsundet Sound around the promontory into where the Ullsfjord cuts inland toward the south. Further in, it divides into Kjosenfjord toward the east and Sørfjord toward the south. The distance of travel round trip was almost twenty miles.

Alfred owned a remodeled dory without a deck. A small wheelhouse was built toward the front of the boat, close to the motor. Below the wheelhouse a modest little cabin was embodied. They called the boat *Bloffsen,* but its official mark was "AKT-T28 TD." Her crew, in addition to Alfred, was his son Jon, who lived in a neighboring house on the south side of Løvli farm, and Peder Nilsen from Svarvaren a little further south.

Monday mornings, it was Alfred's habit to sail into Jøvika Sound. On this Sunday he changed his schedule. He and Jan had come to a possible solution. They would put to sea late Sunday evening after dark, and plot a course for Nordkjosen, in Ullsfjord. From there Jan could ski by way of Lyngen, with Sweden as his final objective. Alfred would bring his usual crew. Earlier in the day he had sent his daughter Astrid with a message to Peder Nilsen. She walked south on the beach along the fjord, then cut across a field below Peder's home, and knocked on the door.

"Mr. Nilsen is it possible for you to come a little earlier today? The weather forecast is not promising and Papa said they could not postpone the fishing trip to Jøvika until Monday morning as planned earlier."

"No problem. I'll be there."

Peder, a husband and father, worked a small farm in Svarvaren in addition to being part of *Bloffsen*'s crew. Just at this time Peder and his wife were deeply sorrowing. Their two-year-old son Norman had accidentally burned his foot on the wood stove. The burn got infected and fever set in. They took him to the hospital in Tromsø, but little Norman never returned home.

This crushing sorrow enveloped the Nilsens when Astrid came visiting them. Nonetheless Peder was a kind, remarkable human being, sober minded and selfless. He would never turn his back on anyone who needed him, no matter what the situation. He liked working unnoticed. He was a good friend, honorable and courteous.

Peder had an early afternoon dinner with his wife before he went northward. When he reached Løvli farm, Alfred was out in the farmyard pacing back and forth, chewing tobacco and spitting. He did not say a word to Peder though he had seen him coming. Peder guessed something was wrong.

Alfred was aware Peder knew the Toftefjord story. Suddenly he turned to him and shared his burden. During the night a stranger had come, the only survivor from the *Brattholm* tragedy in Toftefjord. He was on a desperate flight from the Germans and was trying to reach Sweden. Lockertsen wondered if Peder would help with the further transport of this man. Peder expressed instant willingness to help. They agreed they would transport him to Tyttebærvika (Lingonberry Cove) in Kjosen.

Later that afternoon the weather changed and strong wind gusts brought snow showers and awful visibility. In reality, the weather was in their favor since they had to travel across Grøtsundet Sound in the channel where the German patrol boat traveled. Between four and five p.m. they made ready. Jan wore his uniform and he was wearing a thick, Russian style leather cap. A few days earlier Alvin had found it on the beach. It had been washed and dried, and he gave it to Jan.

Jan was eager to leave, knowing he would soon be able to try out the skis and ski boots he had received at Bjørnskar. Peder noticed the boots were just a smidgen too small, and he was concerned the cold would harm Jan's already disfigured foot. He cut soles to fit inside the boots made from cellulose. Cellulose was a material easily obtainable during the war and used for many purposes; it is the chief substance composing the cell walls of fibers of all plant tissue. He stuffed the soles into Jan's boots. Though they crowded Jan's feet, Peder hoped they would prevent the cold from penetrating the bottom of his boots.

The dock at Løvli from which <u>*Bloffsen*</u> *set out.*

Anatona readied several small food packs and Jan put them in every pocket of his uniform. He accepted a small knapsack this time. It was filled with a change of clothing and extra food.

The wind nipped at the four men as they made their way down to the dock. Alvin followed all the way to the wharf but was not allowed to go aboard. He thought this had been a most action-packed Sunday.

Bloffsen's rope was unfastened and Alfred went into the wheelhouse and navigated the boat into the open waters. Jan spent most of his time below with Alfred's son. Amid their small talk, Jan readied and polished his pistol.

The heavy snowdrifts and wind and *Bloffsen* with no lanterns were ominous signs. Intermittently the snowfall ceased, the sky cleared, and at that moment the brilliant stars and moon shone forth. The celestial bodies are brighter up close to the North Pole, and there was no place for *Bloffsen* to hide during those moments. Peder kept watch in those brief intervals of cessation. He could dimly make out the patrol boat pressing toward Grøtnesodden. The Germans aboard the patrol boat knew most of the fishing vessels that went back and forth in these waters; seldom were any of them stopped. If they were called toward the patrol boat, it was usually on the way in from the sea, and most likely because the Germans wanted to buy some of their newly caught fish.

The men had loaded a sizeable quantity of fishing nets and other fishing gear aboard *Bloffsen*. They intended to hide Jan under it should the German patrol stop them. Jan insisted this was too risky for them, and felt the Germans would assuredly look underneath the fishnets if they were hunting an escapee. Instead he had Alfred navigate close to land, so that he could slither right into the water and swim to shore without the Germans discovering him. They did as Jan wished, but no one believed he would survive on the mainland very long after such a swim. Coming ashore soaking wet, in deep snow and freezing wind where the houses were scarce, and no one to give him help, he surely would freeze to death in such a situation.

Even Alfred could not help. It would be impossible for him to turn towards the shore after a German inspection, they would at once become suspicious of them. At the first opportunity after sailing around the northern end of Ullstind Peak, they set the course into the Ullsfjord, relieved that the most dangerous area was behind them. They had made good time and were a little earlier than expected. As a result Alfred slowed *Bloffsen*, not wanting to arrive in Kjosen before midnight. They wanted to take advantage of the darkness.

The men worked their way to the innermost section of the fjord before they ventured over toward the eastside. A short distance past Storsteinnes, on the north side of Kjosenfjord was Tyttebærvika. A deserted place, Lockertsen owned a small boathouse in the cove with fishing yarns draped over wooden racks in front. He headed *Bloffsen* straight in that direction.

Near midnight they reached the boathouse. The tide was out, and *Bloffsen*'s motor was shut down some distance from the shore, the water being too shallow to continue all the way in. All the men were willing to bring Jan ashore, but Jan asked Peder to help him these last remaining yards.

Aboard *Bloffsen* they had a small dinghy. It was hard for Jan to say goodbye again, to people he had gained such respect for and to whom he owed so much. He climbed over the railing into the ready dinghy, seated himself in the stern, and was handed the skis and the poles. On his back he had his little knapsack.

Rocks were everywhere. Peder rowed carefully, but they kept colliding with them. At last he pushed with one oar on the bottom to help move them along. Even that only worked for a few yards before the boat stranded. He jumped into the icy water and dragged Jan and the boat as far as possible. Then he went back and got Jan's skis, poles and the knapsack and brought them over by the boathouse. He re-entered the water, and carried Jan on his back, an arm around each of his legs, and with Jan's arms around his neck. When they reached the boathouse Peder turned his back to the boathouse and the ladder enabling Jan to climb up dry-shod. Jan was of a much larger stature than Peder but Peder kept a good balance amidst the slippery rocks while bringing him ashore in the dark. Peder now returned to the dingy, waded into the water and dragged it to safety on the shore.

The two men visited under the cover of the fishnet for about one hour. Peder mentioned some relatives he had in Lyngseidet, and suggested Jan look them up should he have difficulties. He gave Jan good pointers and directions. He also updated him about the surrounding terrain, where he should go, and where there might be danger.

When the subtle light from the midnight sun became visible in stark contrast to the serrated mountain peaks in the distance, Jan reached out and clasped Peder's hand firmly, "I know no names," he assured him. Peder understood it to mean that if Jan was taken a prisoner he could not reveal any names, because he did not know them, and they did not have to be concerned.

"No German will ever catch me," he continued. In his gun he had one cartridge left, saved for himself should it be necessary. Jan heartily thanked Peder, and slipped away into the darkness on his skis.

A NARROW ESCAPE

April 5, 1943: The loneliness of Tyttebærvika (*Lingonberry*) seeped into Peder as he stood and watched Jan vanish into the shadows. Jan had come into his life only a few hours earlier but he had left a deep impression. The two men had communicated spirit to spirit, and with his whole being Peder wanted Jan to reach Sweden unharmed. Having just lost his son Norman, Peder did not want to lose his newfound friend as well.

A narrow motor-road snaked along the Kjosenfjord a few feet up from the shore. Traffic was sparse on this road. Sometimes

Peder Nilsen, 1999

Peder Nilsen being interviewed by Tore Haug.

the whole night could pass without a car being seen. A few miles ahead Lyngseidet Village was crawling with Germans and who could know when they would show?

Jan was jubilant. For the first time since Toftefjord he did not have to fight the elements and wade through deep snow or cross mountain plateaus. Ahead lay the open snow-covered road with great skiing conditions. It was the middle of the night and running into people was not a concern. Should he notice approaching car lights it would be an easy thing to fade into the woods bordering the road. In truth this was the first time he felt a road beneath him since he broke away from the Germans. He had food and other necessities in his knapsack. The weather was fairly good, and he was an excellent skier. Re-energized by the circumstances and the hope of soon reaching Sweden, Jan glided across the smooth roads. Sheltered by the darkness he moved rapidly toward Kjosen at the end of the fjord, not quite four miles from Tyttebærvika.

Jan was able to move so quickly that it surprised him. A feeling bordering on euphoria filled his being. His every need was met; he had dry clothes and plenty of food. While people slept he would work his way through the populated areas. During the days he would seek cover in barns and boathouses along the way and ski mostly at night. With this extraordinary speed he would be at the Swedish border in no time.

His first goal was to get through the villages of Kjosen and Lyngseidet, then ski along the magnificent Lyngenfjord south toward Elvebakken, a small snugly populated area five miles from Lyngseidet.

Jan remembered Peder's words: "You must stay off the road going east toward Lyngseidet, Jan. You will be safer back up in the hillsides."

"I'm sure you are right about that," Jan had agreed.

"German soldiers as well as the Norwegians will find it peculiar to meet a skier on the road during the night hours. And be aware that in Kjosen there is a road barrier. To pass it, people have to call the guard, a German soldier. He is up at a nearby house. He comes down to check the person's identification card to see if all is in order before they are allowed to enter the village. You know what you have to do, Jan," Peder had warned.

Jan passed through the barrier unnoticed.

During the nearly two miles between Kjosen and Lyngseidet Village, Jan climbed the incline hidden away from the built-up areas on several occasions.

As Jan neared Lyngseidet, one of his ski bindings snapped. Although it took him a while to fix it, his watch showed the time to be 4:30 a.m. Jan felt confident he could get through Lyngseidet before people began to stir. But his confidence was misplaced. The watch had been along on three swims in salt water and through many wet storms. Jan neared Lyngseidet center with a marvelous elongated downhill road enabling him to click along at a good speed. Suddenly, two-dozen rowdy German soldiers poured out of a school and swarmed into the road blocking it. The soldiers carried plates and utensils instead of grenades and guns—they were heading for breakfast.

Jan couldn't stop abruptly without having the whole troop pounce on him. Having no where else to go, he did what all Norwegians do when skiing and they meet up against people. He kept up his speed and shouted, "Tracks! Tracks!" The soldiers did not move fast enough and Jan was right on top of them. He pushed his way through them shouting "Tracks! Tracks." trying his best not to act flustered.

The soldiers must have been half asleep. They neither resisted nor tried to stop him. Jan was amazed they didn't notice he was wearing a Norwegian Navy uniform with "NAVY" and "NORWAY" insignias emblazoned on his shoulder. It all happened so fast that they, like Jan, probably had no time to react.

Immediately after skiing through the troop, Jan neared an even steeper downhill road a few hundred yards ahead. The road approached a crossroad down by the fjord. Jan saw another barrier in the middle of the crossroads with only a narrow passageway open on the left. Three German soldiers were inspecting identification cards of Norwegian civilians.

Jan butted his skis to slow down and veered slightly off the road, coming almost to a standstill. A few yards ahead, he saw a narrow road turning to the right in the direction of a small cottage not far from the barrier. Jan seized the narrow road with his skis, moving as naturally as possible so as not to show the fear of a hunted man. He forced himself to appear relaxed, as if he was going about insignificant business.

This little side road and his quick decision to take it saved Jan. He continued to move away from the main road and the German guards, and worked his way up the mountain slope. After a while, Jan felt safe enough to stop and think the situation through. He could see the mountain slopes were too close to the German guards and the fjord, and he had to be careful not to reveal himself. Jan remembered the map he had studied which showed an old Sami summer trail used in times past when their reindeer flocks were on the move. This trail went from Lyngseidet over into Lyngsdalen Valley and Furuflaten. Jan was confident he could follow this same road on skis.

His original plan was to follow the road along the fjord – first to Elvebakken, then later along the road past Pollfjellet Mountain in the direction of the village of Furuflaten. Jan planned to travel only when his surroundings looked safe and mostly at night.

After his narrow escapes with the Germans that morning, he reconsidered. The area was crawling with Germans, and the first plan no longer seemed prudent.

ALONE IN THE MOUNTAINS

April 5, 1943: Jan began his ascent into the high mountain plateau in the early morning hours. He climbed diagonally up the hillside in a southerly direction and stayed well away from the built-up areas of Lyngseidet and other small settlements. He had decided to take the Sami summer road toward Lyngsdalen Valley and Furuflaten.

Some distance up, Jan reached the Fyenelv River. He stayed close to the riverbed. The hilly terrain rose continually, and in the end, the river became but a small creek hidden under the deep snow and impossible to follow. In his steady climb he had risen some 1500 feet above the fjord. To the west he saw the mighty peaks of Kavringen and Kvalvik.

The sun shone brightly and below him, to the east, shimmered Lyngenfjord. Staying oriented in this landscape would be easy with such good visibility. Jan hoped to travel far while the weather was so clear. When he reached the top of the plateau, the terrain stayed fairly level for the next two miles.

Jan maintained a southerly direction, working his way around the tall peaks. He then turned west in toward Kvalvik Mountain's south wall. From here the Kvalvik Valley spread out. Jan scanned the landscape and saw no other possibility but to cross the valley. He worked his way down the abrupt slope toward the Kvalvik River, crossed it, and began climbing the south wall of the valley. Viewed from the plateau on the north side, it had looked fairly simple but he found the valley to be much steeper than he'd thought.

The south wall was too precipitous to use his skis in a herringbone fashion; instead, Jan had to side step his way up from the river. This slowed him down considerably. The Kvalvik Valley forged its way toward the Lyngenfjord in the east. Jan admired and was invigorated by the lofty view.

His own situation stood in stark contrast to the power and the magnificence of the nature spread before him. Jan had always enjoyed spending time in the mountains. The mountain ranges here in the Troms District, interspersed with sharp jagged peaks and glaciers, were quite different from the ones he'd roamed before the war in southern Norway. The many mountain hikes he had enjoyed with his parents and siblings during his childhood taught him to love and respect nature.

When he reached Kvalvik Valley, a second valley, possibly Fugledalen, stretched southward. He felt that was the direction he needed to follow. Jan could not remember all the details from the map, but he believed it would take him in the direction of Lyngsdalen Valley.

Steep mountains bordered Fugledalen Valley on both sides. Jan passed to the east by Bredalsfjellet Mountain and the Vestbreen Glacier. The rugged, varied terrain amazed him and he guessed that the mountain wall he saw to the east was part of Rundfjellet Mountain. The Fugledalen Valley eventually blended with another wide valley that Jan neared as he continued his southerly trek.

The majestic terrain thrilled him, but it also slowed him up. In the midst of this beauty he was taken off guard when the wind suddenly bore down on him. Until now, not even the smallest breeze had whispered by him. Within minutes, the snow whipped around him at an alarming speed. The mountain peaks he'd admired moments earlier were now cloaked in ominous clouds. Steel-gray clouds moved in fast and tumbled down the mountainside. Before Jan had time to think or plan, he was in the midst of the storm's fury. The downwind was unbearable. He struggled to keep his balance. The heavy mist and the whirling snow became so thick Jan could not see the tips of his skis. Sharp snow particles scraped his face.

Jan turned his back to the wind and crouched to a half-sitting position but it gave him no relief. The wind blew straight through his clothes and chilled his flesh. He had to keep moving. His only escape was to descend the mountain and find his way back to the sea.

Even as Jan inched his way forward, the ground beneath him began to slant steeply downward. He worried that the skis would just take off, perhaps over a cliff? The snow gales made seeing ahead impossible. But Jan remembered that at the end of the Bredals Lake, the vertical mountain wall sheared down to a small flat plateau. Jan feared he might be right on the edge, but he had no way of knowing. He was caught in the fury of the penetrating wind and whirling snow. Like a helpless toddler, Jan fumbled around lost in a world of giant mountains and glaciers.

How to avoid the edge? "Snowballs!" exclaimed Jan. Now and then the raging wind ceased for a moment to gather strength for its next onslaught. In those fleeting moments, Jan would throw a snowball a few meters ahead. It was impossible to follow its trail in the thick snow, but he strained, listening for its muffled landing. If Jan didn't hear it hit the ground, he reasoned he was too close to the edge of steep and dangerous terrain.

It was a tedious process. Jan threw many snowballs during the storm. Many times he retreated and edged his way forward far away from what he believed to be a precipice, all the while descending steeply. Jan methodically worked his way down the treacherous mountain. He had no idea how steep the mountain was, but he had to side step most of the way down. Jan couldn't see where he had come from or where he was going. After many hours he felt the terrain flatten beneath him. He crossed the even plateau where, without knowing, he was nearing the edge of another precipice, which ended in Lyngsdalen Valley 450 feet further down. The terrain before him was even more difficult than that above. The loose snow rushed madly away from beneath his skis. He leaned heavily on his poles and sidestepped gingerly as he kept moving downward. When he threw a snowball he seldom heard it fall anymore. Perhaps they had outlived their usefulness? The ground unexpectedly evened out once more.

Jan wondered how far he had come. Could he possibly be in Lyngsdalen Valley? It was pure guesswork; he did not know. If he stopped concentrating for even a moment, he became aware of his suffering body. His wounded foot pained him and his hands were stiff and frozen. Even after all his struggles, the possibility remained that he could still freeze to death in the wilderness unless he could find a way out soon.

The chill he had felt after going ashore to Vårøya had eased somewhat, but now it returned in full force. At the time he thought it impossible to ever be that cold again, but the dreadful freezing had returned. Jan trembled uncontrollably.

Overcome by bitter cold and exhaustion, Jan yearned to stop and rest. But there was no place to hide – and besides, if he did, he would surely freeze to death.

"Ski on Jan," he said to himself. "Somewhere you will get down to the sea." His strong will and naturally confident attitude enabled him to forge ahead yard by yard.

The terrain became extremely smooth and he wondered if he had reached a lake. It felt good to ski across this smooth surface. His skiing quickened and a gentle hope began to rise. It wasn't long before the ground rose again. The snow became powdery and he sank deep. He used considerable strength pushing hard on his poles to keep moving.

SCORM in Lyngsdalen Valley

April 5, 1943: Without realizing it, Jan had reached the base of Lyngsdalen Valley. He fumbled around totally bewildered; his sense of direction was gone. In his disorientation Jan began the upward climb. The incline escalated with each step, forcing him to turn his skis and tramp sideways up the gradient.

Jan's foot throbbed with pain. He yearned for relief. The raging wind stirred up the snow around him and icy particles abraded Jan's face and eyes. The sharp Arctic air chilled his lungs - each breath he took smarted.

Jan had no idea he was climbing the lower part of a precipitous mountain stretching upward 500 feet. The mountain was encircled by other snowy giants, except where it butted up to the Lyngsdalen Valley from where Jan had come. Some were over 5000 feet high. No matter where he turned, the snow and fog engulfed him and he could not get oriented in this murky gray and white world. Jan's body was numb. His blood felt as if it had turned to ice.

The buoyant optimism he had felt leaving Kjosen a few hours earlier evaporated. It would be so easy to give up here. No one would blame him. His strength was waning and maybe it was best to end it all. But negative thoughts never lingered long in Jan's mind. "Where am I? There will be a way out! I must find a way!"

The precipitous mountain he faced was weighted down with deep, loose spring snow. Jan could not see it. Suddenly snow, ice and dirt broke loose and moved down the mountain, slowly at first, then rushing madly toward Jan. There was no escape.

The avalanche roared downhill, deafening and awe-inspiring. Helpless, Jan did not know in which direction to move nor did he grasp what was happening. He was offered up, a sacrifice to the crushing snow masses.

The mountain of snow swept him off his feet, catapulting him down, backwards, sideways, then head first. Tossed like a rag doll, Jan flipped, jerked, and was propelled ever downward until he landed on the valley floor he had crossed a short while earlier.

All went black.

View of Lyngsdalen.

Jan opened frost-covered eyelids. His breathing was shallow and came in short spurts. As if through a foggy glass, all he could see was white snow wherever he looked. His mind was vacant. The snow masses enveloped him. Only his head and one arm were free. It wasn't clear to him what had happened, but he'd received a concussion. No matter how hard he tried to focus, he could not remember. The last thing he recalled was how he carefully worked his way down the mountainside. He didn't recollect crossing the valley floor or that he was on his way up the opposite mountain.

Jan struggled to remember. Slowly his consciousness returned. He knew he must have received a terrible blow to his head, but he did not know how long he'd been unconscious. Nausea swept over him and he was clammy and disoriented. Struggling to free himself from the snow masses, Jan discovered both of his ski poles were gone, and one of his skis. The other ski was broken in half, with part of it still fastened to his boot. His mitten and cap were gone. Red spots dotted the snow. Jan touched his face. He looked at his fingers, covered with his own blood. He realized he'd survived an avalanche.

Jan looked around and tried to focus. He saw nothing but high mountain peaks and snow. Where was his knapsack? Gone, and all the food with it. Jan was isolated in a world of snow and ice.

The last few hours before the avalanche Jan had managed to keep moving ahead though his ability to see was impaired. Working his way down precipitous cliffs, being able to see only a yard ahead, he had arrived in Lyngsdalen Valley without knowing it. Unwittingly, he had turned right across the valley floor. He'd gone further into the wilderness and up into the mountains on the opposite side instead of turning left toward the sea. Jan was lost. The raging snowstorm had blinded him, making it impossible to know in which direction he was moving. All he knew was that he had to keep moving.

The unseen power that had preserved him so many times before, again kept him alive against the odds. Yet, life seemed to be at cross-purposes. He was alive, but barely. Nonetheless, in his wretched, deplorable condition Jan was driven to continue onward.

The part of his face that had rested against the snow was scraped and bloody. It burned and stung. The avalanche had also robbed him of his mittens. His hands were turning blue. The boots that Einar Sørensen had given him at Bjørnskar cramped his feet, and the thin socks were not on a par with the Arctic weather. He blessed Peder Nilsen for making him the cellulose soles. Without them…it was too much to think about.

Jan turned from the mountains and headed east across the flat valley floor. Each step depleted his strength. Sometimes he sank so deep into the snow that he had to dig around his leg to free himself or use his hands to lift his leg out. His fighting spirit stirred him on.

"Onward Jan. You must keep walking," he told himself.

Jan battled against the frigid elements for hours. When he tried to orient himself to his surroundings, the white terrain and white vertical mountains blinded him. He was able to make out that the valley had narrowed. Towering mountains stood guard like sentinels on each side. The sound of a rushing river was near and he followed close. The terrain was hilly and rough, up for a few feet, then down, then up.

Jan tried to concentrate but felt like a spectator watching his own drama.

And the cold—the bitter cold penetrated every nerve, every cell of his body. He knew he had to get warm. He came to a large rock and, in his despair, he began digging with his bare hands, down, down. He crawled in, but the bitter cold intensified. It was hopeless. Lying there, Jan knew he would freeze to death. He struggled out of the dent.

Despondency overshadowed him again. It would be so easy to give in. Nature would do the rest, and it probably would not take long.

"Jan, keep walking. You must keep walking!" he demanded of himself.

He trudged through the snow, sinking down to his hips, pulling himself back out again. He fought for his life minute by minute. Eternity could not last this long.

"Jan, you must keep walking."

"Walk!"

What happened during the night when darkness fell was not clear to him. His thoughts blurred. He only knew that if he stopped he would die. Wet, and frozen clear through, beset with pain, Jan forced his body to obey.

"Don't stop! You will die if you do!"

"Just one more step!"

"And another. And another. And another…"

His inner voice refused to give him peace until he obeyed.

"Where am I? Where am I going?"

He lost all sense of direction in the avalanche. Jan waded through the snow hour after hour. He became aware a new day was dawning. His mind raced, and then it abruptly stood still. He battled to stay alert.

He had won against the hostile night, but the weather conditions did not improve. Several times he tried to dig himself down in the snow, but was unable. The next day came and Jan still fought the elements and his demise.

He continued wandering, but he did not know where he was going. He only felt snow, ice, cold and wind. He had no goal anymore.

"Walk!"

As the day joined with the evening, he heard voices. He didn't see anyone. But the voices were real, and he thought he knew them.

"Yes, it is I. Over here! Yes! It is I, Jan!"

He exerted his last ounce of strength to move toward them.

The voices kept calling for him. But they did not answer when he called back to them. Nonetheless, they instilled in him courage and fortitude to continue. As the night shadows crept in over Jan and eclipsed the confined valley, Jan grappled with reality.

"Am I losing my mind? Maybe I am sleepwalking and dreaming? Am I really wandering about in a storm, alone somewhere in the Arctic? How will it all end?"

Reality had slowly merged with imagination. The nightmare he was living got jumbled up with the voices. At that moment the *Brattholm* men walked toward him. One by one they came close.

"Jan!"

"*Ja*, Per, it is I!"

"Jan!"

"I have missed you terribly!"

"Jan!"

"*Ja*, You can see me, can't you, Sigurd?"

"Over this way. It is I!"

Jan plunged forward trying to grab his pant leg.

"Over here. Oh please!"

Jan cried into the howling storm.

April 8, 1943: During the afternoon the weather eased. The heavy clouds loosened their grip on the mountains and a pale glow of blue sky came into view. Jan barely saw the mighty bordering mountain walls.

He was in a valley that continued downward, ever downward. "Was it moving toward the fjord? People? And hope?"

Jan continued to follow the valley, staying close to the ravine. The voices he'd heard so clearly earlier came and went. In the end he tried not to pay attention to them. They never answered his call anyway. The snow was deep. In places he sank to his waist and felt imprisoned when he did. He dug and twisted and turned to free himself, just to take the next step only to have the same thing happen all over again. But something deep inside urged him on.

"Walk!"

"What am I doing here? Where am I?"

"Jan, you must keep walking."

"Per! Is it really you this time?"

"Keep walking!"

"Why are my eyes burning? Why do they hurt so when I try to open them? Why are the mountains so dim?"

The answers never came.

About four miles from the avalanche in Lyngsdalen Valley, Jan emerged at the upper end of Furuflaten. The river rushed headlong down to the village and Jan eagerly followed along as fast he was able. He reached a clump of birch trees and wandered helplessly. A steep gradient rose before him. He gathered there was a plateau not too far up because he could make out the black marks of many birch trunks. He climbed upward, slid backwards, but continued on.

His whole body was wracked with pain. Hunger pangs continually gnawed at him. His hands were frozen stiff and blue. He hardly felt his feet anymore, but his eyes caused him the greatest agony. "How much longer can I hold out? Is there an end to the misery?"

He reached the plateau and could distinguish a dark block a few feet ahead of him. He pushed forward. It was almost within reach. A wall! A wall!

Loving hands

April 8, 1943: The Lyngsdalen Valley cuts a deep and narrow channel into the mighty massifs guarding it on either side. The valley's head, near the immense glaciers, is spread wide. Winter cloaks the valley with a covering of pure white at the feet of the impressive mountain peaks Jiehkkevarri and Balggesvarri, tapering off as it weaves its way four miles eastward in a relaxed "S." At its final point, the valley gives way to the Lyngenfjord. Close to the fjord, the valley opens up wide again and creates space for scattered homes near the water's edge up to the highest plateau in the lower valley. This is the country settlement of Furuflaten.

On the north side, the steep rock wall of Pollfjellet Mountain rises up more than 3600 feet. The vertical mountain wall on the east plummets headlong into the Lyngenfjord. Far down along the water's edge, the narrow road curves with the coastline and connects Furuflaten to the hamlet of Lyngseidet nine miles further north.

The area at the foot of Pollfjellet is extremely dangerous in the winter, because of sudden violent snow slides. The snow masses crash down, one after another, and block the roads. Since open travel year round between Furuflaten and Lyngseidet was of strategic importance, the Germans felt it imperative to keep this thoroughfare open throughout the year. Subsequent to a snow slide, the Germans marshaled manpower to quickly remove the snow and keep the traffic moving.

Because of this, many German and conscripted Austrian soldiers were stationed in Furuflaten. They were quartered at the country school. Near the local road, there was a large depository filled with snow removal equipment and other machinery needed to keep it open. On the road outside of the depository, armed soldiers stood guard.

Uppermost in Furuflaten, on a nearly flat plateau, was the site of the Grønvoll farm. Marius, thirty-three, lived here with his widowed mother and two of his sisters. Gudrun was a few years younger than Marius and Ingeborg was a teenager.

Straight across the farmyard from Marius lived another sister, Hanna. She was married and had two sons of her own, Johan, 16, and Ottar, a couple of years younger. They lived in an old, grayish-worn log cabin with a small enclosure that stored overcoats, boots, and food. The ceiling was low and the one-room cabin had only one door, which opened up toward Marius' house.

The Pedersen family had just enjoyed a weekday meal together in their unpretentious little home. Hanna's husband Alfred was away at Lofoten, fishing. The kitchen table still held a plate of potato peels and fish scraps, leftovers from their just-finished dinner.

They heard something scratching along the wall outside their cabin. Unable to make out what it was, they listened more intently. The door bolt began to move, it creaked and grated, but did not open. The scratching along the wall repeated itself as it moved further away, before it moved back towards the bolt again. There were no windows by the door, so they couldn't look out. Hanna's frightened eyes stared at the door.

"Johan, open the door quickly!" The boy did as he was told.

Hanna gasped! She stepped back and let out a stifled scream, half covering her face with her hands. A frightening being tumbled in, took a couple of faltering steps and ended up standing, barely, in the middle of the room. His body swayed from side to side. His filthy clothes were soaked. He had no cap. Particles of ice, dried blood and sedimentary grains of rock clung to scruffy coal-black hair and stubs of beard, white with frost. His face was all scratched up, dirty and bloody. His eyes were nearly swollen closed, bloodshot and watering. Frost clung to his eyelashes. Dried blood and scabs covered his cracked blue lips and his breathing was heavy and came in short spurts. He groaned and trembled violently.

His boots were entombed in ice that extended well up his legs. It was obviously difficult for the creature to open his swollen eyelids, fire-red around the edges, but he exerted himself, and two horizontal slits appeared.

He spied the plate with the potato peel and fish scraps on the kitchen table. The frozen man toddled over to the table and sank down on a nearby chair. The chair slid toward the wall and he lay half diagonally against the table, grabbing the leftovers and cramming them into his mouth with both of his bluish swollen hands - a starving man out of control. Frightened, Hanna and the children stood speechless, staring at the creature half-lying at their kitchen table. They were watching Jan Baalsrud.

"Johan, run to fetch Uncle Marius." Johan took a couple of seconds to react, then dashed through the door and toward Uncle Marius' house a few feet below the farmyard.

Johan took the four steps up to the door in one big jump.

"What's the matter Johan? It's not like you not to come in. Come on in!" encouraged his Aunt Gudrun.

"Uncle Marius you must come at once, there is a fugitive in our house!"

Marius did not believe him at first. He was sure Johan was teasing him. They had fun outsmarting each other at times. Having delivered his message, Johan darted back to his home.

As he watched Johan sprint across the farmyard, Marius was not quite sure whether or not the boy was teasing. It all sounded a little unbelievable that a fugitive would come to their house, the uppermost house in the valley.

Still unsure, Marius decided to make an errand to the barn. On his way there, he would have to pass Hanna's house. As he drew close to the little cabin, Hanna appeared on her front steps and frantically motioned for him to come in, "You have to hurry Marius!"

He realized Johan had been telling the truth and rushed to his sister's side.

Jan was lying on the floor with a mouth full of leftovers. His remaining strength had deserted him and he had fallen from the chair to the floor.

Marius stood motionless inside the entrance door, gaping at the heap of human being on the floor. Terror stricken, Hanna and her sons looked

to Marius then to Jan and back to Marius. They felt totally helpless and
bewildered.

"What shall we do, Marius?" Hanna got her voice back. "Who is this
man?"

Marius sized up the situation and what to do. Ingeborg and Gudrun
joined them from across the way. Marius stopped them in the entryway
amid the winter boots, work clothes and coats hanging on pegs.

"We have a very ill man in the kitchen. Please wait here a minute,"
Marius said.

He pondered what to do with the ill stranger. The young man looked
like a prisoner of war, tortured to the brink of death. He could not have
known that this time it was the forces of nature that had been at work, not
the Gestapo.

The ghostlike chafed face starkly contrasted with the disheveled coal-
black hair and beard, covered with frost and ice just now beginning to
melt. Jan covered his eyes with his hands shielding them from the light. He
had difficulty keeping them open. It looked like someone or some thing
had dragged him across the ground, as scraped up as his face and hands
were. But the worst was his ice-covered boots and legs. Marius was
simply stunned.

When Jan fell, Hanna thought he was dead. The fish scraps still filled
his mouth; he had not the strength to swallow before sinking to the floor.
She leaned over him to see if he was still breathing.

Marius took control of the situation. Flashes of the rumors he'd heard
about Toftefjord ran through his mind. He called for his sisters in the
anteroom. They were anxious to help.

"What if the Germans should come?" Hanna went in and out of shock.

"They are so close, aren't they Uncle Marius? What shall we do?"
Ottar asked.

"Yes, they are near. But we will find a way to help this man. We must
do this," Marius whispered.

Jan struggled to say a few words. It was difficult to understand him as
he struggled to move his lips. "I am on my way to Balsfjord. Are there any
Germans around here?" He tried to keep his eyes open while he was
speaking.

"You are among friends, and have nothing to worry about," Marius tried to ease his fears.

"What is your name? My name is Marius Grønvoll."

Jan ignored the question about his name. "Did you say there are no Germans around here?" Jan was anxious.

"You only have to worry about getting well. We'll take care of you."

The family went to work to try and save him. Marius started by chipping the ice off Jan's legs and boots. Hanna heated water on the wood-burning stove. He had to be cleaned up. The boots had frozen to his feet and were whittled off in small pieces. The socks were cut off in strips. The sight of his feet and legs was shocking! The girls became queasy. They had never seen flesh with such terrifying colors, mostly an off-color blue, but in places covered with darker bluish-black-purplish spots. Other parts were a white-rosy marble-like color. Despite his agony, Jan didn't complain as the family worked feverishly to try and bring circulation back into his body.

Hanna and Marius got him cleaned up and changed his clothing. Gudrun and Ingeborg gathered pails of snow; they knew the best treatment for frostbite was to rub and massage the affected area with snow. It made no difference if they touched the ice or his legs, the temperature was the same.

Marius stayed in command. He placed Hanna's son Johan outside to keep watch. No one could be allowed to surprise them. The cabin had no place where they could hide Jan. Clear to them all was that they were laboring under the threat of a death sentence. The Germans had brought fear to the settlement in Furuflaten with their many posters attached to telephone poles and anywhere there was room, warnings to anyone who worked against them that should they be discovered the result would be death by an execution squad.

The girls began their work. Taking a leg each, they rubbed and massaged as gently as they could. Jan moaned, but it had to be done; it was the only chance to get his blood circulating again. Their backs hurt, their hands were chilled and yet they kept at it, hour after hour. Hanna and Marius took their turns. Jan was massaged continuously into the early morning hours. When one tired, another took over. They were encouraged when Jan first began to respond; how they wanted to save this man.

Gradually he was able to say a few words. Marius quickly gained his trust. Jan said his hometown was Oslo where his family lived and that he was the only survivor from *Brattholm.*

Marius was now able to put all the pieces together; this was a fugitive from the Gestapo! "Incomprehensible that this man is still alive," he told himself. Even at that, Marius was completely in the dark about how many times Jan had escaped death, nor did he have any knowledge of the mental agony Jan had already lived through. All Marius knew was that this man needed help, and as long as it was humanly possible, he vowed he would be there for him.

Two courageous men, Jan and Marius instantly bonded. The head of the Furuflaten underground, Marius wondered, "Was it just chance that led Jan to me?" Marius did not think so. Once Marius gave his heart to a person, or a cause, he was fiercely loyal. He cared about people. A warm, loving human being who knew when to help, Marius never pushed himself on people and only stepped in when needed. If someone was in need, no risk, no German, no threat of death, could stand in his way.

When he graduated from elementary school at the age of thirteen, his education was over; so like most of the other young men at that time he had to help supplement the family income. The early 1900's were an extremely difficult time economically for the people of northern Norway. Marius helped his parents provide the necessities of life by fishing, but he also had a deep interest in photography and writing, and after awhile became a reporter for the newspaper *Tromsø.*

Marius' lack of education, however, was not a hindrance to his curious mind. He was well read, and was familiar with the works of the Norwegian literary giants. He often quoted from memory the works of Ibsen, Welhaven and Bjørnson, as well as Kipling and others.

Marius deeply loved Norway. Extremely patriotic, he was a leader, respected and trusted by the two hundred people in Furuflaten. To him, it was his civic duty to help another Norwegian in need.

That evening, Marius took a break and returned to his home across the farmyard to eat dinner with his mother. Filled with love and concern for her children and grandchildren, she was skeptical about helping this stranger. There were no blind spots in her eyes - she knew the danger and what it might do to her family.

Marius sat down next to her and in his warm understanding way explained the situation. When she resisted, he asked her, "If I, your own son, should end up wounded and helpless in Oslo – and no one would come to my assistance – what would you do?" His mother turned silent, looked admiringly at her son who had displayed such wisdom, and said not a word. After a brief interval she expressed her change of mind. Her son was doing that which he ought to be doing, that which was good and decent. She agreed with her Marius. The stranger had to be taken care of, no matter what the cost. She looked at him with moist eyes and patted his hand.

"Son, you are a good man. We must do that which is right. You have my blessing."

The situation was extremely tense at the Grønvoll farm. Many Germans were quartered at Solhov School in Lyngseidet, the German headquarters for the whole Eastern Front, and only nine miles away. And down in Furuflaten, close to the fjord, the Germans had confiscated the local school, which was now being used for a German billet. The soldiers, when not busy, milled around Furuflaten, and it was not unusual for them to come unannounced to the farm to purchase eggs and milk. The Grønvolls tried to avoid selling to their enemy, but most often the choice was not theirs.

Marius, Hanna and the two girls counseled together and made the decision to give their all to help Jan to freedom. The safest place to hide him was in the barn, up in the hayloft where there was presently an abundance of hay. No one but the family was to know about this; not even their nearest neighbor could know they were hiding and aiding a fugitive.

The girls had done their best for Jan, tending his hands, feet and legs. Old clothing, sheets and such were scarce during these days when any old piece of clothing was altered for many different uses, but having gathered what could be found, the girls and Hanna tore them into strips. A salve with a cod-liver oil base, a healing compound much used by Norwegians, was applied to Jan's body where needed, after which the strips of sterilized cloth were wound around his affected limbs until they were completely protected.

His general condition was so poor and his pain so insufferable that he was totally helpless, unable to stand on his own legs. The situation looked bleak. Even after all the Grønvolls' efforts, Jan's atrocious suffering in the mountains had taken its toll.

in the hayloft

In one of the outbuildings was an old sled. Around two in the morning, Marius and the two girls lifted Jan onto the sled. Johan kept watch outside, and when all was pronounced clear, they pulled Jan across the farmyard in the dark. They towed and pushed him up the steep barn bridge. The barn was furthest away from the other buildings in the farmyard, and the barn bridge, the only way they could get him up into to the hayloft, was in the opposite direction from their neighbors, facing Lyngsdalen Valley from where Jan had come.

Marius had brought an old mattress up earlier and placed it in the far corner of the hayloft. He and his sisters transferred Jan to the mattress and tucked wool blankets around him. They left him there, hidden behind the haystacks. All went home, but none of them slept. Throughout the night Marius pondered and the girls were frightened. What would happen to them if the Germans came and found Jan? Of a truth, they knew, but they were too frightened to share their thoughts with one another. Morning emerged without the girls having been able to squelch their fears. The experience was all too traumatic for them.

The assignment given to the saboteurs in Shetland was code-named "Martin." The Grønvolls decided to call Jan by that name. He had been in the hayloft for a couple of days, and in spite of the Grønvolls' nurturing, Jan's feet didn't show any signs of improvement. He remained unable to stand on them. Marius puzzled over what to do next.

During the many days Jan was detained in the mountains, snow blindness had set in. His cornea and eye membranes were damaged and inflamed, infected by the reflection of the sun's ultraviolet rays on the snow. His eyes pained him terribly. Sunlight caused a burning sensation. Tears flowed continually. His red, swollen eyelids were roughly attached to one another. When he tried to open them, only a narrow slit appeared, but it enabled him to hazily see the people around him and some of the surroundings. Relief came only when he closed his eyes.

Gudrun and Ingeborg's main assignment was to bring food to Jan in the barn. To be sure, they never took the barn-bridge up to the hayloft. No unnecessary tracks were to be made in the snow. Instead they went in through the barn door, past the cow barn, up the ladder and through the hatch in the ceiling up to the hayloft. They were aware that Jan always kept the loaded pistol close by his side; when they neared the top of the stepladder, they called out, "Martin, I am bringing your food." Three times a day they brought him food. Gudrun often prepared and cooked the food, such as potatoes and other root vegetables, meat, fish and tea if available. Whatever the family ate they shared with Jan.

Being young, it was a highlight of Gudrun and Ingeborg's day to go and visit with this commando soldier. He was good at camouflaging his own pain and the sorrows he carried. At the same time, they were shy and reserved, and hardly dared exchange any words with him. They knew, above all, he needed to rest. The girls did not know how much their visits meant to him. Jan always had a smile and a friendly comment for them. He felt their selflessness and their eagerness to help him. Jan was overwhelmed with indescribable gratitude when he saw these beautiful genuine girls who risked so much on his behalf. The world and its cruel ways had not, to a great extent, intruded upon Furuflaten.

Helpless, ill, and at the point of death, he had been brought into the safety of this barn and had been shown the greatest of care and concern. It was unavoidable that Jan had become very fond of the Grønvolls and all who had helped him.

Likewise, the girls felt pride each time they visited the hayloft with food for Jan. Knowing they played a small part in saving the life of a Norwegian saboteur, taking him away from the Gestapo so to speak, made their hearts joyful. In spite of that, they were careful not to spend too much time with him. They wanted to be sure he got the rest he needed.

Marius felt unsafe. During periods of good weather, without snowfall, the German and Austrian soldiers living at the school in the valley did not have much to do with their time. The road between the Pollfjell Mountain and Lyngseidet did not have to be cleared and plowed on those days, and the soldiers' days seemed tiresomely long. To lessen their boredom, they would ski up into the countryside, and they often made their treks close behind Marius' barn where there was good skiing in the sloped fields.

Jan's tracks still remained in the snow; they led straight to the farmyard only a few hundred feet away. Marius thought with great alarm of the consequences should the soldiers discover them.

The day after Jan came to the Grønvoll farm, Marius decided to do something about the tracks. He put his own boots on and followed in Jan's footsteps from the barnyard down the steep hillside towards the riverbed. Marius made a frightening discovery; the trail revealed a fight for life beyond anything he could have comprehended.

A short distance from the farm, Marius noticed Jan's tracks disappeared into a circle in among a grove of stunted, windblown birch trees. Jan had walked round and round in circles! He must have been partially unconscious, Marius thought, unable to see much, but determined not to lie down and die. He had to keep himself erect; he had to keep walking. If he stopped, the exhaustion would overtake him; he would sink into the snow and perish.

Marius saw before him, like a moving picture, the unsteady stride of two feet transformed into two hunks of ice. He felt Jan's pain, fright, exhaustion and despair, and his struggle for consciousness. In many places he noted how the footprints had taken off from the circle. Jan's trail showed confused side trips from the pressed-down circle; a couple of them turned close to the Grønvolls' barn before they took off down into the valley. Totally bewildered, Jan had fought for his life in a circle. He had spent hours around and in between the birch trees.

Jan had been near the farm without ever knowing how close he had been to relief. Marius realized the man in his barn was no run-of-the-mill soldier. Eager to help Jan anyway he could, Marius retraced his footsteps back to the farmyard. Let the Germans come. Let them ask about the mysterious tracks in the snow! He would have no problem explaining that as a farmer he, from time to time, had to go up into the valley for wood. Marius hurried to the hayloft.

Marius Grønvoll

"Hello Martin, it's me, Marius!" he called out, as he neared the top of the ladder leading to the loft. Excited by his discovery, the farmer laid out for Jan his visit to Lyngsdalen in great detail. Jan was overcome by the news. It all seemed so distant and hazy. All he remembered was the one thing that had remained crystal clear during his fight against fatigue: if he had not been able to place one foot in front of the other, or if he had sat down to rest, he would never have been able to get up—and would have lain there and frozen to death.

Jan did not want to die.

This helped Marius understand why Jan had continued for hours in the circle among the birch trees. Jan expressed his appreciation for all Marius' family was doing for him, and his concern for them. The resistance leader's answer was simple and direct. "It might cost me my life, but what of it? You have to say 'Yes' or 'No' to life."

Marius gave a resounding "Yes" to helping Jan.

Everyone on the Grønvoll farm, especially the young girls, fought a constant battle with fear. Ingeborg, the youngest, was almost in shock. Jan's appearance and need for help had torn the safety net of the farm away from her in a dramatic way; it was a difficult experience for her. The war had now entangled her family. Any talk about death and danger and risk terrified her. The adults' concerned and troubled looks only added to her fears. Ingeborg knew they were afraid the Germans would raid the farm. She also knew they were afraid for what might happen to Jan, and also the family, should the Germans find Jan in the hayloft. They didn't talk about it, but the fear hovered over all of them. It was in the air around them. Ingeborg could even see it in their actions: the many times they looked out the kitchen window and scanned the country lane leading to their house, and how they tensed when the telephone rang. Yet she knew that no matter how afraid her family was, they would never think of turning their backs on Jan, or on any human being in need just to save themselves. Ingeborg was near tears continually, and food held no temptation for her. She tried to act brave like the rest of her family.

Jan was thankful for the help showered upon him and was thrilled with the comfortable mattress behind the haystack. He felt safe. He slept mostly for the four days and nights he had been at Grønvoll farm. He had had no strength when he arrived here; sleep had been a welcome gift.

Marius, as often as he could and when he felt it was safe, entered through the hatch and visited with him. Jointly they made their plans. They had so much to share and tell one another. Marius was able to reiterate the Tromsø rumors and what he had heard about the fate of Jan's friends. Jan lay still and listened, saddened, as again the terrible tragedy was verified. Jan surmised that the two men taken prisoner were Moursund and Knudsen.

The merchant at Bromnes, a few days after the battle in Toftefjord, had received a package in the mail. The package held a rope with a noose in one end. On a torn off paper slip it said:

> "This rope is meant for you. Should it be too difficult for you to use, I will be happy to come and assist you."

The sender was anonymous and nothing else happened.

After the Toftefjord tragedy, the Germans had been around the district arresting people, looking for radios. They imprisoned family members of young men who had been able to escape to Sweden.

German *Schnell* boats patrolled the fjord often around the inlets of Furuflaten. It was risky for Jan to remain in the barn for long. Sooner or later the rumor mill would begin to buzz. Even if the Germans didn't figure out that the elusive Jan was in their midst, Marius' neighbors would soon begin to wonder about all the trips to the barn.

One could not expect everyone to be tight-lipped – that would be a fatal mistake.

BUSY DAYS ON
GRØNVOLL FARM

The ghastly man that had fallen through Hanna Pedersen's door a few days earlier was not horrifying anymore. He was not a stranger, but a friend. Tending Jan and taking food to the barn three times a day was not a chore, but a highlight for Gudrun and Ingeborg as intense and bright as the summer midnight sun.

The young women were filled with pride each time they returned from the barn. They admired Jan's courage and fortitude and were impressed with his knowledge and his work as a saboteur. The Gestapo was hunting him. Yet they were the ones who had him.

As strong and skillful as Jan was, now when he was in danger and vulnerable, he depended on them. This brought them happiness. Each morning they looked forward to their visits with him, though they were usually brief. Jan had brought with him glimpses of a world they knew little about, a world they had only read about. He made that world real to them. And sometimes Jan wanted to talk. They were all young, they all had dreams and hopes for the future, and they enjoyed sharing them. Their lives had been divergent, but now they met at a crossroad. Jan needed caring and tenderness; he had experienced the evil and terror war brought. Gudrun and Ingeborg needed a chance to serve and to show compassion, which is so much a part of a woman's heart. Jan's and the young women's needs met as moments of gentleness in a cruel world. It was good for all of them to make new friends.

As the days passed, a routine of sorts developed; having Jan hidden in the barn was not as frightful as it had in the beginning. They were, of course, still aware of the danger, but a quiet peace settled back over the Grønvoll farm as everyone went about their daily chores.

One day, the peaceful atmosphere was shattered. Within seconds, horror replaced the tranquility and paralyzed all in the little log cabin. Two German soldiers with shotguns over their shoulders were headed straight for the cabin where Marius was visiting with Hanna. As the soldiers crossed the farmyard, Marius went out to greet them.

They told him they had come to re-examine the farm for illegal radios. In 1941 the Germans attempted to confiscate all the radios across Norway. Many Norwegians hid their radios rather than give them up. Aware of this, the Germans carried out raids unexpectedly, often revisiting places they had been just a short time earlier. The laws were strict; no one was allowed to listen to a radio. Heaven forbid that a Norwegian should hear the enemy's messages from London! If caught, the punishment was swift and cruel - torture or the concentration camp, or both.

Though they had recently ransacked the Grønvoll farm, the soldiers announced they'd returned to re-examine the barn. The girls froze. Someone must have reported them - they had been betrayed! Jan would be found and shot! And so would they. Ingeborg could not help herself; tears streamed down her ashen cheeks. She went to the bedroom and sat down in a corner to hide. All was over.

Marius and Gudrun were told to come to the barn with the soldiers. The soldiers walked two steps behind them. It was difficult to keep a nonchalant appearance. Gudrun also fought tears. A few years older than her sister in the cabin, Gudrun was still just a young woman. As they neared the barn she wanted to shout, to tell Jan to run away. She knew it would be impossible; poor Jan could not even stand on his feet, much less run.

The cow barn and the piles of hay were meticulously inspected. The Germans poked their guns into places they could not get to and lifted and pushed farm tools aside. The stress became unbearable.

Marius stood and watched them dispassionately with his hands in his pocket. His face did not reveal the fright within. They neared the stepladder and one soldier began his ascent. He pressed his helmeted head against the hatch, lifted it up and peeked around the hayloft. The hatch was heavy and he grunted trying to hold both his gun ready for action and the hatch up with his head. With great effort he took one more step – and another; his upper body came through the hatchway. He turned in every direction, breathed heavy and groaned, irritated by the heavy hatch leaning on him. Below, retreating a few steps, Marius and Gudrun stood helpless next to the other soldier glancing upward. The German soldier turned and studied their faces, holding the gun ready. The siblings thought for sure it all was over.

The future flashed before their eyes: they would be executed, as would Grandmother, Hanna, Ingeborg, Johan and Ottar. Even their innocent neighbors would be imprisoned or shipped off to concentration camp somewhere in Germany. Their beloved Furuflaten village might be burned to the ground. No one would have a home to return to. Jan would be the first one they would grab. They would haul him in for interrogation and torture.

The German atop the ladder fumed and hollered, coughed and spit. He took a step back down on the ladder, stooped and the hatch slammed shut. Down on the floor he brushed the dust and chaff off his uniform.

"No need to ransack up there," he commented to his buddy. "There is only some dried-up hay." He turned to Marius and Gudrun.

"*Danke*," thank you. "We hope we have not interrupted your day," he said in broken Norwegian. The soldiers clicked their heels, and nodded stiffly.

"No problem."

The inspection was over and the soldiers left.

Had the soldier not been slothful, he would have found the catch of his military career, an enemy commando.

The plans for Jan's continued flight could not be put off. The unseen power that protected Jan from the beginning had sheltered him yet again. As Marius looked ahead, his duty seemed impossible – nonetheless, he would find a way. If Jan had been well and could walk without help, things would be different. But it was too much to expect that Jan could recover quickly. His cheerful manner covered much of his anguish but it all would take time.

Hanna and the girls continued their nurturing care of Jan. He lay in the barn bandaged up, unable to stand and unable to see much. And in this condition, it was Marius' duty to find a way to get him to Sweden past the German guardposts. Obviously there was no time to waste; the just-completed inspection was proof of that. This challenge was Marius' greatest test.

Marius thought and schemed the whole day through and into the evening. He had many ideas but one by one he rejected them.

Then one idea burst forth. "Could it be possible?" He headed to the barn to share it with his friend. This was too important and risky not to discuss with him. Jan listened intently. He agreed that the plan Marius presented was daring. They would need help from several courageous men and a generous portion of good luck to succeed. But what other choice did they have? Jan was grateful that Marius would even have such thoughts. After all, he could not just take off on skis anymore.

Marius went to work. Their plan was to remove Jan from the barn during the darkest of night, pull him on a sled down the valley to the fjord, then row him diagonally across the Lyngenfjord toward the northeast, a little over six miles.

On the opposite shore in Revdal, a short distance from the water's edge stood a little log hut. It was the only remains of a burned-down farm except for the scarred fireplace clinging to a broken-off chimney jutting heavenward where the farmhouse had stood. The untrimmed grass poked through the snow in small tufts here and there. A deserted spot five miles from the nearest neighbor, it was an ideal hiding place.

No road passed through the little place called Revdal, quiet except for the whispering waves and the rushing wind. The little windowless hut could be Jan's hiding place – a place no one would suspect, stranger than anyone *could* expect, and surely no one *would* inspect. Jan would be safe in the hut until they worked out the next phase of his journey to Sweden.

From Furuflaten, Marius could see the log hut with his bare eyes. It was a little black speck just back of the water's edge. It stood a few hundred feet north of two rivers which plunged down the steep mountainside and emptied into the fjord. The mountain towered nearly

3000 feet behind the hut. Close to the plateau, a narrow valley snuggled into the granite masses. The gorge was called Revdal (Fox Valley), like the little place by the fjord, named after the many foxes which made their homes there.

On the other side of the Revdal mountain plateau, the massive mountains drop steeply, fringed by the elongated Manndalen Valley, stretching into the interior from the Kåfjord. Marius planned to enlist some men from the Manndalen Valley to help get Jan to Sweden. Deep within, he hoped that Jan would improve enough to be able to ski along with them, but that was a wish, not reality. By human standards the flight seemed almost impossible, but desperate men seek desperate solutions.

Even with this hopelessness, Marius never considered quitting; he was not that kind of a man. In a brief time, strong ties had formed between him and Jan. He had tremendous compassion for his new friend, mixed with genuine admiration. Saving Jan was not an option anymore. Marius had determined many days ago to give his all to save Jan, even his life. He had promised Jan that if he had to die, he would not die alone.

The three siblings at Grønvoll farm had another sister, Petra Solberg. She lived a short distance away with her husband. She knew nothing about Jan, and was not told. She was trustworthy, like the rest of her family, but everyone involved felt that the fewer people who knew about Jan, the better the chances of keeping the secret. They felt no need to involve people unnecessarily and risk their lives.

Like most Norwegian women, Petra was an expert knitter. Most Norwegians knit for pleasure, but during the war they did so out of necessity. Gudrun knew that Petra prided herself on knitting her husband's long underwear, doing all she could to keep him warm and comfortable during the Arctic winters. One day, Gudrun got the sneaky idea to pay her sister Petra a visit; this would be a different kind of a visit. She realized her plan was not kind, but the need was desperate. As Gudrun set out on the 15-minute walk to her sister's home, she hoped that when she told Petra the whole story in the future, she would be forgiven.

Happy to see Gudrun, Petra welcomed her warmly, ushering her in to the living room where she set the coffee table with home baked goodies and a warm drink. They talked of everyday things and shared thoughts and happenings as sisters are apt to do. This time, however, Gudrun's heart was not in the visit. She could not get her mind off her brother-in-law's long underwear. Petra's husband was a powerfully built man just about Jan's size, and his underwear would fit Jan perfectly.

Gudrun consoled herself that Jan had to have that well-knitted underwear, knitted with gray yarn, if he was to stay warm on the terrifying journey ahead. As Petra chatted, Gudrun knew she couldn't ask for a pair outright. Petra had two pairs for her husband. While he wore one, the other was washed and hung to dry on the clothesline stretched between the inside walls of the little outbuilding not far from the main farmhouse.

It would be difficult to get her hands on them, but Gudrun had a quick mind and was determined. She parted from her sister and set out in the direction of her home. Nightfall covered her as she rushed back to the outbuilding, snatched the long underwear off the line, crammed it under her winter coat, and dashed all the way home.

Jan had his long warm underwear.

As for Petra, her hatred for the Germans grew. The following morning when she went to retrieve the underwear and discovered it was gone, she immediately "knew" it was in German hands. In telling her sister Gudrun about the incident later, Petra vowed she would never forgive them!

A TENDER FAREWELL

The resistance group in Furuflaten received an important assignment. Many men were needed and all had to be tight-lipped. Marius realized how essential it was to find the right people.

Marius had several reliable friends, some from his boyhood days. One young man, Olaf Lanes, was only 17 years old. Olaf lived at the northern end of the village. A powerfully strong young man with broad shoulders, Olaf was energetic and trustworthy. His father Hans owned a fishing boat, and Olaf had gone fishing with him in Lofoten many seasons already.

Amandus Lillevoll, an unmarried farmer and skipper of his own fishing vessel, was a few years older than was Marius. Amandus was reserved, but had a strong will and always finished what he set out to do. Following his father's death, he took over the responsibility of supporting his mother and sister. He had a great wit and enjoyed telling stories. Marius wanted him to join the group because he was tough, energetic and trustworthy. But Amandus was still fishing in Lofoten.

Alfon Hansen, 30 years old and Amandus' cousin, had attended Solhov folk high school in Lyngseidet. His interest was carpentry and he was a skilled craftsman. He also was strong and dependable.

The fourth man Marius wanted for his team was Alvin Larsen, a wise and physically powerful twenty-five-year old who never shunned hard work. When he turned thirteen, Alvin began accompanying his father on frequent fishing trips to the Lofoten Islands. He got his coastal captain's license when he was only eighteen years old. The rough Arctic seas and climate coupled with heavy work had molded him into a mentally and physically strong man. Alvin preferred to live on the sea.

Olav Bakkevold, the oldest of the men Marius sought, lived on a small farm north of the river. He too was unmarried. Like the other men at Furuflaten, he often fished to help with living expenses. And like the others, he was patriotic and dependable.

Artur Olsen was a post official in Furuflaten. Marius hoped for his help during Jan's transport down to the fjord. In addition to these men, the resistance leader involved teacher Longva. To a man, all stood ready to help.

Monday, 12 April 1943: The plan was to remove Jan from the barn during the night. The next phase of his flight to freedom was risky but necessary. He had felt safe at the Grønvoll farm, hidden behind the hay up in the barn, and strong ties had formed between Jan and the Grønvolls.

The leave-taking disheartened Jan. The success of the transfer rested on Marius' shoulders. He came to the barn to wash Jan up. Gudrun and Ingeborg heated water on the wood-burning stove and carried it up to him. Jan would leave with new undergarments, hand knit of pure wool. Jan tried hard to act upbeat and uncomplaining, but Marius sensed his low spirits.

"I am also despairing, Jan. I would have liked for you to stay on," said Marius.

"Don't worry, I'll do fine. And I am impatient to get closer to Sweden."

"I wish I could stay with you all the way, my friend."

"It's just that I…I hate goodbyes. All of you have become dear to me. I am so indebted, Marius."

"Nonsense Jan, we are just happy you found us. We've got to get ready now."

In the late evening, Olav Bakkevold and Alfon Hansen arrived. Still snow-blind and too ill to stand on his feet, Jan was bundled up in wool blankets and placed on the sled. His jovial spirit evaporated. The resistance workers opened the barn door just enough to get the short sled through. Jan's head and bandaged feet hung over the ends. The wounded commando was too weak to hold his head up, so Gudrun and Ingeborg bent over and cradled it in their hands. They rushed sideways down the steep barn bridge while the three men controlled the sled's descent.

Jan cried.

The five shadows hurried across the farmyard, pulling the sled bearing a bundled up and strapped down Jan. The men guided the sled from the front while Gudrun and Ingeborg steadied the back. The girls strained to support Jan's head, stooped over as they were.

At the end of the farmyard, they veered the sled to the left, ending up in a long, narrow hollow bordered by scattered trees and bushes. Further down they crossed a belt of crusty snow leading to the moraine-covered riverbed. A few darkened homes revealed no activity.

Creeping among large rocks, bushes and scraggly trees, they hurried downward to the sea. The chill wind swept over them unnoticed. Though the darkness shielded them, their senses stayed alert to any hazard.

Two places along the route were particularly dangerous: the school where the German soldiers were quartered, and the warehouse near the local road, guarded by the Germans. Key pieces of apparatus, machinery and snow removal equipment were kept safe in the storehouse. The narrow two-lane country road that snaked its way along the water through Furuflaten was the Germans' main supply route to Finland and the Eastern Front. It had to be kept open; therefore, they guarded the snow removal equipment very protectively.

Marius had surveyed the escape route several times in advance. He knew every foot of it, and what he and his friends faced. They had met and worked out detailed plans.

Artur Olsen had been sent out in advance to stand guard on the moraine hill north of the river. The river ran underneath the road bridge and spilled out into the sea. The bridge was near where the German guard was stationed. Artur's exact position had been carefully chosen. An armed soldier kept watch down on the road, walking between the bridge and the store at Hamvik. From his lookout point, Artur could see the bridge. When the German soldier turned by the bridge to go south, Artur was to strike a match as a signal.

Johan, Hanna's son, had been eager to help Jan in some way. He was proud that his Uncle Marius had asked him to be part of this effort. Uncle

Marius had loaned his flashlight to him. And to have a flashlight - with batteries - was something unusual in war-torn Norway of 1943. Johan was excited to be on a par with the adults.

Quietly, the young man trudged through the snow. Johan crawled up the moraine hill to his appointed place on the south side of the river. His heart pounded as he peered into the darkness, alert to danger. Johan felt the tension more than did the others, perhaps because of his youth. He kept looking behind him. Unusual noises seemed to come from everywhere. All was quiet.

The small country store a little further down was a sociable place. Friends and neighbors met and chatted about happenings in their village. These days, the havoc the war caused always crept into their conversation. Before the war, the men-folk centered their conversation on fishing vessels or their latest catch important to their livelihood. They focused on the success or failure of their crops and livestock, weather being all-important here in the Arctic. The latest news of world or around Norway was also important to them.

The women looked forward to gathering at the store. They discussed new ideas on homemaking and rearing children. These were women of substance for the most part. By and large their men were fishermen, often spending weeks or months away fishing, while the women cared for children and attended to farm duties.

Most walked to the country store, though some bicycled. In the wintertime they used kick sleds or skis. The country store was their meeting place, a place for sharing the latest goings-on in their lives, stories they were bursting to pass on, joyful tales.

Closed tonight, the townsfolk safely home, the country store lay quiet.

A shadowy figure stood near the store. Wearing a leather cap with earflaps tied underneath his chin, a homemade knitted sweater and scarf, teacher Longva kept his hands warm inside knitted mittens. Standing guard with matchbox in hand, he would strike a match to signal danger to the five pulling Jan.

Marius had placed teacher Longva by the country store because it gave a good overview of the paths on which they were transporting Jan. Marius, Olav, Alfon and the girls neared the end of the hollow. The land spread flat at the bottom of the moraine riverbed. The closely guarded school where the Germans slept sat on top of a ten-foot embankment. A soldier kept watch close by. All they could see of him was the upper part of his rifle and his helmet moving along the snow mound.

Gudrun Grønvoll

The five crept gingerly along the riverbank below the soldier, all hoping that the sound of the rushing river drowned out the scraping of the sled. Marius had described the escape to Jan in detail. Jan knew their location, and he wanted to assure the girls. It was clear they were nervous by the way they looked around, glanced up at the snow bank and at each other.

"We are almost there, girls. They cannot hear us because of the river," said Jan, though he was not totally convinced of that himself.

The off duty soldiers in the school were lethargic and heedless. None of them had any idea of the daring activity playing out below them. Raucous laughter erupted from the school and over the snow bank. It jolted Marius and the others. The German soldiers were enjoying their time off.

Carefully, Marius' group distanced themselves from the school, and when they neared the county road, they stopped in a thicket. A German soldier a short distance away was guarding the warehouse.

Gudrun and Ingeborg parted company with the others. They walked boldly out into the road and conversed loudly as if sharing an exciting experience. They headed straight for the soldier with the machine gun.

"*Guten Abend,*" good evening, they smiled.

Ingeborg Grønvoll

The soldier was somewhat surprised that the two Norwegian girls would talk to him. He was pleased with this interruption, breaking the monotony of his watch.

"Guten Abend," the soldier smiled broadly. "What are you young girls doing out so late at night?" he continued in German.

The girls shrugged their shoulders and laughed.

"Ich nicht verstehen," We don't understand. Ingeborg tried out the few German words she knew.

"Aah!" the soldier nodded and eagerly labored to make himself understood in his broken Norwegian.

The girls kept him busy pretending they had a difficult time understanding him. Slowly they turned southward. The soldier accompanied them. They chatted as they distanced themselves and the guard from the sled. Reaching a narrow path, they stopped and talked a few more minutes.

The soldier by the bridge had turned. Artur lit the match. Marius hardly saw the weak flame north of the river. Gudrun and Ingeborg turned off on the side road.

"Auf wiedersehen." They waved.

"Auf wiedersehen." The soldier saluted the girls.

Marius checked the road. Clear of Germans, it was time to pull Jan across. The men crouched around him.

"Let's go!"

They darted across the road and rushed down the embankment on the other side into the safety of another thicket, stopping only momentarily to catch their breaths. The boat lay ready by the shore, oars, sail and mast tucked away in the bottom. Jan was freed from the sled and lifted into the boat. Like Viking king Olav Tryggvason's warship, *Ormen Lange*, The Long Serpent, the boat carrying Jan headed into the wind, swallowed by the darkness.

Ingeborg and Gudrun turned to go home. The wind played with their hair. Gudrun brushed a few strands away from her face with a mitten-covered hand. Ingeborg pulled her knitted cap further down her face. She could not bear to look at her sister.

"Did you see how careworn and sad Jan looked?" ventured Ingeborg.

"Ja."

"I hope he will make it." Ingeborg sniffled.

"He will."

In their sadness it was difficult to find words. They walked on in silence, the snow crackling underfoot. In the short time Jan had been at the farm, he and the girls had grown very close. The girls' deep love for Jan had grown out of the care they had given him. They admired his strength and courage and they had suffered with him in his pain.

Jan, on the other hand, loved the girls because of their wholesome youthfulness. When he needed tenderness and a listening heart, one or the other was there. When he needed care it was offered to him. During the brief moments they shared, the sisters helped Jan forget his ordeal and he loved them for that. The girls reminded Jan of his family and happier times.

"Do you remember how emotional Jan was when he said, 'I have ruined everything for all of you?'"

"*Ja*."

"I don't think he did; do you, Gudrun?"

"No. We are Norwegians and we must help each other."

The tears that had been brimming spilled over and flowed in a steady stream.

"Why does it hurt so much, Gudrun?"

"Because we love him."

They went home to an empty barn.

*"The tragedy of war is that
it uses man's best to
do man's worst"*

— Harry Emerson Fosdick

hotel savoy

April 12, 1943: Thoughts of the farewell scene at Furuflaten filled Jan's mind as they crossed the Lyngenfjord. The tender moments stayed with him and made him melancholy.

When the boat was pulled up over the small rocks on the east side of the Lyngenfjord, new hope filled him. Freedom was one step closer.

His eyes were slowly healing. They did not water as much anymore, the swelling was nearly gone, and the redness was beginning to disappear. But the shooting pains in his feet made it impossible for him to walk or stand, even with help. The men lifted him out of the boat. Jan wanted to help.

"Relax Jan, we'll handle this."

"This is no problem. You're not that heavy!" They chuckled.

Olav pushed the boat back in the water and rowed away from the hut. He would wait further south by the Innerelva River until the men returned. They did not want someone discovering a boat lying at the very door of Jan's hiding place.

Marius and Alfon were careful not to cause Jan additional pain. They carried him the short distance up toward the old log hut and paused by the door. Jan was placed in a sitting position on a knapsack.

From the snow pile where they stood to the threshold of the entrance, it was another couple of feet. There were no steps. Marius stretched to remove the bolt and the door squeaked open. The darkness made it impossible to distinguish any contours. Marius climbed up and crouched to get through the door. The small door opening only reached to the top of his chest.

With outstretched arms he felt his way around the room. On the south wall his knees bumped into something resembling a small cot. As his eyes adjusted to the dark he made out the outline of long narrow boards with a slight edge. It could be used as a makeshift bed. Several articles, some of them farm implements, lay strewn around the floor. The wood cot was much shorter than was Jan, but Marius was sure it could be used. Jan's helpers added a couple of the wooden planks which lay on the floor and gathered some loose hay stacked in one corner of the hut. They lifted Jan into the cottage and up into the makeshift bed.

His friends at Grønvoll farm had packed a knapsack with food, some alcohol and a small kerosene burner so he could heat his food. The men laid it all out neatly within easy reach of his bunk.

Marius and Alfon were troubled over leaving him. Jan reassured them he was comfortable and would be fine until they returned.

"Take care, Jan. We'll be back in a couple of days and bring you a little extra food."

"*Ja, takk for alt,*" thanks for everything. Give my best greetings to everyone."

"So long, Jan."

By the water's edge they signaled Olav to come pick them up.

Jan felt good. He was happy with his new living quarters and expressed his gratitude to Marius. He was dry and he had a roof overhead, food, and clothes, even a kerosene burner. Most important though, he knew he had good friends that would stand by him no matter what. And he was nearer to the Swedish border than he had been yesterday.

Jan moved the planks beneath him a little and felt rather contented. Far away from the Germans, he could relax a little and again reminisce over the happy time he had spent in Furuflaten.

Jan expected his feet to improve quickly. Before long Marius would return, as he had promised, and with his help he would climb the mountain behind the hut toward the east. When he reached Sweden, Jan knew his suffering and fear would be a thing of the past.

Hour after hour he philosophized in the dark. The sharp light that forced its way through the cracks between the logs and around the ceiling told him that a new day had dawned. The details in his surroundings became more visible. On the floor and in the corners there were thick layers of dust, hay and cobwebs. The wall planks were carved into square beams by ax. The workmanship varied, allowing the daylight to break through the large cracks. Moss had been stuffed into the larger cracks, but even at that, the hut was far from being well insulated. About four feet above his head there was a heavy crossbar between the walls. Jan could not figure out its usefulness. The ceiling was made from flat, wide boards.

The hut was about nine feet long and six feet wide. As Jan lay there, hour after hour, he discovered new details of workmanship. It gave his mind something to mull over. Every board and beam had different size knots and patterns as he compared them with each other. Soon he knew them all. As he familiarized himself with the hut he felt more at home and he began to feel safe and comfortable.

Jan kept his mind busy learning all about his surroundings. His thoughts also wandered back to his earlier life and the happy times he'd experienced as a youth in Oslo with his friends and family. Reliving these scenes of happiness calmed him, and at the same time, infused him with a longing for home and family. Often he reviewed the reasons for ending up in this hut and he rehashed every detail of how the war had come to Norway.

Past midnight, April 15, 1943: As promised, the men from Furuflaten returned to the hut two days later.

"*Hallo* Jan, how are you doing?" Their cheery voices greeted him before the door was fully open.

"I am doing great. It's like living at Hotel Savoy!" They all shared a hearty laugh.

Jan felt good, and he was happy and expressed gratitude for his new living quarters. His foot still bothered him, but it was nothing he could not live with. He expected it to keep improving.

Marius had attempted to reach the doctor in Lyngseidet to learn more about frostbite, but the doctor had been away. Instead, the bus driver, Lars Utgård, drove to Tromsø in an unsuccessful effort to get professional advice.

"Let's wait a few more days, Jan."

Hoping that his feet would continue to heal, they agreed to return in another few days with more food and provisions. The plan still was that

Jan, with Marius' help, would make it over the mountains on his own two feet.

Once more they said goodbye, but seeing how well Jan was doing, it was easier for them this time. They had to cross the fjord and return home before the people in Furuflaten began their day.

Another day forced its light through the cracks in the hut. Jan's legs suddenly hurt terribly. The burning sensation and throbbing increased at a startling pace, and did not let up. Never before in his whole life had he ever felt such terrifying pain. An unexplainable inner alarm took hold of Jan. Within an hour pain and fear wholly overpowered him. He groaned. Jan pulled up to a sitting position, then laid back down, turned over, rolled

Hotel Savoy stands close to Lyngenfjord.

from side to side and back again. He cried out for relief, but the pain only intensified.

Grabbing his legs just below the knees he squeezed hard. It gave him slight relief. He pulled the bandages off his feet. Horrified, he saw his toes were a dark grayish-black. When he stroked them he could not feel his own touch. The large toe on his right foot was pitch black and the skin was cracking. Fluid trickled out, some clear, some yellowish and thick.

"Oh my - my feet! Gangrene! No! Yes - it is gangrene!"

He knew the consequences of gangrene, but at that moment he did not want to believe it. He knew how quickly it could spread, and that it could end in death. Alone in this dim place with not a friend to turn to for help or comfort, he panicked. Even his trusted friend Marius would not be back for another couple of days.

For three days Jan suffered through agonizing pain. Sleep was impossible. As the minutes turned to hours and the hours into days he could only lie there and struggle with his pain.

Surely Marius would come soon; did he not promise he would be back in three days?

No one came.

A new day dawned and dragged on, then night came; Jan's suffering continued. Another new day and another night came and moved onward. Five days had passed since Marius and Alfon's last visit. Jan gave in to his fate. For him all hope was gone. He assumed the Germans had arrested his friends, and no one else had any idea of his whereabouts. He would die here in this little hut, a slow painful death.

Amandus Lillevoll returned home to Furuflaten from a fishing excursion in the Lofoten Islands two days after Jan had been taken to Revdal. He ran into Marius and two other men on his way home.

"Amandus I need to talk to you. It is a rather serious matter." Marius looked earnest.

"Go ahead, I have time." Amandus studied Marius as he explained about Jan.

"Frankly, dear friend, I am in desperate need of help. Would you be able to help us get him to Sweden?"

But Amandus had heard of the happenings in Toftefjord and felt that it was too risky.

"I have to think about this Marius. This is not child's play."

"Take your time, it might mean our very lives," said Marius.

Amandus pondered the pros and cons, and what to do.

"I'll take the risk. I'll help you," was his final answer.

Furuflaten, April 20, 1943: A dreadful spring storm made it impossible to cross the Lyngenfjord. Finally on April 20 the weather eased. Alfon and Amandus packed their knapsacks. They would have to cross the fjord in daylight; they needed to get food to Jan. At Røykeneset, straight across from Furuflaten, was a German guard post. From there they could observe the whole fjord. Even Revdal to the north behind Foraneset was in their field of vision. The men were uneasy; there was no place to hide.

Alfon and Amandus took fishing gear along and stopped often, pretending to fish. They were concerned that the Germans might have found Jan by now. They had not seen him for several days.

They came ashore on the sandbank south of the Revdal hut and hid among the tall turf.

"I'll run over the grassland," Alfon suggested since he knew Jan from before. He worked his way over to the hut. Jan was armed, and kept the gun close by his side. They had agreed that they would knock three times on the wall when they came. He knocked and heard creaks from within. He waved for Amandus to enter.

Jan crawled from his cot, pulled himself across the floor and opened the door.

He greeted Alfon warmly and shook hands with Amandus.

"We've brought you some food."

"All I have left over is bread crust. It will taste good. Thanks."

They noticed how pale and worn Jan looked. He showed them his feet — all his toes and both heels were black.

"If this is gangrene, I am finished. I am too young, I don't wish to die."

The men looked at his feet in horror.

"Is it possible to reach a doctor when you get home and bring him to me?"

Jan was in despair. It hurt them to leave him, but time was of an essence. They "fished" their way back home across the fjord and contacted a doctor.

The doctor did not have the courage to cross the fjord with them to Revdal.

Wednesday, April 21, 1943: Jan shuddered with pain. Big drops of sweat trickled down his face. In an instant his body chilled, then it turned hot again, and back to cold. Fever ravaged. All he could do was watch his murky gray toes turn black and new cracks appear on the skin. But it was the stench, the putrid stench that rolled over him in waves and nauseated him, that scared him the most. His feet were rotting away! "If I could only lose consciousness and allow death to come unnoticed," he thought.

With all his might he pulled his knees close up to him, grabbed his ankles and pressed them against the back of his thighs. This helped to relieve the pain somewhat. At intervals he had to let go and rest, then he repeated his efforts for fleeting moments of respite from the excruciating pain.

As he struggled emotionally with his situation, his inner will again came to the forefront. He had been close to death many times and somehow he had survived. Lying there in his lonely state, a thought formed in his mind. He pondered his circumstances and what, if anything, he could do to change them. His legs would soon be covered with black spots as the gangrene worked its way upward.

"I have to stop it! I refuse to die here in this hut!" Jan began to fight back. He was still not willing to give up on life and he told himself he would not give in to inaction, pain or panic. He would *will* himself to function, even to take drastic steps.

He looked around. His eyes fell on the sheath knife close by. He stared at it. Grabbing the wooden edge of his bunk with one hand, he pushed the boards beneath him until he came to a half-sitting position, with the other. The sheath knife was on the makeshift stand next to the bunk. He pulled it out of its sheath and laid it on the bunk with the handle toward him. He calmly folded the bed covering aside toward the wall. Jan bent forward and examined his feet, focusing on his large toe. It was all black, including the rough edges on the bottom where the gunshot wound had begun to grow together. He squeezed the toe in several spots but he felt nothing.

Jan's mind was made up.

"What other chance do I have?" he asked himself. No better answer came to him so he reached for the alcohol bottle. Pouring some into his hands, he rubbed it between his fingers and over his hands and wrists. He put the bottle to his lips and took a couple of large gulps.

Jan repeated the procedure twice. The second time he poured a little alcohol over the knife blade and rubbed it clean. He took a few more gulps for final courage and to hopefully soothe the pain.

Two, three times he rubbed his large toe with alcohol. He took a firm hold of it with his left hand. Jan picked up the knife and resolutely held it. He placed the blade of the knife where he felt it to be the best angle. Sweat resurfaced on his forehead.

Jan began to cut. He inched his way ahead as the blood began to trickle out, grateful the bleeding was much less than he had imagined. The knife butted up against the joint. Jan continued the sawing motion and then quickly cut the last piece of skin, severing the toe from his body. He was shivering and dripping wet.

Jan placed the toe by a crack in the wall timber, and then fell backwards in his crude bed. His chest heaved with each breath and moan. The knife fell from his hand onto the floor. With his elbow he wiped his soaked brow. With trembling hands he covered his face and wept.

Minutes later his clarity of mind returned. He again pulled himself up on his elbows. With alcohol he washed his hands, the knife, and then carefully dabbed his toe. The first joint of the next toe was black; with his left thumb and index finger he grabbed hold on each side of the nail. It was easy to place the knife blade now that the large toe had been removed.

Though the edge of the knife was in place, Jan was unable to slit the skin and had to start sawing before the blood was released.

His head shook - his whole body shuddered. Sweat poured from his twisted face – but Jan's hand held steady. Half of the joint was cut when he had to stop. The pain was intense – alcohol was not the best pain reliever.

"You must finish the job, Jan!"

He began to saw again. Jan broke the last piece of the joint and pushed it to the side. The cut gaped. The knife moved easier. The tip of the toe fell into the folds of the covering together with the knife. Jan fell backwards.

Outside the wind howled and beat Lyngenfjord into a fury. Huge white-capped waves angrily flogged the shore near the little hut. Snowdrifts engulfed Jan's shelter, leaving just the upper walls and the roof visible. The whirling snow crashed into boulders and the bare trees leeward thrashed all about as the forceful wind gusts pounced on them.

Jan was oblivious to the storm.

On the opposite side of the fjord, a restless Marius and his friends had to return home. The raging sea was too dangerous. Their little boat was no match for the colossal waves and the wind; they would never reach Jan. Marius could dimly make out the black mountain wall close to the hut, only five miles away. It was so close, yet in this weather so very far.

Several more black spots had to be removed. Jan cut, fell, and cut again several times. No one could have stopped him. His only chance for life was to mutilate his own body. The nightmare lasted several hours.

Motionless, Jan lay on his back. His right arm hung over the edge of the cot. Close by him on the floor was a bloody knife.

Thursday, April 22, 1943: Soon after 2 a.m., Marius and two men hurried from the boat up to the hut. Since Alfon's and Amandus' last visit with Jan, Marius had been frantic. He ran in front the last few steps, knocked three times on the door and rushed in.

"Hello Jan! Have you been waiting for us?"

The moonless April night blinded Jan when Marius opened the door and disrupted his aloneness. He groaned and shaded his half-shut eyes with a hand blotched with dried blood. Even the early morning light pained him. It took minutes before his eyes adjusted to the change after the days of darkness.

A foul odor greeted Jan's visitors. The stench rolled through the door, so fetid it nauseated them. They turned toward the door for a breath of fresh air.

"Jan!" Marius moved toward the cot. No response. The farmer looked down on his haggard friend, moved the blanket aside and gasped. Then he saw the bloody knife on the floor. His eyes traveled to the crack on the wall. A black toe!

Jan did not move. He was dirty and bloody, and his skin resembled a corpse. The sores from his incisions had not healed, and secretions mixed with blood seeped out. The offensive smell filled the tiny hut. Below Jan's knees, his legs and ankles had turned brownish-red.

With the arrival of his enthusiastic friends, a glimmer of hope returned to Jan's wasted body and desolate spirit.

"We're here to take care of you Jan."

Jan moved and slowly opened his eyes. The men cleaned him up and fed him some of the food they had brought. In time the conversation turned to small talk. Jan quickened. Even seriously ill, he was able to find hope in the smallest things. The Furuflaten men were amazed at what their visits did for him. Their visit had restored a flicker of hope to him before they left him alone again.

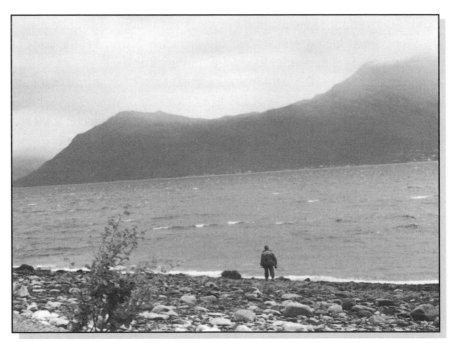

View from Hotel Savoy across Lyngenfjord toward Furuflaten.

ḣAPPENIṇGS Iṇ
LOFOCEṇ iSLAṇDS

On April 24, 1940, Reichskommissar Terboven became Hitler's highest civil authority in occupied Norway. A man explicitly trusted by the Fuehrer, and into whose hands were poured unlimited, concentrated power.

Lofoten Islands, March 4, 1943: The British and Norwegian forces launched a successful raid in northern Norway, in the Lofoten Islands.

Immediately following the raid in Svolvær, Reichskommissar Terboven flew from Oslo to Lofoten for briefing. Terboven's punishment of the people of Svolvær was swift; several innocent hostages were taken and many homes were burned to the ground.

Two young men from the village of Furuflaten, one of them Alvin Larsen, were in the Lofoten Islands at the time of the raid, having just purchased a fishing boat.

Subsequent to Terboven's terrorism of the people of Svolvær, he did something unusual for him. Terboven expressed a wish to see some of the Norwegian fishermen in action. The Germans used huge amounts of fish to feed their soldiers. In spite of his power, Terboven felt it essential and beneficial to have a good relationship with the fishermen. Alvin was among those chosen to be present for Terboven.

A few men were gathered in a fisherman's shelter repairing fishnets when Terboven appeared. He explained he was curious to learn a little of their everyday life.

Terboven was feared. His power was absolute. He was of medium build and slender of stature with a rather handsome face; his dark piercing eyes looked through unframed glasses. While in the fisherman's shelter he displayed a congenial demeanor, and he was almost likeable had his reputation not preceded him.

As he was leaving he stopped abruptly in the doorway, turned toward the fishermen and placed one hand on his hip, the other above his head on the doorframe.

"Do you have any special wishes? Or perhaps, I could serve you in some way?"

A hush fell over the men, they all had wishes but only one dared voice them. Alvin had a blazing desire that could not be extinguished: "I would like for my fishing boat never to be requisitioned into German service," he said, looking straight at Terboven.

The Germans' common practice was to take possession of whatever they desired and they had confiscated many fishing vessels. Terboven lingered momentarily without saying a word, saluted and left.

Reichskommissar Terboven in Lofoten.

There was a stir of excitement in Alvin's home when, several days later, an envelope with the *Reichskommissar*'s logo came. Alvin, a little uneasy perhaps, pulled out a document bearing the German eagle, Terboven's signature and stamp. It stated that Alvin and his companion's fishing vessel were not ever to be requisitioned into the German service. Alvin let out a howl. With such a document he could take his fishing boat anywhere.

Later when German patrol boats stopped him for inspection, from out of nowhere as they often did, Alvin gleefully produced his valuable document. As soon as Terboven's signature and stamp were noted, the military boots clicked together and a rigid military greeting was afforded. Alvin and his crew sailed on triumphant.

GEARING UP FOR REVDAL

While Jan languished in the log hut at Revdal, Marius constantly devised ideas on how to best transport him to Sweden. It was an overwhelming challenge. Jan was extremely ill, and Marius knew that the most comfortable way for Jan to be transported would be by car or truck, along the main road. Even before completing the thought, Marius knew they would not be able to pass the German border guards leaving Norway, nor cross the northwest corner of occupied Finland without being discovered. It was useless to think he would ever reach Sweden by that route.

As the days elapsed, Marius realized that only one way was left open to them, the mountains. The task would be Herculean for the resistance workers to pull off, and for Jan, almost merciless. But it was Jan's only chance for survival. And, without daring, how would they know that it could not be done? They had to try. There was no alternative.

It became obvious to Marius that transporting Jan to Sweden was too risky and too big of a job for the men of Furuflaten alone. They needed to contact the other men working within the resistance movement in the neighboring localities.

Telephones in these outlying areas were few; only party lines were available. Telephones were extremely dangerous to use for illegal work because people listened in. Any veiled stories could be embellished and passed on to other itchy ears.

State roads were non-existent in Birtavärre, Olderdalen and Manndalen Valley. Many of the people central to the resistance movement lived in these places, and a tight-knit communication system was essential to their success. Sometimes because of the distances between localities, it took days before a message reached its intended recipient.

Soon after Alvin returned from Lofoten, he was pulled into the midst of the master plan to rescue Jan. With Reichskommissar Terboven's blessing, unknown to him of course, the document he had granted Alvin suited him superbly. The task of delivering messages among the fjords and inland waters of the Troms District became Alvin's job.

Alvin readily agreed to have his boat at Marius' disposal and suggested they bring along Alfon Hansen. Being a commercial fisherman had its advantages. Once the season was over, or when they came home for a break, the time was theirs to do with as they pleased. Alvin felt good about using his boat in Norway's service.

Furuflaten, April 19, 1943: Alvin Larsen, Marius Grønvoll and Alfon Hansen readied to leave Furuflaten for their inland trip. Alvin called his girlfriend and apologized that he had to break their date, but promised to make it up to her. Alfon told one of his funny stories to his mother before leaving the house. He enjoyed seeing her laugh. Marius was the last to come aboard, having had to finish up some barn chores before leaving.

It was good weather with a brisk wind, and the men were in good spirits as Alvin took to the tiller and set the boat out to sea.

"Jaja." The words came quickly. "When several Norwegians band together, the green devils don't stand a chance," Alfon laughed contagiously.

"You're right. We are going to snatch Jan from the Gestapo yet," Marius agreed.

They crossed the Lyngenfjord and sailed northwest around the tip of Odden. The wind was picking up a bit and it felt good; the air smelled of seaweed and fish, always invigorating to the men. Crossing Kåfjord they soon reached Olderdalen, where they met with resistance member Peder Bergmo and discussed the possibilities of securing help to transport Jan to Sweden.

"No problem. Count me in."

Peder was the contact person for Manndalen, Birtavärre and Olderdalen.

They sailed south to Birtavärre, innermost in the fjord where the Bjørn brothers lived. Stalwarts in the resistance movement, and always willing to offer all they could, the brothers offered advice and provided help whenever it was needed.

Continuing on, they cruised northwest to Manndalen and met with teacher Nordnes, a tall handsome man with deep set clear blue eyes in his early forties. The positive answer came as expected. Many alternatives for transporting Jan were discussed with all of these men. Ultimately, however, they all reached the same conclusion. Satisfied with their work, Alvin's crew returned home from their outing.

Marius now had a well-defined plan. The men from Furuflaten would bring Jan, tied to a sled, up the Revdal Mountains in back of the little log hut. At a designated spot up on the mountain plateau, they would deliver him to the more rested and vigorous Manndalen men, who would come up on skis from the opposite side of the mountains. The Manndalen men would be responsible for Jan's safe passage to Sweden. The plan would be put into action as soon as it was practical and the weather was accommodating. They had to move swiftly. Marius set the day for April 24 and they were to meet at midnight. A message was sent via teacher Leigland at Lyngseidet on to Peder Bergmo in Olderdalen. Jan's life hung in the balance. He was in desperate need of proper medical treatment.

The Solhov School was located a short way up from the Lyngenfjord in the southern part of the village of Lyngseidet, some nine miles from Furuflaten. The school was famed in the Troms District because of its excellent curriculum and also because its majestic building was the largest wooden structure in northern Norway at the time. The Germans had confiscated the building and installed their headquarters unit for the entire Eastern Front. As the building was strictly guarded, no one approached it without a just cause. The school caretaker, however, lived in one of the wings of the building.

As the preparations for Jan's further transport continued under the strictest secrecy, caretaker Jensen was called on to help. An excellent carpenter, Jensen was assigned to make a strong wood sled sturdy and of adequate size to transport Jan on.

In a basement corner of Solhov School was Jensen's modest carpenter shop. A small carpenter's bench squeezed up against the corner window and made it possible for him to partially see the school grounds outside.

One of his shop walls adjoined one of the soldiers' quarters. They came and went at all times of the day and sometimes they dropped in on Jensen for a chat while he worked. Despite these circumstances, on his little workbench he managed to build an excellent ski sled, 6 feet long, 4 inches high and 22 inches wide. It was suitable for a grown man to lie down on.

A couple of days after Alvin and his friends' boat trip to secure aid for Jan's transport, Jensen had the sled ready. Alvin had been given the task of transporting the sled to Furuflaten. One of Alvin's uncles, Johan Johansen, also owned a fishing boat and just that day he was with his son in Lyngseidet to repair the boat's motor. Alvin knew this, jumped on his bicycle and pedaled quickly toward Lyngseidet.

He went straight to the "lion's den" – the German headquarters at Solhov School. Like Daniel of old, Alvin went undaunted and filled with faith. It was a threatening situation but he believed the outcome would be favorable. He hastened over to one of the guards. Knowing a little German he said, *"Guten tag,"* Good day.

"Guten tag," replied the guard.

"Ich suche Jensen," I have a meeting with Caretaker Jensen.

The soldier quickly understood; nevertheless, he was a little annoyed at being disturbed but brushed it off.

"Danke sehr," thank you, said Alvin.

All the soldiers knew of Jensen, but regarded the carpenter as harmless. As a result he didn't question Alvin further. He gave the go-ahead with a nod of his head and waved him over in the direction of the stairs leading to the large windowed entrance door. Alvin thanked him, closed the heavy doors behind him, and continued down the few steps to the basement. As he walked along the corridor, he noticed the guardroom door ajar where some soldiers were relaxing; they paid no attention to him.

Jensen waved Alvin on and closed the door behind him to the workshop. The sled was ready to be moved. But knowing an assembled sled would lead to many questions, Jensen had constructed it like a building set. He carefully explained to Alvin how to piece it together.

"Easy to transport, easy to assemble," he whispered.

They tied the twelve-foot long un-planed boards together into a pile. These planks were quite a bit longer then the rest of the pieces so that both ends could be stuffed with the un-planed sawed-off pieces for the wooden braces, making it all look like 12 foot long planks when tied together and wrapped. The package was extremely heavy, but also fragile, so had to be handled with care.

The two men decided it was best for Alvin to bicycle ahead down to the docks in Lyngseidet to wait by his uncle's boat.

The workbench at Solhov School where Caretaker Jensen made the sled on which Jan lay when he was taken up into Revdal Mountains.

"Auf weidersehen," one of the soldiers waved through the cracked door as he walked back down the hall.

"Auf weidersehen."

Within half an hour Jensen arrived with the horse and sleigh and a long well-wrapped package of wooden planks destined for Furuflaten, and eventually to be Jan's transportation to Sweden.

Soldiers patrolled the Lyngseidet dock. The air coming off the fjord was biting cold, but their compensation was the magnificent view of the Lyngen Alps in the distance. The tide was out and Alvin struggled to get the cumbersome package down into the boat, which lay several meters lower than the edge of the dock. The German guard saw his predicament, removed his machine gun which, up to now, had been loosely flung over his shoulder, and carefully placed it on the dock.

"Ich helfe," I will help, he said, hurrying over to Alvin. With care, the two placed the valuable package up in the bow of the boat.

Quivering nerves never disturbed Alvin; he was a feisty young man. On the contrary, he was stable, wise and daring. With his cheerful disposition, both friends and strangers took an instant liking to him.

"And where is the crew to the boat?" the soldier queried.

"They'll be along shortly. I'm just hitching a ride with them."

Alvin crawled back up on the dock and chatted with the soldier in his broken German. With a thick German burr, the soldier made an effort to speak Norwegian. A pleasant conversation ensued.

"I long for my family and home in Germany. May the war soon end so I can return to my homeland." The soldier was melancholy.

Alvin agreed. He fumbled through his pockets as if trying to find a cigarette, though he didn't have any. The soldier unbuttoned the breast pocket of his uniform, took out a package of cigarettes and seemed pleased to offer one to him, though he was forbidden to smoke on duty.

Soon Alvin's uncle and his son arrived, ready to return to Furuflaten.

"I guess I can come along?" Alvin queried.

"Ka har du der?" What have you got there? His uncle stared, and pointed at the long package up in front of the boat.

"Just some material from Solhov School."

"You are a lucky man to have contact with Jensen." His uncle removed his cap, smiled and scratched his head. "There is such a shortage of material these days."

Alvin lifted his bicycle and put it down on the deck. They loosened the ropes, and as the boat distanced itself from the dock, Alvin raised his hand and thanked the soldier for his kindness.

"Bitte sehr," My pleasure! The soldier saluted.

Arriving at Furuflaten, the package was left aboard the boat.

Furuflaten, April 22, 1943: Alvin's friend, Hans Olsen, picked up the package with the twelve-foot-long boards and loaded it into his rowboat. He rowed along the coast a little further south in the village. Upon his arrival Alvin was waiting. They wrapped the set in burlap and hid it in a secure place close by the water's edge. It would be picked up again when they set out toward Revdal to transport Jan.

Replica of the sled.

ON THE OTHER SIDE OF THE FJORD

Kåfjord, Lyngenfjord's 15-mile arm, stretches southeast toward the mountainous village of Birtavärre at the head of the fjord. Birtavärre lies on the southeast side of Manndalen Valley; to the north lies Olderdalen Valley. West across the Lyngenfjord lies Lyngseidet and nine miles south of Lyngseidet lies Furuflaten. These communities form sort of a quadrangle on the map.

Daring patriots from each village were active in the resistance movement. Each village had established its own sensitive and secret communication nets. Communicating by telephone was risky because one

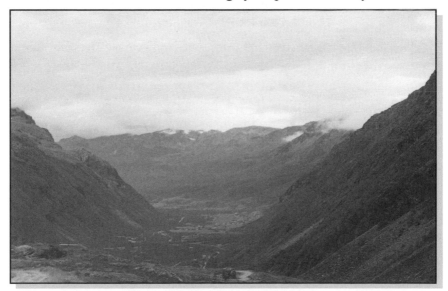

Kåfjorddalen Valley

never knew who would be listening in. The only roads were between Furuflaten and Lyngseidet. There were none between Manndalen, Birtavärre and Olderdalen. A ferry ran between Olderdalen and Lyngseidet and sometimes it was utilized to send secret messages. Other times the resistance members rowed half way out into the Kåfjord between Olderdalen and Manndalen to meet and exchange messages. From Samuelsberg, on the outskirts of Manndalen, over to Olderdalen, the distance was around four miles to row midways into the fjord.

Peder Bergmo, a thirty-one-year old father of five, lived in Olderdalen. His oldest son Asmund was only six. Peder was known as a loving and attentive dad, firm, but fair. He appreciated nature's beauty and loved to be outdoors in any season.

In 1943 Peder managed the communal office for medical insurance. A compassionate man, he cared deeply for the poor, and anyone who faced difficult times. He was of great service to many in the rural community when hard times or disaster struck in its varied forms.

In his youth Peder become acquainted with the Bjørn brothers in Birtavärre. Through this friendship he was later drawn into the resistance movement when the war came. As time passed, he became the leader of the group in Olderdalen. He was the key person in the village's connection with the schoolmaster Leigland in Lyngseidet.

After Jan Baalsrud arrived in Furuflaten, resistance leaders in the area discussed plans for his evacuation to Sweden. In Olderdalen, there were rumors that fundraising to obtain money for Jan's transport to Sweden had begun. The Gestapo got a whiff of this, and Peder Bergmo was arrested and imprisoned in Tromsø. Suddenly his wife was left alone to care for their young children, fearing all the while for her husband's life.

Sheriff Marvold heard about Peder's arrest. He and Peder had been in the same class all through folk school and had spent much time together in their youth. Marvold took pity on his old school chum and his family. Being friendly with the Germans, he traveled to Tromsø and sought out the Gestapo. Since Marvold had an in with the Gestapo and they trusted him, he tried them out.

"You have Peder Bergmo from Olderdalen imprisoned here. I believe you have the wrong man."

The Gestapo agent straightened up and stared at Marvold. "Are you questioning our judgment?" The sheriff ignored the question. "Peder is a school buddy of mine, a father of five. He keeps busy seeing to the need of the villagers through his work and he is law abiding!"

They discussed the issue back and forth without coming to an agreement. When Marvold readied to leave he turned and resolutely stated, "I vouch for this man."

After a short imprisonment, Peder was set free. He returned to Olderdalen, and unafraid despite his misadventure, he continued his work with the underground.

In Manndalen, it was a 43-year-old bachelor, Aslak Fossvoll, and teacher Nordnes who were the contact persons. Aslak was totally trustworthy and an extremely polite man. He owned a small farm that he nurtured with care. He loved nothing more than fishing in the clear streams of the nearby majestic mountains, with his faithful dog by his side. People in the valley said that if you saw Aslak you would also see his dog. The two were inseparable and often went out into the wilds together. Aslak was happiest if no one knew where they were going.

Peder Nordnes was Manndalen's revered folk-school teacher. The rural community considered him a man of sterling character. He was a tall, well-built man and very strong, with Nordic blond hair and intelligent blue eyes. Like Aslak, he was unmarried. All the youth in the valley had had him as a teacher, and he was greatly respected. He had impeccable manners and was known for his ability and willingness to cooperate with others.

When Marius, Alfon and Alvin visited Olderdalen, Birtavärre and Manndalen on April 19, they had worked with these men and made plans for Jan's transport to Sweden. The final date for putting the plan into action was the only thing that was not set.

Furuflaten 23 April 1943: Marius decided it was the right time to carry out the well-laid plans to begin Jan's transfer to Sweden. The weather, something that always had to be considered in the North, was good. The wind was calm and it was not too cold - and all the men were ready. On that day, Marius sent a message via Lyngseidet to Peder Bergmo in Olderdalen. It read, "He will be delivered to the Manndalen men early Saturday, April 25, between two and four in the morning."

Moskogaisa

Ankerlia

Ankerlia and Moskogaisa Mountains

Peder Bergmo was working at his office when Marius' message arrived. There was no way he could just close his office and leave, since people depended on him to be there. At the end of the workday, it was too late to reach the Manndalen men and organize the climb up to the Revdal Mountains. The men hadn't been sought out and told in advance in order to keep the plan secret. If someone should make a slip it could be catastrophic for all. No one was to know anything before the time was ripe.

Olderdalen, April 24, 1943: It was early morning when Peder set course for Manndalen. He rowed across Kåfjord and tied his little boat at Samuelsberg, at the edge of Manndalen. Time was of the essence – he had only one day to find four men who were able and willing to take on this dangerous assignment.

A chill wind blasted Peder as he walked briskly toward the post office to inquire of a trusted friend as to whom he should approach. He received names of people who could possibly help. Another friend loaned Peder his horse to make his trip around the hilly village faster and easier.

From the post office, Peder went straight to the school to see teacher Nordnes, who also was helpful with names. Teacher Nordnes himself desired to be part of the team, but felt he was not in good enough condition for the fatiguing climb. Teacher Nordnes was plagued with a stiff body and was often wracked with pain. He felt that his participation would be a hindrance and possibly cause failure for all.

After Peder left Teacher Nordnes he went to Aslak Fossvoll. As the leader of the resistance movement in the village, he would surely be the right man to ask for help.

The two men discussed able-bodied men who could make the hike. After a short discussion, they both knew they had the right man. Peder left Aslak.

The horse trotted along the wintry road to Hans Oppevold's little house further up in the valley. There Peder found that Hans had cut his foot the day before while working in the woods. It was impossible for him to take on the assignment.

By the time Peder left Oppervoll's home, it was late afternoon and he had yet to find the men he needed for the job. The next man that Aslak had suggested Peder see lived nearby. Peder gave the horse a little rap with the reins and in a small gallop headed toward Nils Nilsen's house. The horse slowed down after awhile, and Peder had to continually smack the horse with the reins to hurry him on. The horse leaped ahead and kept up the speed once more. Time was short.

Nilsen was a tireless and hard working man. Married with a house full of children, his friends called him "Nigo." He ran a small farm and fished on the side for extra income. Everyone admired his ability to handle strenuous work and his diligence long after all others quit. He was a man who could work hard for 48 hours without a bite to eat. On the other hand, Nigo could easily eat a whole loaf of homemade bread once he got started. His unbeatable optimism, no matter the situation, was also well known.

Nigo was working outside when Peder arrived. Peder explained the urgency and the secrecy of his message and Nigo brought him over to a quiet place away from the children. As quickly as possible, Peder laid out what needed to be done and the danger of it all.

"*Ja*, I'll go," Nigo responded, without a moment's hesitation. He knew the mountains, the terrain and the danger at this time of the year; he asked for a companion, one who was both strong and persevering.

Peder was elated knowing Nigo would see this assignment through, but he needed one more man. He had started out from Olderdalen early in the morning and worked all day. Now the day was gone. And Peder Bergmo had been unable to find two men who could climb up to Jan in the Revdal Mountains. He had to leave the responsibility to find the second man with the Manndalen men. Knowing they would not be able to meet the Furuflaten men up in the Revdal Mountains at the appointed time, Peder's heart was heavy. He returned the horse back to its owner and walked down to the dock. He climbed into the rowboat and began the journey home. The rowing home seemed extra long and strenuous.

On the west side of the Revdal Mountains, the Furuflaten men had already begun their climb up from Hotel Savoy with Jan tied to a sled.

pushed to the brink

The tranquil spring evening with its warm breeze was welcome respite from the harsh winter storms. Quiet waves gently lapped the shore and vanished over nearby rocks. A few puffy clouds hung suspended midway up the nearby mountains.

Despite the peace that surrounded them, Marius Grønvoll, Alvin Larsen, Olaf Lanes and Amandus Lillevoll were apprehensive. They motioned to one another and spoke in whispers when they had to communicate. German soldiers were quartered at Furuflaten School a short distance into the village. The young men hoped the soldiers were unwinding for the day. On the village road a short way from the docks, a lone German soldier patrolled; he might hear any accidental noise. The village was quieting down with families relaxing at home. This was the evening the three men had prepared for. This was the evening Jan had been waiting for.

The men, to the minute of the prearranged time, brought the long wrapped package with the sled material aboard Amandus Lillevoll's boat. Inaudibly they rowed out into the fjord, knowing the first few hundred meters were the most perilous. The open water magnified every small sound and could easily be heard in the village.

Cautiously they slipped the oars into the water. Drops formed on the oars and fell back into the water like tinkling silver bells. Too big a splash could give them all away. With the stealth of their Viking ancestors, the Furuflaten men glided smoothly into the nocturnal shadows of the unknown future.

Tension eased as they distanced themselves from the land. Once they were well out in the fjord they felt safe in raising the mast and sail, a noisy proposition. Knowing they would be easier to spot from land, they had waited to hoist the sail for as long as possible.

The wind was almost still and the sail provided little momentum to the boat's forward thrust. But Jan's friends were prepared for any contingency and their sail had a totally different purpose. Should a German patrol boat surprise them, they would have difficulty explaining the long package in the bottom of the boat. Under such circumstances, they planned to sink the package, to which they had attached a heavy rock. Next, they would get their fishing lines out.

As an added camouflage they had brought *nakkeskudd,* which literally means a shot in the head from the back. *Nakkeskudd* was Furuflaten's own homemade brew, a hard liquor with caraway seeds added. The drink derived its name from the violent effect it had on the bodies of those who dared. They had brought several bottles. The plan was to pretend as if they were on a genuine rabble-rousing party out in the fjord.

If necessary, they would pour a little *nakkeskudd* on their clothes; they would take a gulp or two as well. All this, designed to fool the Germans, would happen quickly and *behind* the sail. Surely the Germans would find nothing suspicious aboard their boat: only provisions, fish gear and liquor. As it turned out, the Norwegians pulled the boat up on the shore opposite Furuflaten, in Revdal, after an hour of hard rowing and without incident.

A stone's throw away from the beach, up a small incline, stood the forsaken wood hut almost buried in snowdrift. Within, an ill friend wasted away, yet the hut sat there gawking over the fjord, utterly void of human feelings, dark and threatening.

Behind the rough wood door, Jan battled in solitude against pain and fear. Even after his self-operation, the pain in his feet troubled him. Loneliness pricked his heart and never let go. Unfulfilled longing for human contact made the wound deeper and the solitude harder to bear. For Jan, panic was never far removed. Sometimes it prevailed.

During the day a few rays of light crept through the narrow cracks around the doorframe and along the wall, but they were narrow and sparse.

From his cot, Jan pulled out some of the moss which had been stuffed into tiny fissures of the walls to prevent drafts. These gaps were miniscule, the size of small coins. He mused over which spot of moss he should remove next. These small openings had been his only source of light. In some places where he had pulled the moss out, no light came through. The soldier realized the snowdrifts reached far up the wall.

Jan yearned for news from his friends. His recurring worry was that something had happened to them. He was genuinely concerned that the Germans had arrested them, and that they would be tortured. All he wanted was a hint of them, a small piece of encouragement to make his own burden easier to carry. Jan drifted in and out of consciousness from the pain.

Icy fingers of fear left him little hope. Why this prolonged suffering? What was its purpose? Why had he not perished in Toftefjord with his friends? Why could he not just die now?

Agonizing in his bed, Jan felt forsaken. He did not know that only a few feet away four men trudged through the snow toward the hut. They carried clothing, a couple of wool blankets, an old military sleeping bag, food, drink and some cigarettes. Olaf carried coils of rope over his shoulders.

Alvin brought the long package with the unplaned boards. He fought his way a little past the cottage, up towards the incline, and put the package down. The muscles in his arms ached and his neck felt stiff. Alvin stretched and bent from side to side to loosen up after toting the heavy load. Above, he discerned the outline of clouds hanging low up against the mountainside. He thought back to the kind German soldier who had helped him earlier in Lyngseidet. He had been unaware, of course, of the package contents. The soldier, a young man about his own age, who longed for his own home and loved ones, had been so trusting. Alvin opened the package and set the pieces out in order. Jensen's directions on how to assemble the sled were excellent. Screws, bolts, boards and runners fit together perfectly and swiftly completed the ski sled. Alvin laid down on it to try its strength. He stretched out; it was both long and wide enough and sturdy.

Earlier in the day Alvin rummaged through his house to find the Navy jacket he had worn with pride. It had hung in the back of the closet since his leave in 1940. He had never been recalled. Tonight he dressed in his uniform jacket once again. Alvin tried it on in front of the small mirror at home and was pleased with how well it fit. He looked good. He knew Jan was wearing a Navy uniform. Alvin hoped dressing in a Navy outfit would contribute to Jan's well being, and make him more relaxed and comfortable.

Marius opened the door to the hut; Amandus and Olaf were right behind. Jan was very ill. The putrid smell of rotting flesh still lingered in the air. The men tried to cheer him. After all, he would soon be on his way to Sweden.

"We will get you out of here as soon as you have eaten, Jan."

"Before too long, we will have you in Sweden. The Manndalen men are meeting us up on the plateau."

"By the way, my family sends warm greetings and wishes you their heartfelt best," Marius added.

Jan barely managed a smile.

The men went to work. They cleaned him up and tended to his feet. They changed his clothes and disposed of the waste. With something warm to drink and a slice or two of bread, a little of Jan's strength returned. Mingling with his friends cheered him. They reassured him that his worst trials were behind him. Jan's inherent optimism began to return.

His admiration for these men, these courageous giants, knew no limits. His gratitude for their sacrifices and the risks they were taking overwhelmed him. He was keenly aware that these men had put their own safety and comfort aside to save *his* life, and by so doing they might give up their own. They wanted neither payment nor praise for their effort. Their reward, as they had expressed it, was in seeing him brought to safety. Most of them did not even know him. Life, even in the midst of the relentless trials and evils of the war, was good. His mood and confidence rose.

A short time earlier, Jan felt like he'd reached the end of his road; with a little food to comfort him, tenderness, warm friendship and joviality, his outlook changed to near euphoria. His friends had brought with them a plan of action, a new hope. Jan had learned that one cannot live without hope. With the faith and hope the men brought, Jan returned to the man he really was, a courageous man who could withstand most anything, a gentle man who possessed the strength of the granite mountains he had traversed.

The men bumped into each other as they readied Jan. They removed the door from its hinges and put it out of the way. Six strong arms gently lifted Jan out from the contracted bunk bed. There were no stair steps but Alvin stood in the snow outside, ready to help, and they lifted him down toward him. Soon they placed Jan on the waiting sled. The fresh sea breeze was like a tonic. Jan began to feel alive!

This was the first time Jan and Alvin met. Alvin bent down toward him with outstretched hand.

"I have been looking forward to this meeting. My name is Alvin Larsen, I live in Furuflaten."

Jan slowly reached Alvin's hand and held it in both of his.

"Many thanks for joining us." Jan smiled warmly.

"I'm just happy to be of help."

"I see you are also a Navy man." Hotel Savoy launched a lifelong friendship between the two soldiers.

The resistance men wrapped Jan in two blankets and placed him in the sleeping bag. They then tied him securely to the sled, intertwining the ropes in and around the braces of the sled up to his armpits and down to his ankles. From time to time, especially when they tied his legs and feet down, Jan grimaced—but not a word of complaint escaped his lips. He resembled a mummy tied to the sled as he was, but this was his happy choice. Soon, with the help of his friends, he would be over the mountains and into Sweden where freedom and medical support would end his ordeal. He longed to be there.

The two pairs of skis the men had brought were tied to the side of the sled. Everything had to be absolutely secure for the vertical climb they faced. Jan looked up at the men and again expressed his gratitude for their service to him.

He looked toward the nearly vertical mountain ahead of them.

"If I survive this, I will be able to live through anything," he said.

Shortly before midnight they began their climb up the Revdal Mountains. The path they had chosen was the ravine that tended upward from the hut.

Marius, Alvin, Amandus and Olaf had examined the mountain from the fjord and later from the shore and found it to be the only logical way.

Closest to the fjord, scattered brush dotted the gently sloped terrain. The men reached the thicket where the incline rose sharply all at once. The snow was heavy and deep. In some places they disappeared into the mountain-snow up to their waist. Two of the men were at the front of the sled. Fifteen-foot long ropes were secured to each side of the front of the sled, which two of the Furuflaten men held. A six-foot length of rope was attached to each side of the rear of the sled and held by the other two men. In this way, two men on each side ensured the sled's stability.

The four young men were all in excellent physical condition. In spite of that, they soon realized that the climb would require more energy than they had imagined. They pulled and pushed, slid and fell, and climbed again. All along, they did their best to keep the sled steady to minimize Jan's suffering.

In the midst of the thickets they had difficulty getting the sled through and around the dwarfed timber. Olaf pulled out a small ax and chopped at the stunted trees, clearing the way while the others steadied the sled. These moments gave them brief respite. These were also the times when Amandus kept them all in good humor with his stored-up anecdotes.

"Have you heard…?" or "Did you know…?" he'd begin.

They forged ahead, scrambling over stony outcrops, pulling on boughs, stumps, and exposed roots. Jan helped when he could, grasping at nearby branches and rocks. Sometimes, when the men needed it the most, they'd find a small, strong tree strategically located for them to throw their arms around and pull themselves up with. The complexity of the mountain increased as they scaled upwards, but the men refused to give in.

Just above the tree line they rested on an outcrop. Below the mighty Lyngenfjord came into view. They were amazed at how precipitous the mountain was, compared to their view from below. Each man watched his steps carefully on the ice-encrusted granite. A slip here and the next stopwould be the fjord. Looking backward a few yards on the tracks they'd made, the men saw only air, an abyss, and the fjord below them. The loose snow they had waded through further down now had a crusty surface. When they sank through it up here, it sounded like the crushing of gravel.

The mountain accentuated everything, including itself. It was appallingly rugged and steep. The situation worsened with every few steps. They no longer could just pull and push, though that had been strenuous enough. At present they had to force an entrance to the more difficult passageways, then through absolute determination, the two men in front grabbed a rock or whatever was accessible and pulled themselves up. In a kneeling position, they hoisted the sled up behind them while the two in the rear struggled to lift it up above their heads.

Other times, one man led the way and kicked holes in the crusty snow, providing those who followed a foothold. Cinched down tight, Jan focused on the group's objective, rather than his own pain. When the going was unusually tough or bumpy he let out a stifled groan, but he never complained.

When the men thought they should be nearing the plateau, they discovered that another crest rose higher. The struggle, far from over, tested their faith and determination to the limit. It was too discouraging to look up, better to concentrate on one step or foothold at a time.

The terrain dropped so steeply that the sled hung almost vertically, and the stumps on Jan's foot began to bleed again. Jan thought his feet would burst from the unbearable pain. He frequently lost consciousness; each episode was a moment of relief, then he came to and the horror began yet again. He was torn in his own suffering. How could he complain? His selfless friends were exerting themselves beyond human endurance, but they went on. So must he. But when the pain became utterly insufferable he gave in.

"Is it possible to turn the sleigh?"

They gladly did anything for Jan to give him even a moment's relief.

It eased his pain momentarily as he hung there upside down, suspended in space as it were. Soon the pressure to his brain became overwhelming. Marius and the others returned him to the original position.

The men panted and puffed, spit and pulled, went through the crusty snow, pulled themselves out and pressed upward.

And Jan just hung, tied to the sled.

The time came when the men were spent. They had no more to give. Their arms trembled from exertion; their knees refused to hold them up. The muscles in their legs and thighs cramped and wouldn't respond. Soaked through from perspiration, tumbling in the snow and grappling with the mountain, they were burning hot and thirsty. They prostrated themselves in the snow and closed their eyes. All the while they kept a sure hold on the ropes that kept Jan's sled close by. They lay there, desperately needing rest and renewed strength.

As soon as they laid down, they noticed the freezing wind gusts, more penetrating up here, closer to the plateau. And when physical exertion forced them to stop, their bodies quickly chilled. Only a few moments' relief was all they dared give themselves.

They climbed upwards.

When they reached the edge where the ravine unfolded itself onto the plateau they knew it all would become easier.

The terrain leveled off and they trudged through the snow instead of crawling and clawing. Before they got far, they realized they would have to cross a cleft in the mountain, sideways, beneath a huge overhang of ice. It was vertical and the snow was so hard and cumbersome that the men had to work out minute details each step of the way. They had to force their way through. Because of the gradient they could only place one sled-runner on the snow close into the cleft. Two men sat down and guided it along foot by foot. The other two kicked repeatedly to get a foothold in the iced-over snow while suspending the outside runner in the air.

This way the sled lay perpendicularly. Jan's friends carried the carefully balanced sled over to the other side, one measured step at a time. These were committed men; no obstruction seemed too dangerous, and relinquishing the fight was not part of the plan.

Jan now hung in open air, the determined efforts of the men the only thing between him and a terrible abyss. Even if only one of the men, for one split second, lost his foothold, all five would plummet violently downwards. In long free falls they would be thrown about in a wild breakaway toward the fjord some 2500 feet below. They were somber men struggling to concentrate on their own and their friends' movements. The only words were of the details of their next step.

Jan was, for the most part, quiet except for his occasional moaning. He tackled his own problems as best he could. The excruciating pain continued, almost beyond his ability to endure. Yet through it all, he was aware that his survival depended fully on his friends' endurance.

They had almost reached the plateau when they heard the drone of an airplane. The noise increased rapidly. Almost straight overhead, it reverberated amid the mountaintops. A plane came into view at a low altitude. Alvin recognized the big black swastika painted on its side at once.

"A German Junker!"

Jan reacted like lightning, knowing exactly what to do.

"Throw yourselves face down!"

Hopefully they would look like rocks from the air, and be camouflaged by the mountain terrain. The Junker disappeared as quickly as it had come. They had succeeded.

In those moments Jan felt a heavy responsibility for his friends. The four men knew anything could happen when they took on the commitment to help Jan to freedom. This was just part of their commitment. They were proud to be part of this rescue effort to help a countryman to freedom. It gave a deep purpose to their lives. And to outsmart the Gestapo would bring them many a story to tell after the war. Such thoughts added determination to their endeavors.

The mountain plateau spread before them. Some three hours after they had tied Jan to the sled outside the hut in Revdal they reached their destination.

Like a white carpet, the next 2000 feet lay before them with hardly a rise. In actuality it began with a lengthened gentle downgrade, which flattened out, then gradually eased up to an extended slope where at the end another dark-walled bluff rose straight up.

The sled moved slowly on its own power, the men needed only to guide it along. Across the level plain they were able to pull the sled with two men walking on each side. Here and there they fell through the snow but not as often as earlier. The last steep stretch was difficult, but compared with the cliffs they considered it easy.

The men of Furuflaten were nearing complete exhaustion. But they had accomplished what most would call humanly impossible; their minds and bodies had been pushed to the brink, and they were beginning to pay the price.

In addition to their own exhaustion they were greatly concerned for Jan. He too was totally spent. But he was their inspiration, their reason for completing the deed. He had suffered right along with them in silence. He kept all his fears and pain to himself. Jan was deeply moved and most grateful for their self-sacrifice.

On the south side of the plateau a steep mountain wall rose some 2700 feet. At the foot of this black wall was a large stony wasteland.

"This is the place! We have reached our goal. This is where the men from Manndalen will come!" Marius was jubilant.

They found a level place to rest the sled. For the first time in four hours the resistance men let go of the ropes. They felt free knowing the sled would not rush away from them. Beneath them the babbling river hurried by, but they were safe on thick ice and a layer of snow.

The four men settled down in the snow close by Jan to rest. Even now they did not say much, too exhausted to carry on a conversation. With a quick movement of his arm Olaf pushed his cap back, the brim pointing straight skyward. The others also adjusted their caps and wiped their sweaty faces. They peered across the plateau looking for the men from Manndalen.

Turning away from the plateau they glimpsed the frigid six-mile-wide, Lyngenfjord. Just north of Furuflaten, on the opposite side of the fjord, they observed the outline of the headland jutting out into the fjord. When they moved a few more feet in a northerly direction they could make out the rooftops of their homes in Furuflaten.

The agreement had been to meet between 2 a.m. and 4 a.m. and they became concerned for the men from Manndalen.

Marius questioned if he had the time right. Were they too early, or had the men already been here and left? Were they delayed, or a little lost perhaps? He wondered if something serious had happened to them.

Innumerable thoughts ran through his mind, but none of them gave answers to his questions.

Luckily they had thought to bring two pairs of skis along in case of an emergency. Amandus and Olaf strapped them on and searched for tracks in an ever-widening circle. There was no trace of either man or animal. No one could have been near the place for days. Where were they? Marius asked if they had strength to go toward Manndalen to try and meet up with the other fellows.

"We'll do it."

Rocks and boulders lay sprinkled throughout the plateau as if a giant hand had snatched handfuls and scattered them around. Some rocks were several feet high.

Amandus and Olaf trudged among these rocks into the plateau. They disappeared from sight far up in the inner terrain. Mountain distances seem small until one watches a person moving away. The person gradually shrinks, but is never totally out of sight, until at long last he vanishes. Then one begins to understand the immensity and the power of the mountains.

The men moved in a northeast direction toward Kjerringdal Valley, a precipitous side valley on the west side of Manndalen where they assumed that the men from that side had, or would be coming up.

They skied to the very ridge of the mountain. From here they had an overview of the whole landscape as it stretched before them. They looked up and down the surrounding mountains, back down in the valley and across the valley floor, scraped flat by ancient glaciers. They saw no sign of life. Moreover they saw no tracks. They stood there forlorn, unable to speak. Taken aback, they just looked at each other. The disappointment was acute. All they could do was turn back.

Marius and Alvin tried to hide their restlessness from Jan, but he understood. After about an hour, two forms heading in their direction took shape. Uneasy, Marius knew something was seriously wrong.

As Olaf and Amandus returned and told their story, the other men were filled with misgivings. The mood turned gloomy. All of the men were exhausted. The struggle up the mountain had been difficult, but not without hope. Total bewilderment and disappointment swept over them as they considered this snag in the plan.

The men had an enormous emergency on their hands and they were miles away from shelter and help. A decision had to be made. But what solution could they find? Most choices were eliminated before they were even thought through.

To continue on to Sweden without enough supplies was suicide. Fully expecting to meet the Manndalen men, they had only brought two pairs of skis along for an emergency. Two men could not pull an ill man over the difficult terrain. None had an abundance of strength left after the strenuous climb, and spring snowstorms still raged up here in the mountains.

Jan was too ill to be moved down the mountain. The thought of imprisoning him in the hut again with the appalling memories he had of the place was unbearable. That also would be suicide. Jan was unable to take the stress of the descent in any case. Also, the men themselves were near spent. They shared their thoughts and tried to figure out how best to handle the situation. There was no solution, at least not an easy one.

After much discussion, the four came to the agreement that they had to leave Jan behind in the mountains. Heavy-hearted, they presented the plan to him.

"We have no choice."

"Of course we don't." answered Jan, without a moment's hesitation. "I already came to that conclusion when Olaf and Alfon scouted after the Manndalen men."

"Jan we are so very, very sorry." Marius spoke for all.

"Don't be. You have done everything humanly possible for me. There is no other way. It'll all work out. You'll see." Jan sounded brave.

When they had stopped to rest they were a short distance north of the black mountain wall. They noticed a nine-foot high boulder, which stood out from all the rest midways between them and the wall. It was flat on the south side, and measured roughly 15 feet by 18 feet. It was the only rock of this size and shape in the immediate area. It stood as a sentinel over the landscape. They agreed that this would be a good hiding place for Jan and pulled the sled up the slope towards the rock.

Snowdrifts surrounded the boulder. Toward the east the wind had forged a large gaping hole in the snow, a natural cauldron that almost

The Gentleman Stone

The Gentleman Stone seen toward the east with the river delta on the left.

reached the moss below. A thick snowdrift had formed an overhang from the top of the boulder pointing east, a lid for the cauldron.

The men examined the hole and, using the back ends of their skis, cut large square blocks out of the snow. They cut out a shelf in the snowdrift and into the snowfield southward so that Jan and the sleigh could be pushed sideways onto the shelf, placing his feet toward the rock with his head away from it. They used the snow blocks they had removed to wall up the opening to the shelf, making Jan invisible inside his cave. A small round hole was drilled through the layers of snow so that Jan would have air to breathe.

The remaining food that had not been eaten was gathered. There was a little leftover drink and it was all placed close by him. The snow cave muffled his voice and they could hardly understand him without straining, but they were able to make out Jan's upbeat courage.

"All is well in here," the enthusiastic voice said. "Be careful on that mountain. Get down it safely."

Helpless, the four of them stood there, wanting to encourage him. But they had lost their own courage. Were they signing Jan's death warrant leaving him up here in his condition? They faked optimism for him.

"The Manndalen men are bound to come shortly. If not right away, at least by tomorrow, Jan."

"Good-bye and take care."

"We wish you the best." Empty words meant to be pleasant.

They said their goodbyes through the little opening in the snow, then crawled out of the cauldron. The four young men turned around and looked down on the place where they had left their friend. No one was able to say a word. No one could give an explanation for this turn of events.

The men were bitterly disappointed. They did not cry – they were men of steel, but tonight their eyes were moist, their hearts torn apart. They had concentrated on cheering Jan up as much as possible. Considering the circumstances, they felt this amazing man was in surprisingly good spirits. In the midst of this unthinkable situation, he did his best not to show them he was concerned. This was Jan; he made the impossible seem achievable. They took courage from his resilience.

The Furuflaten men struggled to keep their emotions in check. They stood there on the edge and looked down at the miniscule opening where they were leaving a helplessly ill man; none of them really believed he could survive. They hated themselves.

Near the riverbed, about thirty feet away, they placed a ski pole in the snow. Surely if the Manndalen men showed up they would have an easy time finding Jan with the pole sticking out of the snow. One by one they headed for the abrupt cliffs.

In one big sweep, reality had changed and existence became emptiness and a heavy loss. Marius agonized. He could not be blamed for this mishap; still, a helpless man had been left behind, and he *felt* responsible. Marius had but one desire, to turn back. He did not want to climb down the mountain. He wanted to go back to be with Jan to let him know how much he cared. How could he leave? It all seemed so meaningless, so futile. What kind of a friend had he become?

Revdal, April 25, 1943: It was past 6 a.m. when the exhausted and dispirited men rowed back home to Furuflaten. They had given all that was in them, but it had not been enough. They had failed the courageous man who had put his trust in them. The loss hurt them deeply. Would another door open for them? They would give up all to be able to rescue Jan. They had to find a way.

They rowed on until Hotel Savoy faded on the horizon, until all that was left was a small speck in the snowdrifts across the fjord. Daylight bathed the surroundings. It was the Sabbath and their intent had been to sneak home and get to bed before their families arose, but they knew that plan had also failed. Their strength had dissipated during the ordeal and the rowing was harder and took longer than usual. At this hour all their families would be up. As they neared the shore, they noticed a crowd of people gathered by the dock. A "welcoming committee." The fearless resistance workers cringed at the thought of confronting their friends and families.

The four of them had left the village many times before, and had returned unnoticed. None of their family members knew that they were entangled in illegal and dangerous work. The families were close friends, yet neither parents nor sweethearts had ever been told. During the past evening however, they had begun to wonder.

When they had been unable to find the men the night before, they had become quite concerned. They had spent the early morning hours together and had decided to walk down by the water and there spotted a boat far out in the fjord.

How they had all prayed that it would be their missing men. After a long time, when the boat came close enough, they recognized both the boat and the men. They did not realize how quickly their humble, sincere prayers had been answered. Instead their concern turned to anger.

The men in the boat realized their homecoming would be less than pleasant.

"We have to outsmart the welcoming committee waiting on the shore," Amandus whispered.

The three older men knew they would be held accountable for allowing 17-year-old Olaf to participate in such a rousing party. Once again they were left without a choice. They had to take the responsibility.

The top secret assignment could not be shared. Not an iota of the drama surrounding Jan and his transport up the mountainside could ever be whispered. Their whole trip had been disastrous.

This was just another set of problems to overcome, though far different than anything they could have anticipated.

They rowed to the headway that stuck out into the Lyngenfjord, north of Furuflaten. As courageous as these men were, they were totally unnerved at the thought of telling Olaf's parents that they were responsible for him staying out all night. They did not have the courage to bring him with them toward the welcoming committee. As a result, they put him ashore at the tip of the headland and out of sight of the committee. Olaf walked the long way home. He crept into the village from the north, away from the main road, and stayed a good distance away from the neighboring houses and the people he knew.

The three others sprinkled their clothes with *nakkeskudd;* some ran down their chest. They also gulped down a couple of swallows for courage and let some run down their chins.

Their families had to be convinced that they had partied all night and had enjoyed lots of goodies. Would they believe they could have had fun fishing all night?

When they reached shore, though sober, they enjoyed acting as if drunk with the smell of liquor burning in their noses. Alvin's mother was enraged. She walked down to her son and in a shrill voice, gave him the verbal lesson of his life.

"Son, how could you have left without letting anyone know where you were? I have taught you better than that!"

"Have I not endowed you with any sense? Are you able to understand the grief you have caused everyone? And furthermore, what kind of a man are you? Leaving your sweetheart on a Saturday night to go fishing and partying with other men?" His mother had worked up a full head of steam and quivered with indignation. Not too far off, Alvin's sweetheart stood feeling both humbled and sorrowful.

Alvin straightened up. He went close up to his mother's face and stared right into her eyes. He stood erect, and was deliberately calm - his look unyielding, but friendly. Not for a second did he take his eyes off her and he did not say a word.

His mother quieted down. And in that moment she realized her son was not drunk. But rather, extremely sober! She realized he had tried to act as if he had been carousing, but she knew him too well. His eyes told her. She knew he had been involved in something dangerous, something important and highly secretive. She also knew the war had now invaded their family life. She was silenced without a word being spoken. She did not ask questions. Slowly she turned away and started walking home. Her eyes brimmed with tears. Like Alvin, she knew that secret operations against the Germans were extremely perilous. If something was revealed, the threads could unravel and the whole village could be wiped out. Alvin's mother became part of the small army of people who helped Jan, without being directly involved.

At once she was involved in a secret she knew nothing about, but she had to carry it in silence, a heavy burden for a mother. Women have for centuries been called upon to carry such burdens in wartime. Alvin's mother died before the war ended, and she never knew the story of her son's involvement nor how very courageous he was.

All four men reached their homes without further incident. Each walked off to cope with his anguish. Sadness and weariness were in themselves a heavy load. The men's thoughts dashed back to the plateau and the soldier in the snow cave high up in the Revdal Mountains.

The exact spot where he was could not be picked out from across the fjord, but they could approximate. They worried about every little detail. Was he distraught? Frozen? Scared? Depressed? Or had he succumbed?

Marius in particular had a difficult time. He took full blame for what had happened. Had his instructions not been complete and clear enough? He had never known teacher Nordnes and Aslak Fossvoll not to follow through.

He rushed to the telephone on his return. Resolutely he lifted the receiver and placed each call. Within seconds the lady at the telephone central answered.

"Aslak Fossvoll in Manndalen, please." Marius was in a hurry.

Aslak picked up the phone, and got a clear and firm message. "The fish yarn you ordered is ready to be picked up immediately. It is waiting at the appointed place, dug down in the snow behind a rock."

"We will get it as soon as possible. Thank you." The phone clicked.

Marius looked out from his house in upper Furuflaten. From there he was sure he could see exactly where Jan was. He felt powerless again; his own worthlessness flooded over him. It would make it so much easier if he could only talk with Jan.

Sundays were always peaceful on the Grønvoll farm, a special day. This was not such a Sunday. Thoughts of Jan rolled over Marius and weighed him down with anxiety.

It was amazing how the surroundings had not changed. The mountains and Lyngenfjord lay there untouchable and silent, an overpowering presence.

From left to right: Amandus Lillevold, Olaf Lanes, Alvin Larsen, and Marius Grønvoll, the team that carried Jan up the Revdal Mountain on a sled. Photo 1960.

Che MANNDALEN MEN

Manndalen, a level and narrow valley one and a quarter miles wide and 18 miles long, cuts deeply through the massive surrounding granite mountains. Some of the mountains reach heights of 3500 feet above sea level. The spirited Manndalen River rushes down its hilly center and spills over into Kåfjord Sound. On the northern tip, the valley meets up with the hamlet Samuelsberg, bordering Kåfjord Sound; the innermost valley to the south gradually joins the mountain slopes stretching upwards into mountain walls and ends up on the undulating plateaus.

In 1943, there were no roads connecting the communities with each other in this area, only narrow country roads within the valley itself. Traveling by sea, hiking or skiing over the mountains from a neighboring village was the only way to reach this remote area of the Troms District. The people who lived here were hard working farmers, fishermen and hunters. Tradition passed on through their families taught them to care for one another and any strangers who might enter their village.

Unspoiled by worldly sophistication, the people of Manndalen were fiercely patriotic and fully understood those things that enriched life: family, friendship and the importance of education. For the most part, the war had not intruded much on life in Manndalen, except that necessities and food were more scarce – and ten German soldiers, rather passive men or lazy perhaps, had confiscated the valley's youth center and moved in. The soldiers did not bother with the villagers much, and they frightened no one. However, from time to time, the German soldiers from Lyngseidet came over by boat and performed a house-to-house search. The

Manndalen Valley

Manndalen people were much more respectful of them and concerned when they were in the valley.

The Arctic growing season being short, mainly potatoes and root vegetables were cultivated in Manndalen. Many families also had a few domestic animals, enough for their own needs. Often, many children were born to families in those days, and it was not unusual for siblings to be divided up and taken in by other family members. Peder Isaksen was one of those children, the third of a flock of ten siblings, taken in by his grandparents. Though there were no luxuries, they lived a good life on the little farm they owned. During the summer

Aslak Fossvoll

their cows grazed in the isolated fields around their modest home, or in the wilderness; at close of day the tiny herd was gathered in the barn.

In the late winter of 1941, at the age of twenty, Peder was fishing in the Lofoten fishing grounds some one hundred and twenty miles from Manndalen. He was there when the Svolvær raid took place on March 4.

Following such raids the Germans heaped reprisals on the Norwegians and many chose to escape to England to avoid them. Peder considered escaping, not so much from fear of the Germans, as from wanderlust, and also to possibly help Norway on other fronts. In the end he decided to stay.

Manndalen, Sunday, April 25, 1943: Life in Manndalen continued its traditional rounds. Many of the men were anxious to play a larger part in the war effort. On Sunday afternoon Peder Isaksen left his grandparents' home for a leisurely walk. He passed his good friend Nigo's home and continued down into the valley. A couple of miles from his home he ran into Aslak Fosvoll, who also was the uncle of Peder's betrothed, the pretty, soft-spoken Eliva Hansen. Except for his experience in Lofoten in March of 1941, Peder Isaksen had little feeling for the war raging around them, and no involvement. In the span of a few minutes he became an active player in the game of war. The peaceful days he'd enjoyed became a life of intrigue and fear.

Aslak worked furiously to finish the work he and Peder Bergmo hadn't completed the previous evening. Marius Grønvoll had telephoned early in the morning from Furuflaten, saying urgently, "The fish net is ready to be picked up immediately."

Aslak understood the implications. The soldier the Manndalen men were supposed to have rescued was left out by himself on the frozen, snow covered tundra, waiting. Aslak worked desperately to find someone to go with Nigo, who had readied himself the night before. He had just dropped off his skis for Nigo, who did not own any. They had packed a knapsack full of provisions necessary for the trip into the treacherous mountains and food and drink for the soldier in the snow cave. Aslak had also given Nigo an exact description of the rock where Jan lay. He warned Nigo that the soldier was armed, and that he had to use the agreed upon password, "Hello Gentleman," which they were to shout loud and clear.

Aslak and Peder Isaksen greeted one another and stopped for a chat. Aslak's mind revolved around the soldier in the mountain, and knowing Peder Isaksen to be a trustworthy fellow, he suddenly became thoughtful. He looked straight ahead into the valley while rubbing his chin.

"Peder, would you be willing to take on an assignment for me? It might be a way to earn a few extra *kroner*, but it will be with your own life as a pawn."

"I can't promise you anything before you tell me what this assignment is, Aslak."

Aslak was desperate. There was no more time to lose; the wounded soldier needed to get to Sweden for medical help. The responsibility rested heavy on his shoulders. Assuming Peder would say yes, Aslak took the chance, and brought Peder up to date on the secret mission.

Peder listened intently as he learned of the happenings in Toftefjord and how one of the commando soldiers from *Brattholm* had managed to escape. Now seriously ill, he was hidden in a snow cave up in the Revdal Mountains. It was imperative that he be found before long and transported to Sweden. Once Peder had been filled in, no hesitation clouded his mind.

"If that's the situation, it's okay," he volunteered his readiness right then.

"You can't go into the mountains alone this time of the year, Peder. Nigo is ready to join you. He is ready, packed and waiting," Aslak said. "You have to go tonight."

"No problem. I'll get ready."

Hope and energy returned to Aslak after he spoke with Peder. The heavy burden he had been carrying vanished, and he was filled with triumph.

Peder's leisurely walk ended abruptly. He hurried home with a long quick stride. Memories of childhood lessons to give food and a place to any guest came to his mind. The soldier in the mountain surely was such a guest, even though he had arrived in an unusual and dramatic manner. Peder saw it as his Christian duty to help.

Halfway home Peder dropped in on his friend Nigo who sat ready waiting for word. They agreed to go their separate ways through the village and to meet above the tree line at 10:30 p.m. The two friends gave each other strength of mind and vitality. Both were elated about the mission they had accepted. Finally they would be of service to Norway.

Peder hurried home and changed his clothes. He readied his skis and started for the woods and up into the mountains. The two men went unnoticed as they skied through the Arctic darkness, and met as planned high up on a slope just above the tree line.

It was a difficult climb up the steep mountain, dark and quiet. They advanced steadily, hardly speaking, concentrating on their every move. Young and strong, they made good time. Within two hours they reached the plateau. Ski conditions were good, and it wasn't particularly cold. Only a mild wind caressed the tundra.

Mount Balggesvarri towered in the darkness. They made a path around it and turned slightly southwest to Revdalen. There was still quite a distance to their goal. Not attempting to conserve their energy, they sped along the plateau up over hillocks, and down again from the top of the plateau towards Revdal, dashing along in search of the boulder where the soldier was hidden.

The area they arrived at by following Aslak's instructions was strewn with large boulders and rocks. They hurried from boulder to boulder, searching. Their calls rang out into the dark quiet of the vast mountain plateau, "Hello Gentleman! Hello Gentleman!"

Their voices did not carry far in this immense domain.

The plateau remained silent.

The men of Furuflaten had left no tracks. A rock-to-rock search was of no avail. After two hours of fruitless searching, Peder and Nigo called it quits. It was four in the morning, and they needed to reach Manndalen before six when their neighbors started their barn chores. Would the soldier be able to survive another night? Or was he dead? Their unanswered questions troubled them deeply.

With subdued spirits they climbed back up to the tundra. Once on top, they raced downward to Manndalen and reached home in the early morning hours of April 26.

Manndalen, Monday, April 26, 1943: As soon as prudent, Peder Isaksen and Nigo cautiously contacted Aslak and teacher Nordnes. Both were deeply distressed over hearing the soldier was still in the mountains.

"There are hundreds of boulders and rocks up there," Nigo explained.

"The boulder where Jan is has to be marked clearly if we are to find him," added Peder Isaksen.

Peder Bergmo in Olderdalen had to be contacted at once. Peder Isaksen and teacher Nordnes hurried down through the village and rowed across Kåfjord to find Peder Bergmo. His surprise and shock when he saw them revealed he understood the reason for their visit.

"Will you get a message to Marius?"

"Yes, of course. I'll ferry across to Lyngseidet and take the bus from there to Furuflaten. But I have to find an excuse for leaving this office."

Unable to leave the following day, he troubled over how to get away, concerned the whole while for the soldier in the mountain.

Furuflaten, Wednesday, April 28, 1943: Finally arriving at Furuflaten, Peder Bergmo walked the last few miles to the Grønvoll farm.

"Marius, they didn't find him! The place has to be marked. There are too many boulders and the men are unable to find the place."

Marius grew tense. "Poor Jan! Buried three days in a snow cave. It'll be a miracle if he hasn't frozen to death."

Though Marius believed his friend to be dead, he had to find a way back up into the mountains.

GRAVE CONCERNS FOR JAN

Marius was reassured that the Manndalen men were ready to climb back up into the mountains to rescue Jan and bring him to Sweden as soon as his hiding place was clearly marked. He committed to doing so immediately. He knew, however, that the hike up into the mountain plateau was too dangerous to undertake alone should the mountains and weather reveal their fury.

He thought of his trustworthy buddy Amandus and his sturdy boat. No doubt Amandus would, without any ado, say yes. The weather conditions looked promising. But Marius also had an eye for a beautiful young lady who lived by the fjord at the northern end of Furuflaten village. Olaf Lanes' sister, Agnete, had incredible physical endurance, but beyond that, she had an understanding heart with a deep centered inner strength. Never one to shy away from hard work, she met challenges head on and saw them through to successful endings.

Agnete was admired by many of the young men in the village but it was she and Marius who enjoyed a deep friendship and spent much time together.

Marius felt the pressure of getting Jan to safety and he yearned to share his feelings with Agnete because she would know exactly how he felt, and she was trustworthy. As soon as Peder Bergmo had left for home, he contacted her. Agnete listened quietly to the astonishing story.

"My goodness Marius, I'll go with you," Agnete responded without a moment's hesitation.

"Are you sure Agnete? You understand the risk involved?"

"I understand."

"Our efforts might be in vain. The wounded soldier might already be dead."

"I'll go."

Marius embraced her. "This might be the most important work we will have the opportunity to do in this war."

He had wanted very much for Agnete to come with him and was positive that she could manage the stressful climb and the emotional strain involved.

Hurriedly they changed into their ski clothes and filled their knapsacks with food and provisions. Marius allowed a small flicker of hope to burn. Over and over his mind repeated, "We are coming Jan. Stay alive!"

Always aware that Nazis might be watching, Marius asked Agnete to walk along the beach a short distance from her home and he and Amandus would row and pick her up. The three of them set out across Lyngenfjord.

A good hour passed before they reached Revdal. Skis, poles and

Agnete (Lanes) Grønvoll's identification card

Front   Back knapsacks were taken ashore. This time they chose a different route than the one they had used to transport Jan. Supposedly a few hundred meters south of Hotel Savoy, the climb would be a little easier. Amandus would wait for their return north of the Innerelva River.

Marius and Agnete ascended the first half of the climb rather quickly. As they mounted higher, huge boulders and vertical crags slowed them down. They pulled themselves up by birch trunks and branches and handed their skis and poles to each other enabling them to grip on to the outcrops with both hands. The rushing sound of the river hidden deep in the cleft to the south guided them.

Each mount above them gave the impression that they had reached their goal, only to find another higher one ahead. From their vantage point they could see a good stretch of Lyngenfjord below. Appearances were deceiving in the mountains. Mountaintop followed mountaintop; the plateau was so much higher than the impression they had acquired from the other side of the fjord.

Marius looked up and spotted the vertical mountain wall towards Larsbergfjellet Mountain. It loomed black and ominous against the night sky. The mountaintop they had reached gradually rounded off toward even terrain. From the plateau, the pass higher up became visible.

"Look Agnete!" Marius pointed. "Jan is hidden right inside the opening of that pass." The wind was biting and he tried to sound optimistic, though they still had a long climb ahead. Able to use their skis again, the distance quickly narrowed where the plateau was fairly flat. A few minor knolls here and there did not trouble them as they headed toward the last steep rising. Turning in a southerly direction to come nearer to Innerelva River, they followed the edge of the cleft on the northern side. Two hours of steady and difficult climbing had left them exhausted.

The huge boulder was in sight a few yards ahead on the rocky slope by the precipitous mountain wall. Their bodies tensed; was Jan still alive? Marius sped ahead the last few feet. Agnete followed in his tracks. He unfastened his skis and crawled around to the east side of the boulder. Marius saw that the ski pole they had placed in the snow on their earlier visit had blown down. Snatches of tracks from their last visit were still discernible.

He stood on his knees and began to dig with his hands. Close by, Agnete stood silently shielding her face with mitten-covered hands. The wind was sharp and cold and the snow was packed down hard. Below the whirling snow, and the top layer of new snow, Marius butted up to the snow blocks they had placed three days ago. He kept digging; suddenly the snow collapsed around his arms.

Agnete moved closer to look inside and caught sight of Jan's motionless bearded face.

"Don't sweetheart, move back a bit. I am afraid Jan is dead." Marius gently tugged at her arm.

From within the cave a weak, distraught voice responded, "Oh no! You can't fool an old fox!"

"Jan! Jan! Thank God you're alive! We were afraid we'd find you dead."

"I am okay. I've kept the hope that you would return." Jan whispered.

"We're here to take care of you, Jan. And we've brought you something hot to eat."

To see Jan alive gave new strength to both of them. They dug hard with their remaining energy and pretty soon the snow cave was open.

Agnete crawled into the opening and saw Jan's weary face close-up. Lifeless eyes peered from sunken cheeks and his pitch-black beard rendered his face colorless. Like a mummy, Jan laid on the wood sleigh, tucked into the sleeping bag. Slowly he began to move and freed his arms. Shakily, Jan reached toward Agnete.

He held her hands in his as he studied her face.

"You must be Agnete. Marius has mentioned you a time or two to me in the past." He gradually moved his head and winked at Marius then turned back toward Agnete and flashed a weak smile, "My name is Jan."

Agnete's eyes became moist. Unable to speak, she squeezed his hands.

With both hands Jan took the thermos bottle filled with hot soup. Marius lifted up his head to help him drink.

"I thought you already were safely in Sweden," Marius explained. "It was not until today that I learned that the Manndalen men had not found you. Two men have been up here hunting for you for hours but without luck." Jan just listened.

"Agnete and I are here tonight to mark your place more clearly. As soon as we've returned home, we will send a message on to Manndalen that you are ready. They will pick you up right away and bring you over the border."

With his friends close by, some hot food and the good news, Jan quickened. "This man is amazing," Marius thought as he looked admiringly at Jan. "His fortitude and will to live are astounding!" Marius emptied Jan's sleeping bag of waste and put him back in again.

Agnete placed the food from the knapsacks close by Jan's sled.

"What else can we do for you, Jan?" Marius found his own words rather empty.

"Oh thanks, but nothing really. Well, maybe there is something – a little hot water for a bath?"

Jan's humor had resurfaced – just like it had in the barn.

All laughed, but it was rather subdued. They knew the time for parting was at hand. Jan's friends kneeled near him, against his sled in the snow. Leaving him alone again was painful. Jan lay on his back and stared up at the snow covering above him. No one found the right words.

The whirling snow drifted around the boulder and down into the snow cave. The surrounding plateau was enormous, but the darkness camouflaged Jan's hiding place.

"Promise me, be careful on the way down and get home safely across the fjord." Jan whispered.

Agnete tied the hood tight around her face; she was wet from perspiration from the climb up, and now had chilled off.

A hush fell over all of them.

The whirling snow blew into the cave from all angles.

"Jan, keep up your courage. The men will soon return. We'll keep close track of you," Marius strained to smile at his friend.

"Thanks for all you have done for me." Jan turned his face toward the inner snow wall.

The two gently touched his covered up arm and quietly left and sealed up the cave behind them. Marius crossed two ski poles and stuck them deep into the snow a few meters away from the "Gentleman stone," and tied them crisscross at the top. They had to be clearly seen, especially from the direction in which the Manndalen men would approach. The wind tore at the two of them as they fastened the poles securely in the snow.

The force of the wind would have blown Agnete off her feet if Marius had not been close by to catch her. But even Marius had problems as they clung to each other. Once they left Jan's cave, they could find no shelter and they fought their way across the plateau and over to the mountain ridge. The wind eased a little as they started their descent, a strenuous, demanding climb.

Thursday morning, April 29, 1943: Agnete and Marius had been gone nearly five hours by the time they reached Amandus waiting for them in the boat. The trip home seemed drawn out, and the fjord seemed wider than ever for Marius and Agnete, both struggling to control their emotions. Agnete had been very quiet while they were in the mountains. The vastness of it all overpowered her in the dark. And now she was deeply concerned for Jan.

"Poor Jan is still up here, all alone behind that boulder." With her own hands she had helped Marius seal up his cave. "Will he have the strength to make it through?" Her conscience kept her doubting. "Did they do the right thing when they left him alone, or should one of them have remained with him?" Chilled and despondent, Agnete sat quietly in the back of the boat by herself.

No one in Furuflaten would ever know, at least not until after the war, of the selflessness shown by the three young people during the night – their friends and neighbors still slept as they returned.

Amandus parted from Marius and Agnete when they reached the shore. To avoid discovery at this undesirable hour of the night, they made new plans. Marius and Agnete flung their skis over their shoulders, picked up the other supplies and headed for Lyngspollen some two and a half miles north of Furuflaten. Marius' friend, Kristian Solberg owned a fishing boat with his son Alf. The 48 foot boat was moored at Lyngspollen. The Solbergs lived north of the river about 50 yards from Alvin Larsen's home.

A brisk, biting wind quickened their gait. Weary, Marius and Agnete trudged through the snow alongside the edge of the road in the darkness.

Marius knew the Solbergs well and felt sure they would not mind he had found refuge aboard their boat.

Marius and Agnete crept aboard quickly. In the stern, they placed their skis, the two empty milk pails and the two blankets they had brought from their visit with Jan. Suspicious people in Furuflaten would not find a reason to talk should they be seen when they headed for home.

Marius looked at Agnete. Admiration shone in his eyes. She had endured an arduous ordeal without complaint. Marius noticed she was shivering mercilessly. He picked up one of the blankets and lovingly enfolded Agnete in it as he guided her toward the wheelhouse for shelter. She looked so fragile, yet she had a resolute will coupled with courage. They spoke in whispers.

"Marius do you think Jan has a chance?"

"A slim chance." He studied her face, fraught with concern. He wanted to spare her, yet he could not lie. "It all depends on if the weather holds and if the Manndalen men can find him in time."

They remained silent, each struggling with their own emotions.

When the early dawn pierced the darkness on the Eastern horizon, Marius pointed, "Look Agnete, the morning is breaking. The people of Furuflaten will begin their labors soon."

"*Ja*, that we can be sure of, " she smiled.

"Let's go home, Agnete. I believe it will be safe now." They left behind their skis and the supplies, planning to pick them up later. Marius saw Agnete home. They hugged. "Thank you, Agnete. Thank you."

They stood quietly a moment before she tore herself loose and went inside.

Marius ran up the steep hill toward Alvin Larsen's home. This could not wait until morning. "We have to get to Manndalen in a hurry. Can you possibly take me across the fjord in your fishing boat?"

"I only need a minute." Even without an explanation, Alvin realized the urgency. Marius, between deep breaths, told him the whole story. This early in the morning, it was impossible to disguise their telephone messages, and time was of the essence. Jan was seriously ill.

While Alvin readied, Marius rushed home to change into dry clothes. The boat was tied to a stake a little distance from the shore. Alvin needed

Teacher Nordnes

another man to help with the large boat. He ran to Alfon Hansen's house, the man who had been with them on the trip across the fjord on the 19th of April. It did not take them long to row out to Lyngspollen where the fishing boat was tied up. Marius was waiting on the dock when they came to pick him up; they set course for Manndalen. Crossing the Lyngenfjord, they sailed around the headland into Kåfjord and over to Samuelsberg at the tip of Manndalen. Marius went alone up into the village to talk to teacher Nordnes.

School was in session when Marius arrived. He went straight to the classroom. Nordnes instructed the students to study on their own while the two men went over the plans in muffled voices. Marius drew an outline of where Jan was kept and explained in detail where they could find the "Gentleman stone." He explained how he had crisscrossed two ski poles and placed them a few meters away. Teacher Nordnes nodded and promised they would find Jan this time.

Marius trudged back toward the dock. He could relax – his mission was accomplished. Yet he knew he would have no peace of mind until he was certain that Jan was safely in Sweden. A sudden exhaustion overtook him.

The following day, a German soldier walked briskly up the steep hill leading to the Solberg's home and knocked on the door.

In broken Norwegian he explained that a snowslide was blocking the road between Furuflaten and Lyngseidet. "You me understand?"

"*Ja, ja,*" Alf understood. "But what does that have to do with me?"

"Your boat needed now! Germany needs to bring mail and packages to Olderdalen. We go immediately. Come now, *schnell!*" He motioned for him to come. "We take mail to Olderdalen now."

Alf's good friend Eilif Sørsand was visiting, and offered to come along with them. The German soldier followed after them. The three leaped into the rowboat and rowed the two and a half miles north to Lyngspollen where Alf's fishing vessel lay moored.

Climbing aboard, Alf noticed the skis, milk bottles and blankets. His blood chilled. He knew someone from the underground had been there. How could he explain this? Somehow, the German soldier either didn't notice or found nothing strange about it. They returned southward to Furuflaten.

They docked the boat and the soldier explained he would be gone just a short while. "I pick up mail at blockhouse. You wait here."

Earlier that morning, Agnete, on her return home from the mountains, shared with her brother Olav the expedition she and Marius had made to Jan's cave during the night. She told him they had left their skis and supplies on the Solbergs' boat.

From his kitchen window Olav noticed Alf's boat approaching the dock with a German soldier aboard, and he feared trouble was brewing. He saw the soldier quickly leave the boat. Olav raced to the dock to help his friends. The three young men brought the skis and other provisions ashore and hid them. Alf and Eilif climbed back aboard the boat just before the soldier returned with the mail. They set off for Olderdalen and returned without a hitch.

People in the northland are accustomed to looking after each other and neighbors form warm friendships. Young children especially like to visit with neighboring families. Such a child was Roald. The tousle-headed nine-year old lived close to the Solberg family, and dropped in on Alf's mother, Sigrid, one day.

Roald and Sigrid struck up a nice conversation when Roald suddenly silenced. He twisted and turned while dragging his finger along the edge of the kitchen table, then blurted out, "*Fru* Solberg, did you know that a wounded Norwegian soldier came down from Lyngsdalen Valley? Marius hid him in his barn." Roald was pleased he could share this news with *Fru* Solberg.

"Hush child, what are you saying?"

"They took really good care of him. Marius and his sisters even brought him food every day. But it was too dangerous, so now they have found a new hiding place for him," Roald continued.

Sigrid was stunned. This was dangerous.

"You like Marius a lot don't you?" questioned Sigrid.

"*Å ja!* He is my best grown-up friend. He has taught me how to take care of the animals, and to clean the barn, and..."

"You would never hurt Marius, would you Roald?" interrupted Sigrid.

"Oh no! What do you mean? Why would I want to hurt Marius?"

"You must never – never – never again tell anyone about this." She was stern. "You have never seen or heard anything about this soldier. The Germans will kill Marius and his whole family if they find out about this. We all are in danger. The Germans could kill other families in Furuflaten and burn the village as well. Do you understand me?"

Wordless, Roald stared wide-eyed at Sigrid.

"You must promise that you will never talk to anyone about this until after the war." Sigrid looked intently at the overwhelmed youngster.

"Oh, I promise." Roald's eyes filled with tears.

"Come on boy, let's get your jacket back on and I'll walk you home. And remember this is our special secret." The woman patted the boy on the head as she spoke.

"*Ja,* this is our special secret."

Concerned for Marius and the people of Furuflaten, Sigrid rushed to the Grønvoll farm after she had walked Roald home. She breathlessly poured out Roald's story.

"You must stop him, Marius. We are all at a terrible risk."

"This is dreadful," Marius agreed. "There was nothing we could do. He just dropped in on us unannounced one day when we were caring for Jan. I'll see what I can do."

Sigrid returned home and discussed the matter with Alf.

"Son, you must ski up into Lyngsdalen Valley and erase the soldier's footprints. They lead directly to the Grønvoll farm."

Alf bid farewell to his mother, strapped his skis on and headed for Lyngsdalen Valley.

Down by the riverbed, not far from the Grønvoll's, he found the footprints. Alf noticed that from the riverbed up toward the Grønvoll farm someone had either been frolicking in the snow or had already erased Jan's footsteps, but on the other side of the river and up where the valley curved into the lofty mountains, the tracks were fully visible.

Alf couldn't believe what he saw. Jan's footprints crisscrossed back and forth, traversed the frozen river, continued up the mountain side, turned back down again and crossed back over the river and up the other side. In places, his footprints disappeared and it looked like he had tumbled down the hillside, then re-crossed the river several times. The last mile, the prints revealed that the wounded soldier had dragged himself forward on all fours, lacking the strength to walk upright any longer.

Alf followed the footprints some three miles up into the valley where finally they had been erased by a heavy snowfall. He worked tediously to erase all the prints Jan had left, and returned home weary. An anxious Sigrid greeted him.

"What did you find son?" Alf told his mother the mind-boggling story.

"Are you sure you removed all the evidence? This is very dangerous for everyone in Furuflaten."

"I cannot be sure I got it all, but I did my best."

"Don't you think it would be wise to go back and make certain all the footprints are gone?"

Alf looked at his mother's troubled face and agreed to return. He returned to the valley and made sure every trace of Jan's prints was thoroughly rubbed out, leaving only his own ski tracks. The evening shadows had fallen by the time he finished. An expert skier, Alf reached home without any further incident.

"There is a time for all things,
a time to preach and a time to pray....
There is a time to fight,
and that time is now come."

— Peter Muhlenberg

PEÐER AПÐ ПIGO FIПÐ
ĊHE SПOɯ CAVE

Later that day, Peder Isaksen and Nigo received a long-awaited call from teacher Nordnes. "The fish yarn is completed, and is ready to be picked up."

Both men were anxious and geared up for another trip to the plateau. They met above the tree line when darkness gave them cover, around 11 p.m. They had planned their trip straight up the mountainside toward the west and a bit north of Kjerringdalen Valley, a precipitous side valley to Manndalen. They headed straight for Revdal. Weather conditions were good with excellent skiing. Soon they reached the plateau and could see Revdalen stretch out before it extended downhill toward the west. To the south was the black vertical mountain wall rising upwards nearly 200 feet. North, the landscape was considerably lower and less steep with round hillocks punctuated by small round short valleys.

Below them, the valley floor flattened out and extended ahead with a wide outrun plateau. Under the snow, one might guess it to be a wide river delta or even a marsh. Marshes this high up in the mountains were not unusual and harbored diminutive cloudberry plants, the fruits of which are cherished by summer hikers. Beyond the outrun plateau, the valley shrank to a narrow gap in the surrounding bedrock, which joined the inhospitable mountain wall down toward Lyngenfjorden. At the bottom of the gap, the river plunged over the rocks by the looming mountain wall.

From where Peder and Nigo stood at the top of the Revdal plateau, they could look straight through the narrow chasm into the thin air above Lyngenfjord. Across the fjord on the other side sat stark and mighty Pollfjellet Mountain. Tucked at the base of the massive walls was Furuflaten.

Peder Isaksen

Peder and Nigo continued rapidly down Revdalen Valley, anxious to find Jan. Gradually, way down in the valley, where the terrain dropped steeply, two ski poles took shape in the snow to the left of a large boulder near the mountain wall.

"This time we've found him!"

"Let's go!"

The two men jubilantly pushed off down the rock-strewn plateau, faster than they were comfortable with in this difficult terrain, but tension and concern drove them on. The ski conditions were near ice and it was difficult to keep their speed in check. Every moment counted for the lonely soldier, and Peder and Nigo were eager to reach him and quell his anguish.

When they reached the ski poles, they realized they had not come far enough down into the valley on their prior search. The many hours they spent hunting for him four days ago had been too far up in Revdalen.

The ski poles were tied together at the top and there was no doubt in their mind that this was the place. A few feet to the side of the poles lay a huge boulder so thickly covered with snowdrifts from the mountain winds that it could pass for one of the hillocks in the downward slope they had crossed.

Nigo Nilsen

Hesitantly they looked at the snow masses. It was difficult to believe that a human being could have survived underneath it all for four days - alone, surely frightened, ill and in pain. Wrapped in a sleeping bag, lying on a wooden sleigh and buried in snow, how had he managed? Was he still alive?

There was no movement. They heard no sound except for the wind as it swept over them, and all they could see was snow. The thought that close to their feet, underneath all that snow, lay a Norwegian soldier in flight from the Germans was rather incomprehensible to them.

Nigo, always the optimistic one, always believing in the possible, still believed the soldier alive even after all these days and the cruel circumstances. Peder, a more practical-minded man, was a little more skeptical. He found it hard to believe that anybody could survive under these conditions for five days, particularly a very ill man.

The snow was three feet deep, and even more so in places because of the drifts, which had been blown up against the boulder. They dug with their hands since they had not brought a shovel along. It seemed to them that they were digging a long time. Aware that Jan had a weapon, they continually called the password down into the deep hole, "Hello Gentleman! Hello Gentleman!"

The answer they hoped for did not come. They knelt and kept digging. They stopped for a brief moment and just stared at each other. Even for positive Nigo, hope began to fade.

"Maybe I have been a fool, but I really believed this man made it."

"Hello Gentleman! Hello Gentleman!" It was hopeless, but they could not just leave without seeing for themselves that he really was dead. So many had tried so hard to rescue him, so many wanted Jan to succeed in reaching Sweden.

They had dug down over four feet when a fragile, feeble voice answered their gentleman-call. Even when they stopped calling, the barely perceptible voice continued to answer in a low whisper, "Hello Gentleman, Hello Gentleman, Hello Gentleman!" The men froze.

They dug at top speed, and in record time they freed Jan from his entombment. To their astonishment, as best they could observe, Jan's mind was clear; nonetheless he was terribly weak. He was still dressed in his military clothes inside the military sleeping bag, which lay directly on the sled. He had no other clothing over him.

Inside his cave he had managed to fashion a small shelf about six inches long. On this shelf lay his most prized possession at the moment, a sugar cube! This sugar cube was the only food he had left. Before the Manndalen men arrived, Jan picked it up every so often, sucked on it a couple of times and carefully placed it back on the shelf.

"Were you able to bring a cigarette or two?" Jan wondered. He relaxed as he exhaled and the smoke swirled around him. Not until then was he ready for the food they had brought: some cured meat and bread, and some spirits to warm him up.

Jan eagerly ate the delicious food, recovering strength with each bite. Peder and Nigo tried to make Jan as comfortable as possible. They cared for him in every way, cleaned him up, and fed him until he was satisfied.

Morning neared and Peder and Nigo had to return to the valley before the people in the valley awoke.

It was time to return Jan to his snow shelf. How they hated themselves for having to do it. Peder and Nigo filled in the opening, leaving a small hole for air. They promised Jan that the next night, four men would come from Manndalen to transport him to Sweden and freedom. Jan was greatly comforted, cheered and encouraged by these thoughtful and generous strangers.

They said their goodbyes and Peder and Nigo started their ascent up the steep mountain to the top of the plateau and down again, to Manndalen.

The original plan had been to move Jan by reindeer transport to Sweden, but that seemed all but impossible at this point. They had to pass Skibotn, which was crowded with Germans, and in any case, the helpers were not near the Sami's regular travel route.

Manndalen, 30 April, 1943: It was daybreak when Peder and Nigo came down from the mountain plateau. Soon after, they contacted Aslak Fossvoll and teacher Nordnes. Four men had to retrieve Jan the following night and help transport him to Sweden. Peder Isaksen and Nigo Nilsen would return, and with them would be Nils Brustrøm and Olaf Olsen.

Olaf Olsen was a twenty-three year old farmer who lived on the east side of Manndalen River. A strong youth, a hard worker, dependable and persevering, he felt honored to be asked to help with Jan.

Nils Brustrøm lived on his farm, Brustrøm, highest up in the interior of Manndalen valley. All four were anxious to get Jan to Sweden, knowing that his health was deteriorating rapidly. The men agreed to meet at the usual place just above the tree line at 11 p.m.

That afternoon the wind picked up. They had all hoped for a reprieve from the stormy weather conditions for a few days; after all it was spring.

Towards evening, the wind increased to a moderate gale with a strong storm in the wind gusts.

The four men thought they might still manage the ascent, but the violent snowdrifts blinded them. They arched themselves against the snow and the wind as they inched their way upward. Higher up in Kjerringdalen Valley, the wind increased to such a velocity that it was near impossible to breathe or to keep one's balance. There were no options - they had to return to the valley floor.

Peder and Nigo had promised Jan they would return on this night. But it was impossible; they would not be able to keep their word. In Manndalen to keep your word was a virtue of necessity; it was unthinkable not to. The overpowering weather made it impossible for the young men to follow through on their promise.

Restless, the men could not stop thinking about Jan up on the plateau, helpless and trapped behind the "Gentleman stone."

Later, they tried several different routes, but each ended in disappointment. It was impossible. They could not see their own feet. The wind and the full-blown whiteout forced the four men to turn back. Concern for Jan weighed heavy on all of their minds. In these weather conditions, though, he was better off right where he was – in the snow cave.

May 1, 1943: The storm raged on. The men tried to reach the plateau by a different route. It was no use. They had to turn back.

May 2, 1943: The stormy weather continued. They did not stand a chance of making it. Peder and Nigo worried constantly about Jan, but they were powerless against the tempest.

May 3, 1943: The storm screeched through the valley. The wind howled around the house corners and it was impossible for any human being to be outside. This was the fourth day; none could remember such spring weather. The men decided they had to try to reach Jan. Again they tried an alternate route, but the storm pounded them. No living creature could make it up on the plateau in such weather. Defeated, they returned to the valley. They began to doubt that Jan could have made it through such weather. Anxious as they were for a let-up, they could do nothing but wait inside.

"It might cost me my life,
but what of it? You have to
say 'Yes' or 'No' to life."

— **Marius Grønvoll**

JAN'S SOLITUDE

Encouraged, Jan settled back down by himself after Peder and Nigo had left. Little bursts of happiness ran through him. He looked forward to the new happenings and the plans for his final rescue.

He started thinking about the near future. He decided a large tub filled with hot water and soap was top priority for him. He wanted to soak for hours.

Clean clothes were next on his list. The smelly, filthy clothes he was wearing had long since lost their usefulness. Delicious foods came to his mind - Sweden would have it all. There were many things for his mind to ruminate on. Time would pass quickly; possibly the night would slip by and he would be able to enjoy some sleep. The new day would dawn and quickly turn into night and his friends would return for him.

He discerned that the snow cave darkened early, and thought it amazing how quick night was descending. Soon after came the screeching wind and then he realized it was another Arctic spring storm. The wind came from somewhere behind the boulder and whirled around his snow cave. The darkness thickened and he knew night had come. The wind kept barreling down. The hours hardly moved.

There was no reprieve from the storm. Jan realized the men could not come for him in such weather. It would be impossible for them to fight their way through. Hour after hour snailed by - the storm persisted.

Jan forced himself to think of other things: his family, friends, hikes in the mountains in his youth, his military training, and his hopes for the future.

Jan listened to the wind. Like a raging giant, it took a deep breath, giving him a few seconds of silence; then, with roaring fury, the giant exhaled and the tempestuous wind shrieked with added force around the boulder. The snow whipped around his cave.

Jan lay in his snow-covered bed, listening to the storm; it raged on for four days. He realized he was being buried alive as the wind forced the snowdrift around him up against the boulder. He could not distinguish day from night any longer and the storm became muted. At long last a disquieting stillness settled in. The only sound was his breathing.

The icy cold forced him to keep turning within the sleeping bag so as not to freeze to death. Because of this shifting, painful blisters and raw sores developed on his body. His feet were aching, his toes infected. His body went from shivering to overheating with intermittent fever attacks and sweating, back to freezing. The cold was agonizing. Sleep was impossible. During these fitful days, superficial, shallow periods of sleep for ten to fifteen minutes at a time were his only relief. They recurred when he was too fatigued to fight any longer.

Jan's sufferings continued for three days. Foods and liquids were gone. The men had planned to return within twenty-four hours and Jan had been well supplied for that period. No one had imagined a spring storm of this magnitude. In his wretchedness he was sapped of physical strength and mental fortitude. Rapidly losing weight, an overriding helplessness engulfed him.

As time went on, he heard church bells pealing. At first Jan noticed the barely audible sounds coming from afar, then the volume increased and he became aware that the resonant sound of chiming bells came from the highest mountain peaks. They bounced out across the wilderness and echoed back from a facing mountaintop. The beautiful sounds were muted or intensified depending on which mountain peak sent the melodic sounds back. Church bells had never sounded this celestial before. Jan strained to hear. He did not know he was hallucinating and that the end was near for him.

RESCUED FROM
THE SNOWCAVE

Tuesday, May 4, 1943: The Manndalen men anxiously watched the weather. Early on the morning of May 4 they were able to attempt another climb up to the tundra. There were some Germans in the neighborhood that morning, but nothing could hold the four back now that the weather had cleared.

The route up the steep mountain was tricky and exhausting. With all the new snow, there was a risk of spring avalanches. The four men rubbed their skis with paraffin wax, which made the going easier, but which also gave the skis a tendency to slip backwards. Within three hours they stood in front of the "Gentleman stone."

Hastily they slipped out of their ski-bindings and began removing armsful of snow at a time, continually shouting out the password, "Hello Gentleman!" Soon Jan came into view. He was alive but wretched.

"Jan, we have come to take you to Sweden!"

"There are four of us, and this time we will get you there."

Jan gave a weak smile and the thumbs up sign.

His rescuers were anxious for Jan's welfare after his nine days in the snow cave. Moreover they knew that they were in plain view of Furuflaten and Lyngseidet, where many Germans with powerful binoculars were stationed.

They removed Jan from the sleeping bag and emptied it, hurriedly cleaned him up and put him back in to ward off the cold. Hot soup, bread and coffee revived him once more. They made the soldier comfortable on the sled as best they could, and then fastened him down.

"Si fra, er du klar Jan?," Are you ready Jan?, they asked.

"This is the very moment I have lived for!"

"Are you comfortable?"

"I am anxious to see the Swedish border!" Jan smiled.

The men fastened their skis, put on their knapsacks, and tied the ropes from the sled around their waist. The four worked out how they could best work in unison, braking downhill and pulling together more effectively uphill.

"We are on our way to Sweden!"

"Off to Sweden we go!"

"Off we go to Sweden!" A much weaker but enthusiastic voice came from the sleeping bag.

Ridges and extended valleys made the going across the whole plateau strenuous. In various places, the tundra rolled like waves on a storm-tossed sea, up a knoll, down a dip, then up again.

They moved in a southeasterly direction. Far down on their right, Lyngenfjord reflected steel-gray clouds gathering, and on their left was the precipitous downgrade toward Manndalen Valley.

The most difficult passages were the sharp downward slopes when the sled had a tendency to take off and the men in the back endeavored to slow it down. Drenched with sweat, they stopped for a short breather when they came to some fairly even land.

"How about something hot to drink, Jan?"

"*Ja takk.*"

"Are you okay? You don't say much."

"I am not the one struggling." Jan attempted to flash his handsome, but now tired smile.

His pallid, haggard face told its own story but the only feelings Jan expressed were of gratitude.

On they pushed!

After the men traveled for about four hours toward the border, the wind pounced.

A thick snow squall bore down and engulfed them in a white torrent of flakes. The tips of their skis disappeared in the whiteout. It became difficult to hold their balance. Being familiar with the spring weather conditions in this area, the men from Manndalen knew the storm could stop as suddenly as it had begun. Olaf bent over, "Jan I am going to cover your whole face." Jan nodded.

Unable to see, the men lost all sense of direction. They were fully aware, however, that the three thousand-foot drop to Manndalen Valley was somewhere near and on the other side was Skibotn, filled with Germans. They could only hope they would not stray in that direction.

Olaf Olsen

"Jan, we need to leave you awhile to go and get oriented to our position."

Jan indicated agreement. The Manndalen men discovered they were lost. After about forty minutes they turned back.

While on the way back to Jan, the storm stopped momentarily. Far below them lay Manndalen. They now knew where they were and hurried to get Jan. The wind and snow had erased most of their tracks, making it difficult to find the way back. About an hour after leaving they came to a slight rise. Jan had been snowed under! Some sixty feet from him they stopped cold.

"In all the world... what is this?" Peder pointed to new tracks in the snow—two pairs of fresh ski tracks the wind had not erased yet. The men looked around but they were alone. It was evident the tracks had been made by two German soldiers on a search. None but Germans would be up in the mountains during such weather conditions. The men stood in speechless amazement and watched each other. They backed off from Jan to lay plans.

"No doubt, these tracks were made by Germans. But they are only two, and we are four!"

"If they should come back, let us surrender—Jan also. And when we are led away, let's look for the right opportunity. I'll shout '*Hei!*' then we'll overthrow them. We all have knives." Nigo had it all figured out. The others agreed. Their knives were not particularly sharp, but good enough to complete the job, if necessary.

"There is no need for us to tell Jan about this incident," said Peder.

All were of the same mind. They continued on to Jan.

Someone removed the snow, then the covering from his face. "We are back, Jan!"

"I've never been so happy to see anyone!" Jan beamed.

"You knew we'd be back, didn't you?"

"That's not what I mean. Only moments ago I thought I heard German voices."

The men gaped.

"I was petrified thinking you had become their prisoners."

"How could we get you to Sweden then?" Nigo quipped. They all laughed, but they did wonder why the Germans had not smelled Jan.

The men were grateful the snow squalls had completely covered Jan. If the Germans had seen him, the sled must have just appeared as one of the many snow-covered rocks scattered across the tundra.

Neither Jan nor the men knew at the time that the Germans had increased their patrols and fortified their forces within the inner Troms District and along the Swedish border. For some time the Germans had had indications that someone in the area was trying to escape. The document case retrieved from the waters in Toftefjord contained several papers which revealed certain escape routes toward Sweden. The Germans were convinced it would be in the area of Troms. For that reason, orders had been sent down from German High Command to fortify and intensify the patrols and to be vigilant at all times.

In the mountains, Wednesday, May 5, 1943: The four Manndalen men picked up the ropes and continued further into the wide expanse. The rough terrain slowed them and progress was difficult. They'd pull uphill, then abruptly had to brake going down a steep incline.

It was nearing 5 a.m. The men were on the plateau in upper Manndalen Valley. For twenty hours they had been on the move. It was time to rest and grab something to eat. Quickly they produced from their knapsacks nourishing bread, cured meat, beverages and of course, coffee and cigarettes. They unbuckled Jan and helped him sit up to eat and view the landscape. Suddenly hundreds of reindeer rushed past. These beautiful animals with their broad antlers gather in enormous throngs and at that very moment the clouds parted.

"Majestic! Majestic!" Jan was thrilled.

"Just wait, things will get even better for you, Jan!"

"I have no complaints. You men are my inspiration."

"And you are ours!"

The men had realized for some time that it would be impossible to reach Sweden in one big leap with still another fifteen or twenty miles to go. They discussed how best to work their way to the border. When they had finished eating and packed things away, Nigo suddenly popped up. "I am taking off for Sweden. I have some Sami friends over there, two brothers, and they will probably be able to help us with reindeer transport on the last leg of the journey."

"Nigo you're delirious!" Olaf chuckled. "You are talking about another 85 miles round trip to your Sami friends. You want to ski that by yourself after these twenty hours?"

"No problem. I'll do it!"

They briefly discussed Peder, Nils and Olaf bringing Jan down the Avzevaggi valley a bit where they would keep him until Nigo returned with the reindeer transport from Sweden.

He took off without provisions of any sort. This was typical Nigo, with more endurance than any of them. He didn't give his friends a chance to dissuade him. All they could do was watch his silhouette diminish on the horizon. Like a light-footed reindeer, Nigo disappeared among the mountain ridges.

Nils Brustrøm

When Nigo left, the three men fought their way back some three miles on the plateau uppermost in Avzevaggi, a side valley on the southwest side of Manndalen Valley. Here they began their descent.

They labored to bring Jan downward a distance but the rugged terrain was almost impossible to traverse. The ropes tied to the sled were too short, and several times they had to gingerly lower the sled, letting it hang and sway in the open air. In other places, two of the Manndalen men took a few careful steps down the precipitous mountain while the third lowered the sled after them.

This time Jan suffered excruciatingly, moaning and twisting.

Despite the cold air, the sweat poured off the men.

Foot by foot they descended the rock-ribbed height until they reached a point where a bold-faced wall protruded skyward. The vertical wall blocked the view to the west but it was wide open in all other directions, and it gave shelter from the wind.

Peder, Nils and Olaf were drained. Helpless, they dropped into the snow.

"We probably could go on another little piece, Jan. But we're exhausted and maybe it's best that we leave you here until the reindeer transport comes," said Nils.

"It's just fine here. I am sure I'll be all right for the short while until the reindeer transport comes."

The men built a snow wall around the sled to protect Jan should the wind pick up.

They emptied two of their knapsacks of food, drinks, and cigarettes, putting the items into the other knapsack, which they placed close to Jan.

Jan did not mind sleeping under the open sky. He thought it rather exhilarating after his experience in the snow cave. The men agreed this was the best place for him for the next few hours.

They said their good-byes and left, totally spent, yet encouraged by Jan's upbeat mood. The arduous decent down to the Brustrøms' farm uppermost in Manndalen Valley took them six hours. They arrived in the early afternoon after thirty hours of hard labor in the mountains. Disappointed in the outcome – different than what they had planned – but Jan was a little closer to his goal.

The men flopped as soon as they entered the Brustrøm home. They slept the rest of the day and into the night. Peder and Olaf got up and left in the middle of the night. They walked a few feet from the Brustrøm house and into the icy Manndalen River to avoid leaving any tracks.

BENEATh the sky
in AVZEVAGGi

Avzevaggi, May 6, 1943: Jan stirred and slowly opened his eyes to the bright morning sun. From his sled beneath the black vertical wall, he could see the mountain bluffs nearby and the snow-capped peaks on the horizon. The beauty and splendor of it all filled him with hope and wonder.

He was not sure which mountain the sun was climbing over; he only appreciated its light and its warmth. His happiness was short lived. As the Arctic spring sun raised the temperature, it melted the snow on the ridges and outcrops on the mountain wall above him. The melting snow dripped incessantly down on him and the sleeping bag all through the day. Soon he was soaked, as if covered with a drenched blanket. And when the sun sank behind the mountain crests and the night rolled over him, the melted snow water froze. The sleeping bag became a tomb of ice from which he could not free himself.

The next day the scenario recurred. He cursed the sun that had welcomed him on the first morning and filled him with hope. This was too much. This was more than should be asked of anyone.

Weakness and cold replaced his courage and the warmth. What was left of his toes ached—their putrid smell told him they were rotting away—and he was too weak to do anything about it. The thought of food nauseated him, and he lost still more weight. His mind could not make any sense of it all. Jan was rapidly deteriorating.

Thursday, May 7, 1943: Peder had been up for a couple of hours when he heard the sound of rushing skis in the snow outside his home. As it was mid-morning, Peder assumed it was drunken Germans on their way back to their quarters after an all night brawl. Peder was wrong. It was Nigo returning from his thirty hour, 85-mile trip to Sweden. He had met with his Sami friends, who gave him some food and coffee, but that was all he had eaten since he had left his friends.

Fifty hours of skiing with only a short break in Sweden — Nigo was unbeatable! But even after all his struggles, his Sami friends could not promise him help. The Germans had fortified their borders along the road to Finland and it was the only way into Sweden. The Samis found it too dangerous to transport Jan past the German guards under the circumstances.

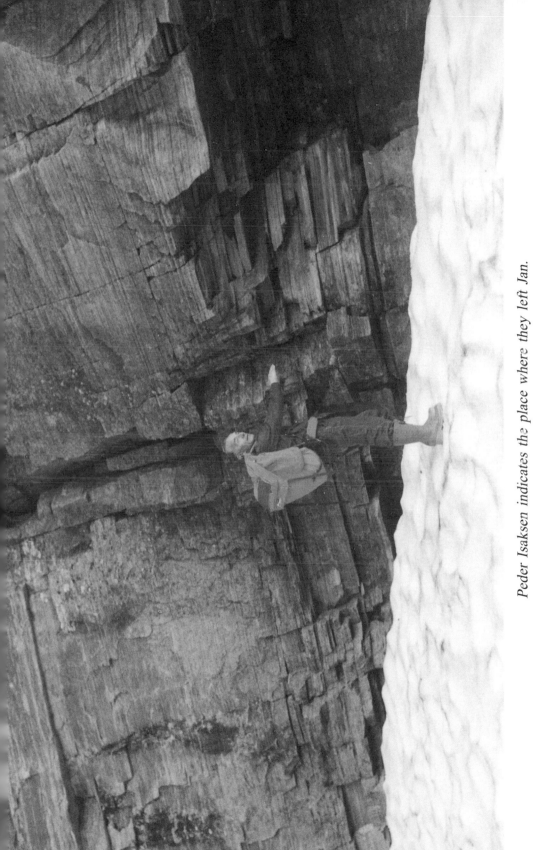

Peder Isaksen indicates the place where they left Jan.

Avzevaggi as it appears from Mannddalen Valley. The arrow indicates where Jan was left.

the spirit of the sami

In the village of Birtavärre, brothers Leif and Rolf Bjørn were the contact persons for the resistance. The brothers had several business interests including a large lumber business, which supplied several areas in the Troms District. In addition, they were shipping agents and had many local contacts. Organizing the escape routes into Sweden from Kåfjorddalen Valley, four miles from Birtavärre, fell to them.

During the war, the Bjørn brothers and Hjalmar Steinnes, a thirty-year-old bachelor in Kåfjorddalen, had developed a close working relationship. Their mutual goal was to defeat Germany. At the time of the German invasion of Norway, Hjalmar was working at Spitsbergen in the Svalbard Islands, a Norwegian possession in the Arctic Ocean. The islands lie about midway between Nordkapp, the northern tip of Norway, and the North Pole.

Hjalmar Steinnes

Long before the invasion of Norway, Hjalmar had developed a hatred for Hitler and all Nazism stood for. Their atrocities caused him to detest Hitler's very name and anything related to him. A born patriot, Hjalmar was anxious to return to the mainland to fight against the German tyranny. With many others he was mobilized at Svalbard. A tramp steamer brought him back to Narvik, south of Tromsø, and he soon involved himself with the resistance movement.

Following the outbreak of the war in northern Norway, a steady stream of refugees crossed the border to Sweden. Hjalmar guided many of them. Kåfjorddalen was isolated but the distance to the Swedish border was only 45 miles. Conversely, precipitous mountains bordered Kåfjorddalen. Refugees had to climb these mountains before reaching the plateau and setting out for Sweden. Kåfjorddalen Valley became one of the main refugee routes across the Norwegian and Finnish wilderness into Sweden.

Border patrols were usually stationed some distance apart and it was not too dangerous to cross. In the early war years, the German soldiers seldom came to Kåfjorddalen Valley. This changed after the Germans confiscated the document case in the battle of Toftefjord and learned that sabotage work was planned against them. Almost immediately, they increased and strengthened their border patrols. After that time the fugitives had to be extremely cautious.

Furthest up in Kåfjorddalen Valley at the lowermost part of Ankerlia Mountain, the Germans had confiscated a small hut owned by the Bjørn brothers, left from the copper mining days. They stationed guards there to keep a lookout for refugees. The forested mountainside was steep, but the trees shielded fugitives and guides climbing the mountain near the hut.

The elongated valley begins at the Kåfjord and stretches eight miles inland. At its narrowest point it is only 450 feet across, but spreads out to about 1000 feet at the widest place. Nearly perpendicular mountains reaching heights of 2700 feet enclose the valley, except to the west where it skirts the fjord.

Winter begins when the first snow falls early in November. The snow stays until April, sometimes May. The heavy downwind from the mountains plays havoc with the snow and forges huge piles several feet high. Torleif Lyngstad says in his book, *"Kåfjord – mennesker, administrasjon og politikk"* that "nature is a master the people of Kåfjord have always accepted."

In 1943 only a few hundred people resided in the valley. The nearest store was three-and-a-half-miles away, Leif and Rolf Bjørn's in Birtavärre.

Birtavärre: Hjalmar and the Bjørn brothers had learned of Jan Baalsrud soon after his arrival in Furuflaten. Messages had been exchanged between established contacts. The Bjørn brothers asked Hjalmar to assist them in securing Sami reindeer transport for the soldier when the time was right.

Some nomadic Samis make Kautokeino their winter home. Their reindeer roam the nearby plateaus. Kautokeino is located in Finnmark County, which borders the Troms District in Northern Norway. In the spring, the Kautokeino Samis move their reindeer to the coast.

The area where the Samis and their reindeer herds roamed is known as Lapland, a vast territory that included the extreme north of Norway, Sweden, Finland and the Kola Peninsula of the Soviet Union. Lapland has no borders and the Sami are free to follow their reindeer herds. The area of Lapland is commonly regarded as the area within the Polar Arctic Circle. The higher, Alpine types mountains in northern Norway and Sweden are known as the *tundra,* with marshes, moors, dwarfed birch trees and rich pastureland which feeds the huge reindeer herds.

Birtavärre, Wednesday May 5, 1943: Hjalmar and the Bjørn brothers held exhaustive discussions on possible solutions on how to best help Jan. They considered bringing him to Kåfjorddalen by boat, but decided it was too chancy. Hjalmar hit on another idea.

"I'll ski over the mountains to find out exactly where they keep him hidden. Then we'll take the next step."

The Bjørn brothers agreed.

Across a narrow country path, a short distance from Hjalmar's home, stood a small red-painted cottage. The cottage stood at the foot of a 2100-foot mountain. John Olav Ballovarre, Hjalmar's faithful helper, lived here with his parents and eight siblings. With his new assignment, Hjalmar headed straight for John Olav's home to ask for his assistance.

John Olav and Hjalmar set off to the mountains that very day for Manndalen, thirteen miles west of Kåfjorddalen. They carried their skis on their shoulders up steep Ankerlia Mountain. When they reached the

Rolf Bjørn

uplands, they put the skis on and set out across the plateau.

One thing the Sami and others in the North Country enjoy is their coffee. It is said that the Samis do not measure journeys in miles but rather in the number of coffee breaks required. Hence, when these two men reached Moskugaise Mountain up on the plateau they had their first coffee, Rika, a coffee substitute made from grains, and the only thing available during the war.

From Moskugaise, they took the path toward the uppermost part of Manndalen. A roughly sketched map of the place where Jan was hidden had been given them.

Nearing Olmmaivaggi, a sudden blinding snowstorm overpowered them. The thick snow made it impossible to see even their ski tips.

"We had best turn back. Maybe we'll make it back to the hut in Moskugaise," John Olav yelled above the howling wind.

After the copper mines closed down in 1919, outdoor lovers had maintained a small hovel from material left after the copper-mining days. Hunters and fishermen alike stopped there for coffee breaks when they came to the uplands.

"Let's do it. We won't find Baalsrud in this soup."

They turned and, with the help of the compass, made their way back to the hut.

The storm increased and nearly lifted the hut off its foundation.

"We can't stay, Hjalmar. Let's try again when the weather clears."

"I agree. It's a terrible night. Let's try to get back down into the valley."

Safely home, the storm stopped abruptly. Hjalmar was exhausted and hungry after the challenging outing. He grabbed a quick bite, changed into dry clothes and set out for the Bjørn brothers in Birtavärre. Deeply disturbed over his report of the unsuccessful trip, the brothers promised to contact him further.

Shortly after Hjalmar's arrival home, two attractive girls from Lyngen visited. Some time earlier he had met them and a young quisling on the ferry from Tromsø. (Vidkun Quisling was a Norwegian Nazi party leader and traitor during WWII. He was executed in 1945. His name is used a label for a person who betrays his or her country by aiding an invading enemy.) Suspicious of Hjalmar's involvement with fugitives and hoping to trap him, the young quisling sent the girls as decoys. The girls told Hjalmar the young man had been called up to the Eastern Front and had asked them to come and see him. "Would he be able to help get the young man to Sweden?"

Uneasy, Hjalmar sensed something seriously wrong. "I'm only a fisherman. I work in the mines," he said. "All those who knew the mountains have escaped already."

"Can't you do anything for him?"

"I don't know what. Let's hope the war ends soon and your friend can return home."

Birtavärre

Three Samis in traditional costume. Nils Siri is in the center.

AT CROSS PURPOSES

Manndalen, Thursday, May 6, 1943: Peder, Nils and Olaf, the Manndalen men, had descended from Avzevaggi the day before Nigo returned from Sweden. Nigo hadn't received a promise of help because the Sami felt the risk was too great at this time. Realizing there would be no Sami transport, they sent an immediate message to the Bjørn brothers in Birtavärre. "Jan is seriously ill, can you help with reindeer transport, now?" The Bjørn brothers forwarded the pressing communication to Hjalmar.

"Please arrange for reindeer transport—post haste!"

By chance, while in Birtavärre, Hjalmar had run into his Sami friend, Nils Juuso, who had just come from Sweden. He relayed that the Siri brothers were camped near Jierta some 35 miles east in the direction of the Reisafjell Mountains. The brothers, who were from Kautokeino, were on the move with their reindeer herd. Hjalmar knew these Sami brothers well. Per and Nils Siri were dependable, honorable men about his own age. He expected they would help him with reindeer transport. At this point, Hjalmar had no idea that Nigo had been to Sweden attempting to get help.

The Bjørn brothers told Hjalmar that Jan was on a ski-sled in Olmmaivaggi.

Manndalen stretches in a southeasterly direction from the country settlement up into the wilderness, which divides into three more side valleys. Jan was not in any of these valleys but on his sled out in the open in Avzevaggi at the highest point of the four side valleys on the opposite side of the Manndalen Valley, in the southwest.

A terrible misunderstanding had taken place.

Hjalmar willingly accepted the assignment to find reindeer transport for Jan. He only asked that the Manndalen men meet him at the place and time they had agreed to, the night between May 9 and 10. Hjalmar skied nearly 90 miles round trip in his search for the Siri brothers' camp, close to Kautokeino. If they were able to come, the Samis needed time to gather their reindeer.

"Tell the Manndalen men not to leave the place in case I am delayed. I am on my way."

Before Hjalmar left, he and the Bjørn brothers discussed the need to compensate the Samis fairly for transporting Jan to Sweden – and for risking their lives. They decided that 3000 *kroner* ($400) was a fair price. Rolf and Leif Bjørn provided the money.

Hjalmar brought with him two of his neighbors, Mons-Peder Gundersen and Einar Løvli, both active in the resistance, as he set out to find the Sami.

The Arctic spring with its light evenings was fast approaching. Soon there would be no darkness at all. Hjalmar was equipped with a rough outline of a map showing where Jan lay hidden. The men carried their skis up through the rugged woodland until they drew above the tree line. From there they continued upland until they reached the plateau. They set out toward Jierta and the Reisafjell Mountains. The snow was crusty, enabling them to move quickly.

By Carajavre, they took their first break in an old turf-hunting hut. Within minutes, fire burned in the old granite pit and they heated the ever-present Rika. Thick slices of homemade rye bread spread with churned butter disappeared quickly.

Satisfied after their break and meal, the men continued their journey. Several hours later, they passed Jierta. But they found neither tracks nor traces of the Sami or their reindeer. Not until they neared Miehtavarri did they see the first *lavvo*, Sami tent. Yelping dogs greeted them and stayed with them until they reached the tent opening.

Inside, Magnus, the oldest of the Siri brothers, sat close by a coal-black steaming kettle of coffee.

Magnus greeted them. *"Boris, boris!"* Welcome, welcome!

His brothers Per and Nils Siri sat on birch branches and shaggy goatskins further back in the tent. They arose and greeted them eagerly.

This time they were served *real* coffee smuggled in from Sweden and delicious Swedish bread. Out came dried reindeer meat. Wielding his sharp hunting knife, Magnus cut the meat into thin slices. After many hours on the plateau, the food tasted fantastic and the men's ferocious appetites were satisfied. It felt good to be among the brothers.

"What brings you to us?" Nils queried.

"I am looking for reindeer transport for a very ill Norwegian soldier hidden in the mountains. He is hunted by the Germans and needs to get to Sweden," Hjalmar explained.

The brothers offered to help without hesitation. Because of his unmarried status, Nils was designated to be the driver. Fatigued after their eight hours in the upland, Hjalmar and his friends slept for five hours while Nils and Per gathered three strong reindeer bucks.

Nils and Hjalmar readied the reindeer bucks and packed the *pulks* with plenty of cured meat, bread and coffee. Pulks are canoe-shaped sleds built from birch wood, set on runners and lined with reindeer skin. They headed for Manndalen to pick up Jan.

With only a moderate mountain breeze and decent snow conditions, they made good time. Nils drove the reindeer further west and closer to the Finnish border than Hjalmar and his friends had come.

By Sumajavrre stood a newly restored cottage the border police used. Hjalmar knew the four police stationed there. They were true *jøssinger*, Norwegian patriots during WWII. The resistance workers still detoured, not wishing to take unnecessary chances on their top-secret mission.

In spite of good weather conditions, riding in a reindeer sled was strenuous. At Smuolkojavret they took a break. Food and coffee always seemed more delicious out on the plateau, especially after an arduous trip. From their resting place, Olmmaivaggi, the side valley where they believed Jan was hidden, was only eight miles away.

Birtavärre, May 9, 1943: While Hjalmar and Nils were in the mountains, the Bjørn brothers, not aware that Nigo had been in Sweden seeking help, sent a message to the Manndalen men: "Reindeer transport from Kautokeino will arrive this coming night. Meet them on the plateau and show them the way to the soldier."

Jan still was at Avzevaggi on the west side of Manndalen Valley. Hjalmar and Nils Siri were on their way to Olmmaivaggi, on the east side of the valley.

Manndalen, May 9, 1943: The Manndalen men were happy to receive the message of the upcoming reindeer transport.

That evening, Peder Isaksen and Peder Pedersen were on their way up to Avzevaggi Plateau to meet with the reindeer transport from Kautokeino. As it was Sunday evening, the two bachelors met people along the road enjoying a stroll.

"Where are you young men going so late on a Sunday night?"

"We are just meeting some young ladies up in the valley."

They all laughed together and there were no more questions.

Following several hours of strenuous climbing they reached Jan. This time the men noticed an emotional change in him. Jan had always been warm and friendly, even in his most difficult moments, but now he seemed to have lost hope.

"I heard church bells chime again. This time they seemed far away," Jan muttered.

They were at a loss for what to tell him, but they tried to cheer him up. They had brought hot coffee and soup in thermoses, but it wasn't enough to warm his spirits.

"We are on the way up to the plateau to meet the Sami. They'll bring you to Sweden, Jan."

Jan's ashen face, hollow cheeks and overgrown black beard frightened them. He had lost weight since they saw him last. His lifeless large blue-gray eyes, framed by thick black eyebrows, manifested his torment all too clearly.

"Will it really happen this time?" A slight hope brushed across Jan's face.

"Yes, Jan. Before long you will be in safety in Sweden. You will get the medical care you need."

Thanks," he whispered, forcing a slight upturn of his lips.

"We're going up to the plateau to meet them and before too many hours we will be back."

Filled with misgivings, the men left Jan, but felt calm knowing the Sami transport would join them on the way down.

In the mountains, Evening, May 9, 1943: Hjalmar and Nils continued to make good time, and arrived early at the agreed upon place. They set the tent up. Coffee in hand made the long wait more pleasant. The kerosene stove was produced and the coffee pot filled with snow. Nils had brought a leather pouch with more of the good Swedish coffee.

Nils' good-natured remarks made him a jovial fellow to be around. Though his mother tongue was Sami, he communicated well in broken Norwegian. When he relaxed, he liked to *joik,* a Sami monotone chant that tells the story of a person or past event.

The reindeer were tied to stakes near bare spots in the snow where there was plenty of silver gray lichen, reindeer moss, for them to eat.

Reindeer bucks scrape away snow with their antlers to find food during the winter. After the older bucks shed their antlers they use their hooves to paw away the snow to get to the lichen if the snow is not too deep. The obtain water by eating snow.

Time dragged on and the Manndalen men did not come. Hjalmar and Nils grew uneasy. They could not understand the delay. At last they began their own search for Jan. For hours they searched in ever-widening circles. The plateau with the scattered boulders stretched out pure white for miles. They found no tracks. No sign of life.

They searched all the way down to the tree line, but to no avail. Repeatedly they studied the rough drawing. They believed they were in the right place. The reindeer were getting restless; the two men moved the animals to better pasture. Worn down from long hours of skiing and intense searching, the men finally went to sleep on the reindeer pelts in the tent.

In the early morning hours of May 10, they started exploring anew. No matter where they skied, or how much they called out, there were no answers. Not a trace of a human being.

"What's the use? They're not in this area," Hjalmar said toward evening.

"We need more information."

"Nils, will you wait here while I make a run back to Birtavärre to contact the Bjørn brothers? They can contact the Manndalen men and find the cause." Hjalmar was downcast.

"What are you thinking of Hjalmar? That's a 26-mile round trip. It doesn't make any sense to wait way out here on the plateau. How could I explain a reindeer transport out here should the German patrols show? It's best I return to my camping ground."

Hjalmar understood his friend. They had hunted and waited for nearly forty-eight hours without success.

"I see your point. We'll try again once I've found the exact location?"

"*Jaja, ja.* I'll work with you."

Past midnight, Hjalmar helped Nils hitch up the reindeer. He paid him the previously agreed upon salary, and they parted. Saddened and exhausted, Hjalmar watched his friend disappear in among the mountain boulders. What had gone wrong? Attaching his own skis, he started on the long way home.

Late evening, May 9, 1943: After leaving Jan, the Manndalen men climbed up to the Avzevaggi Plateau and went another three miles south to where they understood they were to meet the Sami.

The Samis had not arrived yet when Peder and Peder reached the tableland. Chill night winds blew and the men flapped their arms back and forth to keep warm. They continually scanned the landscape. No one was near. And they saw no one coming from afar. They dared not think the worst; as a result they just waited – and searched.

They could not have known that in a side valley two other men spent desperate hours searching also. Their hope rose every time they came around boulders, up bumps, around knolls, or down in dips, only to fall again. They tried to find the man they wanted to get to Sweden.

Peder and Peder waited until early in the morning of the 10th.

Two dispirited young men, nearly overcome with cold and emotional defeat, climbed silently down toward Avzevaggi and Jan.

By the time they returned from their fruitless search for the Sami, Jan was barely able to converse with them.

The men were distraught to see Jan's condition. They could see that Jan needed both medical help and to be gotten out of the weather. Jan's courage to press forward had diminished, and the men determined that Jan had to be moved quickly or they would lose him.

"There will be no reindeer transport." Peder Isaksen had difficulty speaking.

"In time there will be, Jan. Just not yet."

Jan stared into space. A hopeless look crossed his face and his despondency grew. At that moment they felt him disassociating himself from them and his surroundings.

They promised him that the following evening four men would come up with provisions and other necessary things they were able to carry up here to the upper valley.

Something snapped; Jan had reached the end of his tolerance. The five days in Avzevaggi had turned into a prolonged nightmare.

"It is enough," his dejected voice was almost inaudible. "I can't anymore. Let's call it quits. It is more than I can bear."

Watching him filled them with empathy. He was right. The suffering and loneliness he had been through, the uncertainty and the loss of his friends, pain and illness was more than most people could have coped with. Yet he had taken his hard knocks unflinchingly and with heroic valor. And now when he needed them, all they could do was to look down at him, powerless to help.

Except for their presence, they had no meaningful comfort to offer. They tried as best they could to encourage him not to give up.

"We'll stand by you Jan, until you are across the border."

Anguished and frail, Jan lay there helpless and without hope. He just stared out in space. His friends grew resolute. They would save him no matter what the cost.

Peder Isaksen and Peder Pedersen did not have four men ready to make the trip to Sweden at that point, but they also knew something had to be done, and soon. And they knew they would have no difficulty finding such men in the valley. Again they were able to ignite a spark of hope and life in Jan. They started their six-hour downward climb.

Birtavärre, May 10, 1943: When Hjalmar did not return when expected, the Bjørn brothers sent his friend John Olav a message, "Please come and see us at the store in Birtavärre."

"John Olav, what do you think has happened? Do you think the Germans have caught them?" Leif asked with great concern.

"It is hard to know. Maybe after such a long time they have reached Sweden. But even at that they should have been back."

"John Olav, would you mind acting as our liaison and try to find the cause?"

"I'll go. But on my last outing I broke my skis."

"Come back to my house tonight and I'll have skis for you," Rolf said.

When John Olav returned that evening, many guests filled the Bjørn home. Rolf brought him over to a corner in the ante-room filled with shoes and boots. Rolf picked out his own boots. "Use these, and here are my skis."

"Before you leave, come down to the store and I'll have some tobacco for you, John Olav."

"I'll take the road along the riverbed."

He headed for the store on the way home.

Before long he became aware of two Germans behind him on bicycles.

"Now," he thought. "Now it is over! What will I tell them about carrying skis with no snow in the valley?"

But the Germans bicycled right past him. Most likely, John Olav concluded, they were "trading-Germans." From time to time German soldiers came from Spåkenes, a large German fortification. It was not unusual for them to bicycle the 20 miles to Birtavärre to trade their tobacco for home churned butter, mittens and other knitted goods.

Rolf met Hjalmar at the store, and immediately called one of the contact men in Manndalen. He wanted to know if Jan had been brought to Sweden yet.

"Has the fish been picked up?"

The answer was not clear, though it sounded as if Jan hadn't been picked up yet, but soon would be.

"Jan has not been picked up yet." Rolf turned to John Olav. "It is best you go searching. Here is some tobacco, both twist-tobacco and pipe tobacco for you. Good luck!"

John Olav stopped home to prepare for the outing. Without delay, he changed clothes and packed his knapsack. He loved cold, cold milk and always took a quart whenever he went on outings. Next best, he liked to sink his teeth into homemade whole grain bread. The other "must" he carried was a bottle of hard liquor. He did not drink, but it was good to have close by should the need arise. It was always in his sack with his bread and milk, and Rika coffee.

John Olav had never told his parents that he was involved in illegal activities, and they did not pry, but they were suspicious and a little unnerved. Fear of the Germans was very real, something most families learned to live with. John Olav wanted to protect his parents and siblings. Should the Germans come searching their home, his family could with good conscience tell them they did not know his whereabouts.

"Don't wait for me. I do not know when I will return." They asked no questions.

He left the little cottage around 9 p.m. A neighbor saw him and shouted through the window, "Are you heading into the mountains, John Olav?"

"*Ja.* I am heading for Vaddas (a plateau some distance from John Olav's home) to see if the Sami have returned." The Samis' return to the plateaus above Kåfjorddalen Valley was a sure sign of spring.

Skiing along on the upland he noticed a silhouette coming toward him from the direction of Manndalen. He could not make out who it was and thought it might be a German. "Let that be as it may, I will make out," he told himself.

Coming closer he was happy to see it was his friend Hjalmar. He was discouraged and worn out. "We did not find Jan Baalsrud. Nils Siri has promised to wait in upper Manndalen." Hjalmar expressed great concern.

"Do you have any tobacco John Olav?"

"*Ja da,* I can give you some tobacco. Rolf gave me some."

"Do you have any liquor as well?"

"*Ja,* but that you can't have until you have drunk some milk." Hjalmar drank about one fourth of the bottle.

"Tasty! Just what a weary body needed."

"Now my friend, since you've got some milk in you, have a nip so you don't fall asleep." John Olav handed him the bottle. "And don't wait for me, if I don't come home for a while, I have probably gone on to Sweden."

Kåfjorddalen, Monday, May 10, 1943: Hjalmar continued on his way homeward and arrived early the following morning. As soon as he had eaten and changed clothes, he set off toward the Bjørn brothers in Birtavärre. He told his fatiguing, discouraging story. They fell silent at the news. At the same time they knew the Manndalen men had gone up in the mountains to meet them, also in vain. Hjalmar was irritated and frustrated with the miscommunication. He was convinced that the place he and Nils had searched was not the correct one. As usual, the Bjørn brothers remained calm and said they would get to the bottom of it all. He would hear from them.

Hjalmar pondered how the communication between the valleys worked. He knew there were many links and that it was difficult to arrange such a dangerous mission in the midst of spying Nazis, German troops and control points. The *Brattholm* affair was well known, but Jan's escape had to be kept top secret.

Spring pushed forward and with it, the always-radiant midnight sun. But for the men in Manndalen Valley, the moments of darkness were more precious, especially since the Arctic spring robbed them of several minutes of shadows daily.

The Manndalen men's breeding gave them fortitude and resilience. They had gained their strength and character from the rugged mountains enclosing their valley and from the stormy seas. In their homes as children they had been taught honesty, dependability and hard work. They, to a man, had been taught not by words, but by the actions of their parents. By watching the people in the valley they had learned that living meant loving and caring for one another, and that to be a man was more than physical prowess and a flawless personality. A real man was tender and giving and filled with selflessness as well as strength

Manndalen, May 10, 1943: In the lower part of Manndalen, a side valley from where Jan was lying in the open air, the men knew of a cave in the mountain wall from earlier times, located nearly 200 feet up a steep incline from the Manndalen River. Jan's helpers had decided to bring him here until they could arrange the final transport to Sweden.

The resistance members in Manndalen had been working extremely hard when they learned of Jan's misfortune. As soon as they decided to transfer him down to the cave in Skaidijonni, men and women worked to make him as comfortable as possible. The most important for his weary body, they felt, was a good bed. The men began braiding together thick bundles of birch branches. They covered the top of this "mattress" with leaves and hay to make it soft and relaxing. The bed was placed right up against one of the inside walls of the cave, making it impossible to see the mattress from the outside. One had to come into the cave before one discovered anything made by human hands. They felt certain of Jan's safety here.

Aslak Fosvoll went to his sister Helene Mikalsen to ask her assistance. Helene was a widow with three children ranging in age from two to ten years old. She was also an expert at making *grener*—the woven woolen covers that the valley of Manndalen is famed for. Today these *grener* are mostly used for decorative wall hangings. But in days past, the nomadic Sami people would use them as coverlets in their tents. Helene was a Sami, as was Aslak, and the tradition of her people making these *grener* go back hundreds of years in the district of Troms. They were made in the natural colors of the wool, white, gray and black.

"Helene, I need for you to make us two Manndals*grener* as soon as possible. They are for a wounded Norwegian soldier. We are bringing him to Skaidijonni, and we need to keep him warm."

Helene went right to work, never questioning her brother's judgment. She bedded her children down and set up her work in her little kitchen. She worked straight through the night and the next day, stopping only to feed the animals and to meet of her children's basic needs. The first one was ready the day after Jan arrived in the cave, because, as she said, "It is important for him to have a warm cover as soon as possible."

A few days later, the second cover was ready for him. Now he had one to sleep on and one to cover him.

Avzevaggi, May 11, 1943: When the four Manndalen men reached Jan they tied him securely to the sled and fastened the long ropes. They knew this would be extremely difficult for him and they tried to be encouraging and told him of all the preparations made for him by many people in Manndalen Valley.

"We want to make you as happy as possible"

"And you will have a mattress! Well, maybe not as good as in Grand Hotel in Oslo. But the birch branches are braided with love and we think you will be comfortable."

Jan forced a smile. The last thing he wanted to do was to hurt these generous people. But the truth was he had given up.

The five hour descent from Avzevaggi to the cave in Skaidijonni was torturous for both Jan and the Manndalen men. His painful feet, made worse when the sleigh hung almost vertically downward, were unbearable. He was frozen and hungry but unable to eat. And the Manndalen men were tested to the limit as they inched their way down over the craggy, slippery outcrops struggling to handle Jan and the sled with care to minimize his pain and discomfort.

Once they had come down the precipitous mountain in the north, they came directly upon a gentler birch-forested downgrade. It brought them to the edge of another steep incline where the Manndalen River in the valley bottom bordered the bold-faced mountain on the other side. At the edge of the downgrade, a thirty-foot perpendicular gradient led them down to a three-foot wide shelf. They traversed carefully, clinging to dwarfed birch trunks so as not to slip with the sled over the narrow shelf and down into the river far below. The narrow path turned slightly to the left and about another sixty feet ahead was the opening to the cave.

Jan's spirit was bankrupt of hope. *Livsgleden*, the joy of life, had come to naught. Everything seemed futile and he did not care what happened anymore. He allowed his friends to make all the decisions and he let them transport him wherever they wished. Did it really matter? Everyone now knew he would never experience Sweden and freedom again. He pitied his friends who had cared and slaved for him, knowing their dream for him could never be.

Entrance to the cave in Skaidijonni.
The Manndalen River is down the incline on the left.

CONCEALED IN A CAVE
IN SKAIDIJONNI

Skaidijonni, May 11, 1943: Jan was taken to the Skaidijonni cave. The cave had been formed from a large crevice in the interior of the mountain, and it was high enough that a grown person could almost stand upright. It was twenty feet long and had two apertures; the first was within a few feet of the thirty-foot incline they had brought Jan down. This gap was the smallest and most difficult to use as an entrance. At the opening in the lower end, huge boulders formed a natural camouflage in such a way that it was impossible to discover the cave until one was right on top of it.

The roomy cave would be a good shelter from the spring storms. Jan's helpers also felt it was a secure place away from the Nazis. From his bed he had a partial view of the sky and some trees growing near, and from the opening in the back, shafts of light entered the cave. There was room to lay his clothes on the rocks to dry, and when his helpers came, there was enough space for a couple of them to sit on the rock close by him.

The day after Jan was taken to the cave, Peder Isaksen and Aslak Fosvoll made the trip from Manndalen to bring him food and other provisions. Aslak looked forward to meeting the soldier he had heard so much about.

Peder introduced Aslak to Jan. The two men instantly connected. Peder had warned Aslak about Jan's condition, but Aslak was still shocked to see how scrawny and sickly Jan looked with his sunken cheeks and eyes ringed in black.

The upper entrance to the cave in Skaidijonni.

*Author Astrid Karlsen Scott inside the cave. Jan lay close to the left
wall with his feet toward the left corner of the picture.*

"If you have a wish or a need, please don't hesitate to let me know," Aslak offered.

"Thanks, I appreciate it, but my needs are filled with this great bed and sheltered cave."

"We brought clean clothes for you, and we'll help you get cleaned up if you wish."

"It will be good to be clean and dry. Thanks!"

Already a good night's rest had strengthened Jan, and the care given and the kindnesses shown him brought hope back again in small doses.

Aslak helped Jan remove his dirty socks, but the one on his wounded foot was bonded to scabs and dried up blood clinging to his foot – the skin was bluish-black. In Avzevaggi Jan had become aware that what was left of his toes had rotted away. Without a moment's hesitation, Jan took his knife from his pocket and cut off the tissue that clung to the sock and the extra scar tissue left on his foot. He did it without a word.

Aslak and Peder realized Jan was a remarkable man, uncommon in his capacity to tolerate pain and to survive traumatic experiences. They also realized his unique ability to make necessary decisions even in his wretched condition, and to cope with burdens too heavy for many.

They observed how seriously ill he was and wondered how to best handle the crisis. Somehow they had to find a doctor who could come and help Jan, or at least give them advice.

Once back in Manndalen, Aslak and Peder consulted with teacher Nordnes. Manndalen did not have a doctor. The nearest one, who was known as a patriot, kept an office in Lyngseidet. Nordnes' sister worked for the doctor in his office, which gave Nordnes an idea. One morning Nordnes called in and said his sister was ill and she needed for the doctor to come and give her a check up. The doctor intended to do so, but he missed the ferry.

The following day Nordnes called again and said his sister's condition had taken a turn for the worse, and would he please come quickly? When the doctor received the phone call, he called the sheriff, a Nazi, and asked for permission to take the doctor boat across the fjord to see a sick patient in Manndalen. Gasoline was rationed and the Germans maintained strict control of all the comings and goings. Permission was granted and he was on his way.

The doctor found the school in Manndalen and went straight to teacher Nordnes. He handed the teacher Jan's medication, along with a prescription, in case more was needed. Nordnes was also instructed on how best to treat and care for Jan's feet, and how to wrap them. Jan's helpers took him the medication and cared for his feet, following the doctor's instructions.

In the upper part of Manndalen Valley lived Nils Brustrøm with his wife Signe and their three children. To the south of their Finnish-style cottage, a secluded place quite some distance from the nearest neighbor, the valley stretched upward into the foothills, and steep mountains bordered the narrow plains on each side of the house. The Manndalen River flowed a few feet from the cottage and was filled with salmon. Wild fowl and animals lived in the forest. From time to time, reindeer appeared on the horizon high up in the mountains. For the Brustrøm children the place was pure paradise.

Signe and Nils Brustrøm

One evening, that paradise changed forever. Hanna, the youngest child, was four and a half years old at the time. She remembers how she sat close by her father's chair while he was reading the newspaper by the kerosene lamp. He looked up and said to her mother, "The war is coming closer."

"We had better gather as much food as we can then," answered her mother.

Food had been rationed for some time and commodities were scarce. Some people watched to make sure no one got more than their share.

The war caused many to be covetous. Nils was able to buy some sacks of flour and a few other staples.

Many a night little Hanna woke up to the clatter of knitting needles and saw her mother sitting up in bed knitting mittens, socks, and stockings. Nils caught salmon in the river and they traded it for other staples: sugar, grains, flour, and other foods.

They had a few sheep and cows that gave them milk. Signe churned butter and made cheese and *gomme*. They dried and salted their lamb, and during the summer they picked wild strawberries. When fall came, they roamed through the woods and gathered blueberries and lingonberries. From these, Signe made juice and jam. Since they lived close to the wilderness and were an industrious family, they were better off than many, and shared generously with others.

The war moved steadily closer to their valley. When Jan Baalsrud was brought to the cave in Skaidijonni, Nils Brustrøm became involved with helping him, and he began to disappear from the house at regular intervals. Signe constantly prepared food. Hanna's mother stood by the kitchen counter, which was just about Hanna's eye level, pouring food into the transport pails. Nils took the pails and skied up into the valley, sometimes toward the south, other times toward the east up the mountainside, and now and again he crossed the fields straight toward the steep mountain to the west of the valley. It was all a decoy to fool anyone who might see him. The food and provisions were taken to Jan in the cave.

Nils was among the group of helpers that regularly visited Jan with food and other supplies. He was an energetic and happy fellow who loved to tell stories and sing all types of songs both for his family and for Jan. His bright outlook on things was a boon to Jan's sagging spirit and loneliness.

Signe became known as "the cook," since she cooked most of Jan's food. Several other women in the valley helped with the cooking or brought their food to her to be cooked, but Signe prepared it all for transport, and Jan was the grateful recipient. They gave him of the best they had, soups made from fish, dried meat, salted lamb, milk and homemade breads.

Jan expressed concern to his helpers that he was taking the food away from the children and that he would be happy with *fiskesø*, the water that the fish was cooked in. They assured him they had enough to go around.

The helpers liked to have two men go together for safety, but sometimes Nils went by himself. During those times he spent a little extra time visiting with Jan. They talked about family and the news of the war and everyday things. From time to time Nils and the other helpers brought Jan *ukeblader*, weekly magazines, or books to shorten the hours when he was alone. And Nils taught Jan some lively songs, making their times together memorable.

Typically the trip up and back from the cave took about four hours from the Brustrøm house. For safety the trips were most often taken late in the evening, and these excursions often lasted the whole night through.

It was rough and dangerous terrain and provisions hampered their progress occasionally. Usually the helpers took a path close along the out-of-the-way river until they reached just below the cave, where they secured their skis in the snow by the river's edge, then climbed the steep slope up to the cave.

Jan always looked forward to hearing the helpers call out the password, "Hello Gentleman!"

"Hello, hello!"

He was armed since he never knew who might be calling on him. When he heard someone coming he became tense and alert. One could never be sure that the enemy had not followed and spied on his helpers. Jan's gun was beginning to rust because of his swim in the salt water at Toftefjord.

"Nils what are the chances that you can restore this gun?"

"I would think they are pretty good," Nils winked at his friend. He took it home, cleaned and polished the gun and brought it back. Jan's happy countenance when he saw the gun was reward enough for Nils.

"Tusen, tusen takk!" Thousands and thousands of thanks!

When Jan's helpers left, he listened to the last sound of their movements until the stillness of the vast wilderness blended with his own solitude. The sounds of the wind rustling the trees around the cave and the Manndalen River babbling below lightened his burden. A fondness for the place and its people was kindled and Jan felt a new desire to live emerge from somewhere deep within.

Jan had a lot of time to think and often rehashed the events which led to *Brattholm's* mission.

Jan thought of what a difference Eskeland, Blindheim, Salvesen, and he could have made toward the war effort with their planned sabotage actions against the German installations had they not been betrayed. The soldier wanted another chance to fight the Germans. He had to get to Sweden and then back to England. He was beginning to trust that the Manndalen people would be able to get him the rest of the way to freedom, and then he would fight again.

The Germans had an inkling that secret activities were taking place in the inner Troms District, but they had never been able to pin them down. Periodically they sat for hours in secluded areas with their binoculars, scouting for fugitives on their way to Sweden.

One morning, German soldiers crowded into the little Brustrøm house in the upper Manndalen Valley. They had come to arrest Nils but he had gone to take food to Jan with Olav Fossum. When the soldiers spoke to the children in broken Norwegian, the children pretended to not understand them. Signe was told to go and milk the cows. She protested and said they had been milked a short while ago and that there was no more milk. One of the officers reached for his gun belt. Signe grabbed a pail and ran down by the fence to milk the cows. The Germans drank the unstrained hot milk as fast as she could milk it. She was forced to pull the udders until every drop of milk was gone and the animals became fidgety.

Olav's father, Ole, was visiting the Brustrøm farm. In the confusion, he slipped away unnoticed on horseback. He galloped along the river until he reached the valley floor where he knew Nils and Olaf would be returning. On a piece of birch bark he wrote, either in Sami or Finnish, a warning that the Germans were approaching. Nils and Olav discovered the bark and hid in the thick forest. A short while later they heard the Germans as they passed them on the way up the valley. The Germans never returned to look for Nils.

To secure food for Jan every day and to bring him clean and dry clothes was a big operation. His helpers felt that it was important that they stay awhile to break the monotony for him. All involved had their assigned work. They were careful not to send the same people through the valley every day, eliminating the cause for suspicion.

Not only did the men in Manndalen contribute to Jan's welfare but the women did as well. In addition to Helene Mikalsen, who wove the coverlets for Jan, and Signe Brustrøm, who became known as the "cook," there was Eliva, who later married Peder Isaksen. She was a courageous and trustworthy woman who knew about the operation all along and supported the men, as well as helped to obtain food and to cook.

And there were Marie Olsen, Olaf Olsen's sister, and Marie Holm down in Samuelsberg, a small hamlet in Manndalen. She and her husband had run a small grocery store together. When he died, she continued on alone. She was a tremendous help in gaining access to groceries so that the women could prepare food for Jan.

Together with several other women, they all participated in this dangerous work, always performed in secret. A slip of the tongue, one false move, and all their work could unravel before their eyes. The whole village could be burned to the ground.

Isak Solvang

Peder Pedersen

Marie Fossen Olsen

Nils Nilsen

Marie Holm

Eliva (Hansen) Isaksen

At left: Helene Mikalsen and her three children, Magne, Anton and Ella.

At right: The Nilsen brothers. From left: Nigo, Ole and Hans.

the sheriff's assistants

Lyngseidet, May 1943: The tranquil village of Lyngseidet reposes amidst small farms and mountain slopes on three sides; to the west it fringes Lyngenfjord. It is the largest and most populated village in the area, and until the war, a place where tourists loved to come.

During the war, Lyngseidet swarmed with Germans. They were quartered at the village's two schools.

While Jan lay hidden in the cave at Skaidijonni, knowledge of him and the activities surrounding him had somehow seeped out. No one to this day knows how it came about.

Nonetheless, one day during May 1943, a black-clad lady was aboard one of the local ferries writing a letter. When finished, she quickly sealed and stamped it and dropped it in the ferry's mailbox.

The next day a letter arrived at the sheriff's office in Lyngseidet. Three men worked in the office – the sheriff, who was a Nazi, and his assistants, Halvard Halden and Hans Larsen.

On this particular day the sheriff was out of the office when the mail arrived. The two assistants noted the letter that had no return address and had been posted on the ferry. They became suspicious and discussed back and forth how to handle it.

Halvard Halden, one of the sheriff's assistants.

Halvard asked, "What shall we do with this letter?"

"Let's open it," said Hans.

"You know the consequences?"

"*Jaja.* Open it!"

Carefully they opened the letter and removed it contents. They huddled together. It read:

Dear Sheriff,

I want to inform you of a happening in Manndalen, which should be of great interest to you.

Somewhere in the Skaidijonni Mountains, I have been told, a wounded English soldier lies in a cave. Several men and women in Manndalen are nursing him back to health. Daily they take turns bringing him food and provisions.

I believe I know who some of them are and will be happy to share this information with you.

Sincerely,

Fru. ………………….

The two men fell silent and still.

"The sheriff must not see this letter," said Halvard.

"You're absolutely right!" answered Hans.

"Let's take a moment to get our wits about us."

It was a rather chilly day and the black wood burning stove in the corner crackled cheerfully. The same thought occurred to each of them and they nodded to each other.

"Let's burn it!"

"If we do, we must act as if such a letter never arrived in this office."

"I know nothing."

The flames instantly engulfed the letter. Nothing more was heard from the mysterious writer.

The spontaneous, daring decision made by the two patriotic men, Halvard Halden and Hans Larsen, saved Jan Baalsrud and many men and women in Manndalen from certain death. Since so many in Manndalen were involved, many people would have been executed and most likely the village would have been burned to the ground.

Ironically, in the fall of 1944 when the Germans retreated from the Troms District, they followed a "scorched earth" policy. Tore Hauge says in his book, *They Burned Our Homes,* "No one believed that Manndalen would be burned and it came as a shock to all. But the Germans systematically went to work with their gas cans and matches! Within a few days Manndalen was no more."

The one thing the people of Manndalen could be grateful for, despite the suffering and heartache the people endured, was that no lives were lost. And they had the inner satisfaction of having played a major role in Norway's longest escape story from World War II.

None of Jan's benefactors in Manndalen knew anything about the letter. But they were concerned about people noticing the many trips the helpers made up into the mountains, always with filled knapsacks.

Far up in the valley there lived a man who liked to talk. He freely conversed with anyone on any subject, and especially about things which were not his business. It was obvious to Jan's helpers that he was a dangerous man. One of the resistance men, Ludvik Nilsen, visited his home one day for the purpose of getting this man to keep his mouth shut.

"I have learned that you spread rumors about things that are not your business," said Ludvik.

Ludvik Nilsen

"When the sheriff and the Germans come to question you, I am telling you here and now what you are to say. Listen carefully, and then repeat after me verbatim. If you say as much as one word that I have not instructed you, I will return with some men. Your days will be numbered!"

An angry Ludvik dictated, and the man repeated sentence after sentence, verbatim. The man clearly understood what Ludvik meant.

In spite of all the careful planning, the rumors of all the trips the men in the village were making further up into Manndalen still reached Sheriff Marvold's ears in Birtavärre from other sources. Sheriff's assistant Hans Larsen was asked to make the trip across the fjord to Manndalen to try and find the cause of the rumors. According to the rumors, Peder Isaksen was one who had to be investigated.

Hans Larsen came to Peder's home. "Do you know Aslak Fossvoll, Peder Isaksen?"

"Yes, I know Aslak, at least well enough so that when we meet, we visit for a minute or two."

"I have heard that the two of you go into the mountains from time to time. I am not sure what you do up in the mountains, but I assume that you are hunting for the mentally ill man that disappears in the mountains from time to time? Is that right?"

Hans Larsen was a good man and did not want Peder to get in any trouble. Hans was suspicious that Peder was involved in something top-secret, but he tried to help him out of the tough spot by planting another thought in his mind.

"You are right," Peder said. "We continually have to go hunting for the deranged man that disappears all the time."

The sheriff's assistant was satisfied. Once again he had saved Manndalen from a catastrophe.

The village buzzed with whispered rumors. Some guessed some things were going on, others knew. The situation worsened when two quislings from Lyngseidet arrived a couple of days after the sheriff's assistant had been in Manndalen. They came hunting fugitives. They requisitioned a horse down in the valley and started on their way.

What could have been a bad day for Manndalen gave the village people a story to chuckle over for some time.

A young girl was coming down the road, and the quislings asked her for directions to one of the people they planned to interrogate.

"Don't ask me. I don't know anything. I am just a child," the girl said and skipped away.

Next they met an elderly lady on her way to the store. They stopped her and asked if she knew an Olav Olsen. He had escaped from a German camp in Skibotn.

"No. I have lived in this village all my life, but I am not familiar with that name."

The woman was Olav Olsen's mother.

The men continued upwards into the valley and came to a small farm where a man was sawing wood. On one of his feet he had a boot and on the other a *kommag,* a soft boot made of reindeer hide and worn by the Sami. The man was known in the village as a man who was a little confused and muddled.

"We understand you have several sons. Where are they?" the quislings asked.

"*Ja,* I have five sons, and they have all escaped to Sweden. Soon I will follow them." The man was a bachelor and did not have any children.

The men continued up into the valley to find the man who was the easy talker (the same man whom Ludvik Nilsen had visited with a warning). The man himself was not home, but his wife was. The quislings asked when she expected him home.

"That man is crazy, and there is no reason to question him," she said. "He just talks nonsense, and he can be real dangerous if he is pressed. If you're wise you will think twice before you interrogate him," she continued.

The quislings decided to call it a day. They returned the horse to the owner and they confided to him that they thought most of the people in Manndalen were screwballs.

The Brustrøm's home.

*The old wood-burning stove on which
Signe Brustrøm cooked Jan's meals.*

DO NOT ASK ME THIS

Following one of his pleasant visits with Jan, Nils Brustrøm was about to leave the cave.

"What can I bring you the next time I come, Jan?"

"I am remembering Signe's delicious fish soup, maybe with a couple of nibbles of meat?"

"No problem."

"And…" For a split second Jan hesitated.

"Yes Jan? You know we will try and do anything for you."

Jan looked at him pensively.

"Will you cut my rotten toes off?"

Nils' face paled. His mind raced. Speech left him. He just stared at this ill, suffering man who needed help. He weighed it all in his mind. Several times. Quietly he spoke up.

"Oh, Jan! You know I'll do anything for you. But please… don't ask me this. I don't have the heart."

"It's okay. But you'll bring me a sharp sheath knife then?"

"I'll do it."

Nils reflected upon the reason Jan wanted a sharp knife while he plodded homeward along the river. He had no problems guessing how he would use it. Jan soon had both his wishes fulfilled. Nils brought both the delicious fish soup and the sheath knife on his next visit.

Jan devoured the soup with gusto. Both Nils and the other Manndalen men had noticed how Jan, almost imperceptibly, was gradually gaining strength and becoming healthier and more jovial every day. Nils watched him with satisfaction. It was good to see their labors paying off with such a meaningful dividend, though they all realized he was still a very sick man.

Their friendly visit ended, and when Nils parted with Jan, he left the sharp knife.

On his way down from the mountain Nils spotted a German patrol coming up the valley. How could he get out of this tight spot? There was no easy way to explain what errand he had been on - and what about his tracks? He grappled for a solution.

The war had taught Nils to be extremely resourceful. Quickly he removed his knapsack and the transport pail and buried them in a snow heap. He owned a small section of the forest and he started searching for a nice size willow tree. Finding one, he chopped it down, tied it to the rope he always carried with him, and dragged it behind him erasing his own ski tracks. Then he set his path straight in the direction of the Germans.

They saw him coming and the lieutenant raised his arm and signaled him to stop.

"What is your errand here in the woods?" he questioned in broken Norwegian.

Nils smiled with questioning eyes as he studied them. He turned and looked at the tree then turned back and looked at them. Pointing to the tree, and acting somewhat amazed at the question, Nils said, "Surely, you can see for yourselves? I am bringing some nourishment to my sheep. They love the willow bark."

The Germans huddled together in conversation. Nils grew concerned. He could see they were suspicious. A thought hit him like a lightning bolt.

"Follow me to my farm if you have doubts. It is close by. Then you may see for yourself."

The Germans joined him as he moved further down in the valley, away from Jan's cave and toward the Brustrøm farm. Nils gloated inside, thinking what a curious sight they made – him dragging a willow tree and behind him following seven German soldiers on skis with their rifles hung loosely over their shoulders.

Once back at the farm, Nils removed the rope and cut some of the branches off the tree. Luckily for him the sheep gathered quickly as he spread the limbs out on the ground. They wasted no time before they nibbled at the boughs.

"Sehr gut, sehr gut!" Very good, Very good!
The Germans' suspicions had been laid to rest.

Up in the cave Jan made the final plans for his self-operation. What he had started at Hotel Savoy he was about to finish here in the cave in Skaidijonni. As he laid in the open in Avzevaggi, he realized from the feelings in his feet and the stench that the rest of his toes were rotting away. At that time though, Jan was too ill to do anything. He had neither the physical strength nor the unswerving mental resolve needed for such a task.

Over the last few days, though, Jan had been well nursed and fed, and his friends came up from the valley at regular intervals. He was comfortable in his dry bed, and he gained courage and strength from his caring friends. To feel the joy of life return was a source of great encouragement to him. As a result, Jan's basic human character traits also returned.

He clearly understood that the rotten tissue could infect his toes, and this could spread to his lymph glands and cause blood poisoning. He was also fully aware that if blood poisoning set in while he lay here in the cave far away from a doctor's care, he would die.

He knew exactly what to do. Jan had had plenty of time to plan the amputation during the long hours of solitude. He picked up the sharp knife Nils left and started his self-operation anew.

He removed seven toes down by the main joint. The eighth he cut off at the middle joint. The rotten, dead tissue was loosely attached to the knucklebones and just fell off as Jan touched the toes. He was relieved to see the bleeding was not as heavy this time.

Through his ordeals, Jan had become like tempered steel. His conviction that his operation had saved his life strengthened him and left him at peace with himself.

He wrapped his foot in the old rags the men had already brought to the cave and which they used when they changed the bandages on his foot.

Exhausted, Jan lay back on his bed of birch branches. He covered himself up with the wool covering Helene had woven for him. It comforted him.

During the quiet moments that followed, his mind wandered backward in time, which it so often did at these times of solitude. The saboteurs' mission to stop the German bombing of the convoys to the Soviet Union had failed. Jan sorrowed over the many additional crews who by now had probably lost their lives because of it. When he contemplated the failed mission, his fallen comrades always came to mind. Remembering them, his whole being mourned.

It was unavoidable for Jan to think of his comrades without his thoughts drifting homeward to his family and friends in Oslo. What he would not give to just have one word from them, just to know that they were safe. Missing them, his brother Nils and his sister Bitten, made his solitude especially agonizing.

As he lay distressing, he earnestly sought to cope with his physical pain, sorrow and isolation. As so often before, Jan became aware of the wind rustling the trees on the mountainside near to the cave and the murmuring river at the valley bottom—and his spirit calmed.

chE GERMADS iD pURSUic

Nearly two weeks had passed since Hjalmar and Nils' unsuccessful attempt to find Jan.

One evening, Petter Pettersen, an employee at the Bjørns' store, came to Hjalmar with another urgent message for him to meet the brothers at their store. He learned that Jan had been moved to the east side of lower Manndalen Valley, and he was still awaiting transport.

"Will you be willing to take on the assignment one more time?"

"Of course I will." Hjalmar was not a man to say no when he was needed.

That same night he was on his way up Ankerlia Mountain, staying hidden in the forest behind the German hut. On his last trip he had concealed his skis above the tree line. The snow on the mountainside was wet and heavy, but on the upland the ski conditions were good. He needed to reach the Siri brothers before sun-up, and he only stopped once to rest.

Per and Nils Siri greeted him with the usual Sami friendliness. Nils expressed concern about taking on the assignment to transport Jan this late in the season. The ice on the river bordering Sweden was no longer safe and the road above Kilpis in Finland lay wide open for long stretches. Several German military movements had been seen from time to time.

"I recently crossed over to Sweden with seven fugitives," Hjalmar explained. "We were told the Germans military movements usually come in convoys, and far between."

"Well, let's get a map out and see how we can do this then," Nils ventured.

They mapped the route across occupied Norway and Finland and on into neutral Sweden. Out of necessity they sometimes had to cross the wide-open spaces, but whenever possible, they mapped the way through thickets and shrubs.

Nothing but the strongest and fastest reindeer would do. Their trained eyes picked out two of the best among the many.

Early in the morning they harnessed the reindeer to the *pulk*, and each man crawled into his canoe-shaped sled. With good snow conditions holding, they made excellent time and were ahead of schedule. They even had time to eat and relax a little while the reindeer grazed along the way. As they neared the plateau above Manndalen, a flock of about thirty reindeer and some men came into view in the distance. They hurried onward to see who it might be.

Coming closer, they noticed two Sami sleds. The men were running back and forth into the tent. One man in one of the sleds seemed to be getting all the attention. Hjalmar stopped a little ways off while Nils continued on so he could talk with the men. The sled with the man who had drawn all the attention was put in the center of the reindeer flock. Another Sami climbed into the *pulk* with him. Then the entourage of sleds, reindeer and barking dogs began to move.

Somewhat bewildered, Nils returned to Hjalmar to explain.

"One of the men in those sleds is Jan Baalsrud. Aslak and Per Thomas Baal are bringing him to Sweden."

Nils and Hjalmar were astounded. Extremely disappointed, after their best efforts, their many hours of struggles came to naught. Yet in the midst of their discontent they were gratified that Jan had been taken care of and was on his way to Sweden.

The friends shook hands and said farewell to one another. Nils took the reindeer and the sleds and headed east, and Hjalmar noticed the early morning glow of the sun as he attached his skis and headed for home.

Before reaching Kåfjordalen Valley he hid his skis among the trees in Ankerlia Mountain and trudged the rest of the way home. His mother awoke as he entered. By the time he had cleaned up and changed into clean clothes, his mother had breakfast ready for him. He shared the happenings of the last few hours with her and then went to bed in his room in the attic.

Hjalmar had no sooner pulled the covers up when he heard the sound of a motorcycle. It puzzled him. There were connecting roads between Kåfjorddalen to Birtavärre, but none to Olderdalen. Whoever the visitor was, he must have come by boat and motorcycled from the docks up to his home. Hjalmar jumped out of bed and ran to the window. He stiffened as he saw a motorcycle with a sidecar. Two German soldiers walked toward the house and another stood watch by the motorcycle.

Hjalmar jumped into his clothes, grabbed the inner works of the Tandberg battery-super-radio and stuffed it in his jacket. Downstairs loud German voices mingled with his mother's calm voice. Concerned the old floor would creak, he stood as if nailed to the floor for a few seconds. Like a prowling cat, he moved quietly down the steps toward the first floor. His mother and the Germans were now in the living room and he snuck out the front door where the third soldier still held his gun ready by the motorcycle. Though Hjalmar's body felt like a tightrope, he nonchalantly walked toward the barn, hid the radio works in the corner of one of the horse stalls and kicked some hay over it. He came back out and again moved unhurriedly toward the summer barn that lay 120 feet closer to the edge of the forest. While walking this distance, he was within open view of the German guard. He continued in the direction of the forest and sprinted toward the trees as fast as he was able. In the outlying fields there was a hay barn well hidden by the trees. He prepared himself a bed in the hay. Lying there he finally began to relax and fell asleep.

After many hours of sleep he awoke in the middle of the night. His thoughts wandered and he realized what peril he had been in. Had he been arrested and brought in for interrogation and torture, the whole Baalsrud affair might have unraveled. He shuddered at the ghastly circumstances that would have followed, and how many people might have suffered.

His concern grew as he thought of his mother. Had the Germans arrested her? He left the hay barn and carefully moved from the forest toward the farmyard staying extremely alert to his surroundings. He crawled through a window in the back of the house and found his mother still in bed.

The Germans had ransacked every room in the house including the attic. They had opened every closet and searched through every drawer.

"Who else lives here?" the Germans asked.

"I have a husband and a son, but both have been called to work for the Germans in the district of Finnmark (the neighboring district). They very seldom get leave to come home," Hjalmar's mother had told them.

Hjalmar shared the experience of his escape and how he had slept in the summer barn. His mother had only one comment, "The one God wants to preserve is without danger."

Hjalmar knew the only way the Germans had been able to come to Kåfjord with the motorcycle was by boat. He also realized there must have been rumors about Jan Baalsrud and that someone had revealed that Hjalmar had a part in the affair. It was obvious that they had come to pick him up. For now he had been able to escape, and Jan Baalsrud was on his way toward safety in Sweden. Once again, Jan's benefactors were a step ahead of the Gestapo.

EN ROUTE TO FREEDOM

Jan had been in the Skaidijonni cave for seventeen days. In Avzevaggi his life had hung by a fragile thread. The intent of the people of Manndalen had been to nurture him back to a better physical condition. They never wavered in their purpose, but they gave so much more. Daily the men trudged the five miles through the rugged snow-covered terrain to bring him nourishing food prepared lovingly by their women, dry clothes, medical supplies, and reading material. More importantly, they brought him the commodity he needed most of all, the comfort and warmth of their own spirits. They nurtured him back to life by giving him of their time, friendship and their selfless love.

It was now the end of May, and time was running out. The warmth of the midnight sun was melting the snow cover. Jan had to be moved before the good snow conditions disappeared.

Manndalen, Thursday, May 28, 1943: Without notice, a man appeared in the lower Kjerringdal Valley in Manndalen. He was Aslak Baal, one of the two Sami brothers whom Nigo had contacted on his 80 mile round trip to Sweden on May 5.

Aslak's brother, Per Thomas, had remained up on the plateau making ready to bring the soldier across the border. They believed they had found a way to fool the German border guards and were now willing to take the risk to bring Jan to Sweden.

Sami Aslak Baal

Sami Per Thomas Baal

Five men, Aslak Fossvoll, Nigo Nilsen, Hans Nilsen, Isak Solvang and Nils Brustrøm made their way up to Jan's cave during the night of May 28. They carried long ropes to help them with the steep climb to take Jan up to the plateau to meet the Baal brothers. Jan had little desire to leave the safety of the cave and the comfort of his friends' love to face another horrendous climb and uncertainty up on the plateau.

"Is it possible to postpone the leaving a day or two?" he asked.

"Jan this is your chance for freedom. We have to grab it."

Jan knew his friends were right, and he mustered his courage. "I'm ready."

They carried him out to the waiting sled, and again he was securely strapped down.

The memory of the prior suffering he had endured on the sled was still vivid. Jan did his best not to let the others know the fear that abruptly gripped him and nearly overwhelmed him.

The exhausting climb took several hours and morning had dawned when they reached the plateau. Three of the Manndalen men felt the need to leave right away, because all were concerned that someone would start to ask too many questions. The emotional farewell was difficult for all of them.

"The day we hear you are safely in Sweden will be a special day for all of us here in Manndalen, Jan."

"Thank you. I am looking forward to it, but I will miss all of you good people."

They tried to be jovial. "All the women wanted to come up to the plateau to see you off. But we felt someone needed to mind our homes and the youngsters." Everyone laughed.

"Take care, Jan. We're going to miss you dreadfully."

"After this atrocious war is over, you've got to come back to Troms. We'll throw a party out in the open!"

"I look forward to that. How do I thank all of you? Please take care and be safe," said Jan. His voice trembled with emotion. As he said farewell to his rescuers, his eyes grew moist. These people had given so much to him, a stranger. They had given him shelter and food. And they'd given him friendship and hope.

"You too, dear friend. Have a safe journey." They all shook his hand. Jan was unable to do anything but whisper, "*Tusen, tusen...tusen takk,*" Thousands and thousands and thousands of thanks.

The men started down toward Manndalen.

May 29, 1943: Jan remained in the mountains with Aslak Baal, Nils Brustrøm and Nigo Nilsen.

Per Thomas went to gather the reindeer flock. The reindeer would follow Jan all the way to the border. Jan would be hidden in the midst of them and the animals would be his shield and erase the tracks from his *pulk.*

During the night, Jan was brought into the Baal's *laavo,* their Sami tent, to get some good sleep before the final journey.

Saturday, May 30, 1943: In the early morning hours, Aslak and Per Thomas Baal dressed Jan in the traditional Sami fur winter clothing with its bright colorful trimmings of red, yellow, white and cornflower blue. They placed a Sami hat on his head; typical of the Finnish and Norwegian Sami, with four floppy points, it was known as the "hat of the four winds."

The vast white tundra stretched out before them. Jan was tense and fearful that the German patrols would discover them.

"Don't you worry, Jan. We will get you safely to Sweden this time."

Aslak and Per Thomas had their carbine rifles hidden at the bottom of their *pulks.*

"If the Germans should approach us, would you use that gun, Aslak?"

"Absolutely! I will not only shoot, but I will hit my mark as well. Remember, I have been shooting reindeer for years."

"If you should have to kill some Germans and you returned safely to Norway, are you not afraid they will come chasing you?"

"Maybe so, but don't forget Jan, we live in the mountains a lot."

Around 2 a.m. on May 31, the men placed Jan, too ill to manage a pulk by himself, with Per Thomas. The men left their encampment and headed south. At this time of the night the snow was at its firmest and they could make better time. The midnight sun had returned to northern Norway on May 21 and would not set again until July. There was no darkness.

Sitting low in his *pulk,* with Per Thomas, Jan was surrounded by reindeer nostrils snorting hot breath at top speed. The reindeer spread their sure feet wide. Close to Jan's head, their pounding hooves whipped the snow into a small blizzard. Above the snow Jan saw nothing but bouncing reindeer horns, which resembled thick bare tree branches enduring a snowstorm.

The first stretch of their journey brought them to Didnojarvi Lake, about midway between the Manndalen plateau and the Swedish border. They rested here and gathered a few roots to build a fire for their black coffee pot. They also heated up some broth that they enjoyed with some heavy rye bread. The entourage had been able to maintain a nice speed, making good time and they decided to rest out the day in the higher elevation.

Up on the highest plateau, the snow conditions were best and they had a good overview of their surroundings. The reindeer would have a chance to rest and eat before the final push across the border. They expected to cross into Sweden under good conditions in the early morning hours. The men reasoned they had about another four hours or so to travel before they reached the border.

The sun had been dazzling throughout their journey, making the snow crystals sparkle like highly polished diamonds. The unending white upland shimmered. When Aslak gathered roots for the fire for late afternoon-coffee he suddenly went snow blind. The intense pain made him unable to scoop up the snow for the coffee pot. Jan knew well what his friend was experiencing and was filled with empathy.

The three men discussed this new development. Per Thomas said if they were going to get Jan across the border, they had to continue as planned, and leave Aslak behind. Per Thomas would come for him on the way back. Aslak fully agreed, though Jan felt terrible about the situation.

June 1, 1943: The next morning at two, Jan and Per Thomas readied to leave. The snow conditions were holding good and the wind was tolerable. This close to the Finnish border they were nearing the danger zone. The German patrols were stationed within close vicinity of each other and they were on the alert for fugitives.

It was a difficult time for Jan in light of the physical suffering and loneliness he had endured during the last two months, and all that his helpers had sacrificed. Would it now all come to naught as they neared the border?

"Per Thomas, if the Germans come, we cannot, under any circumstances, be taken prisoners." Jan fondled his gun.

"I understand. Take my gun Jan, it is better than yours." He dug out the carbine rifle from the bottom of his *pulk*, and they exchanged weapons.

"And here is my knife. It is sharp and will cut straight through!" He handed Jan the knife.

The men agreed that if a situation should arise where there was no hope for them, Jan should first shoot Per Thomas and then himself. With mixed feelings Jan and Per Thomas left Aslak behind. A mixture of emotions swept over all three of them. They were so close, and yet they could not predict what the next few hours held in store for them.

"På gjensyn," so long, a somber Jan waved, but Aslak could not see.

Coming from the east, they continued south down Sørhellinga toward the lower plateau. In the early morning the reindeer herd reached Lake Coahppejåvri where they stopped for their last rest near the Finnish border. They left the reindeer herd. From here on it would only be Per Thomas and Jan in the one pulk and three of the strongest and fastest reindeer bucks. The third reindeer was brought in case an accident should happen to one of the others.

The two men descended around the Saana Mountain's extended valley. Lake Kilpisjårvi, the last stretch of the crossover to Sweden, was in sight. The men's nerves were taut. Only a few miles to freedom, surely they would make it now. Per Thomas bore down on the bucks; they whizzed headlong across the snow.

Shots rang out!

Again and again the shots flew through the air. Jan twisted around to get a look. "They will never catch us Per Thomas, they are too far behind!"

"May you be right!"

Per Thomas walloped the reindeer with his whip and they lurched forward at breakneck speed.

They came out by Saamivaarat on the Finnish side of the border. A short distance away flowed a brook with a bridge crossing over.

"The Germans have a patrol station close to that bridge," Per Thomas shouted over the pounding hooves.

The Germans, some distance behind them, kept firing as they sped across the snow. "They're lousy skiers!" Per Thomas shouted. He had observed the guards skiing on previous trips.

He set course for the frozen Lake Kilpisjårvi and whooshed onto and over a narrow protruding headland. Another short distance on the lake and they would be in Sweden.

"Freedom! Freedom Jan! You are right, they *could not* catch us!"

Overwrought with emotion, Jan covered his face in the fur raiment. His body trembled.

Per Thomas took Jan to the home of his Sami friends, the brothers Per and Aslak Juhso in Kommavopio, Sweden. From here the brothers took him to Sweden's northernmost farm in Keinovopio, where the August Jensen family warmly received him. These hospitable people had helped many a fugitive in the past.

Jan was tended and fed before he was placed in a sleeping bag, lifted into a riverboat, and carefully tied down. The boat rode low in the water and they wanted him secure. Two men sat in the bow and two in the stern; each rowed with one oar. They followed the river along the Finnish border-river Konkama down to Saarikoski. The rowers had a difficult time maneuvering the strong current between the ice floe and rocks. Jan did not like this trip; he felt uneasy tied down and unable to move. After all he had experienced, he feared that this river trip would not have a happy ending.

The boat made its way through many obstacles until it reached Saarikoski, where the Konkama River widened and turned into a narrow lake. A seaplane had been called in and was on its way. The frozen-over river had to be cleared of ice to enable the plane to land.

Dr. Englund from Vittange, Sweden had been brought in earlier to watch over Jan and he stayed with him while several men worked to keep the ice from closing in.

The plane came in low, landed without mishap and Jan was put aboard. The men had to work quickly - the river was icing up fast and all involved were nervous. A disaster seemed imminent. But the pilot, Norberg, was well seasoned and he pulled the plane up at the last second. He and his navigator, Arne Sundquist, flew to Boden in northwest Sweden, where an ambulance was waiting.

Boden Gardisjon Hospital was under blackout during the night because of the war in neighboring Norway. Nurse Barbro Morin was on duty. A message had preceded Jan, that a fugitive in critical condition would be brought in from Norway sometime during the night.

Jan was lifted from the ambulance onto a stretcher and hurriedly wheeled through the hospital doors down the long, dim corridor. A kerosene lamp burned at the end of the corridor. Barbro Morin watched as Jan was rolled

Nurse Barbro Morin

through the doors. He was lying on his back with his arms under his head. Weary and thin with an ashen face, his long coal-black beard nearly covered all his face but his eyes. He lay there smiling. His chalk-white teeth nearly lit up the corridor.

A robust young soldier when he landed in northern Norway two months earlier, Jan now weighed only 80 pounds.

The attendants unraveled the rags that Jan's feet were wrapped in. Next was a layer of newspapers, a layer of reindeer hair and another layer of newspaper. The stench from his feet nauseated those in attendance. Nurse Barbro and the other hospital personnel were concerned about inflicting pain on Jan as they removed the bandages, but Jan never complained. He only smiled and showed gratitude.

"Don't worry, you won't hurt me."

The condition of his feet was horrid. The putrid smell nearly overwhelmed the nurses. A surgeon with special knowledge in gangrene and transplantation was called in. All were under the watchful eye of Dr. Torben, the hospital's Medical Director. Jan's feet and legs were darkish-blue up to his knees, and his hands were in danger of needing amputation as well, as their color matched his legs and feet.

The doctors told Jan they did not know if they could manage to save his hands and feet, but they would do all they could. They removed as little as possible, then they had to wait and see. The wounds left on the toes Jan himself had amputated were cleaned and trimmed, making them ready for new skin transplantation. Skin from the inside of his thighs was removed to cover the protruding bones on his toes. They healed well and Jan was able to keep the remainder of his feet without further amputation.

"Jan, we had to burn your clothes. They were so filthy they would be impossible to clean. I apologize," the surgeon said when he returned the following day.

"By the way, Baalsrud, while I am here, who amputated your toes? That is one of the finest surgeries I have ever seen."

"Thanks, doctor. I was the surgeon," Jan smiled broadly while the doctor looked at him in stunned silence.

The Swedish police came to question Jan, but the medical director refused because the patient was too weak. Jan was given two weeks, and during this period he prepared his story. The last time he was in Sweden he had been asked to leave and he now decided to tell his story as it was. In the meantime he called the Norwegian consulate in Stockholm and let them know one man from M/K *Brattholm* had survived.

During the several weeks Jan recuperated in the Swedish hospital, he faced many emotional struggles. He yearned for his family, yet he could not call them in occupied Norway. Jan also missed his deceased buddies, and often he thought of the many people in Troms who'd helped save his life.

The appreciation he felt for what the Manndalen men and women had done for him held no bounds. Often, in the solitude of the quiet evenings in his hospital bed, he remembered their many kind deeds and words, and their faces came to him one by one – Peder, Nigo, Nils, Olaf. He thought of the many women who had prepared his meals; he might never know who they all were.

Afterward his mind wandered to his dear friends in Furuflaten, Marius, Alvin, Agnete, Ingeborg, Gudrun and all the others who had risked their lives for him.

And then he remembered his fallen comrades again and the horrors that had taken place in Toftefjord - and he anguished.

Even in Toftefjord helping hands had been outstretched toward him, the Idrupsens and the Pedersens. Jan retraced his steps through the mountains and remembered the Heikas and the stalwart Sørensen men, the Løvlis, and dear Peder Nielsen who carried him on his back. And the Samis Aslak and Per Thomas Baal who had snatched him right out of the Germans' grip and gotten him to Sweden.

The list was overwhelming. His heart swelled with gratitude and he cried soundlessly for the love and selflessness that these people had shown him, a total stranger. These stalwart people had risked their own lives and families and their villages and had shared all they had. How could he ever repay them?

The people of Troms had proven to him that evil could never conquer goodness. Hitler's might and the power of his armies, and the horrors of their brutality, were no match against such people. Evil did not have the muscle to crush the goodness and the decency of the people of northern Norway. Jan had seen freedom in their eyes.

In the end, as all through the world's history, he now knew of a surety, that the light of freedom *would* burst forth to dispel the darkness covering Norway. The land and its people, and all the other lands under the Nazi heel would rise again to the sounds of freedom.

Jan had learned firsthand from these simple, courageous people that evil can never be gruesome enough to chill the love of freedom, nor to stifle the inborn love for our fellow man.

> *"YES, WE LOVE THIS LAND*
> *AS IT RISES*
> *FURROWED, WEATHERED,*
> *O'ER THE SEA WITH*
> *THE THOUSAND HOMES..."*
>
> Bjørnstjerne Bjørnson
> Norway's National Anthem

epilogue

Jan Baalsrud's story did not end when he reached freedom in Sweden.

The war's scars stayed with many of those involved throughout the rest of their lives, especially Jan. He had bouts of depression and nightmares, but Jan, determined and courageous, fought back.

When he returned to the Shetland Islands following his convalescence in Sweden, Jan taught marksmanship to the men of the Linge Company. At war's end, he returned to Norway in the Bergen area, and was involved in taking over the Russian prison camps from the Germans. In September of 1945 he left the Navy.

Jan in the Shetland Islands teaching marksmanship.

When Jan's fallen comrades were taken home to their final resting places, Jan traveled to be with each one of them as they were laid to rest.

In 1947 Jan and others originated The Linge Club, and became its first president, a position he held for many years. He was the first honorary member of *Den Norske Krigs Invalid Forbund*, the Norwegian War Invalid Confederation, and president of the same for eight years. Jan also served as vice-president of the World Federation of War Veterans for six years.

Jan was actively involved in the establishment of the Bæreia Veteran Recreation Institution for War Invalids at Kongsvinger. He was awarded Norway's St. Olav's Medal and the Most Excellent Order of the British Empire, MBO.

Jan suffered constant pain in his legs and feet after his ordeal in the Arctic. Because of this, he returned to the hospital each winter for treatment. It became apparent that Norway's cold winters were too difficult for him to tolerate, and he searched for a home in a warmer climate.

In 1951, Jan married Evie Miller, a Scottish lady from New York. They had one daughter, Liv. When Liv was five years old, Evie died.

In 1959 Jan married Terese Balmesita, a Spanish woman, and in 1962 they bought a farm on Tenerife, an island off the north African Coast.

Jan and Terese grew oranges on their farm. When Jan turned 50, his brother Nils Ivar and some friends in Norway sent him three sows and a boar and he became a successful hog farmer.

Jan died of cancer at Bæreia on December 30, 1987. Because of his many hours of service to the Institution, he stayed bedridden at Bæreia without cost for four months prior to his death.

Jan's wish was to be buried among his friends in northern Norway. His ashes were taken to Manndalen and buried with Aslak Fossvoll in his grave.

Tor Knudsen and Kaare Moursund, the Tromsø resistance leaders, were sent to a concentration camp in Germany where they both died.

Jernberg Kristiansen and Sedolf Andreassen, the half brothers from Grøtøy Island who offered to store *Brattholm's* cargo of explosives and other provisions, were tortured and sent to a concentration camp in Germany where they perished.

Edwin Wikan, the policeman who tried to forestall the telephone call about the *Brattholm* men to the Gestapo, today lives on the outskirts of Tromsø. During the war, he was among the many Norwegian policemen who refused to bow to Hitler's regime. In August of 1943, he was sent to a German concentration camp near Stutthof, Poland.

Edwin was freed on May 3, 1945, and returned to his work as a policeman in Tromsø. During the late summer of 1945, he was placed in charge of excavating the *Brattholm* men slain at Grønnåsen Rifle Range.

Peder Nilsen, who in Tyttebærvika waded from the rowboat to the shore with Jan on his back, lives at Herakleum Retirement Home in Tromsø. He is 87 years old.

Following the war, Peder continued his work as a fisherman and a small farmer. He also worked at a fish processing plant until his retirement. After the death of their first son Norman, Peder and his wife had three more children.

On the day of Norway's Liberation, Peder fixed breakfast and brought it to his wife, who was still in bed. That was the first time she learned of Peder's involvement with Jan Baalsrud.

Einar Sørensen, from Bjørnskar, preceded both his wife and father in death. He died on March 24, 1953. Bernhard lived another seven years until February 2, 1960, and Einar's wife Elna lived until June 12, 1990.

Marius Grønvoll and Agnete Lanes married. They had five children and built another house on the Grønvoll farm at Furuflaten. Marius continued to be a leader in his village and went into business with Alvin Larsen. He worked with their company until his death. Agnete still lives at Grønvoll Farm in Furuflaten.

Eliva Hansen and Peder Isaksen were married in October 1943. They had four children. When the Germans scorched the earth in 1944, Peder and Eliva escaped to a mountain cave not far from their home. The Germans did not burn all the homes at the same time. When the Isaksens returned three days later, they found Germans in their home.

One young soldier found the bed that Peder had built very attractive and wanted it. Peder was furious. "That is my bed!" said Peder, as he yanked the linens off and started dismantling the bed. He and Eliva wrapped it carefully and took it, with a few other belongings, aboard the ferry which evacuated the Manndalen people.

When Peder and Eliva returned to Manndalen after the war, they rebuilt their home and Peder continued as a fisherman and small farmer. Because he was a skilled carpenter, he spent many years helping to rebuild Manndalen. Today Eliva and Peder, both 80 years old, live in Manndalen.

Alvin Larsen married his sweetheart Erna Lanes in October 1943. They had eight children. He continued fishing until 1952. Circumstances changed dramatically after the war and fishing became less profitable. With his two brothers and Marius Grønvoll, Alvin started his own construction company, working on projects all over northern Norway. According to Alvin, they "wanted to help rebuild Norway and be able to feed their families." At 82 years old, Alvin is the same jovial fellow and lives in Furuflaten with his wife.

Haakon Sørensen, the merchant from Bromnes, was given twelve years at hard labor for his betrayal. His citizenship was revoked for ten years and he was ordered to pay back the 5000 *kroner* the Gestapo awarded him. Haakon was released after four years in prison. Until his death in 1990, he lived in Bromnes with his wife. They had no children.

For his betrayal, **Sheriff Hoel** of Karlsøy was sentenced to fourteen years at hard labor. His citizenship was revoked for ten years and he was ordered to return the 500 *kroner* the Gestapo had given him. Both the merchant and the sheriff were ordered to pay the court costs. Aldor Ingebrigtsen, a member of the parliament, helped to get Sheriff Hoel's sentence appraised and he was freed in 1950, having served less than half his sentence. He was 88 years old when he died in 1975.

Jan Baalsrud always said, "I am not the hero. The people in Troms are." It was his lifelong wish that all the people who had helped him would be honored. That has been the goal of the co-authors of this book, to honor the unsung heroes of the Troms district. As we do, we are fully aware that there are so many others throughout Norway and the world who willingly sacrifice to help others, and that Jan and his benefactors are only a symbol of those many others.

Jan Baalsrud Foundation
"Many risked their lives and helped one to freedom"

On June 19, 1989 the Jan Baalsrud Foundation was organized. Established as a private foundation, it received public acknowledgement on October 11, 1990 from the Troms District Governor. The foundation is jointly administered between four municipalities, Kåfjord, Storfjord, Karlsøy and Lyngen. Each community is equally represented in the foundation's leadership and the general assembly.

Jan's brother Nils Ivar Baalsrud, co-founder of the foundation, has served either as president and vice-president since the organization's inception.

The foundation has established Jan Baalsrud-Marsjen, a permanent and annual re-creation of Jan's 125-mile trek through the mountains, with historical markers along the route. The Foundation has also established memorials to the M/K Brattholm men; a stone monument in Toftefjord and a monolith and memorial birch grove near the University of Tromsø.

MAP 1— Jan's escape route from Toftefjord to Mikkelvik.

X   *Brattholm explodes*
I   Swim
II   Swim
III Swim
--- Walking
——   By Boat

MAP 2 — Escape route from
Toftefjord to Veggefjord toward
Karanes

X   *Brattholm* explodes

- - - Walking

—   By Boat

HELGØYA

Ramnbergvika
yt Kvalsneset
in Kvalsneset
Kvalnesholmen
Mølnelvvatnet
Goddalsvatnet
Goddals-
skolten
Raudnesskol
Kjerkevika
Kjerkevik
Törnskjeret
Kjerkevik
Nebbeskjeran
Gåsh
Kjerkh
Helgöy
Engholmen
Mölnes
Tuva
Tjavholmen
Helgöy
Skjåhø en
Gauken
esgrunnen
Finnbyskjeran
Storneset
Svartneset
Ytremolnes

H E L G Ø Y S U N D E T

yt Karaneset
Molneset
76
Elvetaren
Finneset
Avløysingsskjeret
Högöya
Hersöygrunnen
Sandbukta
in Kara-
neset
75
Storbukta
Karanes
Hersöygrunn
Karasundet
Dåvöya
Storegrunnen
Vestresidvåg
7A
Lein-
Skarvskjeran
bugen
Ternneset
Reinöytaren
Langstranda
Myrstad
Sjöstrand
73
Svensklubben
Karlsöygrunnen
Avløysnin
Rosinerholmen
36   37   38   39   40
Gammvikneset Gammvik-
Avløys
bukta
72
Gammvikbukta
nnesgrunnen
Svartneset
Gammvik-
Rosinerholmgrunnen
Håka
aksla
Brennesåss
DÅFJORDEN
Hestholman
Sakariasbukta
Håkabytinden
het Gammvik
Storholmen
Langstrandneset
70
Langstrand
Fin
Gammvi
Geitfjellet
Finnelv
Litleholmen
Jettabukta
Gammvikdalen

MAP 3 — Escape route from Veggefjord to Karanes over the mountains toward Dåfjord.

---   Walking

MAP 4 — Escape route from the
mountains to Dåfjord and continuing
over the mountains to Kopparelv.

--- Walking
— By Boat

MAP 5 — Escape route from Kopparelv to Bjørnskar across Grøtsundet Sound to Løvli and into Ullsfjord.

--- Walking
— By Boat

MAP 6 — Escape route from Ullsfjord to Tyttebærvika on to Lyngseidet and up into the mountains.

--- Walking
— By Boat

MAP 7 — Escape route down from the mountains through Lyngsdalen Valley to Furuflaten across Lyngenfjord to Revdal (Hotel Savoy) up to the Gentleman Stone.

X	Avalanche
—	By Boat
---	Walking

O	Hotel Savoy
☐	Gentleman Stone

MAP 8 — Escape route from the Gentleman Stone to where Nigo left for Sweden and Jan was taken to Avzevaggi. Jan was then moved down to the cave in Skaidijonni and finally up into the mountains where the Baal brothers took him toward the Finnish border.

-- - - - Pulled on a sled
——— Transported from the cave
☐ The cave
X Out in the open in Avzevaggi

▶ The Sami camp

MAP 9 — Escape route towards Lake Coahppejåvri across the Finnish border over Lake Kilpisjärvi, into Sweden and freedom.

— The Sami transport

MAP 10 — Jan's escape route from Toftefjord to Saarikoski, Sweden, where he was picked up by seaplane and flown to the hospital in Boden, Sweden.

SOURCES

Documents:

Jan Baalsrud's report, 1943, Norway's Resistance Museum, Oslo, Norway

Krigsdokumenter, 1943 Bundesarchiv, Militaerarchiv, Freiberg, Germany.

Krigsdokumenter, 1943. Prof. Dr. Peter von Rueden, Militaergeschichtliches Forschungsamt, Potsdam, Germany

Operation Instructions for Martin, 20th March,1943

Articles:

"Hallo, Gentleman!" Holger Raste. Jan Baalsrud Festivalen 8 -15. August 1987

Baalsrud flukt over Ringvassøy, Holger Raste Jan Baalsrud Festivalen 8 -15. August 1987

Grene-vevtradisjon i Nord-Troms, Vårt blad, 8/98

Mange av oss ble aldri tatt, Vi Menn, Nr. 13, May 8, 1979, Kjell Fjørtoft

Med Verdens beste kjørerein, Holger Raste, Jan Baalsrud Festivalen, August 8-15, 1987

Rettsreferat, Avisen Tromsø, September, 18-20 1946

Spreng Bardufoss flyplass og Lyngen-ferga, Vi Menn, Nr.13, March 27, 1979, Kjell Fjørtoft

Books:

Årbok for Karlsøy, Ulf L. Vinje, 1996

Bygd og By i Norge,Troms, Gyldendal Norsk Forlag, Oslo, *Under redaksjon av* Ivan Kristoffersen

De brente våre hjem, Nord-Troms Museum, 1995, Tore Hauge
      & Anders Ole Hauglid
Den annen verdenskrig, J.W. Cappelens Forlag, Oslo, 1949,
      Winston S. Churchill
Greneveving, Kåfjord kommune med hjelp av Manndalen
      Husmaflidslag
Kåfjord – mennesker, administrasjon og politikk, Torleif
      Lyngstad
Kompani Linge, Første bind, Gyldendal Norsk Forlag, Oslo
      1949, Erling Jensen, Per Ratvik, Ragnar Ulstein
Kompani Linge, Annet Bind, Gyldendal Norsk Forlag, Oslo
      1949, Erling Jensen, Per Ratvik, Ragnar Ulstein
Lensmen i Karlsøy, Ulf L. Vinje, 1995
Militær motstand i nord 1940 –1945, Universitetsforlaget, 9001
      Tromsø
*Svensketrafikken–3, Flyktningar til Sverige frå Trøndelag og
      Nord-Norge 1940-1945,* Det Norske samlaget,1977,
      Ragnar Ulstein
Våre Falne, Første bok, Bind-1-4, Grøndahl & Sønn, Oslo 1951,
Den Norske Stat

Interviews:

Andersen, Ingeborg, Bø in Vesterålen, Norway
Andreassen, Alvin, Asker, Norway
Antonsen, Hjalmar, Rebbenes, Norway
Bål, Per Gustav, Troms, Norway
Bål, Sigrid, Troms, Norway
Baalsrud, Nils Ivar, Vormsund, Norway
Ballovarre, John Olav, 9147 Birtavärre (in Sami w/Mikkel
      Bongo) Nordisk Samisk Institutt, Kautokeino, July 13,
      1978 Translated to Norwegian by Torleif Lyngstad, April
      1999, Translated to English by Astrid Karlsen Scott
Ballovarre Vilhelm, Kåfjordalen, Norway
Bergmo, Asmund, Olderdalen, Norway
Bergmo, Erling, Birtavärre , Norway
Brustøm, Gudbrand, Manndalen, Norway

Dalhaug, Asbjørn, Furuflaten, Norway
Dalhaug, Lasse, Furuflaten, Norway
Fjørtoft, Kjell, Tromsø, Norway
Grønnslett, Arvid, Rebbenes, Norway
Grønnvoll, Helge, Furuflaten, Norway
Grønvoll, Agnete, Furuflaten, Norway
Hågensen, Olaug, Tromsø, Norway
Halden, Halvard, Lyngseidet, Norway
Halden, Hans, Lyngseidet, Norway
Hansen, Ragnhild, Dåfjord, Norway
Hauge, Tore, Oteren, Norway
Heika, Arvid, Kopparelv, Norway
Heika, Viggo, Kopparelv, Norway
Henriksen, Thorleif, Tromsø, Norway
Hoel, Grethe, Tromsø, Norway
Idrupsen, Dagmar, Tromsø, Norway
Idrupsen, Halvor, Rebbenes, Norway
Idrupsen, Idrup, Rebbenes, Norway
Isaksen, Eliva, Manndalen, Norway
Isaksen, Peder, Manndalen, Norway
Isaksen, Magne, Trondheim, Norway
Larsen, Alvin, Furuflaten, Norway
Leivseth, Gudrun, Bergen, Norway
Lyngstad, Torleif, Birtavärre, Norway
Mikalsen, Aud, Manndalen, Norway
Mikalsen, Magne, Manndalen, Norway
Morin, Barbro, Kalix, Sweden
Nilsen, Peder, Tromsø, Norway
Olsen, Harald, Dåfjord, Norway
Pedersen, Gunnar, Tromsø, Norway
Raste, Holger, Tromsø, Norway
Ratvik, Johan, Ålesund, Norway
Siri, Berit Anne, Kautokeino, Norway
Solberg, Alf, Tromsø, Norway
Sønsteby, Gunnar, Oslo, Norway

Sørensen, Odd, Tromsø, Norway
Ulstein, Ragnar, Ålesund, Norway
Wikan, Edvin, Kvaløyvågen, Norway

Institutions:
Norway's Resistance Museum, Oslo, Norway
Sameinstituttet, Kautokeino, Norway

Letters:
Brustrøm, Gudbrand, Samuelsberg, Norway
Reinøy, Julius, letter to Magnar Olsen, July 28, 1985, regarding
   M/K Brattholm
Solvang, Hans, letter to Ingolf Sjursnes, Sjursnes, August 8,
   1991
Stilnes, Hanna Brustrøm, Oppegård, Norway
Vågseter, Aud Brustrøm, Skåla, Norway

Maps:
National Geographic
Statkart, Oslo, Norway LA82011 R88334

Photographs:
Kompani Linge, Annet bind, Gyldendal Norsk Forlag, Oslo,
   1949, Erling Jensen, Per Ratvik, Ragnar Ulstein: Fishing
   barrels with machine guns
Kompani Linge, Første bind, Gyldendal Norsk Forlag, Oslo,
   1949, Erling Jensen, Per Ratvik, Ragnar Ulstein: Martin
   Linge, Scalloway Harbor
Krigen i Norge fra Sola til Tromsø, Gyldendal Norsk Forlag:
   Reichskommissar Terboven in Svolvær
Lennsmenn i Karlsøy, Ulf L. Vinje, 1995: Sheriff Hoel
Norwegian Resistance Museum, Oslo, Norway: Josef Terboven
Så vi vant vår rett, Frihetskampen 1940-1945: Nasjonalhjelpen til
   Frihetskampens ofre, E. Ancher, Hanssen

Våre falne — Første bok, Grøndahl & Son, Oslo 1949, Utgitt av
  den norske stat: Lt. Sigurd Eskeland, Sgt. Per Blindheim,
  Sgt.Gabriel Salvesen
Baal, Aslak Family: Per Thomas Baal, Aslak Baal
Baalsrud, Nils Ivar: Jan Baalsrud (Cover), Jan Baalsrud in
  Shetland Islands
Ballovarre, Vilhelm: John Olav Ballovarre
Brustrøm, Gudbrand: Nils Brustrøm, Signe and Nils Brustrøm
Dahlhaug, Asbjørn: Lyngsdalen, Amandus Lillevoll, Olav Lanes,
  Alvin Larsen and Marius Grønvoll, Alfon Hansen
Grønnslett, Arvid: Ludvik Nilsen
Hågensen, Olaug: Haldis Idrupsen, Peder Idrupsen, Olaug
  Hågensen, Dina Pedersen, and Dagmar Idrupsen, Anna
  Pedersen, Idrupsen's home
Halden, Hans: Halvard Halden
Haug, Dr. Tore: The Bromnes store and Anaton Pedersen's
  house, Toftefjord, Island and rock by Vårøya where Jan
  swam to, Vårøya Island, Idrupsen home, Jacoba Jensen's
  home
Isaksen, Eliva and Peder: Aslak Fossvoll, Teacher Nordness,
  Peder and Eliva Isaksen, Nils "Nigo" Nilsen, Olaf Olsen,
  Peder Pedersen, Isak Solvang, Marie (Fossen) Olsen,
  Marie Holm, Ludvik Nilsen
Iversen, Leif Erik: Police station in Tromsø, *M/K Brattholm*
  twisted skeleton on bottom of Toftefjord, Memorial
  Plaque infront of Gestapo Headquarters, Gestapo
  Headquarters, Veggefjord, Solvatnet Lake, Arvid and
  Viggo Heika and Astrid Karlsen Scott, Lyngsneset, The
  dock at Løvli, Peder Nilsen, Workbench at Solhov School,
  Replica of sled, The Gentleman Stone, Gentleman Stone
  seen toward the East, Entrance to Skaidijonni Cave, Upper
  entrance to Skaidijonni Cave, Inside Skaidijonni Cave,
  The Brustrøm home, Brustrøm's old wood-burning stove
Leivseth, Gudrun: Marius Grønvoll, Ingeborg Grønvoll
Lockertsen, Trond: The Lockertsen Family

Lyngstad, Torleif: Ankerlia with Moskugaise, Birtavärre
Mikalsen, Magne: Peder Isaksen by mountain wall in Avzevaggi,
      Helene, Magne, Anton and Ella Mikalsen
Morin, Barbro: Barbro Morin
Eliva Isaksen, Nils E. Nilsen
Raste, Holger: Astrid Karlsen Scott (Cover)
Scott, Astrid Karlsen: Tore Haug (Inside back cover),
      Kåfjorddalen Valley, the Steinnes home, Kåfjord, the
      Sørensen home, Bjørnskar, Toftefjord, Toftefjord where the
      saboteurs came ashore
Steinnes, Inger: Hjalmar Steinnes
Wikan, Edwin: Edwin Wikan, excavation photos of the
      Brattholm's men's graves

Reported
Missing

By the same author

Woe to the Unwary
Torpedo Airmen
The Strike Wings
Target: Hitler's Oil (with Ronald C. Cooke)
Arctic Airmen (with Ernest Schofield)
Failed to Return
An Illustrated History of the RAF
RAF Records in the PRO (with Simon Fowler, Peter Elliott and Christina Goulter)
The Armed Rovers
The RAF in Camera 1903–1939
The RAF in Camera 1939–1945
The RAF in Camera 1945–1995
RAF Coastal Command in Action 1939–1945
RAF: An Illustrated History from 1918
Britain's Rebel Air Force (with Dudley Cowderoy and Andrew Thomas)
The Flight of Rudolf Hess (with Georges van Acker)
RAF in Action 1939–1945
The Battle of Britain
The Battle of the Atlantic
Missing Believed Killed
The Battle for Europe
Ultra versus U-boats

Reported
Missing

Lost Airmen of the Second World War

Roy Conyers Nesbit

Bournemouth Libraries	
ST	
300027635	
Askews	2009
940.548	£19.99

Pen & Sword
AVIATION

First published in Great Britain in 2009 by
Pen & Sword Aviation
an imprint of
Pen & Sword Books Ltd
47 Church Street
Barnsley
South Yorkshire
S70 2AS

Copyright © Roy C. Nesbit 2009

ISBN 978-1-84415-822-5

The right of Roy C. Nesbit to be identified as Author of this Work has
been asserted by him in accordance with the Copyright, Designs and
Patents Act 1988.

A CIP catalogue record for this book is available from the British Library.

All rights reserved. No part of this book may be reproduced or
transmitted in any form or by any means, electronic or mechanical
including photocopying, recording or by any information storage and
retrieval system, without permission from the Publisher in writing.

Typeset in 10pt Palatino by
Mac Style, Beverley, E. Yorkshire

Printed and bound in the UK by
CPI

Pen & Sword Books Ltd incorporates the imprints of Pen & Sword
Aviation, Pen & Sword Maritime, Pen & Sword Military, Wharncliffe
Local History, Pen and Sword Select, Pen and Sword Military Classics and
Leo Cooper.

For a complete list of Pen & Sword titles please contact
PEN & SWORD BOOKS LIMITED
47 Church Street, Barnsley, South Yorkshire, S70 2AS, England
E-mail: enquiries@pen-and-sword.co.uk
Website: www.pen-and-sword.co.uk

Contents

Acknowledgements

My thanks are due to all those who have helped with the research into the six chapters of this book, including those who have provided maps and photographs. They are: Squadron Leader A.H. Aldridge DFC and bar; D. Alsdorf; the late T. Armstrong DFC; W.R. Armstrong; the late Flight Sergeant A.R. Brown DFM; the late Wing Commander G.J. Buxton MBE; T. Carroll; Flight Sergeant W. Carroll; R. Chapman, *Flugzeug Classic*; Ms D. Chapman; Commonwealth War Graves Commission; Squadron Leader J.D. Cowderoy; Mrs Jane Cowderoy; J.G. Cresswell DFC, DFM; J.E. Cvnk, Polish Aircraft Archives; the late Flight Lieutenant W.M. Dunsmore DFC; Warrant Officer J. Eggleston; the late R. Freeman; S. Garrett, Carlton Broadcasting; General Register Office for Scotland; the late Flight Lieutenant P.H. George; Mrs P. George; G. Grad; P. Kuchera; H.L. Grimminger; P. Johnson, The National Archives; Dr E.W. Hawkinson, Eighth Air Force Memorial Museum Foundation; the Reverend. C-J. Heinemann-Grüder; the late A. Henshaw; the late Flight Lieutenant P. Hughes; Dr R. Jaloustre; Flight Lieutenant D.A. Jennings DFC; H. Laage, Volksbund Deutsche Kriegsgräberfürsorge; W. Maxhofer; the late T.A. McGarry DFC; Mrs M.J. Nelson, IPC Media; M. Piala; Colonel M. Pont, US Army Central Identification Laboratory; M. Postletwaite; RAF Personnel Management; C. Richards, Air Historical Branch (RAF); J-L. Roba; J.C. Scutts; the late Corporal N. Shirley DFM; P. Slimek; the late Wing Commander T. Spooner DSO, DFC; N. Stroud, *Aeroplane Monthly*; the late Lieutenant-Colonel E.T. Strever DFC; G. Van Acker; Mrs A. Williams; US National Archives and Records Administration; G.T. Zwanenburg KON, MBE.

Chapter 1

The Enemy Within

On 18 September 1941 a Czech pilot in the RAF, Sergeant Augustin Preucil, took off in a Hurricane from RAF Usworth in County Durham on a training exercise and disappeared without trace. It was not until after the war that the truth became known. Research was initially carried out in 2002 by Richard Chapman, the ex-RAF editorial coordinator for the German magazine *Flugzeug Classic*. He and this author had collaborated for many years on subjects concerning air history and pooled the results of our researches.

Hurricane I serial W9147 of No 55 Operational Training Unit on display during the war at the Museum for Transport and Technology in Berlin. The museum and all its exhibits were later destroyed by Allied bombing. *Author's collection*

The trail began with the examination of a photograph taken in the Berlin Aviation Museum during the war. This showed Hurricane I serial W9147, letter A unit code PA. The only damage visible was to its propeller, where the three tips had broken off. The undercarriage was down, indicating that the pilot had made a reasonably good landing. The markings demonstrated that the Hurricane had last been on the strength of No 55 Operational Training Unit, based at RAF Usworth. How could this machine have arrived, in almost perfect condition, at a prominent German museum? Its RAF record card showed that it was never flown in an operational squadron, and moreover Berlin was well outside the range of any Hurricane. No information was available from the Berlin Aviation Museum, for it was bombed during the war and its contents completely destroyed. The investigation had to begin, surprisingly, in Czechoslovakian records.

Of the many nationalities who served in the wartime RAFVR (RAF Volunteer Reserve), Czech aircrew and ground staff had some of the finest records. They were expatriates who had escaped from German occupation and were fighting for the liberty of a country which was suffering cruel exploitation and extreme hardship. Their achievements are legendary in the RAF's Fighter, Bomber and Coastal Commands, and many of the men ended the war justifiably covered with awards and honours. Others lost their lives in the conflict and their names are commemorated. Yet every country had its traitors in the Second World War, including Britain, and Czechoslovakia was no exception.

Augustin Preucil of the Czech Air Force photographed on a pilots' course at Prostejov in 1937. His forename was often abbreviated to 'Gusta'. *Courtesy of Miroslav Fiala*

Augustin Preucil, known to his family and friends as 'Gusta', was born on 3 July 1914 at Trebsin, near Benesov in Czechoslovakia. He qualified as a pilot in the Czechoslovakian Air Force before the war, his last posting being as an instructor in the 6th Observer Flight, Air Regiment No 1 'T.G. Masaryk' at Letecky, an airfield which still exists.

This country was unfortunate to become one of Hitler's objectives in his quest for *Lebensraum* (living space). After Germany's annexation of the Sudetenland area of north and north-west Czechoslovakia, where many citizens of German origin lived, Prime Minister Neville Chamberlain flew to Munich at the end of September 1938. He

The CKD E-39 was a basic trainer employed by Air Regiment No 1 'T.G. Masaryk' (the first President of the Czechoslovakian Republic). It was powered by a radial engine, commonly an NZ-120 of 120 hp, from the Walter factory in Prague. This machine, E.39.21 coded M11, was photographed before the German occupation of the country, with an unidentified crew. *Photo courtesy of Richard Chapman, Ed. Co-ordinator, Flugzeug Classic, Munich, Germany*

The Letov S.328 was a two-seat biplane used for training air observers at Air Regiment No 1, before the German occupation of Czechoslovakia. It was powered by a Walter Pegasus II.M-2 radial engine of 580 hp. This machine, coded L7, was on the strength of the 6th Air Observer Flight, in which Augustin Preucil served as a pilot. *Photo courtesy of Richard Chapman, Ed. Co-ordinator, Flugzeug Classic, Munich, Germany*

The Bloch MB-151-01 fighter, with a Gnôme-Rhône 14N-11 engine rated at 920 hp, which first flew on 18 August 1938 at Villacoublay near Paris. The Armée de l'Air was equipped with the first batch of these aircraft from November 1939, armed with either two cannons or four machine guns. Some were employed as trainers at Chartres. *Author's collection*

returned waving a piece of paper signed by Adolf Hitler, Benito Mussolini, Edouard Daladier and himself, which he represented as 'peace for our time' in the four major European countries involved. This came as a relief to those desperate to avoid a repetition of the carnage of the First World War, but was treated with extreme scepticism by those with more discernment. Of course, Hitler soon broke his guarantee by occupying Bohemia and Moravia in March 1939, in addition to his other depredations. Slovakia declared itself an independent state, but came under German hegemony.

On the disbandment of the Czechoslovakian Air Force, Preucil was forced to obtain civilian employment and became a tailor and ladies' outfitter. His father, also named Augustin, was a professional tailor. It is evident that the younger Preucil did not object to his country's subjugation, for he applied to join the Luftwaffe. This was rejected, since he had not been born a German national. According to his later testimony, he also attempted to reach Brazil in order to become an airline pilot, but leaving the newly established protectorate was a punishable offence and he was arrested. In the summer of 1939 he was persuaded to work for the Gestapo. A branch of this infamous organization, based in Prague under Kommissar Oscar Fleischer, instructed him to 'escape' to Poland, in order to report on Czech Air Force personnel who had fled to that country.

The newly recruited spy duly crossed the Polish border at Frystat, to the accompaniment of gunfire and shouts which gave authenticity to his 'escape', and reached Cracow. From there, he was sent to Male Bronovice, a nearby camp for Czech personnel. But the Poles were not enthusiastic about accepting Czechs into their air force, for such action might give the Germans an excuse for invasion. In any event, relations between the Poles and Czechoslovakians were not particularly friendly. The Czechs who arrived in their country were shunted off to France, mostly by ship from Danzig to Le Havre. It has to be assumed that Preucil followed this route.

The French were even less accommodating to the Czechs than the Poles. They had an alliance with Poland, dating from 1921, and usually welcomed its citizens. There was also a Treaty of Mutual Assistance with Czechoslovakia, dating from 1925, but in 1939 the country was ruled by Germany and acceptance of refugees from its former armed services could create an international incident. However, there was a neat solution. The Czechs could either join the French Foreign Legion or return to their own country. Many chose the former alternative and were sent to Marseilles where, by an ironic twist of fate, they were indoctrinated by brutal German NCOs in French service. After a period of training, most were sent to Sidi-bel-Abbès in Algeria. Here they led extremely harsh lives as part of the garrison of the country, their force being composed of refugees from many countries.

We do not know if Preucil arrived in France in time to pass through this system, but he certainly did not serve in its Armée de l'Air before the Second World War. But the attitude of the French towards the Czechs changed as war broke out, when those in France or Algeria were permitted to volunteer for the domestic armed services. Preucil joined the Armée de l'Air and was sent on a training course for fighter pilots. This was Course No 6 of the Centre d'Instruction de Chasse at Chartres, about forty-five miles south-west of Paris. Although precise details of his flying activities are not known, the aircraft available for his course were Bloch 151 monoplanes, Fiat CR42 biplanes obtained from Belgium, Morane-Saulnier 405 monoplanes and Dewoitine 500 monoplanes. He remained on this course for seven months. According to one of his instructors, Sergeant Rudolf Zima, he was considered a poor pilot who was far more interested in playing cards and amusing himself than improving his knowledge and skill. This tallies with his secret allegiance with the enemy. It seems probable that he was in touch with an agent of the Sicherheitsdienst (SD), the branch of the German SS Security Service which operated in countries bordering Germany.

Very few Czech aircrew flew operationally when the Wehrmacht invaded France, probably because they had not been sufficiently trained or

Eleven Czech fighter pilots attending Course No 6 at the Centre d'instruction de chasse (CIC) at Chartres in France shortly after the declaration of war. Left to right: B. Kymlicka; J. Kucera; R. Zima; A. Preucil (with a cap in the rear row); J. Pardus; B. Postrekovsky; Tomas Vybiral; Fr. Sticka; A. Vrana; M. Standera; M. Kopecky. *Courtesy of Pavel Slimek*

integrated into squadrons. It seems that, of approximately 1,000 Czech aircrew in France, only 123 flew actively after managing to join squadrons. Preucil was not one of these. When the defeat of France became imminent and even after the country collapsed, many Czechs managed to reach England from various ports, ranging from Cherbourg in the north to Bordeaux in the south-west and Marseilles in the south. Most were encamped at Mérignac, near Bordeaux, and made their escape by sea from there. It is known that Preucil arrived in England, to continue his traitorous activities, and this is the most probable port from which he sailed. However, he told a different story to a young English girl a few months later.

All Czech airmen who reached England, whether flying or ground personnel, were enrolled in the RAFVR. The commissioned officers, NCOs and airmen were first sent to Cosford in Shropshire for an initial course in the RAF, no doubt with some elementary English lessons. Augustin Preucil was no exception, becoming Sergeant No 787344. All personnel records of the RAF in the Second World War are under 'long closure' (probably seventy-five years) at the Personnel Management Agency at RAF Innsworth

President Eduard Beneš of Czechoslovakia visited RAF Honington in Suffolk on 6 August 1940. This was the base for No 311 (Czech) Squadron, which had been formed with Wellington IAs on 29 July 1940. *Author's collection*

in Gloucester and thus are not available to the general public. However, it is possible to trace some of Preucil's movements from information within the Czech Republic, combined with records of RAF squadrons and units at The National Archives at Kew, Surrey.

Unfortunately the records for RAF Cosford in 1940 and 1941 are missing, presumably having been lost or destroyed at some stage in the war. Preucil's next posting was to No 43 Squadron at RAF Usworth in Durham. This squadron assumed training status on 19 September 1940, and Preucil's name appears frequently during the next two months. His flying took place in Hurricane Is on such exercises as formation flying, aerobatics, combat and altitude flying. There were many trainees with Czech and Polish names on this course, but they all disappeared in December 1940.

According to information from the Czech Republic, Preucil was then posted to No 605 (County of Warwick) Squadron, based at RAF Tangmere in Sussex. This was an operational squadron, equipped with Hurricane Is

Pilots of No 312 (Czech) Squadron watching their Hurricane Is at RAF Speke in Lancashire, where the squadron was based from 26 September 1940 to 2 March 1941. *Author's collection*

but in course of receiving the new Hurricane IIA, fitted with the Merlin XX two-stage supercharged engine and about 20 mph faster than its predecessor. There is no mention of Preucil in the squadron records and it must be assumed that he was considered unsuitable and rapidly moved on.

His next posting was to No 10 Maintenance Unit at RAF Hullavington in Wiltshire, which was involved with servicing and testing a wide variety of aircraft, including Hurricanes. Once again, there is no mention of him in the records, for the names of the pilots are seldom given. He was then moved to No 33 Maintenance Unit at RAF Lyneham in Wiltshire. However, there is positive confirmation of his next posting, to No 18 Maintenance Unit at RAF Dumfries in Dumfriesshire, which records him as arriving there on 6 March 1941 from No 33 Maintenance Unit at Lyneham, for ferrying duties. Within this station was No 11 Ferry Flight, but this was disbanded on 1 July 1941 when the aircraft and staff departed for RAF Kemble in Gloucestershire.

One of the pilots of No 312 (Czech) Squadron, a talented violinist, entertaining fellow pilots in the crew room at RAF Speke in Lancashire. Some of the pilots are kitted ready for flying, evidently on standby. *Author's collection*

The records of RAF Kemble do not mention names unless they are senior officers, but we know that it was the home of No 5 Maintenance Unit, which held and serviced many types of aircraft, including Hurricanes. At some unrecorded date, Preucil was posted back to RAF Usworth, this time as a junior instructor at No 55 Operational Training Unit.

According to other information from the Czech Republic, Preucil was constantly in touch with an enemy 'handler' somewhere in the UK while in the RAFVR. It is also understood that the Germans wanted to get their hands on one of the new Hurricane IIs. However, the German spy system in the UK was conducted by the Abwehr under Admiral Wilhelm Canaris, and it proved almost ineffective. The recruits were mostly of very low calibre and their organization was soon infiltrated. The British Radio Security Service (RSS) began to intercept the radio signals sent to and from them in August 1940. By the following December, cryptographers in the Government Code and Cypher School at Bletchley Park in Buckinghamshire had broken the

RAF Usworth in Durham photographed from the north-west on 25 June 1941. Hurricanes of No 55 Operational Training Unit are dispersed around the airfield. *Author's collection*

main hand cypher. In December 1941, the machine cypher was also broken. These achievements contributed to the arrest of all the spies throughout the war, who were interrogated at 'Camp 020'. This was Latchmere House at Ham, between Kingston and Richmond in Surrey. Those who refused to become double agents were executed. If Preucil was in touch with one of these spies before his capture, details are not within the records of MI5, although these have been released and are now in The National Archives.

The date of Preucil's second arrival at Usworth is not recorded but on 2 July 1941, when he was stationed there, he married an English girl of 19, the two having met almost a year before. Of course this young lady knew nothing of his nefarious activities but believed that he was one of the courageous band of Czech pilots who were fighting for the freedom of their country and for the Allied cause. It seems that he told her he had been 'in dogfights with

One of the Czech pilots at an airfield visited by President Eduard Beneš, commissioned as a pilot officer in the RAF Volunteer Reserve and sitting on the edge of the rear cockpit in a Tiger Moth. Although these biplanes were employed primarily as elementary trainers, most operational airfields had one on strength for communication purposes. *Author's collection*

German aircraft' and 'had stolen an aircraft in France and escaped to Spain before reaching England'. The marriage ceremony was attended by other pilots from Usworth, who believed that Preucil was a genuine patriot.

At the time, pilots of all nationalities in the RAF were often known as the 'glamour boys' of the armed services. All were volunteers and the physical standards for acceptance into the aircrew branch of the RAF were extremely high, in the sense that any defects discovered in a stringent medical examination resulted in rejection. In their blue uniforms emblazoned with silver wings or brevets and with the victory in the Battle of Britain to their general credit, they usually enjoyed great popularity among the young ladies of the country. This was inevitably to the irritation of recruits to other branches of the services.

The records of Usworth at this time are quite extraordinary. No 55 OTU was engaged mainly on training Czech and Polish pilots in Hurricanes, and accidents are listed on almost every day. Most of these were fairly minor, but occasionally they resulted in fatalities. Although the date of Preucil's arrival is not recorded, his name appears on 27 July 1941 when he mishandled the fuel system of Hurricane I serial V7608 and force-landed near Houghton-le-Spring, without injury to himself. It is believed that he was reprimanded for carelessness. His flight commander at Chartres, Flight Lieutenant Frantisek Burda, knew him in England and commented that he led a 'sloppy life' and was always in debt.

Preucil's last flight took place on 18 September 1941 in Hurricane I serial W9147. This machine had been on the strength of RAF Usworth since the days when No 43 Squadron was on training status at the station. It appears to have been the personal aircraft of the chief flying instructor, who at this time was a former Battle of Britain pilot, Squadron Leader John Ellis DFC. According to Air Ministry Form No 1180 Accident Record Card, Preucil had flown 173 hours in the RAFVR, of which 163 hours were solo.

Prior to his flight, his young wife noticed that he stuffed his pockets with documents, which seemed unusual but not suspicious. He was on a dogfighting exercise over the sea between Sunderland and West Hartlepool with a Polish sergeant-pilot, who lost sight of the other Hurricane when 'flames were coming out of the radiator'. The time is recorded as 'after 1700 hours', presumably in Greenwich Mean Time.

The observation of the Hurricane being on fire was obviously incorrect, but it must be assumed that Preucil was reported to the Air Ministry as 'missing believed killed'. His name appears on a plaque which commemorates the names of about 500 Czech airmen who gave their lives for freedom during 1939 to 1945, located in the Czechoslovak National

Wellington IC serial L7842 of No 311 (Czech) Squadron, which was shot down by flak on the night of 6/7 February 1941 during a raid on Boulogne, restored and in German markings. A crew member, Pilot Officer Arnost 'Wally' Valenta, was one of the many escapers on 24 March 1944 from a tunnel in the PoW Camp of Stalag Luft III at Sagan. After his recapture, he was murdered by the Gestapo at the end of the month. *Courtesy of G.J. Zwanenburg KON, MBE*

House in West End Lane, London. However, it is not on the list of RAF War Dead at the Commonwealth War Graves Commission, nor is it in the ledgers of the RAF Church of St Clements Dane at Aldwych in London.

It is known that the RAF Chaplain at Usworth visited Preucil's wife and told her that he must have come down somewhere in the sea. He offered to conduct a memorial service for him, but for several weeks she clung to the hope that he was still alive and would be picked up. She was provided with a widow's pension for his death.

To find out what really happened, we must rely largely on contacts from the European mainland. It seemed possible in the course of this research that Preucil might have landed somewhere in the Netherlands. However, Gerrit (Gerrie) J. Zwanenburg KON, MBE, the former Identification and Recovery Officer for the Royal Netherlands Air Force, discovered that there are no German records of such a landing in his country on 18 September 1941. Instead, he managed to trace the record of a German Flak Unit at

Vlissingen (Flushing) in Belgium, near the border with the Netherlands. This recorded an unknown aircraft approaching at 2128 hours Central European Time (two hours in advance of Greenwich Mean Time) on 18 September 1941. The aircraft circled from 2130 to 2133 hours and then flew inland. This time fits reasonably well with the 300 miles Preucil would have flown to reach the locality, maybe at about 190 mph cruising speed. It would have been evening twilight at Flushing, and the aircraft may not have been seen clearly from the ground.

Next, the air historian Georges Van Acker in Belgium traced an account written in French by his colleague Jean-Louis Roba. This was published in *Contact* of 1997, the newsletter of the Belgian Aviation History Association. Jean-Louis obtained some of his information from the records of a German Feldkommandantur in Belgium, as well as the recollections of Didier Campion, a Belgian who was 14 years old at the time. Didier was on holiday with his father near the village of Ortho in the Ardennes when they were approached by a farm worker, out of breath. A British aircraft had landed nearby and someone who spoke English was required. He ran to the site, despite the imminent curfew at 2200 hours, but discovered that the pilot had been 'taken away by the Germans'.

Yet more information came from Lieutenant-Colonel Jules J. Musyck, retired from the Belgian Air Force but writing on behalf of the Air Section of the Brussels Military Museum. The Ortho area where Preucil landed was the base of a Belgian underground service which transmitted information to London. This led to further research, but first it is perhaps necessary to describe the situation in the country when it was overrun by the Wehrmacht after the Blitzkrieg was launched against the Low Countries on 10 May 1940. The Belgian army capitulated seventeen days later on the orders of King Leopold III, who remained in his country and was placed under house arrest. His Cabinet escaped and some of its members eventually reached Britain.

The British War Cabinet approved the formation of Special Operations Executive (SOE) on 22 July 1940, with the objective of 'co-ordinating all action by way of subversion and sabotage against the enemy overseas'. This had resulted in the formation of No 1419 Flight within the RAF, based at Newmarket in Suffolk and equipped with Westland Lysander IIIs to land agents in clearings in western Europe, or to drop them by parachute. On 25 August 1941, this flight had been expanded into No 138 Squadron and been additionally equipped with Armstrong Whitworth Whitley Vs.

Of the prominent Belgians who had arrived in London, SOE had collaborated initially with Fernand Lepage and H. Dadson, who were intent on building up a secret army within their home country and causing sabotage.

However, SOE insisted on keeping control of W/T communications and participating with its agents in the conduct of operations against the enemy. It planned to establish an organizer in all nine provinces of Belgium, each with his own wireless operator while controlling all subversive activities. This arrangement did not work quite so smoothly as hoped, partly because Belgian patriots within their home country were already active with their clandestine cells.

There were over thirty regions of Belgium where these spontaneous underground resistance movements had sprung up after the German occupation. The small local group in the Ortho area was formed on 18 June 1940 by Waltère Dewé, a veteran of the First World War. In this earlier war he had founded the Belgian resistance movement La Dame Blanche and eventually had been awarded the CBE by the British, as had his friend and comrade Herman Chauvin.

On the outbreak of the Second World War, Dewé had been contacted by the Special Intelligence Service (SIS) and asked if he would work again for the British. He had accepted this risky assignment and was given the code-name of 'Cleveland', while his organization was named 'Clarence'. His assistant was a man called André, but he never gave his real name. Their movement was provided with four transmission sets, but these could not receive messages. However, on the night of 12/13 January 1941 the agent Jean Lamy was dropped with a transmitter/receiver near Manhaye in the Ardennes, and regular contact with London began.

Lamy was captured by the Germans on 26 March 1941, when in the course of sending a message. Under torture he was forced to transmit incorrect messages. However, the Clarence network had managed to put information on microfilm and deliver it to the American ambassador in Vichy France, who duly passed it to the British. A new agent as well as a radio operator landed in the area in early August 1941 and joined Clarence. These were Adrien Marquet, code-named 'Mill' and Paul Jacquemin, code-named 'Marble', and genuine contact was resumed. They were still in operation when the stolen Hurricane arrived in their area.

After his landing near the village of Ortho, Preucil was soon discovered and sheltered by local people who believed him to be a genuine Allied airman. Of course, he could speak French fluently after his period in the Armée de l'Air and was soon able to gain their confidence and sympathy. He told them that he had landed after running out of fuel and had been unable to destroy his aircraft for the same reason. They took him to a local farm where he was given some civilian clothes. He then left this home, ostensibly to hide in the woods during the night.

Flak damage to the tail of Wellington IC
serial L7842 of No 311 (Czech) Squadron.
Courtesy of G.J. Zwanenburg KON, MBE

On the following day, the traitor returned with several German troops, part of a contingent who surrounded the area and conducted searches. Two Belgians who had sheltered him, a farrier named Armand Durand and a gamekeeper named Léon Charlier were arrested and doubtless forced to endure appalling cruelties under interrogation. They were eventually shot by the Germans in the National Rifle Range in Brussels on 21 January 1942. A street in Ortho, Rue Armand Durand, still commemorates the life of the Belgian patriot who lived from 1901 to 1942. Charlier's wife and a Belgian named Antoine were given prison sentences.

The renegade must have felt very satisfied with himself in the period after his arrival. His Hurricane was almost intact, although it was not a Mark II, and he had pleased his masters. His adopted country seemed to be winning the war. There was something of an impasse with Britain but the German invasion of Russia had resulted in great victories with enormous territorial gains and it appeared that Moscow would soon be occupied. While the USA remained neutral, victory for the Third Reich, with some accommodation for Britain, seemed certain.

But the British became aware of Preucil's traitorous activities almost immediately. Soon after his landing, 'Mill' sent a clandestine signal in French to the War Office in London. A translation of part of this message reads:

On the following day, the Germans employed fifty men in a fruitless hunt in this district. Soon after they had finished, the pilot left the woods and fraternised with them. He immediately denounced those who had given clothing to him, even disclosing the members of the family. There followed the immediate arrest of four people.

Preucil was sent to Prague, where he was rewarded with 10,000 Reichsmarks, which was a handsome sum in those days. He began work for the Gestapo 'Department N' in this Czech capital. His work was mainly administrative, recording and listing those of his own nationality who were fighting against the Third Reich, but occasionally he helped in the interrogation of Czech war prisoners.

An example of the type of information he intended to extract had already taken place in the Luftwaffe Interrogation Centre at Oberursel near Frankfurt, to which Pilot Officer Frantisek Cigos of No 311 (Czech) Squadron was taken after his Wellington I serial L7842 was shot down on 6/7 February 1941 during a raid on Boulogne. When told in Czech by a Gefreiter (leading aircraftman) to fill in a spurious Red Cross form, Cigos replied in French that he did not understand the language. The German promptly told him that his station was RAF East Wretham, his squadron was No 311 and that his commmanding officer was named Toman-Mares.

Other Czech prisoners of the RAFVR were sent to the Gestapo interrogation centre at Petchka Palace, near Wenceslas Square in Prague, before transfer to PoW camps. One of these was Flight Sergeant Vilem Bufka, who was the pilot and only survivor of Wellington IC serial T2990 of No 311 (Czech) Squadron which had been shot down in the early morning of 23 June 1941 near Niewe Dorp in Holland, during a raid on Bremen. He was greeted by Preucil, who reminded him they had been together in Poland, France and England. Preucil relayed all his knowledge to the Kommissar when the latter entered the room, leaving Bufka sickened. Another was Flight Lieutenant Frantisek Burda, who was shot down in a Spitfire of No 310 (Czech) Squadron on 27 February 1943. Preucil entered the room during the interrogation, dressed immaculately in civilian clothes, and offered him a cigarette. Burda said that he did not know him, but Preucil pointed out that they had served in the same flight at Chartres, together with Standera and Sticka.

No doubt at this stage, Preucil visualized for himself an important place in the hierarchy of his home country when the Third Reich finally won the Second World War. But he must have become apprehensive when the tide of events moved inexorably against his adopted masters. Towards the end of the war, he was employed more and more as a 'stool pigeon' – at

Theresienstadt, the internment camp holding certain Czech civilians, as well as at other camps where captured Czech partisans were held. It is believed that his work cost a number of Czech resistance fighters their lives. Eventually, he must have become convinced that he had backed the wrong side and that retribution was approaching. Nevertheless, he had no opportunity to flee and was arrested by the Allies on 19 May 1945.

This was the time when Czechoslovakia began a brief period of independence, before the Communists seized control in February 1948. In Belgium, it was acknowledged after the Liberation that as many as 18,000 people had been involved in clandestine operations against the Germans, 5,000 as active agents with 13,000 others supporting them. The Gestapo sent Jean Lamy to a concentration camp but he survived the war, although dying some years later. Walthère Dewé did not survive. He was shot and killed in the late afternoon of 14 January 1944 by a Luftwaffe officer while trying to escape from the Gestapo, running out of Kroonlaan towards Flageyplein in Brussels. By this time, he was 64 years of age. Nevertheless, the Belgian underground was never infiltrated by the Gestapo, unlike its equivalent in Holland, but continued its activities until the country was liberated.

Preucil was no more than a minor spy and collaborator during his infamous career, but a thoroughly unpleasant individual. A person who worked primarily against his own nationals and former comrades for financial and other rewards can only be rated as contemptible. It is also clear from information available in the Czech Republic that during the war the British Air Ministry wrote a report about his betrayal of the Belgians who had befriended him, although this has not been released to the general public.

During his trial, Preucil disclosed that he had married an English girl, and gave her maiden name. It seems probable that he was making an attempt to claim British citizenship. If so, it availed nothing, for he was executed in Prague on 14 April 1947. In England, his young widow refused to believe that her husband could have been a traitor. According to newspaper reports of the time, she 'vowed to clear his name', although this did not prove possible.

Chapter 2

The World's First Skyjack

The four crew members of a Bristol Beaufort torpedo bomber which failed to return from an operation from Malta on 28 July 1942 were later shown to have achieved an exploit without parallel in the Second World War.

At this time the people of Malta were near starvation. Supplies of food had dwindled to a trickle and, perhaps equally important, there was little fuel available for cooking. The island was almost bereft of trees while the meagre supplies of oil reaching her harbours had to be husbanded for the armed forces. 'Victory' kitchens had been set up to dole out daily a tiny meal per head, but some of the old and weak were dying. In the officers' and NCOs' messes at RAF Luqa, the daily ration consisted of three slices of bread and a sliver of corned beef, with the occasional luxury of a few tomatoes. Aircrew lost stones in weight, although some of the more enterprising NCOs were able to sneak out to the nearby village of Qormi and supplement their rations with a surreptitious meal of black market pork in an inn presided over by a large Maltese lady with a brood of children.

Among these aircrews, scabies, tick fever and dysentery had become endemic. The men of three Beaufort squadrons had suffered so many casualties in their low-level anti-shipping operations that those who remained fit were sorted into crews irrespective of their squadrons, whether they were from Nos 39, 86 or 217. These survivors were led by Squadron Leader R. Patrick M. Gibbs, DFC and bar, a veteran of No 22 Squadron's operations in the UK. He was a man of extraordinary dash and courage who inspired the utmost respect among his aircrews. Again and again, the Beauforts threw themselves against enemy convoys and, although their losses continued at an appalling rate, they sank ship after ship and damaged others.

The Afrika Korps under Feldmarschall Erwin Rommel had swept across the Western Desert and taken Tobruk on 21 June 1942, sending the British Eighth Army reeling back to the east. It seemed probable that the Axis forces

A bombing attack on the aircraft carrier HMS *Illustrious* in Valletta harbour in January 1941. The warship had already been hit by six bombs on 9 January while escorting a convoy to Malta. She was hit by two more bombs in harbour but slipped out under her own steam and reached Alexandria on 25 January. *Author's collection*

Bombs exploding on Valletta during a daylight raid on 21 January 1942. *Author's collection*

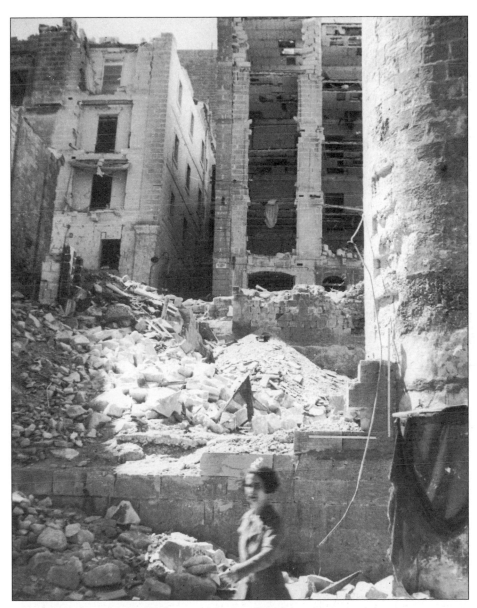

Devastation in a street in Valletta. *Author's collection*

were poised to enter Cairo, but they had been held at a small railway station named El Alamein. Their lines of communication were so extended that the pipelines of supplies, particularly oil, were beginning to dry up.

Rommel and his senior officers were enraged at the failure of the Regia Militare Italiana (Italian Navy) to escort tankers and merchant vessels safely

Bomb damage in Valletta, photographed in March 1942. *The late Wing Commander G.J. Buxton MBE, via Roy C. Nesbit*

Troops of the British Army helping with salvage work in the bombed streets of Valletta in Malta. *Author's collection*

across the Mediterranean. There was a general belief among the Germans that details of sailings were being conveyed to the Allics by Italian traitors. They would have been astonished if they had known that the British had succeeded in decrypting German signals sent by their 'Enigma' system. Dates of sailings were known by the British, as well as details of the cargoes. Thus a relatively small RAF strike force from Malta was able to intercept the convoys, after air reconnaissance had confirmed the sailings, while Allied submarines were also able to pick off the vessels.

The day of 28 July 1942 began when Pilot Officer H. Coldbeck, flying from Malta at 25,000 feet in Spitfire PR IV serial AB300 of No 69 Squadron, spotted an expected target at 0700 hours. He landed back at Luqa 80 minutes later. A merchant vessel, escorted by what looked like two enemy destroyers, was creeping down the west coast of Greece, the route then favoured by the Italians to keep their distance from the wasps' nest of Malta. These convoys might have used the harbour facilities of Tobruk, which was nearer the Axis front line than the more westerly ports of Tripoli and

The airfield of Luqa in Malta, blasted by bombs, photographed by a German reconnaissance aircraft in 1942. *Author's collection*

A squad of soldiers filling in craters after a bombing attack on the airfields of Malta. *Author's collection*

Benghazi, but it was not yet fully serviceable and under frequent air attack by the RAF.

The vessels spotted by Coldbeck were the armed transport *Monviso* of 5,552 tons, built two years before in Genoa and carrying a mixed cargo of war supplies. She was escorted by the Italian destroyer *Freccia* of 1,206 tons, armed with four 120 mm guns and four 37 mm flak guns. The other escort was the modern torpedo boat *Calliope* of 679 tons, armed with three 100 mm guns as well as six 37 mm and two 13 mm flak guns. These three vessels could put up a very powerful defence against attacking aircraft. They had set out the day before from Brindisi and their destination was Benghazi.

Nine Beauforts had been racked up with Mark XII torpedoes to attack this target. They were led by Squadron Leader Gibbs, accompanied by his brilliant navigator, Flight Sergeant John Creswell. Time of take-off was 0910 hours and the torpedo-carrying aircraft were without long-range fighter escort, although a lone Baltimore I serial AG734 of No 69 Squadron,

A Mark XII torpedo with a contact warhead being loaded in the bomb-bay of a Beaufort I, at Luqa in August 1943. *Courtesy of the late T.A. McGarry DFC, via Roy C. Nesbit*

A Beaufort II over Luqa in Malta. *Courtesy of the late T.A. McGarry DFC, via Roy C. Nesbit*

with a crew of four captained by Pilot Officer D. Munro, was detailed to fly at high level above the strike aircraft and photograph the results of the attack.

One of the Beaufort crews was captained by a South African, Lieutenant Edward T. Strever. He was a very tall, athletic man, born in 1920 in Germiston near Johannesburg. He had worked in an accountant's office before the war but in addition had seen service as a company sergeant-major in the volunteer part-time services. On the outbreak of war, he transferred to the SAAF and began training in the RAF as an air gunner, but an opportunity to train as a pilot in the Rhodesian Air Training Group arose when a ship carrying trainees from Britain was sunk in the Atlantic. After qualifying as a pilot, Strever was commissioned in the SAAF and then seconded to the RAF. He came to Britain and converted on to Beauforts at the Operational Training Unit (OTU) at Chivenor in North Devon and then passed through the Torpedo Training Unit (TTU) at Abbotsinch in Ayrshire. His next move was to No 217 Squadron at Leuchars in Fife, shortly before this squadron flew out to Malta in early June 1942.

The navigator in the crew was a Liverpudlian, Pilot Officer William M. Dunsmore. He was a burly man, older than the average flyer at 32 years, and had had some experience pre-war in the Civil Flying Corps. After joining the RAF, he had passed through Air Observer's Navigation School at West Freugh near Stranraer and then joined Strever at Chivenor and Abbotsinch.

Strever and Dunsmore had already lost the other two members of their original crew. During an attack on the Italian battle fleet on 13 June, their air gunner, Sergeant Bob Gray, had been wounded. When flying temporarily with another crew, their wireless operator, Sergeant Dick Ellis, had failed to return.

The replacements for these two wireless operators/air gunners were both New Zealanders. Sergeant John A. Wilkinson was aged 22 and came from the Mahia Peninsula near Gisborne on North Island, where he had worked on a farm. Sergeant A. Raymond Brown was aged 26 and had worked on both the railways and the land in his town of Timaru on South Island. The two men were of similar build, nearly 6 feet tall and with very powerful physiques. Both had attended Air Gunnery School near London in Ontario, part of the Empire Air Training Group in Canada. They had met in late 1941 at the Wireless School in Cranwell, before going on to Chivenor and Abbotsinch. They had been part of a crew captained by an Australian, Pilot Officer B.J. McSharry, but he had been badly wounded during an anti-shipping attack in the previous month.

The account that follows is based on the first-hand testimony of three of this Beaufort crew. A severe air raid on Malta was in progress when the crews walked out to their aircraft in the dispersal pens at Luqa. Just before they reached these pens, a Spitfire came in low, weaving drunkenly, and

Sergeants Wilkinson (left) and Brown, the two WOp/AGs who participated in the skyjacking of the Cant, photographed inside a Beaufort. *Courtesy of the late A. Raymond Brown DFM, via Roy C. Nesbit*

struck a stone wall not 50 yards away. One of its elliptical wings cartwheeled through the air in front of them. Nevertheless the nine Beauforts took off on time and formed up behind their leader, Squadron Leader Gibbs, heading on an intercept course which took them towards Sapienza on the south-west tip of Greece.

Strever was operationally experienced and flew as number two in the formation, on the starboard wing of the leader. He was in Beaufort I serial L9820, armed with two Browning machine guns in the turret, two Vickers machine guns in the nose and another Browning in the port wing. It was a most uncomfortable flight. In the blazing heat of midsummer, the switch of the pilot's cabin heater had stuck in the 'on' position. Strever sat and sweltered while Dunsmore occasionally stuck the cardboard cover of his navigator's log out of the starboard window in an attempt to deflect cool air on to his pilot. Fitted with two enormous and ungainly air filters above their Taurus engines to protect them from sand particles, the Beauforts could barely achieve a cruising speed of 120 knots. Wilkinson turned his turret systematically, keeping a watchful eye for the sight of any enemy aircraft. Brown sat in front of his wireless set, listening for signals from Luqa. He also switched on his Air to Surface-Vessel (ASV) radar set, for this was one of the Beauforts in which the instrument was fitted.

Eventually Brown saw some images about seventy miles away, probably the small Greek islands south of Sapienza. As the Beauforts neared the coast of Greece, the ASV could be switched to short-range. At almost midday, three objects showed up to starboard, about ten miles away. These were obviously the enemy vessels. Gibbs turned and led the formation south-east down the coast towards this target, hoping to take the enemy by surprise by attacking from an easterly direction.

Gibbs made straight for the merchant vessel but the attackers had been spotted and the Italian captain took evasive action by turning to port, thus presenting only a narrow bow shot to torpedoes. Behind Gibbs, Strever could see flak like stones splashing into the sea, but most unusually there did not seem to be any tracer in this fire and thus the spectacle appeared less alarming to him. He accelerated to the torpedo-dropping speed of 140 knots and aimed carefully at the bows. In the nose of the Beaufort, Dunsmore opened fire with his two Vickers at the enemy gunners.

'Torpedo dropped,' called Strever to his crew. Ahead of him, Gibbs flew straight over the ship while Strever, now skimming just above the surface of the sea, turned slightly to starboard and flew down the length of the vessel. Standing in the waist hatch on the port side, Brown could see the Italian crew on the deck, and even the glint of the sun on the brass buttons of their uniforms. The gun crews were firing point-blank at them, but the Beaufort men could not see the trajectory of the flak.

The Beaufort suddenly shuddered and a stream of smoke poured from its port engine, which began to bang and rattle. Strever flew towards Gibbs, while Dunsmore scrambled up beside him.

'My God, the other engine's had it,' said Dunsmore, looking out to starboard at an engine streaming oil. Strever caught up with Gibbs and waggled his wings in farewell, before turning back to the Greek coast.

'This is it, boys!' shouted Strever over the intercom. 'Prepare for ditching!' Both engines were still giving power, although they shook terribly and the whole aircraft vibrated alarmingly. Strever managed to gain height to about 300 feet but there was no opportunity to turn into wind so as to lessen the shock of impact. He tried to approach the sea parallel to the line of troughs, the least dangerous method of ditching. Wilkinson backed out of his turret and braced himself, facing backwards while sitting on the Elsan pan. Brown leant backwards and braced one leg against his wireless set and the other against the side of the aircraft to minimize the chance of smashing his head on impact. He had already sent out a distress signal and clamped down his transmitter on a continuous note, although he had little confidence that it could be heard in Malta. Strever wound back his trim, throttled back, applied half flaps and eased back the control column. 'Everyone at ditching stations!' he shouted. 'Ditching now!'

Dunsmore had scooped up his maps and charts and stuffed them in his navigator's canvas bag, together with a Very pistol, in the expectation that they would be useful in the dinghy or when 'on the run' in Greece. He began scrambling back over the seat beside the pilot so as to sit with his back against the main spar. But he never made it.

The landing was exactly as they had been told to expect at OTU. The first contact with the sea was quite light. and the Beaufort then bounced. The second was a bone-shaking, reverberating crash, as the rear of the open bomb-bay, which had accommodated the torpedo, caught in the sea. Then everything went silent. Dunsmore careered past Strever towards the nose, gashing his right arm. Wilkinson leant out of the port hatch and pulled the toggle in the wing, releasing the dinghy. The CO_2 bottle functioned and the 'Type H' round dinghy appeared, right side up. Wilkinson got in it, followed by Brown, and neither of them even got their feet wet. Behind them, they could see the tail unit of the Beaufort, broken away and bobbing in the swell, but the main part of the aircraft had tilted forward with the nose in the sea and there was no sign of either pilot or navigator.

Sergeant Bill Carroll (right) of No 217 Squadron in a Beaufort flying to Ceylon. He was originally scheduled to fly as air gunner in a Beaufort which was shot down during the attack off Greece on 28 July 1942, but was replaced at the last moment. *Courtesy of Arthur H. Aldridge DFC and bar*

Green water smashed into the pilot's cockpit while Strever was unstrapping himself, and closed over his head. Dunsmore recovered from his backward plunge and wrenched open the top escape hatch, sticking his head above water. Strever hammered at the back of Dunsmore's knees and began shoving him upwards. The two sergeants saw the navigator emerge, still clutching his canvas bag. Strever, an expert swimmer, popped up a few moments later. The dinghy soon carried all four crew members. Brown cut the retaining rope free from the Beaufort, just before the latter gurgled and disappeared.

Another aircraft was shot down by flak on this strike. This was Beaufort II serial AW296 flown by Pilot Officer E.C.F. Dawson, with a Canadian navigator, Flight Sergeant E.P. 'Doc' Sutherland. The wireless operator/air gunners scheduled to join them were Sergeant Alan Still and Sergeant Bill Carroll, both of whom had been part of the crew that had torpedoed and sunk the Italian heavy cruiser *Trento* on 15 July 1942 during an attack on the main Italian battle fleet. On this occasion, Alan Still opted to go in the turret. At the last moment, Bill Carroll was ousted by a wrathful Pilot Officer R.I.C. Head, who asserted his rights as part of Dawson's normal crew.

Head's determination was to cost him dear. As they approached the convoy, Alan Still saw oil streaming from the port engine, which must have been hit by flak. Head tapped him on the shoulder, motioning him out of the turret. As he backed out, the Beaufort hit the water and he shot forward, injuring Head's leg. Nevertheless the two men released the dinghy and got into it. They were joined by Dawson, but Sutherland must have been trapped and went down with the aircraft. Sitting in their dinghy, the three men saw the remaining seven Beauforts heading back to Malta. They also saw an Italian Cant Z.506B floatplane circling overhead and wondered if it

A Cant Z.506B floatplane of the Regia Aeronautica taking off. *Author's collection*

was an air-sea rescue aircraft, but it ignored them. Shortly afterwards, the torpedo boat *Calliope* picked them up and took them to the nearby harbour of Navarino, where they were treated in hospital before being transferred to a PoW camp in Italy.

'Let's see what we've got on board,' said Strever. The store was not over-bountiful but it contained some tins of tomato juice, a supply of water, distress signals, a topping-up pump and two aluminium paddles. The crew could see the shore and decided to make for it. Away to their port was a prominent tower which, had they known at the time, was built to celebrate the Independence of Greece following the victory of the British, French and Russian fleets over those of the Turkish and Egyptian in Navarino Bay in 1827.

The four men bent themselves to the task. They were strong and tough but could make no progress in paddling through the choppy sea. They even tried putting out the sea drogue at one stage, hoping it would enable them to achieve a constant direction. They paddled and sweated but the coast remained a tantalizing five miles away. Unfortunately they did not realize that four stabilizing pockets were still in position underneath their dinghy and should have been pulled inboard in the same way as a retractable keelboard. A strong offshore wind, known in those parts as the *Gregale*, or Greek wind, also seems to have impeded them. At one stage a Macchi MC202 fighter flew low over the dinghy. They watched it with some anxiety, for attacks on downed airmen were not completely unknown.

'If that Macchi makes a pass at us, then nip over the side quickly,' Strever told his crew. 'Get down as far below the surface as you can – he can't fire at us for more than a few seconds.'

But the fighter flew off and soon afterwards a different sound was heard approaching. It proved to be a tri-motored Cant Z.506B floatplane, and it circled overhead. Originally built for civil transport, the military version was named 'Airone', or 'Heron' in English. The fuselage and wings were all wood, covered in fabric, but the two large floats were metal. It was nearly 87 feet in wingspan, 63 feet long, and powered by three Alfa Romeo AR126 RC34 nine–cylinder radial engines of 750 hp. It cruised at about 110 knots, was armed with up to four machine guns and could carry a bomb load of 2,650 lb. There were up to five in the crew and it was mainly employed on naval reconnaissance, anti–submarine work and air-sea rescue.

The Beaufort men watched the floatplane with intense curiosity while it circled and finally landed about 30 yards away. They quickly dumped Dunsmore's maps, charts and Very pistol over the side. The crew of the Cant beckoned them, but since paddling had proved so ineffective Strever dived over the side and swam strongly towards the floatplane. He returned a few minutes later holding the end of a rope. They tied this to the dinghy and the crew of the Cant hauled them in. These Italians spoke little English but did not seem antagonistic and even gave the Beaufort men a cigarette apiece, which they smoked gratefully while standing on the wing. Then they were shepherded aboard and made to sit in a well in the middle of the fuselage, their captors being armed with handguns. A bandage was applied to Dunsmore's arm but the injury proved slight and not seriously inconvenient.

The Italians indicated that the heavy swell and choppy sea prevented take-off, for they appeared to be carrying a full load of depth charges as well as the four extra passengers. The pilot taxied to the lee of the small islands near Sapienza. A landing craft appeared to their starboard, full of German soldiers waving their rifles and apparently engaged on some form of amphibious exercise. It was a strange sight to see the enemy, fully armed and at such close waters. However, the sea was calmer close to the shore and the floatplane made a long run into the air.

The prisoners inspected the interior of the Cant speculatively. There were two pilots in tandem on the left, with the first pilot in front. In another well in the nose was a flight engineer. Behind the two pilots was the navigator's seat and to the rear was the wireless operator. Above was a turret with a single gun, apparently the equivalent of a 0.50 inch, but this appeared to be operated manually rather than hydraulically.

The Cant began to fly in a northerly direction, judging from the coastline and the direction of the sun. After about two hours, it arrived at what seemed to be an island and landed in a large inlet, almost enclosed by land. It motored to a jetty and the four Beaufort men were ushered off and into an interrogation room, where they were pleased to find that the questions were both courteous and perfunctory. The whole atmosphere was almost friendly. Aircrew flying from Malta usually wore their blue battledress tops and khaki shorts in an unmilitary combination. The Italians noticed that those worn by Strever and Dunsmore were still wet and provided some civilian clothes while these were sent away for drying.

Next, the four captives were escorted by the Italians into an officers' mess. At first they could hardly believe their eyes or noses. By the standards of Malta, a sumptuous meal was set before them – steak, tomatoes, spaghetti and vegetables, to be washed down with red wine. They were all young and resilient, and any shock of their experiences and predicament had already gone. They set to with a will. Then cigarettes were handed to them and their captors proposed a further diversion with a few rubbers of bridge. This game was apparently popular in the mess, but the Italians were disappointed to learn that the prisoners did not know how to play it. Instead there was table tennis, and the friendliness was enhanced by a visit from an Italian admiral, who congratulated Strever and told them that the merchant vessel had been damaged and 'beached'.

In fact, the *Monviso* had been hit by a torpedo and towed into the port of Navarino. The crew of the photo-reconnaissance Blackburn Baltimore had witnessed the entire strike, seen the two Beauforts shot down and the two RAF dinghies with their occupants. They had also seen two unidentified enemy aircraft, which were probably the escorting Cant floatplanes. A hit on the merchant vessel was also seen and reported, as was the towing to Navarino. In the event, the merchant vessel was not severely damaged, for she was rapidly repaired and set off again on 2 August, escorted by the destroyers *Alpino* and *Corrazione*, headed almost due south for Benghazi. But she was sunk on the following day when near her destination by two torpedoes fired by the submarine HMS *Thorn*. Italian warships from Benghazi rescued 241 of her crew and other military personnel on board. Only six men were lost.

Meanwhile, the prisoners were allotted quarters for the night, the two officers in one room and the two sergeants in another. They were warned not to try to escape, for there were armed guards outside with orders to shoot. If they had to go to the *gabinetto*, they should call the guards. But they were too replete with food and far too tired to make any such attempt, although the idea was uppermost in their minds. Strever discussed the possibility with Dunsmore, guessing that they would be sent north and then to Italy by train. He proposed that they should try to jump off somewhere and make their way to the Middle East. The two sergeants found themselves in a room with a map of the area on a wall. They examined this curiously and guessed that they were on the island of Corfu. This belief was assumed to have been correct for many years but more recent research into Italian records has established the fact that they were in the port of Prevesa, nearby on the mainland of Greece. Both men were also determined to escape somehow. But all four men slept as though stunned, after the day's exertions.

The crew of Beaufort I serial L9820 of No 217 Squadron who skyjacked Cant Z.506B of 159° Squadriglio on 29 July 1942 and flew it to Malta with the Italian crew as captives. Left to right: Sergeant John A. Wilkinson (WOp/AG); Sergeant A. Raymond Brown (WOp/AG); Pilot Officer William M. Dunsmore (navigator); Lieutenant Edward T. Strever of the SAAF (pilot). *Courtesy of John G. Creswell, DFC, DFM*

Back in Malta during the evening, Bill Carroll sat alone in the café in the tiny village of Qormi. He was drinking the fiery alcohol named *ambid*, diluted with lemonade, and eating a meal of black market pork. There was nobody to share his repast. Most of his closest friends from the sergeants' mess at Luqa had been lost during the operations of the last two months. His navigator, Vince Aspinall, was in hospital with dysentery. Alan Still, Wilkie and Brownie had failed to return from today's strike, although there was a report that two dinghies had been spotted. He should have been on the operation himself. They loved to talk, those redoubtable NCOs, the discussions often involving flying and the personalities of the crews. Their talk might expand a little after a few drinks but so did the comradeship. Tonight, it was utterly miserable being on his own.

A boy of 10 years, the bright son of the proprietess, asked Carroll where his friends were. He replied that they were all sick, not wanting to discuss the matter. The boy disappeared but returned a few minutes later with his ample-girthed mother.

'You buy eggs and milk for sick friends,' said the boy, offering these precious foodstuffs.

'I'll buy those six eggs,' said Carroll. 'But you must keep the milk for the babies.' The boy translated for his mother, who laughed and joggled her large breasts with her hands. Carroll asked what she was saying.

'She say she got plenty of milk,' replied the boy. Carroll could not help laughing, but he still refused the milk and bought only the eggs. He walked back to Luqa, feeling lonely and miserable once more.

At Prevesa, the four prisoners slept heavily in their guarded quarters. On awakening, they were taken again to the officers' mess and given a hearty breakfast, during which they were able to discuss quietly their plans for escape. But their hopes were shattered when they were told they were about to be taken to Taranto by aircraft, not by train.

The two officers were given their uniforms, all dried out, and Strever was surprised to find that his captors had overlooked a tiny escaper's compass he had secreted in the small pocket near the waistband of his battledress. Dunsmore had another of these compasses hidden in his cap badge. The four men were taken to the jetty where they had landed the previous afternoon, and in front of them was a newish-looking Cant Z.506B, manned by another Italian crew. Although they were not aware of the fact, it was serial MM45432 of 139° Squadriglio, 82 Gruppo, Regia Marina (the Italian equivalent of the RAF's Coastal Command). This was one of two squadrons of Cants at Prevesa engaged on escorting convoys to ports in Libya.

The farewell was like a film première. The Beaufort crew were lined up and a battery of Italian airmen stood in front of them, clicking cameras. One generous photographer handed each prisoner a packet of twenty cigarettes labelled *Tre Stelle*. The idea caught on in a trice and the astonished foursome were showered with packets. Strever tried to express their gratitude and was told that they were just small presents, for they were going to Taranto where conditions would be far worse for them.

After the goodbyes they were taken to the port waist hatch of the Cant and made to sit in the familiar well amidships below the turret. Five Italians followed them and closed the hatch. Wilkinson was biting his lip with disappointment, for the prospect of escaping from a train had vanished. Unlike the more outgoing Brown, he was rather a quiet and withdrawn person who seldom expressed his innermost thoughts.

'Do you reckon you can fly this thing, Ted?' he whispered to Strever.

'Any pilot can fly any aircraft once it's in the air,' replied the South African.

'Maybe we can take on these jokers,' said Wilkinson. 'Are you all with me?'

'You bet I am,' replied Strever. Brown and Dunsmore nodded agreement.

'*Non parlare*! *Non parlare*!' the Italians shouted at them.

The first pilot, Tenente (Lieutenant) Gaetana Mastrodicasa, sat in the forward seat on the left. Behind him sat the second pilot, Tenente Alessandro Chafari. In front of them, a flight engineer slouched in the nose. A smallish corporal who seemed to be an army man looked suspiciously at the captives. He was armed with a large revolver, in a holster on his belt. Between this guard and the Beaufort men was a wireless operator on the right, with his wireless set on his left. There was no navigator.

Strever saw a large bottle containing machine oil on the floor of the fuselage and began to edge towards it, for it might be used as a weapon, but it was snatched away by the wireless operator. The Cant taxied into the large bay, almost enclosed by the sea. At 0915 hours it took off and began to climb in the direction of Taranto, about an hour and a half away.

The floatplane droned westwards through the blue Mediterranean sky. After a while, Wilkinson smiled gently at the wireless operator in front of him. He pointed to the wireless badge on his blue RAF battledress, a hand grasping flying sparks, and then pointed at the wireless set. The Italian smiled back, acknowledging their common bond, but he did not recognize the falsity of Wilkinson's friendship or the tension that was building up among the captives. Slightly in front of them, the corporal guard eyed the Beaufort men occasionally, but did not draw his revolver. Some time later he began to look pale from airsickness, apparently unused to flying in a service aircraft jolting in the convectional upcurrents of a hot summer's day.

'Spitfire!' Wilkinson yelled suddenly, pointing out of the window to starboard. The wireless operator jerked his head round. His eyes were widening in horror at the dreadful predicament, but they immediately glazed over when Wilkinson's fist smashed into the side of his jaw. Back home in New Zealand, Wilkinson had driven a six-horse team on a farm. He was a brawny young man and his enormous hands grew out of wrists which were the thickness of an average man's forearms. The Italian was knocked out and slumping to the floor when Strever caught him and yanked him backwards into the arms of Brown and Dunsmore. This left Wilkinson to tackle the man they wanted, the airsick guard. His two great hands flashed forward and grabbed the gun and holster on the guard's belt, tearing both free with a savage jerk. In the same movement he threw them to Strever.

The heavy 0.45 inch revolver was out of its holster and in Strever's right hand within a couple of seconds of Wilkinson's first blow. The dumbfounded

Army personnel helping RAF fitters and armourers to refuel and re-arm a Spitfire in a blast pen at Takali in Malta. *Author's collection*

guard, a 45-year-old Corsican of no great stature, was pulled to the rear by the powerful New Zealander. Strever flipped the safety catch of the revolver to 'on'. 'Right, now we've got it made,' he thought, gleefully.

'Look out, that joker's got one!' yelled Wilkinson. The first pilot, Mastrodicasa, had heard the commotion and dived into the sunken well in the nose, drawing a 0.32 inch Beretta automatic and pointing it over the edge at Strever. The South African was suddenly conscious of his height and the size of his body's target. He did not want to fire at the head and eyes of the Italian captain, for immediately behind him was the centre of the Cant's three engines and a bullet in the wrong place might have brought the machine down in the sea. At the same time, Mastrodicasa did not fire, for in the rear were three of his comrades, under the control of the Beaufort men. For a long second, Strever and Mastrodicasa looked at each other in indecision.

The fates were on the side of the Beaufort men. The flight engineer, sitting on the edge of the step facing forwards into the well, had evidently been dozing. There was no work for him, since the Cant was flying back to Taranto for a maintenance check and the entire crew was going on leave. He woke from his dreams of sunny Italy to see his captain alongside him, apparently having gone berserk. The engineer decided he was in the wrong place and began to back hastily out of the nose. For a moment, his body blocked the line of fire between the two men and his backside presented an inviting target. Strever and Wilkinson charged forward and two large-sized shoes rammed into the engineer's posterior, pitching him forward on to his captain. The two Italians were disentangled from each other by powerful arms and bundled unceremoniously to the rear of the fuselage, where Brown and Dunsmore were busy tying up and guarding their erstwhile captors. At first, Strever and Wilkinson could not find the Beretta, although they made certain it was not in the hands of the Italians.

Strever then turned his attention to the second pilot. Chafari had formed his own idea about how to deal with the situation. He had put the control column forward and was diving towards the sea, where he hoped to land and cut the engines. But a large revolver was thrust under his nose.

'Up! Up!' said Strever, jerking the revolver upwards to emphasize his words. Chafari was no linguist, but the meaning was clear. He looked into the fierce eyes of the tall officer beside him and sullenly opened the throttles. The Cant rose into the air again.

At last the Beretta was discovered in the well of the nose and Strever picked it up, before passing the corporal's revolver to Wilkinson. He left Chafari at the controls and moved back to the other four Italians, by then safely tied up with their own belts. Brown and Dunsmore had found some

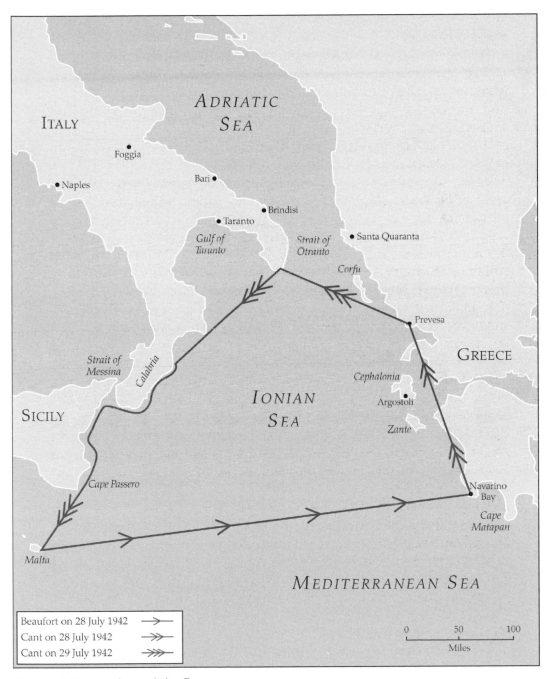

Tracks of the Beaufort and the Cants.

wrenches and were standing guard over them. The Italians looked at Strever with trepidation.

'Africa?' they asked. 'No *benzina*!'

Strever pointed his pistol at the flight engineer, motioned towards the petrol cocks and made a threat that he would never have kept.

'No *benzina* and you're dead!' he said grimly. The flight engineer understood and nodded his head miserably.

'Not Africa,' said Strever. 'Malta!'

'Malta!' howled the Italians. 'Spitfire! Spitfire!'

'Don't worry about Spitfires,' grinned Strever. 'Wilkie, come up beside me, face backwards and cover the second pilot and the rest of them.'

Strever walked forward and slid into the first pilot's seat, taking over the controls. He began to fly the Cant like a Beaufort, skimming just above the surface of the sea. The Italians groaned in protest, indicating that the floats would hit the water, but the South African knew how to fly in this fashion and was intent on keeping under any radar screen.

Dunsmore hunted for maps and charts, without success. It seemed incredible but there were none on board, any more than there was a navigator. They guessed that the crew must have been following a radio beam to Taranto. Brown looked at the wireless set but he and Wilkinson decided to leave it alone, for fear of somehow alerting Italian or German radio controllers. Brown went into the turret and familiarized himself with the free-handling machine gun, in case he had to fire it.

The crew decided to head due west and pick up the coastline of Italy, then dogleg onwards until they reached Cape Passero, the most southerly point of Sicily, from which they remembered that the track over the sea to Malta was about 220°.

A tiny dot appeared on the horizon, away to port. It was an aircraft on an intercept course and Strever watched it carefully, not wishing to arouse suspicion. The outline of the aircraft became clearer as their paths converged. It was a Junkers Ju52 transport heading for Italy and flying at 300 feet. The German aircraft passed close behind them and Strever waggled his wings amicably, while Brown spun the turret around in RAF fashion, to indicate a friendly greeting. The German pilot waggled his wings in response and their paths diverged.

Unsure of their position, the Beaufort men strained their eyes for the Italian coast, waiting impatiently for it to appear. At last mountains rose above the summer haze and Strever flew south and then west. The sweeps and bays seemed never-ending as they worked their way towards Cape Passero in a series of doglegs, but they were not familiar with the coastline and had to fly entirely by guesswork.

The flight engineer indicated that he wanted to adjust the petrol cocks and was released. Brown and Dunsmore stood by him threateningly while he turned knobs and levers, although they had no idea of the control system for the petrol. The Corsican guard was looking so green in the face that Dunsmore, who had occasionally suffered from airsickness himself, released the little man and stood beside him beside the open window hatch. Mastrodicasa and the wireless operator seemed resentful of the release from bondage of their two comrades. The Beaufort men eventually untied them as well, for they seemed suitably subdued and were no match for four hefty young men armed with handguns and wrenches.

At last the Cant reached what appeared to be the southerly tip of Sicily and Strever set course on 220° for Malta, the crew praying that their guesswork was correct. Dunsmore had drawn a rough map from memory but was not convinced that it was accurate enough. The flight time from Sicily to Malta should be only half an hour, and the Cant had already been

Spitfire pilots led by Wing Commander P. Prosser Hanks, the commanding officer of the Luqa Spitfire Wing, scrambling to their aircraft from a bomb-blasted building. They seem amused by the presence of the photographer. *Author's collection*

in the air for over three hours. Strever's mind was in a turmoil when eventually some radio masts appeared ahead. Beaufort crews were not allowed to approach Malta from the north, the direction from which enemy aircraft appeared, and he could not recognize the coastline.

'Can that be Malta?' he wondered. 'What if it isn't?'

Suddenly, Dunsmore shouted: 'My God, look at that!' A thousand feet above them, four Spitfires were in line astern, and the leading fighter was dipping its starboard wing.

Bill Carroll had been released from stand-by at Luqa during the morning of 29 July and was free to enjoy whatever attractions the island of Malta had to offer. A 'Queen Mary' transport came through the airfield, the huge low-loader which could carry an aircraft provided its wings were removed. Carroll jumped on board, for it was headed for Sliema near Valletta, where there was a chance of a dip in the sea, provided there were no jellyfish around. These had been known to sting sailors into insensibility after their ships had been torpedoed. It was a bright hot day, ideal for swimming. But Carroll heard an unusual drone and looked up at the sky. A tri-motored floatplane, obviously Italian, was approaching low over the sea, and above it Spitfires were peeling off to attack.

'That idiot won't get far,' thought Carroll, as the floatplane headed south-west in the direction of St Paul's Bay. The rattle of machine-gun and cannon fire began.

A thousand feet above, Flying Officer 'Dickie' Sherwood of No 603 Squadron looked with curiosity at the Italian floatplane. He could recognize it as a Cant Z.506B and see the Italian markings, but could not understand what an unescorted reconnaissance aircraft was doing in clear daylight at low level around Malta. He wondered if it had been fitted with a torpedo and was about to make an attack. Leading his flight of Spitfires out of the sun, he dived on the intruder.

The danger of Spitfires had been driven out of Strever's mind during the final approach to Malta, for all his attention had been concentrated on recognition of the island. He had intended to land on the sea at the first sight of an RAF fighter and wave a surrender signal, but he had left it too late. Ahead was St Paul's Bay, where the apostle had been shipwrecked in AD 60 when on his way from Caesarea in Roman Palestine to confinement in Rome.

To Strever's port the flight of Spitfires was screaming down on them. Dunsmore took off his singlet, the only white article he could find and waved it from the top hatch, but his action was ineffective. The South

Captors and prisoners on the wings of the skyjacked Cant in St Paul's Bay in Malta, photographed from the approaching air-sea rescue craft. *Courtesy of the late William M. Dunsmore DFC, via Roy C. Nesbit*

African slipped out of his seat and grabbed Mastrodicasa, thrusting him behind the controls. 'Land!' he said, motioning with his hand. 'Land!'

In the second pilot's seat, Chafari had already anticipated this order and begun to throttle back. A burst of fire from the first Spitfire raised a line of splashes 30 yards in front of them. The aim of the second Spitfire was a little more accurate, and the sea boiled with cannon and machine-gun fire only 15 yards in front of the decelerating Cant. Mastrodicasa was turning to starboard, into wind, and throttling right back, when the third Spitfire attacked. This was flown by Strever's friend Bill Young from Bulawayo and it caught the Cant in the port wing, shredding the fabric and leaving forty holes in the wooden airframe. The Italian pilot landed and cut the engines. Strever looked at Wilkinson in relief. They had made it.

All nine occupants of the Cant clambered out on the wing and the Beaufort men waved to the Spitfires. Circling above, the fighter pilots could tell that these peculiar Italians must be surrendering, and they set off for their base of Takali in Malta. The Beaufort men were exultant at their success and the Italians seemed resigned to their fate. Chafari even produced some wine from a suitcase and handed a bottle around. He said he had been going on leave, and now would not be seeing his newly born baby. The Beaufort men and the Italians warmed to each other. Brown slipped inside the fuselage once more

The air-sea rescue craft that collected the captors and prisoners from the skyjacked Cant. *Courtesy of the late William M. Dunsmore DFC, via Roy C. Nesbit*

and got busy with a small screwdriver he had found, removing four aircraft clocks with the quick efficiency of an inveterate souvenir hunter, for distribution to his crew.

There was only one RAF air-sea rescue launch on that side of the island and it was almost an hour before it arrived. A gunner sat inside the aircraft turret fitted in the bows, levelling twin Brownings at the men on the wings of the Cant.

'It's all right!' called the escapers. 'We're RAF!'

'I don't give a cuss what you are!' came the reply. 'Don't move!'

But as the launch drew alongside, they could see the nine men more plainly.

'Blimey, you really are RAF!' one of them exclaimed. 'We thought it was old Mussolini coming to give himself up!'

There was general jubilation and the crew of the launch tried to take the Cant in tow towards St Paul's Bay, but the aircraft kept weather-cocking into wind and progress was painfully slow.

Arriving in the air-sea rescue craft at St Paul's Bay in Malta, the Italian flight engineer looks at an RAF officer while Sergeant John Wilkinson, cigarette in mouth, talks to an Army officer. *Courtesy of the late William M. Dunsmore DFC, via Roy C. Nesbit*

'Let's start up the engines again and try to taxi in,' suggested Strever. But Mastrodicasa shook his head. 'No *benzina*,' he said. The last drop of petrol had been used up during the landing, after a flight of nearly four hours.

Eventually the captors and their prisoners landed at a small cove in St Paul's Bay. News of their arrival had already reached the Maltese and a crowd of excited civilians had gathered. They hated the Italians and rushed threateningly towards them. There might have been a lynching if Strever had not drawn his pistol and kept them at bay until an army escort closed around the group. These took the Italian prisoners to an officers' rest camp nearby and the Beaufort men did their best to repay hospitality by giving them the scanty meal which was all the island could provide. Then Strever insisted on joining the escort as far as the PoW cage, where he shook hands with all of the prisoners and wished them well.

The four Beaufort men were then debriefed and taken back to a rapturous welcome at Luqa. Brown was able to stop a telegram notifying his parents in New Zealand that he was missing. Their billets had been cleared out and their few valuables were ready to be sent to their homes. But, as was the custom in that deprived environment, their clothing and other items of kit had been dispersed among the fellow flyers in their squadron. One by one, their grinning friends came to see them, returning these piece by piece. It was good to be back.

Prisoners and captors in friendly mood in Malta. Left to right: Pilot Officer Bill Dunsmore, Corsican guard, Italian flight engineer, Lieutenant Ted Strever, Tenente Mastrodicasa, Sergeant John Wilkinson, Tenente Chafari, Sergeant Ray Brown, Italian wireless operator. *Courtesy of the late A. Raymond Brown DFM, via Roy C. Nesbit*

The Italian prisoners arriving at Waterloo Station in London under armed guard. Carrying the valise is Tenente Chafari, the second pilot of the Cant. To his left, wearing the forage cap, is the wireless operator, while to his right is the flight engineer. *Courtesy of the late William M. Dunsmore DFC, via Roy C. Nesbit*

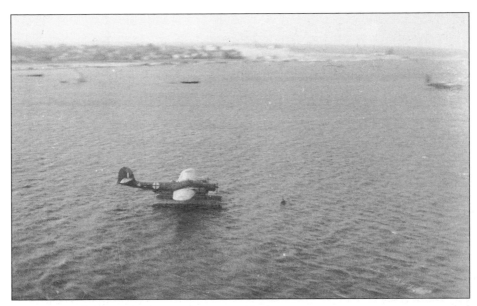

Cant Z.506B serial MM45432 of 139° Squadriglio, moored in Kalafrana Bay in Malta after being skyjacked on 29 July 1942 by Lieutenant Ted Strever and his crew of No 217 Squadron. It has been painted with RAF roundels and air-to-sea rescue crosses. *Courtesy of the late Tom Armstrong DFC, via Roy C. Nesbit*

The captured Cant Z.506B with RAF markings at harbour in Malta. *Courtesy of the late William M. Dunsmore DFC, via Roy C. Nesbit*

Postscript

The Cant was pressed into service as an air-sea rescue aircraft by the RAF at the seaplane base of Kalafrana in Malta, until this was found to be too dangerous and it was sent to Egypt. The Italians were mystified at the loss of an aircraft on what should have been a safe route. Two days after the skyjacking, a Beaufort of No 86 Squadron flown by another South African, Sergeant L. Clifford Thompson, was shot down off the coast of Greece. The crew managed to get into their dinghy but were later picked up by the Italians. Their rescuers told the men that warships were looking for the crew of a missing floatplane. Thompson, known as 'Potty', later became a neighbour and close friend of Strever in South Africa.

All four of Strever's crew received immediate awards. The two officers received DFCs and the two sergeants DFMs, gazetted on 4 September 1942. On 16 November 1942 the Air Member for Training, Air Marshal Sir A. Guy R. Garrod, issued a table of RAF operational casualties. This assessed that the aircrews who flew in torpedo-carrying aircraft stood only a 17.5 per cent chance of surviving a single tour, and a mere 3 per cent chance of surviving two. These were by far the worst figures for any of the RAF's activities in any Command.

Strever was involved in a major crash at Vavuniya in Ceylon on 1 November 1944, when flying as a passenger in a Beaufighter to take over command of No 211 Squadron in Burma. He was badly burnt but recovered and was eventually promoted to lieutenant-colonel. The four Beaufort men survived the war and returned home afterwards, but all of them have since died.

Ted Strever (left) in 1994, with a painting by Axel Dietz of the skyjacked Cant being attacked by Spitfires over Malta. It was presented by his friend Dudley Cowderoy, also a former RAF pilot. At the time, Ted Strever was still flying his own light aircraft over Southern Africa, a Cessna 180. *Courtesy of Jane Cowderoy*

Chapter 3

Death of a Maverick

The mystery of the disappearance on 12 April 1944 of the RAF's most remarkable reconnaissance pilot in the Second World War was finally resolved in 2003, following a discovery in Germany and a detailed examination.

Adrian Warburton was born in Middlesbrough on 10 March 1918, the son of Commander Geoffrey Warburton DSO, RN, and his wife Muriel. He and

Adrian Warburton photographed in Malta while wearing a combination of RAF battledress (without badges of rank) and khaki slacks. *Author's collection*

his elder sister Alison went to local schools in Bournemouth, where their grandparents lived. The family eventually moved to the London area but Adrian's further education took place at St Edward's School in Oxford. Earlier pupils at this school were Douglas Bader and Guy Gibson, later to become famous RAF pilots. After leaving school, Adrian Warburton worked in a firm of accountants in the City of London and also joined the Territorial Army. On 14 January 1939 he entered the RAF with a short-service commission.

His initial flying training took place at RAF Prestwick, where he was rated as average. He was then posted to No 8 Flying Training School at RAF Hullavington, where he trained on Hawker Harts. Although awarded his wings, he

Eileen 'Betty' A.M. Mitchell, a National Beauty Queen who married Adrian Warburton in 1939. *The late Tony Spooner collection*

was rated as below average. In September 1939 he arrived at Coastal Command's Torpedo Training Unit at Gosport. In late October he was posted to No 22 Squadron at Thorney Island in Hampshire, which was equipped with Vickers Vildebeests but about to convert to the new Bristol Beaufort. A few days later he married an attractive divorcée several years older than himself, Eileen 'Betty' A.M. Mitchell. He was too young to receive a marriage allowance from the RAF and seems to have made no financial provision for her. Indeed, the marriage began to break up almost immediately.

In April 1940, No 22 Squadron moved from Thorney Island to North Coates in Lincolnshire. Within the squadron, Warburton became known as a loner with a disregard for RAF authority. There are no records of him taking part in operations. Instead, he was sent on various courses, including a long session with No 2 School of General Reconnaissance at RAF Squires Gate in Lancashire. Although classed as an indifferent pilot, it later transpired that he could handle a machine with great panache and moreover seemed impervious to fear.

Warburton came into prominence after 6 September 1940, when three Martin Marylands arrived in Malta to form No 431 General Reconnaissance Flight, having been flown from North Coates by pilots of No 22 Squadron. These machines were part of a batch that had been ordered from the USA by the French Air Force, and the RAF pilots had converted on to them when serving with No 22 Squadron. Their arrival gave Malta a long-range PR facility which had hitherto been absent. They could cover targets such as Brindisi and Taranto in Italy, the Sicilian ports of Messina and Palermo, the Libyan ports of Tripoli and Benghazi, and even range as far as the eastern Mediterranean. Warburton was considered so unsafe with the Maryland that he was not allowed to fly one to Malta but instead acted as navigator. It was only the illness of another pilot that gave him a chance to demonstrate his prowess.

The Commander-in-Chief of the Mediterranean Fleet, Admiral Sir Arthur Cunningham, had decided to launch an attack with Swordfish torpedo bombers from the carrier HMS *Illustrious* against the Italian fleet at Taranto, and the Marylands were being employed on advance photo-reconnaissance. On 10 November 1940, Warburton carried out one of the final flights for this purpose. He made three runs over the harbour at extreme low level, in the face of intense flak, and then returned to Luqa with a ship's aerial trailing from his tailwheel. The crew reported that the balloon defences were down, and their photographs showed five battleships, fourteen cruisers and twenty-seven destroyers in the port. During the night of 11/12 November, the Swordfish sank one battleship and damaged two more, one so severely that it had to be beached. Two Swordfish were lost.

On 10 January 1941, No 431 Flight became No 69 Squadron and was equipped with PR Hurricanes as well as Marylands. By the end of the following December, Flying Officer Warburton had flown 155 sorties in these machines and been awarded the DFC and bar. He and his crew had been in combat with enemy aircraft and had even carried out bombing raids. Due for a rest, he was posted to No 223 Squadron at RAF Shandur in Egypt, a training unit which was engaged on converting crews to Marylands, Blenheims and Bostons. However, the posting was not to his liking and in early November he contrived to join No 2 Photographic Reconnaissance Unit at Heliopolis.

During the previous September, this PR unit had acquired two Beaufighters, which had been stripped of their cannons and armour plate before being fitted with F24 cameras. They formed a small flight under Flight Lieutenant R.G.M. 'Johnny' Walker, together with ground photographers who had volunteered as aircrew. Operating from the forward airfield of Fuka, Walker and Warburton flew over distant targets such as Crete. Then came a call for photographs of beach landing sites in Sicily. On 29 December 1941, the two pilots set off for Malta, via Timini, west of Tobruk. They carried another pilot, Flying Officer 'Benjie' White, and three airmen photographers.

Corporal Norman Shirley, DFM, who flew from Malta as a cameraman with Adrian Warburton. *Courtesy of the late Norman Shirley*

Christina Ratcliffe, the cabaret dancer who later worked in the RAF Operations Room in Malta and became Adrian Warburton's girlfriend. *The late Tony Spooner collection*

Malta was enduring intense air attacks in late 1941. The Air Officer Commanding-in-Chief, Air Vice-Marshal Hugh Pughe Lloyd, regarded all aircraft landing on the island as coming under his command indefinitely. Moreover, he had missed the services of his favourite reconnaissance pilot. The ground crews also idolized 'Warby', not only for his flying achievements but because he socialized with them on terms of equality. This unorthodox behaviour did not meet with the approval of some RAF officers on the island.

Lloyd cancelled the operations over the Sicilian beaches. Instead, the Beaufighters were sent to ports such as Tripoli, Taranto, Messina and Palermo, as well as Sicilian airfields. At the end of six weeks, Warburton was awarded the DSO while two photographers, Corporal Norman Shirley and Leading Aircraftman Ron Hadden, received DFMs. Shirley, who frequently flew with Warburton, though wounded himself had pulled another pilot, Benjie White, from a burning Beaufighter when it crashlanded at Luqa.

The remaining Beaufighter was flown back to No 2 PRU at Heliopolis by Flight Lieutenant Warburton, together with Hadden and Shirley. By this time, March 1942, he was genuinely in need of a rest. He managed to find an ancient Hawker Hind and took off for a fortnight to Haifa in Palestine, where his father was stationed as a Commander in the Royal Navy. Unfortunately he crashed en route, wrecking the machine but walking unharmed across the desert to safety.

It was well known that Warburton found no shortage of girlfriends in Malta, Haifa or Egypt. Of athletic build, handsome, blue-eyed, blond-haired and wearing his medals, he fascinated women. His long-term girlfriend in Malta was Christina Ratcliffe, a vivacious and attractive young lady from Cheshire who worked on plotting duties in the underground RAF Operations Room, part of the Malta Command Centre at Lascaris in Valletta. She had been a dancer in a cabaret in Valletta, engaged to a French airman who was lost on a photo-reconnaissance sortie, and this had brought her in touch with Warburton. Fluent in French and of high intelligence, she proved invaluable as a civilian in RAF service.

Back in Heliopolis, Warburton flew non-operationally with No 2 PRU for several weeks. He also converted on to the Spitfire PR IV, which had arrived in the unit. Then he began flying sorties in these machines or sometimes in Beaufighters, covering such targets as Athens, Piraeus, Salamis, Rhodes and other Greek islands. At one time, when Rommel's Afrika Korps was nearing Cairo, he flew Beaufighters to RAF Lydda in Palestine with six women packed in each machine, evacuating them to safety. He also made flights in company with the so-called 'Halpro force' of B-24 Liberators of the USAAF, which was stationed in Egypt.

In August 1942, Warburton was posted back to Malta, to take command of No 69 Squadron with the rank of squadron leader. He arrived there on the 11th of the month, to find that Air Vice-Marshal Sir Keith Park had taken over as Air Officer Commanding-in-Chief. By then, No 69 Squadron had become a hybrid unit which consisted of A Flight with PR Baltimores, B Flight with Spitfire PR IVs and C Flight with Wellington VIIIs modified to carry torpedoes. However, it was woefully short of pilots and aircrews, following severe losses. There was near starvation on the island and the forces were desperately short of military supplies. But relief was en route, in the form of the surviving merchant ships from a convoy, which had fought its way from Gibraltar under operation 'Pedestal'.

Warburton's arrival coincided with this dramatic operation and he lost no time in getting back into the air in a Spitfire. There was a strong possibility

A Lockheed F–4 photo–reconnaissance aircraft of the USAAF's 3rd Group in a blast pen in RAF Luqa, Malta. The first of these aircraft arrived on the island on 3 March 1943, flown by an American pilot from Castel Benito in Libya. *Courtesy of William H. Armstrong*

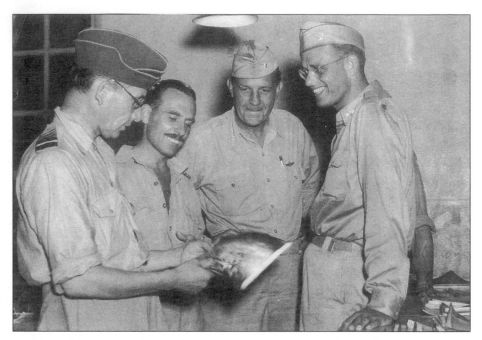

British and American officers discussing air photographs prior to the invasion of the Italian mainland in September 1943. Left to right: Air Chief Marshal Sir Arthur Tedder (Air Commander-in-Chief Mediterranean Air Command); Squadron Leader S.R. Walton (Photographic Officer); Brigadier-General Patrick W. Timberlake (Director of Operations, USAAF); Colonel Elliot Roosevelt (Commander, Northwest African Photographic Reconnaissance Wing). *Courtesy of Warrant Officer J.R. Eggleston, RAF (Ret'd)*

Wing Commander Adrian Warburton, DSO and bar, DFC and bar, DFC (USA), wearing an RAF blue battledress. He appears to be wearing the shoulder tabs of a group captain in this photograph, but in fact they are those of a wing commander on a khaki background. *Author's collection*

A Spitfire PR XI and a Lockheed F-5E, both with American markings, serving with the 7th Photographic Group of the US Eighth Air Force. *Author's collection*

that Italian heavy cruisers would attempt to finish off what was left of the convoy. He flew over Taranto and on the next day made two flights over Messina and Palermo, and over the sea between Sardinia and Tunisia. Four enemy cruisers and attendant destroyers were spotted, steering south near the west of Sicily. Three of Warburton's Wellington VIIIs were then despatched, sending messages *en clair* to a fictitious force of Liberators and calling them to attack. The Italians turned away to Messina, but two cruisers were torpedoed and badly damaged by a British submarine before they reached port.

Operational flying continued. One extraordinary episode took place on 14 October 1942, when Warburton was engaged on photographing three Beaufighters of No 227 Squadron making a bombing attack on an Italian convoy consisting of a merchant ship and the torpedo boat *Medici*. Two of these Beaufighters were shot down, but the crew of one, flown by Pilot Officer J.M. Bryce, got into their dinghy. Despite a torrent of flak, Warburton flew round the Italian warship, waggling the wings of his Spitfire, until the captain understood that he was leading them to a rescue. The two RAF men were picked up by the warship and became PoWs.

The Battle of El Alamein opened on 23 October 1942. The Axis forces went into full retreat, and the Anglo-American invasion of north-west Africa began on 7 November. In this period, Warburton was awarded a second bar to his DFC. Then, on 15 November, he failed to return from an operation in a PR Spitfire over Algeria. His father was notified of his loss, but Warburton landed back in Malta six days later. He had been attacked by several Messerschmitt Bf109s while over the coast but had managed to nurse his shattered Spitfire to the airfield of Bône, which had been occupied by British paratroops only two days before. The aircraft was wrecked in the crash-landing but he walked away unharmed, after removing an undamaged camera magazine. A French aircraft flew him to the airfield at Maison Blanche, near Algiers, and from there he had obtained a lift in a Halifax to Gibraltar. Once there, he had managed to find a spare Spitfire VB to fly to Malta via Algiers and Bône, and during this sortie had shot down a Junkers Ju88. Meanwhile, his promotion to wing commander had come through.

Operational flying continued unabated and there are many stories of Warburton's exploits in the next few months. On 8 February 1943, the Spitfires of No 69 Squadron's B Flight were formed into No 683 Squadron under Warburton. The other two flights remained in No 69 Squadron, which was taken over by Squadron Leader R.C. Mackay in the following month. Warburton took a leave in England during March and on his return found that the North African Photo-Reconnaissance Wing had been formed, as part of the preparation for the invasion of southern Europe. It embraced all the RAF and USAAF PR squadrons in the Mediterranean Air Command, including No 60 (SAAF) Squadron.

Air Marshal Sir Arthur Coningham, photographed when an Air Vice-Marshal. On 23 July 1943, when Air Officer Commanding the Northwest African Tactical Air Forces, he sent a personal letter of appreciation to Wing Commander Adrian Warburton. *Author's collection*

This brought him into contact with Lieutenant-Colonel Elliot Roosevelt, a son of the US President, who commanded the new wing from his headquarters at La Marsa, near Tunis. The Americans were puzzled by Warburton, who did not fit the usual mould of RAF senior officers. His hair was too long, his well-worn uniform consisted of a mixture of RAF blue and khaki, and he carried a Luger pistol in a holster as well as a knife stuck in the top of one of his scuffed desert boots. But his expertise, reputation and decorations were such that he soon became accepted by them.

On 14 May 1943, the Axis forces in north-west Africa surrendered and the invasion of Sicily became the next priority of the Allied forces in the Mediterranean. In advance, the heavily defended island of Pantellaria had to be rendered ineffective, and Warburton brought back some astonishing low-level photographs. These earned him the award of an American DFC.

Then Warburton led the photo-reconnaissance of the landing beaches in Sicily, flying a Spitfire XI. Immediately after the island was invaded, on 9/10 July 1943, personal letters of appreciation were sent to him from the General Officer Commander-in-Chief of 15 Army Group, General Sir Harold Alexander, and the Air Officer Commanding the Northwest African Tactical Air Force, Air Marshal Sir Arthur Coningham. It is not surprising that he was awarded a bar to his DSO.

The next stage after the occupation of Sicily was the invasion of the Italian mainland. Here again, Warburton and his squadron carried out photo-reconnaissance of the beaches. However, a few weeks after Italy surrendered to the Allies on 8 September, he was posted back to the UK. By this time, he was recognized as the premier PR pilot of the war.

His stay in the UK did not last long, for he was sent back to command the RAF's new No 336 Wing at La Marsa in Tunisia, formed on 30 October 1943 under the North African Photographic Reconnaissance Wing. This consisted of No 680 Squadron in Egypt and No 682 Squadron at La Marsa, both of which were equipped with Spitfire PR IXs in addition to the older machines. No 683 Squadron in Malta also came under the new wing, with Spitfire PR IXs and Mosquito PR IVs. Lastly, No 60 (SAAF) Squadron, by then at Ariana in Tunisia and equipped with Mosquito PR IVs and PR IXs, joined the wing. The purpose of this wing was to provide strategic and tactical PR support for the Italian campaign.

Warburton's phenomenal luck ran out in the evening of 26 November. He had been presented with a personal jeep by Elliot Roosevelt, but he ran off the road and turned it over, causing major injuries to himself. His pelvis was fractured and he was taken to a military hospital in Carthage, where he remained in plaster for several weeks before being transferred to another hospital in Algiers. His recovery was slow and inevitably he was relieved of his command. He remained in hospital until late January 1944, and was still not fully fit when he discharged himself.

On 25 January 1944, Elliot Roosevelt was posted to England with the rank of full colonel. His task was to begin forming a strategic PR capability within the US Eighth Air Force. Ilis unit was equipped with Lockheed F-5 Lightnings (the PR variation of the P-38 Lightning fighter-bomber) and a few Spitfire PRs obtained from the RAF. This eventually formed part of the 106th (Photo-Reconnaissance) Group, comprising both the USAAF and the RAF strategic PR squadrons. Roosevelt asked for Warburton to be

The headquarters of the 325th Reconnaissance Wing of the US Eighth Air Force at High Wycombe in Buckinghamshire. *Author's collection*

appointed as his deputy in his headquarters at Mount Farm in Oxfordshire, close to the RAF PR headquarters at Benson.

Warburton duly arrived to take up his new duties but it was not until 1 April 1944 that he was officially appointed, with the title of RAF Liaison Officer to the US 7th Photo-Reconnaissance Group. It should be noted that the American 'Group' was the equivalent of an RAF 'Wing'. According to contemporary accounts, he seemed very depressed, but he may have been suffering from the latent effects of his accident. However, he arranged to carry out an operation in an F–5 Lightning, having had limited experience in the aircraft while in North Africa.

In the morning of 12 April 1944, Adrian Warburton took off from Mount Farm in Lockheed F–5B serial 42-67325 of the 27th Squadron to photograph targets in southern Germany. His mission was No BB22, but his targets are not listed in the official American records. It was thought that one objective might have been the ball-bearing plant at Schweinfurt, about forty-five miles north-west of Nuremberg. This was the target on that day

The Lockheed F-5A photo–reconnaissance aircraft, as seen in this photograph, was an adaptation of the Lockheed P-38C single-seat fighter. It was powered by two Allison V-1710-51/53 engines, each of 1,150 hp, and the armament was replaced by four K-17 cameras. *Author's collection*

Ground crews of the 7th Photographic Group, US Eighth Air Force, at Mount Farm in Oxfordshire, working on a Lockheed F-5E photo–reconnaissance aircraft. *Author's collection*

It is believed that the Lockheed F–5B flown by Wing Commander Adrian Warburton was brought down by 20 mm explosive shells fired from Lechfeld airfield. This version of the defences against low-flying aircraft was the deadly 'quad gun', which fired shells at the rate of about 1,000 per minute. *Author's collection*

for 97 B-17 Fortresses of the 1st Bombardment Division of the US Eighth Air Force, escorted by P-38 Lightnings, P-47 Thunderbolts and P-51 Mustangs. However, this force encountered dense clouds before reaching the French coast and aborted the mission.

Another F-5 on this operation was flown by an experienced pilot in these machines, Captain Carl Chapman. His F-5B was serial 42-68205 and his mission over southern Germany was No BB21, to photograph the airfields of Erding, Landau-Ganacker, Regensburg-Obertraubling (where the new Me262 jet fighter was being produced), Schwäbisch-Hall and Straubing. Both F-5s were to be escorted by eight P-51s of the 357th Fighter Group, although in the event only two of these managed to make contact.

The two F-5s flew in company before splitting up for their separate targets. Chapman carried out his photography and headed for a position where he was scheduled to rendezvous with Warburton and then fly on to Alghero in Sardinia, which had been occupied by the Allies. He circled for a while, calling on the R/T, but when Warburton did not show up flew on to Sardinia and returned to Mount Farm later in the day, his mission, No BB23, to photograph French airfields.

The disappearance of Warburton caused a stir, coupled with recriminations for allowing the operation. Various speculations followed. He had

A distant photograph of Lockheed F-5B serial 42-67325 flown by Wing Commander Adrian Warburton, still smouldering and under guard by a soldier of the Wehrmacht, after crashing on 12 April 1944 on a field near Egling in southern Germany. *Author's collection*

not recovered from his injuries and had crashed or baled out somewhere. He had committed suicide, following his bout of depression. He had slammed into the Swiss Alps or come down in the Tyrrhenian Sea before reaching Sardinia. His aircraft had broken up in severe turbulence. He had set course for San Severo, near Foggia in southern Italy, where his old squadron, No 683, was based. He had flown back to Malta, where his aircraft was hidden by ground crews and he lived in secrecy with his girlfriend, Christina Ratcliffe. These speculations were fuelled by the fact that his parents were not notified of his disappearance for over a fortnight. However, this was not unusual at a time when extensive enquiries were being made by the authorities.

After the war, Warburton's wife Eileen was presented with his medals at Buckingham Palace, but she generously gave them to his parents. Warburton did not receive the public adulation that was accorded to other war aces, although his memory was perpetuated in Malta. He is recorded as having 'no known grave' by the Commonwealth War Graves Commission. The mystery of his death seemed insoluble.

On 19 August 2002 a German historian in the Landsberg district of southern Germany, Dr Anton Huber, began to excavate a site in a field

The excavation team busy at the crash site of the Lockheed F-5B in Egling, together with a mechanical digger. They excavated an area of about 12 metres by 3 metres, down to a depth of 3.8 metres. *Hermann Laage collection*

Press reporters and witnesses of the crash looking at the first components excavated from the crater in August 2002. *Courtesy of Cesar-Siedel, via Richard Chapman*

Gefangenenlager: 7 870	Staatsangehörigkeit: ÜSA	Nr. der Liste:
Gefangenen-Nr.:		Seite der Liste:
Name: Unbekannt	Beruf:	
Vornamen:	Religion:	
	Dienstgrad: Flg.	
Geburtstag u. Geburtsort:	Truppenteil: Masch. Lightning	
	Komp. usw.	Matr.-Nr.
Vorname des Vaters:		
	Ort und Tag der Gefangennahme oder Internierung:	
Familienname der Mutter:		
	Verwundungen, Verletzungen oder Tod:	
Name u. Anschrift der zu benachrichtigenden Person:		
	wann und von wo zugegangen:	
Aufenthalt u. Veränderungen: ✠ 12. 4. 44/1145 zw. Egling u. Künzelbach		

A German record of the crash of a Lightning near Egling at 1145 hours on 12 April 1944. The machine was correctly assumed to have been American; the name of the pilot was unknown.

south-east of Egling on the River Paar, where an Allied aircraft was reported to have crashed at about 1145 hours local time on 12 April 1944. Witnesses, who were boys at the time, stated that it came from the direction of Lechfeld airfield, flying low and trailing smoke. Lechfeld was where four Me262 jet fighters were being tested. The aircraft dived into soft earth, causing a fairly shallow crater. The Wehrmacht found the wreck but most of the parts on the surface were pushed into the crater. Some of this wreckage, including a wing and one of the engines, was cleared in 1951/52 during land consolidation work.

This excavation was initiated by the British researcher Frank G. Dorber, who believed that the wreckage was the machine flown by Warburton. Also associated with the dig was David Roath of the US Army Memorial Affairs Activity Europe (USAMAAE). The work was coordinated by Hermann Laage of Volksbund Deutsche Kriegsgraberfürsorge (VDK), the German War Graves Commission, which is responsible for maintaining 3.2 million German war graves throughout the world. Much of the information that follows was provided by Hermann Laage.

Dr Huber located the site with the help of a field map and air photography provided by the US Army. The aircraft had come down in a field at Egling owned by the farmer Herr Braumüller, and the remains had sunk to a depth of 11–12 feet. However, he recovered an Allison V-1710 engine from the port wing; this was number AF 42-9475 and a plate indicates that it was installed in an F-5 Lightning, which later transpired were part of Warburton's machine. There was a propeller, apparently grazed by two bullets. A length of film was found. This was burnt at both ends and about 10 inches wide; the standard American K-17 camera had a 9 x 9 inch exposure format.

There was a fragment from a sleeveless pullover. Dr Huber also recovered over 100 postcranial elements, ranging in size from less than half an inch to approximately 5 inches, constituting some 15 per cent of a skeleton. These remains were highly fragmented and partly calcinated. Their overall appearance indicated that Warburton had been killed by a burst of flak. It is interesting to note that there was little evidence of glass, whereas aircraft crash sites are usually studded with such fragments. This indicated that the canopy over the cockpit had been blown away by flak, jettisoned, or more probably removed by those who sealed off the area and examined the cockpit area of the wreckage.

Following this excavation, a military funeral took place on 14 May 2003 at a cemetery in Durnbach, south of Munich. It was attended by Warburton's wife, Mrs Eileen 'Betty' Westcott, who had remarried but had been widowed

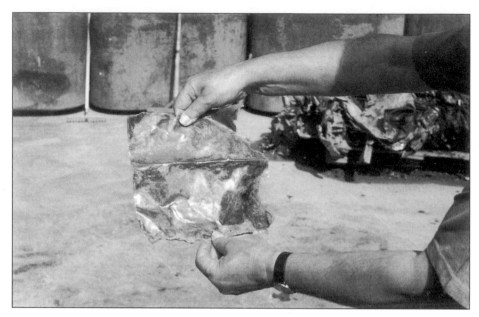

A scrap of camera film, about 10 inches wide, which was found partially folded within the wreckage. *Photo via Richard Chapman, Ed. Co-ordinator,* Flugzeug Classic, *Munich, Germany*

Parts of the aircraft recovered, including port propeller, crankshaft, pistons and other components. *Photo via Richard Chapman, Ed. Co-ordinator,* Flugzeug Classic, *Munich, Germany*

Part of the cockpit control, including the undercarriage selector lever, a throttle and a propeller control shaft. *Photo via Richard Chapman, Ed. Co-ordinator,* Flugzeug Classic, *Munich, Germany*

The human remains recovered in 2002 from the crash site at Egling were placed in this small casket, ready to be taken away for burial. The anthropologist at the US Army Memorial Affairs reported that these consisted mainly of small fragments of the cranium, part of an ulna, part of a femur, and small remains of toes. All were badly burnt from a fire in the aircraft. *Hermann Laage collection*

for the second time and was living in Australia. This seemed to close the matter; but three questions persisted. How was this aircraft brought down? What were the precise targets he was ordered to photograph? Was there any truth in the belief that some part of the pilot's body was recovered by the Germans at the time and buried in the graveyard of St Johannes Baptist Church, about a mile from the scene of the crash?

According to the Deceased Personnel File of the USAMAAE, the aircraft was brought down by heavy flak, but Hermann Laage considers that to be unlikely. The Heimatflak (local Anti-Aircraft Division) probably poured shells at the lone Lockheed F-5B but it was manned only by Flakhelfers (auxiliary gunners) who were either very young Russian recruits or old reservists, notoriously inaccurate and capable of firing only box barrages. Its generals were eager to claim credit for successes, for these meant promotion and decorations, keeping them away from the perils of the Eastern Front. Warburton was a specialist in medium and low-level reconnaissance, and there is very strong evidence that his aircraft was hit by medium flak over Lechfeld airfield. Its defences consisted of 37 mm flak guns, deservedly named *Jaboschreck* (fighter-blaster) by their crews. These were fully automatic, fitted with sophisticated sighting and could traverse quickly. It is clear that the Lightning was brought down by fire from this airfield, for its commander immediately despatched a detail in the direction of its path and this team duly arrived at the crash site.

Herr Gottfried Grad of Egling, photographed in 2003. As a schoolboy, he was one of a crowd of civilians who witnessed the removal of body parts from the cockpit of the Lockheed F-5B that crashed on 12 April 1944 in a field at Egling. *Courtesy of Herr Gottfried Grad*

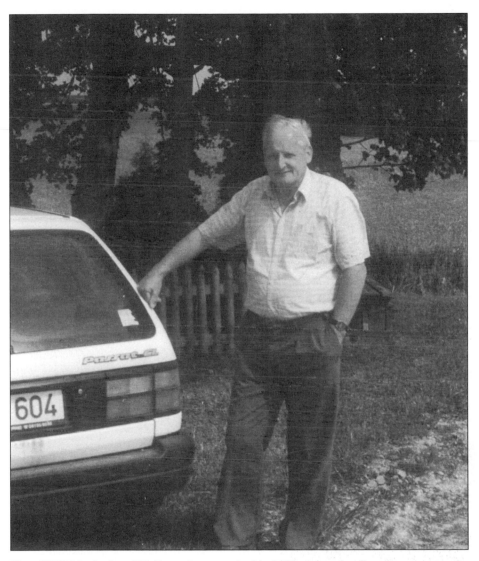

Herr Willi Maxhofer of Egling, photographed in 2003. As a schoolboy, he was one of a crowd of civilians who witnessed the removal of body parts from the cockpit of the Lockheed F-5B that crashed on 12 April 1944 in a field at Egling. *Courtesy of Herr Willi Maxhofer*

As to whether some part of Warburton's body was buried by the Germans, Hermann Laage obtained some vital information from two respected local citizens who were schoolboys at the time. These are Herr Willi Maxhofer and Herr Gottfried Grad, both from Egling. They were on their way home from school when they heard the resounding crash of guns from Lechheld and then saw the stricken aircraft trailing smoke and flames. Soldiers of the Luftwaffe and the Feldgendarmerie (Field Police) arrived quickly and sealed off the crash site, but the boys were able to watch events as part of the crowd outside the cordon. They saw medics wrapping up 'a limb dripping with blood and taking it to a troop carrier'. Another witness, whose name has been lost, saw 'a tuft of hair on a piece of skull'; it is known that Warburton's hair was fair.

These human remains were probably taken to a sick bay for examination. Of course, it would have been necessary for the military to have found out whether the pilot had been killed, was lying there wounded, or had even baled out and was evading capture. In spite of the guards and the strict prohibition, photographs were taken of the crashed aircraft. Some children were also able to loot parts of the aircraft, such as instruments.

Subsequently, Hermann Laage tried to find out what had happened to the human remains which had been removed from the site. He telephoned the clergyman in charge of St Johannes Baptist Church at Kaufering and asked him to check his register of burials, only to be told that all records of Allied casualties were handed over to a provisional German War Graves Commission at the end of the war and that in turn these were handed to an Allied Commission. However, a *Grabmeldung* (Grave Report) dated 4 June 1946 is available, showing that 'approximately seven' Allied airmen were buried in the church. It has been confirmed by the Commonwealth War Graves Commission that this includes seven men from a Handley Page Halifax II of No 77 Squadron, shot down on the night of 6/7 September 1943 during a raid on Munich, but there are no records of the burial of any other airman.

Thus this part of the mystery of Warburton's last flight cannot be resolved, unless there is information under 'long closure' not yet released to the public. Nevertheless, from a commonsense point of view it seems extremely unlikely that those who inspected the crashed Lockheed F-5B would have ignored the cockpit area and done nothing about recovery of some body parts. It is certainly understood by those citizens of Egling who are old enough to remember the incident that these were interred in the communal grave for Allied airmen at the church in Kaufering. These include Herr Johannes Heiss, a young gravedigger, although he had been drafted into the army at the time of the crash.

As mentioned above, the American records do not list Warburton's targets and they may never be known precisely. However, part of the answer can be provided from a very authorative source, namely Flight Officer Constance Babington Smith of the WAAF. This remarkable young lady had formed the

The church of St Johannes Bapt. in the village of Kaufering, a few miles from the field where Adrian Warburton crashed on 12 April 1944. *Courtesy of Daniela Chapman, 'Chapman Fotografie', Kaufbeuren, Germany*

Gemeinde ... Kaufering.   Formblatt 1

Lfd. Nr. ... 2.

Von den Bürgermeistern sind alle auf ihrem Gemeindegebiet befindlichen Gräber von alliierten und deutschen Soldaten, Kriegs
gefangenen, männlichen und weiblichen Angehörigen des Militärgefolges und Unbekannten zu melden.

Datum 4.6.1946

Ausgestellt durch ...... Gemeinde Kaufering.

Grabmeldung

Nationalität des Toten ... Engländer

Familienname ... unbekannt.	Begräbnisort, Gemeinde Kaufering.
Vorname ... unbekannt.	Kreis ...... Landsberg/Lech.
Dienstgrad ... unbekannt.	Provinz Oberbay ...... Staat Bayern.
Truppenteil ... Luftwaffe	bei Feldgrab: Lageangabe
Feldpostnummer unbekannt.	Entfernung ...... Meter, Himmelsrichtung
Erkennungsmarke (volle Aufschrift) ... unbekannt.	von ...... (nächste größere Ortschaft)
	(Wenn Skizze der Grablage, Rückseite benützen)
Geburtstag ... unbekannt.	Kriegerfriedhof / Gemeindefriedhof*). Kaufering.
Geburtsort, Staat ... unbekannt.	Einzelgrab / Sammelgrab (mit einem gemeinsamen Grabzeichen)
Todestag ...	Nr. ...... Reihe ...... Feld ...
Todesort, Staat Kaufering, (Oberbay)	Anzahl der Toten im Sammelgrab: ungefähr 7.
Todesursache*): gefallen, Art der Verwundung / verstorben, Art	Grabbild / Negativ an Angehörige gesandt am
der Krankheit / Unfall	Umgebettet am
	nach
Selbstmord, mit / ohne Bewilligung militärischer Ehren*)	
erschossen, Urteilsgrund	Grab-Nr. ...... Reihe ...... Feld
Anschrift der Angehörigen unbekannt.	Umbettungsprotokoll ausgestellt durch
	Weitere Angaben, z. B. Identifizierung, Zeichen von Unbe
	kannten, Type und Nummer des Flugzeugs und Motors, Anzahl
	der Besatzung (auch Rückseite benützen):
Angehörige benachrichtigt am	
Bei Alliierten: gemeldet am zum letztenmal	
am 3.Juni 1946	
Nachlaß*) abgesandt am	

*) Nichtzutreffendes streichen   Möglichst mit Schreibmaschine ausfüllen und Fragen lückenlos beantworten

Bombardur Verlagsanstalt

This 'Grave Report' of 4 June 1946 recorded the discovery of unknown British airmen in the graveyard of the church at Kaufering. It also recorded that there were 'approximately seven' of them.

A corner of the graveyard of the church of St Johannes Bapt. where Allied airmen were buried during the war. These were understood to have included 'the pilot from Egling' who crashed on 12 April 1944. The site is now occupied by other graves. *Courtesy of Daniela Chapman, 'Chapman Fotografie', Kaufbeuren, Germany*

Herr Heiss, a farmer of Kaufering, photo-graphed in 2003. In his youth he dug graves at the church of St Johannes Bapt. and understood that 'the pilot from Egling' who crashed on 12 April 1944 was buried there. *Courtesy of Daniela Chapman, 'Chapman Fotografie', Kaufbeuren, Germany*

Two 'line overlap' reconnaissance photographs of Lechfeld airfield taken on 13 April 1944, showing damage during an attack by ninety-three Liberators of the US Eighth Air Force, escorted by fighters. The circled numbers 1 to 14 show hits on barracks, workshops, hangars and small buildings, while that marked 15 shows a damaged aircraft. © *The National Archives ref: AIR 40/600*

Constance Babington Smith joined the WAAF in July 1940 and after six months as a teleprinter operator was commissioned as a photographic interpreter. She began the Aircraft Section of the Central Interpretation Unit alone in April 1941 and was in charge of the unit throughout its expansion until 1945. She prepared training and reference material and lectured regularly to interpreters at the RAF Staff College and the Empire Flying School. She was Mentioned in Despatches in January 1942 and awarded the MBE in 1945. *Author's collection*

A photograph released in October 1943, showing B-17 Fortresses of the US Eighth Air Force flying through a flak barrage while bombing an enemy airfield. *Author's collection*

B-17 Fortresses of the 447th Bomb Group, US Eighth Air Force, based at Rattlesham in Suffolk. *Author's collection*

Aircraft Section of the Central Interpretation Unit in April 1941 and remained in charge of it in April 1944, by which time it had been renamed the Allied Interpretation Unit and was based at Medmenham in Buckinghamshire. She liaised with senior RAF and USAAF officers, frequently lectured on the subject of air photography, and was in a position to know the purpose of Warburton's flight. In her book *Evidence in Camera*, which describes a number of Warburton's sorties, she states 'he was going to photograph some German airfields on the way out, and more targets on the way back'.

In the south of Germany there is a vast plain in which Kaufering and Lechfeld airfields were situated. It is clear that these two major airfields were among Warburton's targets, since they were close together and he was brought down by fire from the latter. Moreover, something significant was happening in this area, and this was known to Allied Intelligence. To explain this, one has to compare the development of jet aircraft in the Luftwaffe with that of the RAF.

The RAF's first experimental jet aircraft, the Gloster E.28/39, was invented by Frank Whittle and made its maiden flight on 15 May 1941. No 616 Squadron was equipped with the Gloster Meteor 1 from 12 July 1944. Similar research was taking place in Germany, and in some ways was more advanced. The first German jet aircraft was the Heinkel He 178, designed by Hans-Joachim Pabst von Obain and fitted with an HeS-3B turbojet: this first flew on 24 August 1939. However, the Reichsluftfahrtministerium (RLM or German Air Ministry) was not interested in this project and so the machine was not developed. Instead, it was Professor Wilhelm (Willy) Emil Messerschmitt who was asked by the RLM to design an aircraft fitted with a new turbojet engine being developed by Junkers, later known as the Jumo 004B. Three prototypes were ordered in early 1940, and the first all-jet flight took place on 18 July 1942 in Messerschmitt Me 262VE.

The service version of this aircraft, the Me 262A *Schwalbe* (Swallow) went into production but output was delayed for several reasons. One was the devastation of Messerschmitt's assembly plant at Regensburg, near Munich, on 17 August 1943 by B-17 Flying Fortresses of the US Eighth Air Force. Then a very heavy attack on Augsburg by RAF Bomber Command on the night of 25/26 February 1944 caused much damage to Messerschmitt's component factory. Other attacks were made on the factories making the jet engines. Another major reason was Hitler's insistence that the machine should be converted from a fighter to a light bomber, for use against the Allied forces when they invaded western Europe. This was a role for which it was unsuited.

The existence of the Me 262 had become known to British Intelligence. Ever since she had first suspected the presence of V-2 rockets at Peenemünde in the summer of 1942, Constance Babington Smith had been looking for scorch marks caused by jet aircraft taking off from German airfields. Some fan-shaped marks disclosed the possibility of twin-engined jets. She discussed these findings with Group Captain Frank Whittle in the summer of 1943 and compared them with special photographs of marks made by Gloster Meteor prototypes on RAF airfields. At the end of January 1944 she was able to identify an Me 262 on the airfield of Augsburg and another on the airfield of Lechfeld.

There were other means of gathering such information. In the volumes *British Intelligence in the Second World War*, by F.H. Hinsley *et al.*, it is recorded that decrypts of Enigma signals on 7 February 1944 disclosed the

A Messerschmitt 262A-1a jet fighter of III./EJG 2 (Ergänzungs-Jagdgeschwader or Fighter Replacement Group) on the ramp at Lechfeld airfield in late October 1944. *Author's collection*

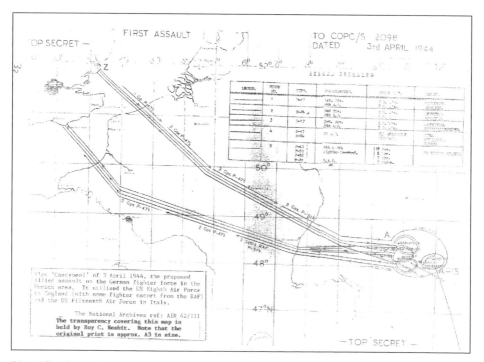

Plan 'Candypeel' of 3 April 1944, the proposed Allied assault on the German fighter force in the Munich area. It utilized the US Eighth Air Force in England (with some fighter escort from the RAF) and the US Fifteenth Air Force in Italy. © *The National Archives ref: AIR 42/111*

An enlargement of part of a photograph showing the start of the runway at Rheine, west of Osnabrück. It shows scorch marks caused by jet engines starting up before take-off, as well as bomb craters. The photograph is undated but Me262s of the staff unit Stab/Kampfgeschwader 51 Edelweiss were based there from 25 February 1944 to 20 March 1945 and its squadrons became operational in July 1944. *Author's collection*

fact that German Army specialists were being transferred from the Balkans to work on jet-propelled aircraft. Another signal on 22 February 1944 revealed that the Luftwaffe was seeking highly qualified pilots for training on the Me 262 and on the Arado Ar 234 jet bomber, which was also under construction. Further information came from German PoWs. One of these, who had been employed in the Messerschmitt factory at Augsburg, stated in March 1944 that facilities were being dispersed as a result of Allied bombing.

Thus more photo-reconnaissance was required by the Allies. The area to which Warburton and Chapman headed was an ideal site for testing the Me 262 and its engines. In early April 1944 an operational convention had been formed there, the Kommando Thierfelder. This had also attracted the attention of the Allies, and the threat of the Luftwaffe regaining air supremacy had galvanized them into action. By 3 April 1944, they had drawn up a plan code-named 'Candypeel', in which the US Eighth Air Force in England and the US Fifteenth Air Force in Italy would combine to smash the airfields in southern Germany where the new German jet aircraft were being tested. This was only a preliminary plan, for the US Eighth Air Force made a heavy raid on Lechfeld on 13 April 1944, the day after Warburton was shot down. Thereafter, as recorded in *British Intelligence in the Second World War*, 'from April 1944, PR visited Lechfeld every few

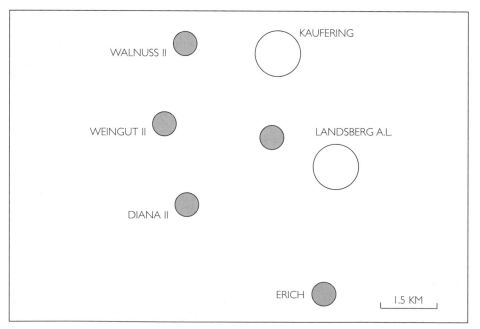

A map showing the location of the *Grossbunkers* in the vicinity of Landsberg.

Work in progress on one of the six *Grossbunkers*, partially underground, intended for the dispersal of aircraft production in the Kaufering district of southern Germany. Each bunker was 400 metres long and 26 metres high. There were five floors within a bunker, each protected by a ceiling of five metres of concrete and 38 mm of armoured plating. The roof was 18 metres thick and intended to be concealed by trees. *Hermann Laage collection*

days'. These photographs revealed more Me 262s, although by May 1944 'Germany had produced only thirteen'.

Yet there was even more in this area to challenge Allied supremacy in the skies. Lechfeld Plain was planned to become the location of a group of *Grossbunker* projects. Fortifications similar to those on the 'Atlantic Wall' were built with frantic haste near the airfield, facilitated by large gravel deposits in the locality. Work on these began on 18 June 1944, when the first draft of Jewish slave labourers arrived from Auschwitz-Birkenau and were housed in concentration camps erected around the town of Landsberg am Lec. Large batches of other victims were then sent from Dachau.

Huge installations were built, partly underground and able to resist every conventional weapon of the day. The area north of Munich was prepared as a focal point for German air defence, and as one of the last redoubts of the Third Reich. It is not known in precise detail what each *Grossbunker* was intended to house, but certainly there were to be underground command posts, aircraft production and assembly plants, hospitals and even hangars. Their main function was to provide facilities for aircraft production – the Me 262, the Dornier Do 335B-2 nightfighter and the Focke-Wulf Ta 152 interceptor. They were given innocuous code-names, such as 'Weingut' (vineyard), 'Walnuss' (walnut) and 'Diana'. They were 400 metres long and their dome-shaped concrete roofs were intended to be 18 metres thick.

Lieutenant-Colonel Edward F. Seiller of the US 12 Armoured Division, with his helmet removed, ordering German civilians from the town of Hurlach to bury the corpses of slave labourers at Lager IV, Kaufering, on 29 April 1945. © *US National Archives and Records Administration # 111-SC 208 385*

The trial of Johann Baptist Eichelsdörfer, the last commandant of Kaufering IV sub-camp. He was sentenced to death and hanged on 29 May 1946. © *US National Archives and Records Administration # 111-SC 223 878*

The conditions under which the slave labourers worked were cruel and sadistic. Forced to endure sixteen-hour shifts, they lived in filthy conditions and were routinely starved and beaten. It is difficult to understand how humanity can sink to this level of brutality. Yet the whole project came to nothing, for the nearby airfields were constantly bombed by the Allies.

After D-Day, the medium bombers of the US Ninth Air Force joined in the attacks, while their escorting fighters strafed aircraft and ground installations throughout southern Germany.

The camps at Kaufering were liberated by the 12th Armoured Division of the US Seventh Army on 27 April 1945. The Americans found them littered with the bodies of slave labourers. Their commander, Lieutenant-Colonel Edward F. Seiller, ordered German civilians in the nearby town of Hurlach to bury the corpses. The exact death toll is not known, but it is estimated that about half the 29,000 slaves employed died of hunger, overwork and beatings. The main perpetrators of this atrocity did not escape justice. Commandants, sub-commandants and other officials were brought to trial. Some were convicted and hanged, while others were given long sentences of hard labour.

Adrian Warburton DSO and bar, DFC and bar, DFC (USA) was commemorated in a moving ceremony exactly sixty years after his death.

The Guard of Honour from the RAF and the USAAF arriving at Berinsfield in Oxfordshire on 12 April 2004 for the ceremony to commemorate the 60th anniversary of Wing Commander Adrian Warburton's death. They were headed by two standard-bearers from the RAF Association's Wantage District and Oxford branches, with a standard-bearer from the Royal British Legion between them. *Anne Williams collection*

This took place on 12 April 2004 at Berinsfield, formerly the location of RAF Mount Farm in Oxfordshire, and was supported by the Berinsfield Parish Council and the Ridgeway Military and Aviation Research Group. Guards of honour from the USAAF at RAF Croughton and the RAF at Benson were present, along with standard-bearers from the RAF Association and the Royal British Legion. A memorial stone was unveiled by Warburton's 92-year-old widow, Mrs Eileen 'Betty' Westcott. There was also a display of the wreckage of some of his aircraft, brought over from Germany. More than 100 people attended the ceremony.

Warburton flew the phenomenal total of over 350 photo-reconnaissance missions in the Mediterranean theatre of war. Air Chief Marshal Sir Arthur Tedder, the Air Commander-in-Chief of the Mediterranean Air Command, described him as 'the most valuable pilot in the RAF'.

Chapter 4

The Last Months of St-Ex

The disappearance of the famous aviator Antoine de Saint-Exupéry on 31 July 1944 has been one of the most puzzling of air mysteries. However, it is now possible to explain the circumstances with the aid of information from German sources.

St-Ex ended his long exile in the USA on 13 April 1943 when he boarded the liner SS *Stirling Castle* in New York harbour, en route to North Africa. Aged 42, he had achieved fame as a pilot, writer, mathematician, inventor and philosopher. He had served in the French Air Force in the 1920s and then as a commercial pilot on African and South American routes. Despite serious injuries sustained in crashes, he rejoined the French Air Force on the outbreak of the Second World War and flew on many sorties as a photo-reconnaissance pilot over the Western Front. After the fall of France, he escaped to North Africa and eventually reached the USA. His account of these missions in his book *Flight to Arras* had been acclaimed in the United States. It had also been read in Vichy France and clandestinely in Occupied France, where his name became a symbol of hope for ultimate liberation. His book *The Little Prince*, also written while in exile, was read mainly by children and became one of the most popular ever published.

The *Stirling Castle* was part of a convoy of thirty ships carrying 50,000 American troops to North Africa. By this time, the tide of war had swung decisively against the Axis. The Wehrmacht had sustained a massive defeat at Stalingrad during the previous winter, the German homeland was being bombed remorselessly by the RAF and the USAAF, Anglo-American troops had crushed the German-controlled forces in French North Africa under operation 'Torch', while the remaining German and Italian forces were being mopped up in Tunisia.

The next major phase of the war had been decided during a meeting of the leaders of Britain, the USA and China at Casablanca in January 1943. This was to concentrate forces in the Mediterranean and to knock Italy out

The three-power conference at Casablanca in January 1943 resulted in important decisions for the conduct of the war in the Mediterranean. Bottom row, left to right: Generalissimo Chiang Kai-Shek; President Franklin Roosevelt; Prime Minister Winston Churchill; Madame Chiang Kai-Shek. Top row: General Chang Chen; Lieutenant-General Ling Wei; Lieutenant-General B.B. Somervell; Lieutenant-General J.W. Stilwell; General H.A.P. Arnold; Field Marshal Sir John Dill; Admiral Lord Louis Mountbatten; Major General Carton de Wiart. *Author's collection*

of the war. A new Allied command structure had been formed in the theatre for this purpose. On 17 February 1943, General Dwight D. Eisenhower had been appointed Supreme Commander for this enterprise, the invasion of Sicily, with General Sir Harold Alexander as his deputy. The Allied naval forces came under Admiral Sir Andrew Cunningham, while Air Marshal Sir Arthur Tedder had been appointed as Air Officer Commanding the new Mediterranean Air Command. Within the latter, the new and powerful Northwest African Air Forces came under the command of Major-General Carl Spaatz of the USAAF.

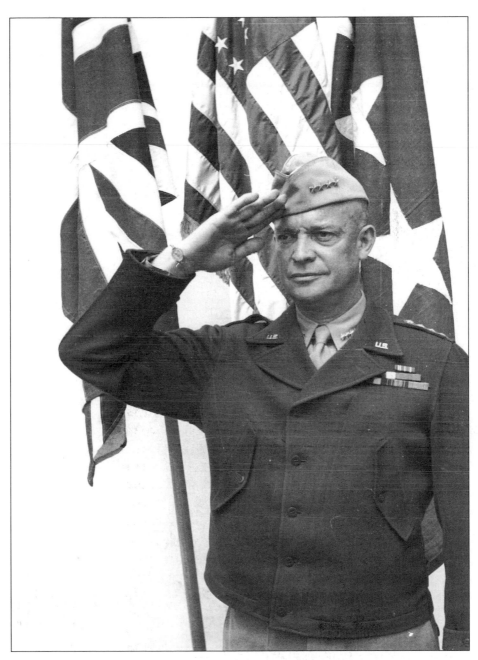

General Dwight D. Eisenhower, who had been appointed at the Casablanca Conference as the Supreme Commander for Operation 'Husky' (the Allied invasion of Sicily), photographed in May 1943. *Author's collection*

Meanwhile, Germany had responded to defeats in North Africa by occupying Vichy France. St-Ex was determined to participate in the liberation of his country, which everyone knew was a forthcoming objective. Although far older than the average for Allied reconnaissance pilots, he had some influential friends. One of these was Colonel William J. Donovan, the head of the US Office of Strategic Services (OSS), the forerunner of the Central Intelligence Agency (CIA), which was created in 1947. Another was General René Chambe, on the staff of General Henri Giraud, who with General Charles de Gaulle jointly headed the French forces in North Africa.

General Charles de Gaulle (right), the leader of the Fighting French since the fall of France in 1940, arrived by air in North Africa on 30 May 1943. He was photographed shaking hands with Commander-in-Chief of the French Forces in North Africa, General Henri Giraud, who was engaged on re-equipping and re-arming his troops. One outcome was the formation of a new French Committee for National Liberation. *Author's collection*

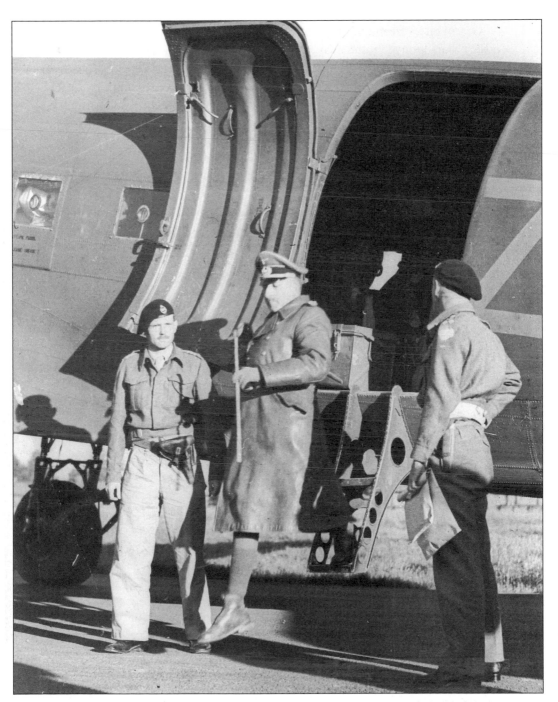

General Jürgen von Armin, the commander of the Axis force in Tunisia who surrendered to the Fourth Indian Division on 12 May 1943, arriving in England as a prisoner of war four days later. *Author's collection*

Shortly before his arrival in North Africa, St-Ex had been reassigned on 1 May 1943 as a capitaine in the French squadron in which he had served in 1939/40, Groupe II/33. This small unit was based at Laghouat in Algeria and commanded by another old friend, Capitaine René Gavoille. It was still equipped with the same machines, single-engined Caudron-Simouns and twin-engined Bloch 174s, although these were about to be replaced.

This French unit formed part of the North African Photographic Reconnaissance Wing (NAPRW), based at La Marsa in Tunisia and commanded by a son of the US President, Colonel Elliot Roosevelt (an American wing commander groups, the reverse of the RAF's nomenclature). The US contribution to this wing consisted of the 3rd Photographic Group, equipped with the Lockheed F-5As of the 5th and 12th Squadrons and the

Winston Churchill flew to Libya after the Axis forces in North Africa capitulated on 13 May 1943, to thank the Eighth Army on behalf of the King. He was greeted at Castel Benito airport by General Sir Bernard Montgomery. *Author's collection*

B-17 Fortresses of the 15th Squadron. The RAF's contribution to the wing consisted of the Spitfire PR IVs and PR XIs of No 682 Squadron.

In this period, the NAPRW was responsible for all photography west of Longitude 12° East, which included Sardinia, Corsica, the south of France and north-west Italy. East of this line, photo-reconnaissance of Sicily and the Italian mainland was carried out by RAF and SAAF squadrons based in Malta, while Greece was covered by an RAF squadron based in Egypt. The NAPRW also commanded the North African Central Intelligence Unit (NACIU) staffed by ground photographers and photo-interpreters. This unit was responsible for the printing and interpretation of all reconnaissance photographs. St-Ex referred to interpreters as experts whose work was akin to that of micro-biologists. Their information formed a vital part of Allied tactics and strategy, being fed directly to the Supreme Commander.

On arrival in Algiers on 4 May 1943, St-Ex parked his luggage in the home of a friend, Doctor Georges Pélissier, who had treated him for injuries received years before. He arrived at Groupe II/33 on the evening of the following day and received an ecstatic welcome from his comrades at Laghouat airfield, being hailed as a national hero. He took off soon afterwards in a Bloch 174 in order to refamiliarize himself with the controls and handling characteristics, and flew to Bou-Sada airfield, near Algiers. Unfortunately, he wrecked the Bloch on the end of this airfield, apparently since he forgot to lower the undercarriage when approaching to land, although he was unhurt.

The arrival of St-Ex at II/33 coincided with the squadron's conversion to the Lockheed F-5A, a photo-reconnaissance version of the Lockheed P-38G Lightning. The guns of the single-seater P-38G had been removed from the nacelle nose and replaced with up to five K-17 cameras which the pilot operated electrically, either singly or collectively. The F-5A had a top speed of about 400 mph, about 75 mph more than the Bloch 174, and was able to outstrip many fighters of the Luftwaffe. When carrying drop-tanks, it had a range of about 1,750 miles, and was thus suitable for the strategic tasks ahead in this theatre of war. However, it had far more controls than the Bloch 174 and the training period was more exacting, especially for French pilots who had not been flying for some time and were not familiar with instruction manuals or tuition in English. The squadron moved to its new base at La Marsa near Tunis, the centre for these operations, where the US 5th and 12th Squadrons were already based with their F-5As.

St-Ex was not considered a suitable pilot for flying the F-5A, on account of his age. However, he decided to enhance his position by visiting General Henri Giraud via his friend René Chambe, for the former wielded

Commandant (Major) Antoine de Saint-Exupéry in his flying gear. *John Phillips collection*

A Lockheed P-38 Lightning of the USAAF. The photographic reconnaissance versions of this machine were designated F-4 and F-5. *Author's collection*

considerable influence since he had commanded the main sector of the Maginot Line during the attack by the Wehrmacht in 1940 and had escaped from a German PoW camp after his capture. In June 1940, the Comité Français de Libération Nationale (CFLN) had been formed in London by General Charles de Gaulle. This had been transferred to Algiers after Operation 'Torch', with Giraud and de Gaulle recognized by Britain and America as its joint heads, although de Gaulle did not arrive in North Africa until 30 May 1943.

Meanwhile, the Free French Air Force in North Africa, with its proud emblem of the Cross of Lorraine, came under the authority of Giraud. St-Ex and Giraud do not seem to have been impressed with each other at their meeting, although St-Ex was asked to make a short propaganda tour of the

A Caudron-Simoun of the Free French Air Force's Group II/33, photographed at Blida in Northern Algeria by the RAF in early 1943. *Mark Postlethwaite collection www.ww2images.com*

General Sir Harold Alexander, Deputy Supreme Commander for the invasion of Sicily, pointing to a map of Italy with a group of Allied photo-reconnaissance officers. This was at the headquarters of the North African Reconnaissance Wing at La Marsa, prior to the invasion. General Alexander was responsible for much of the detailed planning. *Jack H. Eggleston collection*

Sticks of bombs exploding as Martin B-26 Marauders of the US Twelfth Air Force attack the airfield of Alghero in Sardinia on 25 May 1943. This destruction of enemy aircraft and airfield installations was one of the preludes to the Allied invasion of Sicily on 10 July 1943. *Author's collection*

The Italian island fortress of Pantelleria being battered by Consolidated B-24 Liberators of the US Ninth Air Force in late May 1943, as one of the preliminaries to the Allied invasion of Sicily on 10 July 1943. The aircraft in the photograph are turning away from flak bursts while bombs explode on their targets. *Author's collection*

French army messes in North Africa. He carried out these duties for the next few days by flying from place to place in a Caudron-Simoun.

St-Ex arrived at La Marsa on 4 June 1943, and made his first training flight in an F-5A four days later. He was a stocky man and felt cramped in the confined space of the cockpit. There were no major disasters, although he seems to have misunderstood the altimeter reading and flown too high without using his oxygen mask. Training continued in company with other French pilots, with the American instructors becoming impatient with those pupils who had difficulty in grasping their expressions. On a personal basis, St-Ex got on reasonably well with the Americans, partly because he had developed an admiration for their country during his long exile. On 22 June 1943, he was promoted to the rank of Commandant (Major). Exactly a week

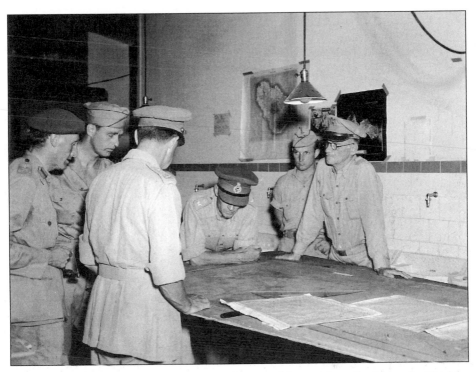

A group of senior officers examining a photographic mosaic at La Marsa in Tunisia. Left to right: Brigadier T.S. Avery (British Eighth Army); Colonel Elliot Roosevelt (Commander, North African Photographic Reconnaissance Wing); General Sir Harold Alexander (Deputy Supreme Commander in Mediterranean theatre of war); unidentified British major-general; Lieutenant-Colonel Frank Dunn (Commander, 3rd Photographic Group); Major-General Carl Spaatz (Commander-in-Chief Northwest African Air Forces). The heavily fortified island of Pantelleria, shown on the wall, surrendered to the British 3rd Infantry Brigade on 11 June 1943, after a heavy air raid and bombardment from the sea. *Jack H. Eggleston collection*

later, on his 43rd birthday, he was delighted to be cleared by a French medical examination for long-distance and high-altitude missions.

Meanwhile, the business of war continued. The small Italian islands of Pantelleria and Lampedusa had already fallen to the Allies, and the invasion of Sicily under the code-name of Operation 'Husky' began on 9/10 July 1943. This colossal enterprise involved over 2,000 vessels, with the Western Task Force carrying troops of the US Seventh Army under General George Patton while the Eastern Task Force carried troops of the British Eighth Army under General Sir Bernard Montgomery. Over 250 squadrons of the Allied Air Command supported the landings, greatly outnumbering the serviceable aircraft of the Luftwaffe and the Regia Aeronautica. These

General Dwight D. Eisenhower (Allied Commander-in-Chief in the North African Theatre) at the air film negative library of the Northwest African Photographic Reconnaissance Wing at La Marsa in Tunisia, with Squadron Leader S.R. 'Wally' Walton and Colonel Elliot Roosevelt smiling at him. *Jack H. Eggleston collection*

This part of the Allied invasion fleet, which consisted of over 2,000 vessels anchored off North Africa, was photographed from a Consolidated Catalina. The entire fleet set off for Sicily in the afternoon of 9 July 1943. *Author's collection*

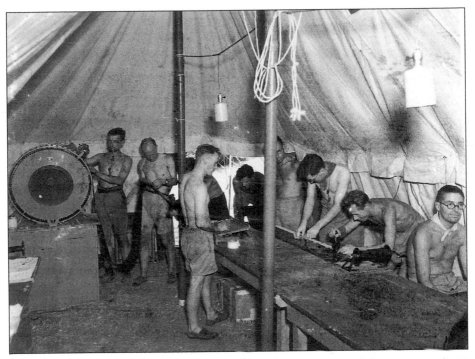

Drying and numbering films in a photographic tent at Lentini in Sicily in 1943. *Jack H. Eggleston collection*

landings were preceded during the night by glider-borne British troops and American paratroops, but these did not go well. As a result of darkness and poor navigation, over half the British gliders were released over the sea, while the American paratroops were dropped in widely scattered areas.

However, all the seaborne landings were successful and the troops began to fight their way inland against determined opposition, especially from the Wehrmacht. Airfields were captured and Allied aircraft began to occupy them. They included photo-reconnaissance Spitfire VBs of No 40 (SAAF) Squadron from Malta, engaged on short-range tactical work. For air reconnaissance, this period is notable for the arrival in Sicily of J-type trailers of the RAF. These were mobile darkrooms designed for the rapid processing and printing of air photographs, powered by generators. The trailers carried tents which could be erected quickly for additional working space. These facilities were extremely useful for photo-interpretation and the provision of intelligence for the tactical situations faced by the ground forces. The J-type trailers were soon followed by photographic semi-trailers, which improved the facilities even further.

On 23 August 1943, General Dwight D. Eisenhower visited the headquarters of General Sir Bernard Montgomery in Sicily, where he invested him with America's highest military order, that of Commander of the Legion of Honor Merit. After the ceremony, the two men viewed the Italian mainland from Messina. *Author's collection*

Troops and trucks of the British Eighth Army going ashore on the toe of Italy from landing craft on 3 September 1943. The date was exactly four years after Britain entered the Second World War. *Author's collection*

   While these events were taking place, St-Ex continued his training on F-5As at La Marsa. Having finished the course, with its ground instruction and practical flying, he was considered ready to begin operational sorties. The first took place on 27 July 1943, a long-distance photo-reconnaissance flight from La Marsa to a stretch of the French coastline from the east of Marseilles to the east of Toulon, evidently one of the preliminaries to the eventual invasion by the Allies. This involved flying at an altitude of about 30,000 feet, first skirting round to the west of Sardinia and Corsica, held by the Axis forces, and then flying a series of parallel tracks over the target area. It afforded his first view of his beloved homeland for years, albeit from high altitude from which little could be seen except the bursts of heavy flak which greeted him, but it must have been an emotional

On 9 September 1943, assault troops of the US Fifth Army had stormed ashore on the beaches of Salerno, south-east of Naples. Eleven days later, when this photograph was taken, troops of the British Eighth Army had advanced up the western coast of Italy and linked up with them. Landing operations were still continuing while the Germans were retreating from the coastal areas. *Author's collection*

experience. The sortie lasted almost six hours and he returned with the required photographs in the magazines of his K–17 cameras.

His happy frame of mind following this success did not last long. On 1 August 1943, he took off for a second mission but had to return within an hour following engine trouble. On landing back at La Marsa, he failed to apply his hydraulic brakes early enough and ran off the end of the 6,000-foot runway. The undercarriage collapsed and the port wing hit an obstacle. The aircraft slewed round and crashed, wrecking both engines. Although St-Ex was unhurt, the F–5A was a complete write-off. The accident was witnessed by Lieutenant-Colonel Harold Willis, who was on the staff of the

Northwest African Air Forces under Major-General Carl Spaatz. He reprimanded St-Ex in forceful terms and recommended to Spaatz that he be grounded.

Groupe II/33 was a small unit, probably less than a flight in RAF terms, and it seems to have been allocated the older and less airworthy F-5As. Possibly the accident could have been attributed to a mechanical fault, but these machines were valued at about 80,000 dollars, a considerable sum in those days, and were not in prolific supply. St-Ex's record in training had not been good and Lieutenant-Colonel Frank Dunn, who commanded the NAPRW's 3rd Reconnaissance Group with its F-5As and B-17s, agreed with Willis.

General René Bouscat, Commander of the French Air Force, reading a citation at Alghero in Sardinia, accompanied by General Ira C. Eaker, Commander-in-Chief of the Mediterranean Air Force. *John Phillips collection*

Of course, St-Ex was dismayed when he was told of this decision, and pulled all possible strings to effect his reinstatement. When none of these produced the desired result, he organized a lavish dinner in a Tunisian villa on 4 August for members of his squadron and some senior American officers of the 3rd Photographic Group. There were a series of courses and a constant flow of wine. When he felt the time was ripe, he tried to influence Lieutenant-Colonel Frank Dunn by telling him dramatically 'I want to die for France!' This failed to produce a sympathetic response and he repeated his statement later in the evening. On this occasion, Dunn (who had the nickname of 'Dynamite') responded with typical North American bluntness. He said, 'I don't care if you die for France or not, but you're not going to do it in one of our airplanes!'

At this stage, St-Ex was placed in the French Reserve list of officers, without pay and living on his private means. Sunk in despondency, he took up residence in Algiers with his friend Dr Georges Pélissier. He rejected a proposition that he should return to the USA, and continued to lobby influential friends to effect his reinstatement as an operational pilot in Groupe II/33. One of these was Colonel William J. Donovan, who had arrived in North Africa with the objective of supporting the Maquis, the underground movement engaged on fighting the German occupying forces in France. When this failed to produce any result, he tackled his friend General René Chambe, on the staff of General Giraud. In turn, Giraud lobbied General Dwight D. Eisenhower, apparently to the exasperation of the latter.

Giraud's authority was on the wane in this period, while the star of de Gaulle was on the rise among the French forces as well as with the British and Americans. St-Ex had never followed de Gaulle and thought him a most unsuitable person to lead the French nation, while in turn de Gaulle did not favour him. No authority was granted for a return to Groupe II/33. In frustration, St-Ex decided to move away from the congested area of Algiers and accepted an offer from another friend, Dr Henri Comte, to stay with him in his villa in a congenial suburb of Casablanca. This proved so comfortable that he remained there for a month, concentrating on writing.

Meanwhile, the war in the Mediterranean continued at an accelerated pace. The Axis forces were cleared out of Sicily by 17 August 1943. Many Italian prisoners were taken by the Allies but the Germans retreated in good order and crossed to the mainland, leaving almost 1,000 wrecked aircraft behind them. By then, the Italians had had enough of the war and so the vanguard of the British Eighth Army encountered little opposition when the men crossed the Straits of Messina on 3 September and began to occupy the toe of Italy. The terms of an armistice with Italy were signed on 8 September, and a day later troops of the US Fifth Army, together with British divisions, landed at Salerno in Campania. By then, the Fifth Army was commanded by Lieutenant-General Mark W. Clark and the men faced a stiff fight from German troops. British forces from the south linked up with them eleven days later.

Thus one of the main objectives of the Casablanca conference had been achieved, the elimination of Italy from the war. In fact, the puppet government of the country changed direction completely and declared war against Germany. It had already deposed and imprisoned the dictator Benito Mussolini, but he was skilfully rescued by German parachutists on 12 September 1943. Allied advances in Italy continued, and on 1 October British troops entered Naples. These were closely followed by two Mobile Field Photographic Sections of the RAF, which had arrived on the mainland

General Mark W. Clark, in command of the US Fifth Army, arriving by Douglas C-47 Dakota at an airfield in Italy. An Auster light aircraft can be seen behind his tall figure. *Author's collection*

Robert Heichele, trainee fighter pilot in the Luftwaffe. *Origin of photo unknown*

via Sicily. One of these travelled up the west coast of Italy and the other on the east coast, giving immediate facilities for developing and printing reconnaissance photographs taken from the air.

During these Allied advances, the Germans decided that their occupation of the Italian island of Sardinia and the French island of Corsica was no longer tenable. They evacuated both by the end of September, leaving behind wrecked airfields. Although the American 3rd Photo-Reconnaissance Wing, with its French Groupe II/33, remained in the Tunisian airfield of La Marsa for the time being, it was obvious that eventually the Allies would restore the airfields on these two islands and that they would provide bases which would bring the aircraft far closer to targets in the south of France.

The Fw 190D-9, known to German pilots as the 'Dora', was fitted with a Jumo 213-E engine and an MW-30 power-boost. It had a distinctive extended fuselage. The first prototype flew in March 1942 and Allied pilots reported spotting 'long-nosed' Fw 190s towards the end of 1943. The first operational unit to be fully equipped with Fw 190D-9s was III./Jagdgeschwader 54 in September 1944. *Mark Postlethwaite collection www.ww2images.com*

Despite their initial successes, the Allied troops faced a brutal and bloody struggle up the Italian peninsula, against determined opposition. The German forces were strongly reinforced and led by the experienced and resourceful Generalfeldmarschall Albert Kesselring, whose rank was the equivalent to that of Marshal of the RAF or a Five Star General in the USA. He was aged 48 and had served as a soldier in the First World War before becoming Chief of the General Staff of the Luftwaffe in 1936. From December 1941 he had commanded Luftflotte 2 in the Mediterranean, but he had relinquished this command in 1943 to concentrate on commanding the ground forces.

St-Ex had returned to Algeria and was able to keep informed of the Allied progress from newspapers, broadcasts, news items in cinemas, and from personal contacts with some of the military personnel directly involved. He became increasingly morose at his exclusion from operational flying. Nevertheless, he was not solitary, being lionized by Algerian society and invited to many social functions. He also spent much time writing books in the home of Georges Pélissier, but seems to have drunk more heavily than usual.

In November 1943, a reorganization of the American photo-reconnaissance units took place when the 3rd Photographic Group was joined by the 5th Photographic Group. At first, the latter consisted solely of the 23rd Squadron, equipped with Lockheed F-5s, but the French Groupe II/33 was eventually placed under its command. The new 90th Photographic Wing was formed to control these two groups, within the overall command of NAPRW. This development might have given St-Ex an opportunity for reinstatement under a new commander, but he was in no condition for application: on 5 November he had fallen down some steps in Algiers and injured himself quite badly. He believed he had broken his vertebra, despite X-ray evidence to the contrary, and argued the matter with Pélissier. However, a recovery took place, albeit slowly and painfully.

On 8 December 1943, the US 3rd Photographic Group moved from La Marsa in Tunisia to San Severo near Foggia in south-east Italy, while the US 5th Photographic Group moved to Pomigliano near Naples, on the west coast. Thus the latter, including the French II/33, could carry out operations over the south of France from its advanced base. At this time, NAPRW was renamed the Mediterranean Allied Photographic Wing (MAPRW).

During this period, the fighting on the Italian mainland had reached a stalemate, despite overwhelming Allied air superiority. The Germans had skilfully occupied strong positions across the peninsula in a rugged terrain

Colonel Karl 'Pop' Polifka, a renowned American photo-reconnaissance pilot with much experience of flying Lockheed F-4s and F-5s. On 25 January 1944, he took over command of the Mediterranean Allied Photographic Reconnaissance Wing from Colonel Elliot Roosevelt, who was posted to England to take over command of the Reconnaissance Wing of the US Eighth Air Force. *Author's collection*

which favoured defence, the so-called 'Gustav Line'. The British Eighth Army attempted to penetrate this line in the centre while the American Fifth Army battled in the west. Their efforts were hampered by the onset of an unusually severe winter, which restricted both ground and air operations. All this proved a disappointment to the Allies, who had expected to sweep forward and occupy Rome by this time.

Some major changes in the Allied High Command took place on 1 January 1944. The Supreme Commander, General Dwight D. Eisenhower, left for England to assume a new role as the Supreme Commander for the invasion of Normandy; he was replaced in Italy by General Sir H. Maitland Wilson. Eisenhower was joined in England by General Sir Bernard Montgomery, who became the Commander of the British and Canadian 21st Army Group in this great endeavour; he was replaced by General Sir Oliver W.H. Leese, while the armies were grouped under the title of 'Allied Armies in Italy'.

Of particular significance for St-Ex were two other replacements which followed soon afterwards. Air Chief Marshal Sir Arthur W. Tedder relinquished his post as Commander-in-Chief of the Mediterranean Air Command on 17 January to take up a new post in England as Deputy Supreme Commander to Eisenhower; his place in Italy was taken over by General Ira C. Eaker of the USAAF. The Commander of MAPRW, Colonel

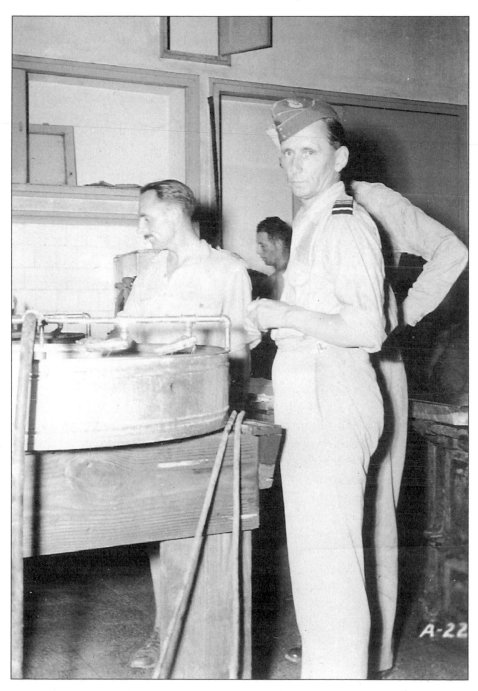

Air Chief Marshal Sir Arthur Tedder (Commander-in-Chief of the Mediterranean Air Command) with Squadron Leader S.W. 'Wally' Walton (Photographic Officer) at San Severo in Italy in early January 1944. *Jack H. Eggleston collection*

Elliot Roosevelt, left Italy on 23 January to command the photo-reconnaissance squadrons of the US Eighth Air Force in England. He was replaced by Colonel Karl L. Polifka of the USAAF, a pilot in Lockheed F-5s who had achieved much distinction in the Pacific theatre; he proved a very popular choice among the squadron members.

Sufficiently recovered from the injuries sustained in his fall of 5 November, St-Ex was fervently eager to resume operational flying. The changes in the top command seemed to offer an opportunity for another appeal; but he had no means to travel from Algiers to war-torn Italy for any interviews. However, encouragement was provided by Colonel Paul Rockwell, one of the senior members of the USAAF's French Liaison Section in the Mediterranean. He had developed a friendship with St-Ex and agreed to recommend to General Eaker his reinstatement with Groupe II/33.

The war in Italy continued. General Wilson attempted on 22 January to outflank the German defences by landing two attack forces, American and British, at the ports of Anzio and Nettuno on the west coast. Heavily supported by naval and air power, these were initially successful and seemed to offer a path to Rome, but were stalled by skilful German reaction when the American generals failed to exploit their advantages. A further attempt at a breakthrough was made by intense bombing of German positions up to 15 February, but these solely put paid to any possibility of a German counter-attack. The later bombing of Monte Cassino reduced the monastery to a heap of rubble but failed to achieve an immediate advantage.

St-Ex was offered another opportunity after John Phillips, a young American war correspondent for the influential magazine *Life*, arrived in Algiers in late February. He agreed to provide magazine articles if Phillips would use his influence to effect his reinstatement in Groupe II/33. Phillips eventually flew to Naples and reported to Colonel John McCrary, who was in charge of the USAAF press in Italy, but obtained no immediate result. In the meantime, St-Ex was assigned to another French squadron, Groupe I/22, which was equipped with Martin B-26 Marauder medium bombers and based at Villacidro in Sardinia, but only as a co-pilot. His pay recommenced on 1 April, but this posting did not suit his aspirations and he protested vehemently.

Phillips managed to bring St-Ex to Naples later in April and introduced him to McCrary, who agreed to use his influence with General Eaker, provided St-Ex would write a chapter for a book he was compiling. The deal was struck, though the men had to await a decision from the Commander-in-Chief. Returning to Algiers at the end of April, St-Ex attended a lunch

St-Ex in his tent on the airfield at Alghero in Sardinia, writing while smoking a cigarette. *John Phillips collection*

arranged by Henri Frenay, a hero of the Maquis (by then officially named Forces Françaises de l'Intérieur, or FFI) together with others of the Resistance Movement. Already familiar with some details from his friend William J. Donovan of the OSS, St-Ex was deeply moved by their stories of sacrifices and even offered to be parachuted into France and to fight with them. This was refused, but then the assent to rejoin Groupe II/33 arrived from Eaker, although it is understood that the Commander-in-Chief recommended that he should fly only six sorties.

St-Ex arrived back in his unit on 16 May 1944, at a time when it was based at Alghero near the west coast of Sardinia. He landed as a passenger in a B-26 Martin Marauder, accompanied by the war correspondent John Phillips, and was welcomed as a national hero by his countrymen. The squadron had been equipped with new Lockheed F-5Bs, the reconnaissance version of the P-38J Lightning fighter, and was primarily engaged on missions over the south coast of France in advance of the Allied landings. It was still commanded by St-Ex's friend René Gavoille and attached to the 23rd Squadron of the US 5th Photographic Group. Living conditions were somewhat sparse, the officers being housed in bare cottages and the other ranks in tents, for the facilities had been heavily bombed by the Allies before the occupation of the island.

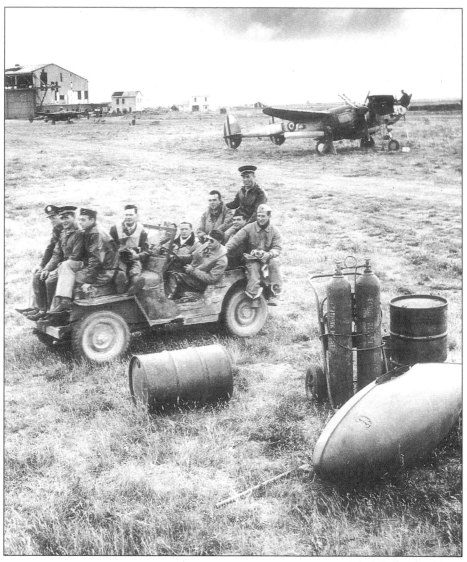

Some of the French of Groupe II/33, including St-Ex, in a Jeep on the airfield at Alghero in Sardinia, with one of their Lockheed F-5s in the background. *John Phillips collection*

At first, St-Ex had to refamiliarize himself with the controls and handling characteristics of the Lockheed F-5, but there were no catastrophes during this period. The F-5B had a greater fuel capacity than its F-5A predecessor, as well as power-boosted ailerons and a flat bulletproof windscreen, but some of the older F-5As had been retained for retraining purposes. John

Top right: St-Ex being helped into his flying suit preparatory to take-off in a Lockheed F-5. *John Phillips collection*

Opposite left: St-Ex clipping on his parachute at Alghero in Sardinia, watched by a fellow member of Groupe II/33. *John Phillips collection*

Left: St-Ex at the controls of a Lockheed F-5. *John Phillips collection*

A Lockheed F-5 of Groupe II/33 taking off from Alghero in Sardinia. *John Phillips collection*

Phillips remained on the station for about a fortnight, taking some unique photographs with his Rollieflex camera. St-Ex's first long-distance flight took place on the day after Phillips's departure, 31 May, with a trip to Maison-Blanche in Algeria and returning two days later without mishaps. There was encouraging news on his return, for the Allies had at last broken through the German lines in Italy and occupied Rome.

In contrast, he met bad luck on his first operational flight, which took place on 6 June to the area of Marseilles, since his port engine caught fire on the outward journey and he was forced to turn back. He managed to land safely, despite a large hole burnt in the engine cowling. During the evening, the men on the station learnt that the Allies had landed in Normandy. It was an emotional time for the French, for this seemed to be the beginning of the liberation of their country.

Bad weather in the region grounded all aircraft in the next few days. St-Ex made his next sortie on 14 June, photographing a target near Rodez, north of Albi in south-west France. All went smoothly despite some cloud, and he landed safely with the photographs in the K-17 cameras of his Lockheed F-5B. The distances on these sorties were far shorter than those from La Marsa in Tunisia, but they still required precise flying. The pilot usually had to fly a series of parallel tracks at high altitude over the target, with his cameras taking a series of exposures overlapping each other by about 60 per cent, to provide stereo cover in 'line overlaps'. The cameras could be fitted with the A5 magazines each containing 190 exposures, or the A5A magazines with 100 exposures. The prints might be constructed to provide an enlarged mosaic for interpreters to identify enemy aircraft or positions such as gun emplacements. Flying at 30,000 feet without pressurized cabins was gruelling enough for young pilots but could be painful for a man of almost 44 years who had suffered numerous injuries.

On his 44th birthday, 29 June, St-Ex managed to persuade Gavoille that he should replace him on a sortie to Annecy, south of Geneva. This was the area where he had spent his boyhood in his family home, having been born not far away in Lyons. Moreover, he was intensely interested in the flight, for near the target was a major resistance centre for the Maquis in the mountainous plateau of the Vercors. This plateau is shaped like a jagged triangle with a perpendicular length of about forty miles, with peaks rising to about 6,000 feet. After the fall of France, it had formed a refuge in the resistance movement for trained soldiers and for young men who wished to avoid forced labour under the Germans. The rugged area provided many hiding places as well as natural defences.

By June 1944, over 3,000 Maquisards had gathered in the Vercors, helped by specialists in partisan warfare from the American OSS and the British SOE. They were being supplied with light weapons dropped from USAAF B-24 Liberators based in North Africa. The intention was to build an airstrip near the small town of Vassieux, where Allied transport aircraft could land. Under Operation 'Montagnard' (Mountaineer), this constituted a threat to the rear of enemy defences in the south of France. The Maquis force was commanded by Major François Huet: one of his officers, Captain Jean Prévost, was a close friend of St-Ex and had published St-Ex's first literary work. He was also a trained soldier, physically strong, who had spent some time before the war in New York, where he had been recruited by Colonel Bill Donovan for the fledgling OSS.

St-Ex took off for Annecy. All went well until he reached the area of Avignon, when his port engine began spluttering so badly that he was forced to close it down and feather the propeller. The machine could fly on one engine, but this made it an easy target for enemy fighters. He headed north-east for the Vercors, where there were friends on the ground if he was forced to bale out. However, he seems to have become disorientated for he continued too far east, until he neared Turin, by this time at about 8,000 feet. Even more ominous, he saw an enemy fighter in his rear view mirror and resigned himself to being blasted out of the sky. Yet nothing happened and he turned south-east, passing over Genoa without incident. He was then informed by ground control that he should switch on his IFF (Identification Friend or Foe) radar and head for Bastia in the north of Corsica. He landed there safely, where the photographs in his cameras confirmed the astonishing story of his flight.

Following this strange episode, St-Ex took a short leave in North Africa, when in La Marsa on 8 July, he had discussions with a number of French pilots who had formed a 'Groupe Patrie' intent on acquiring transport aircraft capable of carrying heavy weapons to their embattled comrades in the Vercors. However, the plan came to nothing, for the aircraft could not be found and in any event the airstrip at Vassieux had not been built.

Back in Alghero, St-Ex's next operational flight took place on 11 July. This was an attempt to photograph objectives near Lyons, but cloud covered the area and he was forced to return without results. On 14 July, France's Bastille Day, St-Ex experienced a major problem on a flight to targets near Annecy. His oxygen supply failed and brought on a fainting spell, but he managed to return safely to Alghero. This was a day when a major attempt was made to bring support to the Maquis, for the US Eighth Air Force in England despatched 359 B-17 Fortresses without long-distance fighter escort to drop supplies to groups in southern France. Of these, seventy-two Fortresses headed for the Vercors and dropped about 740 containers, with the parachutes emblazoned in the blue, red and white of the French national colours. The containers were welcomed by the Maquisards, but they did not include any of the heavy weapons so urgently required. Moreover, the men were hampered while collecting them, being strafed by Italian fighter aircraft serving in the Luftwaffe, Fiat G-50s and Reggiane Re 2001s.

This air drop prompted the Wehrmacht to take a more active role against the Maquis in the Vercors. On 15 July, their forces attempted to gain a foothold on the plateau by attacking the small town of St-Nizier in the north. This was defended by Maquis units led by Jean Prévost, who at first drove off the attackers with bazooka fire but had to retreat when the Germans returned with increased numbers.

In Alghero, the US 23rd Squadron and the French Groupe II/33 were preparing to move north to Borgo airfield in Corsica: this was accomplished on 17 July. On the following day, St-Ex flew on another sortie over the south of France. His targets are not recorded but it is known that he returned with his mission accomplished. On 20 July, he flew to Algiers for another discussion with Colonel Bill Donovan and, according to the latter, expressed a wish to serve full-time for the OSS; it seems probable that they discussed the situation in the Vercors.

He did not return to Borgo until 26 July, and in the meantime the Germans intensified their operations in that region. Their assault began on 21 July with their 157th Gebirgsdivision (Mountain Division) attacking from Grenoble in the north as well as scaling steep mountain passes in the east. Backing these were some units of the 9th Panzer Division, a Sicherheitsregiment (Security Regiment) of Military Police, and a number of Osttruppen (troops from Eastern Europe and Asia). Overhead flew about thirty Fiat G-50s or Reggiane 2001s in the fighter/bomber role. In addition, twenty Dornier Do 17s towed DFS assault gliders of Luftlandgeschwader 1 (Airborne Landing Group) from Lyons-Bron, heading for the incomplete airstrip at Vassieux.

Despite the loss of two gliders from ground fire, about 150 Fallschirmjäger (Combat Group) Schäfer stormed the large village and its surrounding hamlets, giving the Germans a stronghold in the centre of the Vercors. Elsewhere, most of the defences were smashed by the attackers, but the partisans in the northern region of Valchevrière, commanded by Jean

Prévost, held out and even counter-attacked. Battles continued. In the morning of 23 July the fighter-bombers attacked defences on the plateau while a second wave of twenty DFS 230 and Gotha Go 244 gliders brought in Ostlegionen (Eastern Troops) as well as 20 mm flak guns. No help arrived for the defenders and their cause was lost. François Huet gave orders to disperse and sent a signal to Algiers calling the authorities 'cowards and criminals'. The survivors were hunted by the Germans and on 31 July Jean Prévost and his small band were killed, probably in an ambush.

Meanwhile, the two F-5 photo-reconnaissance squadrons at Borgo continued their work. On 30 July, Captain Gavoille took off for a target in the Alps but was forced to turn back when it was covered with cloud. When returning over the sea he met another F-5, flown by Lieutenant Eugene Meredith of the US 23rd Squadron, which was returning from a sortie north of Marseilles. The two aircraft parted company but shortly afterwards Gavoille heard Meredith call over the R/T 'I'm being fired on! I'm going in!' Nothing more was heard: it was assumed he had been shot down by an enemy fighter.

On 31 July, St-Ex took off at about 0845 hours in Lockheed F-5B serial 43-68223 for targets in the Annecy-Grenoble area. The exact locations are not recorded but they were undoubtedly slightly to the north of the Vercors area. Like Meredith, he never returned. No R/T message from him was heard at Borgo airfield and he was listed as 'missing' about two hours after his fuel would have been exhausted, to the sorrow of his comrades in Groupe II/33.

Various speculations about his disappearance followed, but nothing convincing arrived until March 1948 when St-Ex's main publisher, Gaston Gallimard, received a letter from a German pastor, Hermann Korth, who had read about the matter in a magazine. This correspondent had served as a Luftwaffe intelligence officer in Italy, covering an area that included the south of France at the time St-Ex was lost. He had checked his records and found that the only enemy aircraft shot down on 31 July 1944 was over the sea when approaching Corsica, and that the time and place corresponded with the position where St-Ex would have been on his return flight. The German aircraft involved was a Focke-Wulf based at Avignon.

This account was dismissed by researchers who believed that Hermann Korth was confusing his record with the loss of Meredith on the previous day, although Korth firmly denied this. Moreover, as this author can verify from personal experience, if a German fighter scored a success against an enemy aircraft on a certain day, the unit commander would often seek to repeat the victory on the next day.

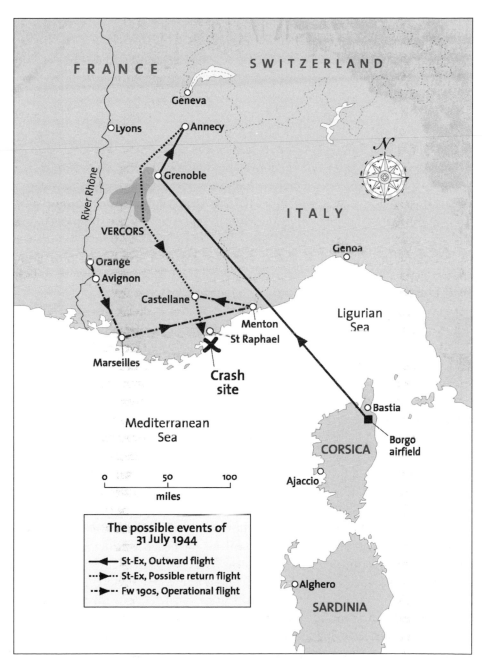

Maggie Nelson 2008 via Aeroplane *magazine www.aeroplanemonthly.com*

The facts are that two German fighter units were based at Avignon at the time, often operating from the nearby airfield of Orange. These were Nahauflärungsgruppe (Reconnaissance Group) 12 equipped with Fw 190s, and Jagdgruppe (Fighter Group) 200 equipped with Fw 190s and Messerschmitt Bf 109s.

In 1972 the German magazine *Der Landser* published in its 725th edition a letter written on 1 August 1944 by a German pilot, Robert Heichele, to his friend Leutnant Wilhelm Manz, a pilot serving in 4/Jagdgeschwader 3 (a Squadron in a Fighter Wing) and who had been shot down twice on Germany's western front. Heichele had the rank of Oberfänrich, a cadet at an advanced stage of training before being commissioned as a Leutnant, and was serving with Nahauflärungsgruppe based at Avignon. Such cadets could also be engaged on operational flights.

This letter describes an operation on 31 July, when Heichele knew nothing about St-Ex. He took off from Orange at 1102 hours, in company with another Fw 190 flown by Feldwebel (Sergeant) Högel, with orders to fly between Marseilles and Menton on the border of Italy, hunting for enemy aircraft. They completed this leg of their mission and were over Castellane on their return flight when they saw a P-38 Lightning, which was probably a reconnaissance aircraft, flying about 1,000 metres above them. To their surprise, this aircraft dived at great speed towards them and then flew past.

It then states he was flying 'a marvellous bird', an Fw 190D-9 fitted with a Jumbo 213 engine with cooled fuel, which was capable of increasing speed for a short period by injecting a mixture of water and methanol. Thanks to this supplementary power, he was able to get between 150 to 200 metres behind the P-38. He fired but missed. After several passes, he fired again but missed once more. Then the P-38 changed direction and dived even further. He followed and got to about 50 metres behind it, firing yet again. The P-38 dived lower, leaving a trail of white smoke. It crossed the coast at low altitude and then flames streamed from the starboard engine. When about ten kilometres south of St Raphael, the starboard wing hit the sea. The P-38 spun several times and plunged below the water. The time was 1205 hours.

The events described in this letter fit the return flight that St-Ex would have made, both in terms of time and place. After finishing his mapping mission in the Annecy–Grenoble area, St-Ex probably made a minor diversion over the Vercors, where he knew in general terms that his comrades were fighting a desperate battle against overwhelming German forces. He was entitled to take photographs with the unused lengths of film in the magazines of his K–17 cameras, for these would otherwise have gone to waste in the development process. Then he would have been extremely anxious to return to base and his route would have taken him close to Castellane, on an unexpected interception course with the Fw 190s. Having spotted these, a dive at maximum speed was a logical manoeuvre – he hoped to shoot past them and escape at low level before they could turn and catch him.

Thus evidence seems to vindicate Hauptmann (Captain) Hermann Korth and Oberfänrich Robert Heichele, but their statements cannot be checked. Heichele was killed in Avignon on 21 August 1944, during a ground attack by the Maquis. The letter allegedly written by him can no longer be found. Towards the end of the war, Oberkommando der Luftwaffe (Luftwaffe High Command) ordered all units to destroy their war diaries. Most complied: there are no operational records of the destruction of the Lockheeds flown by either Eugene Meredith or Antoine de Saint-Exupéry.

Some German historians believe that the Heichele letter is a hoax, since records of the aircraft at Avignon do exist and do not mention Fw 190D-9s. They also dispute the assertions of Allied pilots who reported seeing 'long-nosed' Fw 190s from late 1943 onwards, and state that these fighters were never employed in operational units until September 1944. They do not believe that a single early-production Fw 190D-9 could have been on detachment at either Avignon or Orange for conversion and training purposes.

Whatever the truth of these matters, it can be said with certainty that Antoine de Saint-Exupéry died in the way that he always wished, in the liberation of his country.

Chapter 5

Lancaster Overdue

A photograph published in the July/August 1999 issue of the German aviation magazine *Jet & Prop* showed an RAF prisoner together with his captors. His name was Flying Officer George and the location was Bargstedt, near Stade in north-west Germany. The reader who sent it, Dietrich Alsdorp, wanted to know what had happened to the prisoner. The editor of *Jet & Prop* was interested enough to research the circumstances, with some help from this author.

One of the photographs which prompted the enquiry into the fate of the other crew members of Lancaster 'A' of No 83 Squadron. It shows the navigator, Flying Officer Phil George, holding his parachute while under guard at Bargstedt, near Stade. *Dietrich Alsdorf collection*

On 25 September 1944, Air Chief Marshal Sir Arthur Harris received a directive requiring Bomber Command to concentrate on destroying Germany's synthetic oil plants and its transport system. Although Harris opposed this policy, contending that the area bombing of German cities was the best method of bringing the war to an end, he grudgingly diverted some of his Command's efforts to these objectives.

The photograph in *Jet & Prop* was a result of this oil campaign. Bomber Command devoted the night of 11/12 November 1944 to attacks on the Rhenania-Ossag refinery at Harburg, across the Elbe from Hamburg, and the Hoesch Benzin refinery in the Wambel district of Dortmund in the Ruhr. No 5 Group was ordered to attack Harburg with 237 Lancasters and eight Mosquitos, and among these was the marker force of No 83 (Pathfinder) Squadron at Coningsby in Lincolnshire. Nos 1 and 8 Groups despatched 209 Lancasters and nineteen Mosquitos to Dortmund. The other groups were ordered to stand by for possible daylight operations in support of the Allied ground forces, which were attempting to break into western Germany.

This was the first occasion that Bomber Command had visited Harburg, although the US Eighth Air Force had already made six daylight attacks on the oil targets in the summer and autumn of 1944. Lancaster III letters OL-A serial PB188 was one of twelve from No 83 Squadron that took off on this attack, at 1638 hours. The crew was one of the most experienced in the squadron. The pilot was an Australian, Flight Lieutenant David (Curly) Jennings DFC. His navigator was British, Flying Officer Phil George. The wireless operator was another Australian, Flying Officer Peter (Bill) Hughes. A third Australian was the mid-upper gunner, Pilot Officer Brian Hayes DFM. The rear gunner was British, Pilot Officer Albert Mathews DFC, as were both the flight engineer, Flight Sergeant Stanley Burleigh, and the bomb aimer/radar operator, Warrant Officer H.W. (Bert) Turton. In fact the bomb sight was not intended to be used, for the load was to be dropped by 'blind marking', using the *G-H* radar system fitted in such specialized aircraft.

Six of the seven men in the crew survived to become prisoners. Three were located by the *Jet & Prop* enquiry while another had subsequently died but left a vivid account. Thus the events of the flight could be reconstructed from their recollections. The crew had been briefed to back up the target indicators dropped by the Master Bomber in one of the Mosquitos, with the unenviable job of orbiting the target area from 1900 hours until the main bomber stream arrived fifteen minutes later. They were also given the additional duty of 'Command Wind Broadcaster', which meant that the navigator Phil George had to calculate the wind velocity en route to the target and pass the

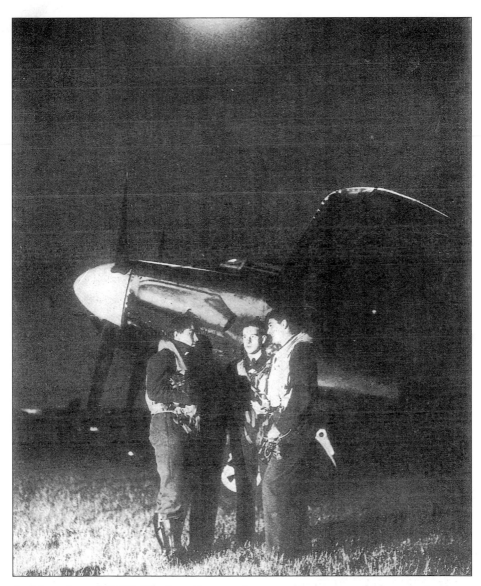

A Mosquito of RAF Bomber Command preparatory to a night operation over Germany, and port wing of a Lancaster in January 1945. *Author's collection*

information to the wireless operator Bill Hughes, who would transmit it to Bomber Command Headquarters for relaying to all aircraft in the operation.

The Lancaster was loaded with two green flares, a red target indicator, a medium capacity bomb of 1,000 lb with a twelve-hour delay and seven more such bombs with ominous six-day delays.

The route to the target took the Lancaster over the North Sea to the coast of Germany and then up the River Elbe to the target. The usual routine was followed in the early part of the flight. The navigation lights and Identification Friend or Foe (IFF) were switched off, the guns tested with short bursts into the sea, and all instruments were checked. The oxygen system was checked at 10,000 feet and all crew members were connected

A Lancaster II being loaded with 500 lb high–explosive bombs. *Author's collection*

The new 12,000 lb bomb carried by Lancasters, alongside 500 lb and 1,000 lb bombs, photographed in March 1944. *Author's collection*

with it. Phil George made his calculations and discovered that the forecast wind was incorrect, so that an increase in speed was required. This information was radioed to Bomber Command, and all other aircraft were informed.

The flying time to Harburg after crossing the coast was about twelve minutes. By this time the Lancaster was at 23,000 feet. The flight engineer,

Snow being cleared from the runway of an RAF airfield and swept from the port wing of a Lancaster in January 1945. *Author's collection*

Stanley Burleigh, had moved into the front turret. It became evident that the defenders had located the approaching bomber stream on their radar, for searchlights were weaving around their blue master lights. David Jennings put the Lancaster into a constant weave, seeing bursts of flak to starboard. Yellow flares ahead on the port bow indicated a probable assembly point for night-fighters. Bert Turton reported six aircraft on his radar screen, but since these were on the same heading they were assumed to be RAF. The flak became more intense as they neared the target. From the rear turret, Albert Mathews reported aircraft going down in flames a couple of miles behind, followed by huge flashes as their bombs exploded.

Bill Hughes searched the frequencies on his wireless set for enemy voices directing night-fighters. To his surprise he heard a woman giving these and drowned out her voice with blasts of engine noises every ten seconds. But this action did not stop the enemy activity, for the gunners soon reported night-fighters in the vicinity. David Jennings was alert for directions and was not surprised when Albert Mathews warned that an enemy aircraft was tracking them, after Bert Turton had picked it up on his radar screen. He was told to be ready to 'corkscrew port'. When receiving the word 'go', he banked the Lancaster 90 degrees and descended by 2,000 feet, then levelled out and skidded into a climbing turn. The gunners reported cannon fire streaking above the aircraft. By then they were eight minutes away from the target and this manoeuvre was repeated twice more before they reached it, after successfully shaking off their pursuers.

David Jennings regained altitude to 23,000 feet and encountered a myriad of searchlights. Then came a sudden and tremendous crash as a salvo of

Lancaster OT-L of No 83 Squadron, heading towards a target somewhere in Germany.
Jeremy C. Scutts collection

heavy flak exploded around them. The Lancaster filled with smoke, the starboard engines and wing caught fire and spurts of flame appeared on the port wing. He ordered the fire extinguishers to be used but these proved ineffective. Then he put the machine into a dive in the hope of putting out the fires, but these remained just as fierce when he pulled out. He ordered Bill Hughes to report the situation to base but was told that both the wireless set and the radar were shattered.

From behind the curtain that sheltered his navigator's position, Phil George saw that a large section of the roof overhead had disappeared. He climbed over the main spar to see that flames were spreading along the fuselage, causing ammunition in boxes and oxygen bottles in the racks to explode in all directions. It was clear that the bomb load could explode at any moment and Jennings gave the order to bale out.

All seven men left the blazing Lancaster as best they could. The front and rear gunners turned their turrets and fell out backwards through the openings. Brian Hayes was wedged in his mid-upper turret, wearing heavy flying gear, but struggled out to find that his parachute pack underneath him was scorched. Nevertheless he clipped it on and looked towards the entry door at the rear of the starboard side: this appeared to be jammed, and the area around it was burning. He clambered forward over the burning bomb bay and managed to leave through the front escape hatch. Bert Turton and Phil George also left by this hatch, the latter, at 6 feet 2 inches, barely able to squeeze through with a forward roll. Bill Hughes, who described the inferno in the fuselage as 'like a gas ring', saw Phil disappear. He dashed to the rear door, with the flames searing his face and hands, and managed to wrench it open in time to dive out. The captain left his pilot's seat and saw that everyone seemed to have left. He also made his way to the front hatch and baled out, from a height he estimated at 20,000 feet.

David Jennings passed out, possibly from lack of oxygen, but came to when descending through three layers of clouds. He kept brushing off snowflakes to prevent his clothes from becoming wet. Then he crashed through trees and was left suspended above the ground. After a while in this awkward situation he heard voices and a light was shone in his direction. A voice said '*Kamerad*' and a rifle with a bayonet was pointed at him. He pushed the release button on his harness and fell about ten feet to the ground. The jolt jerked false teeth from his mouth and he used his lighter to

The Gasthof Zur Linde, photographed fifty-three years after Flying Officer Phil George's capture. He was taken to this inn and given glasses of beer by foreign workers, but left them untouched since he did not drink alcohol in those days. *Dietrich Alsdorf collection*

search for them. He had fallen on a farm at the edge of a pine forest and was taken to a guard house about a mile away, where he was searched and his personal equipment removed.

Phil George also remembers descending through layers of cloud. Since the heating in the Lancaster had its outlet near the navigator's chart table, he was wearing only his battledress, without extra flying clothes, and thus became extremely cold. He instinctively clung to the parachute shrouds and his hands froze to them. His memory of landing and its immediate aftermath is hazy but he now knows that he fell near the village of Bargstedt, where he was captured. It seems that he was taken the following morning to a local *Gasthof* (inn), under guard by the Volkssturm (home guard). He remembers the local ladies eyeing his parachute material with interest and foreign workers arriving, some of whom gave him a surreptitious V sign and even bought beer for him. Thus his treatment was not too bad and he was soon reunited with other crew members.

Bill Hughes also passed out when he baled out of the rear door on the starboard side. He was still in free fall when he came to, at a height he estimated at 4,000 feet, and pulled the ripcord. The parachute opened and he could see lights all around but the ground below was jet black. Then he plunged into water, for he had fallen into a canal of about twenty feet wide. He unclipped his parachute harness and swam to the bank, to find many houses. The target area was visible from searchlights and flak, so he headed in the opposite direction, running down a couple of streets and then past paddocks. A stick of bombs fell about 75 yards away, sending him flying. The main bomber force had arrived and the sky was a mass of flashes and thunderous explosions. He kept on, half running, blundering into trees and even falling into an icy cold creek. It began snowing heavily as he entered a forest, but the moon began to shine through the clouds. He headed east by the stars. His face was agonizingly hot and he sat down and rubbed snow into it, without effect. Some condensed milk from a tube in his escape kit gave it some relief.

When dawn came he could see his hands, horribly burnt with even a bare knuckle bone showing. He had no hair on his head and his clothes were partly burnt away. He eventually walked or crawled to over fifteen miles from where he had landed. His face had swollen up like a balloon, his bottom lip was terribly gashed and he could not see out of one eye. He fell asleep but was woken up in bright sunlight, with dogs barking and soldiers yelling while pointing their guns at him. He stood up and surrendered. '*Alles kaput*', they kept saying, and marched him to a barn where they relieved him of all his possessions. Then he was told to march on, under guard. A

The mid-upper turret in a Lancaster. Pilot Officer Brian Hayes DFM, jammed with his bulky flying suit, had difficulty extricating himself from his turret when Lancaster A of No 83 Squadron was hit and set on fire. *Jeremy C. Scutts collection*

German got off his bike and began to hit him, knocking him to the ground, but one of the guards hit this assailant on the head with his rifle. They arrived at another small village, where he was locked up in a room.

Brian Hayes waited until he was in an upright position before pulling the ripcord of his burnt parachute, offering up a very quick prayer as he did so. To his intense relief, the canopy opened and the harness took his weight. He hit the ground with a great jolt, causing pains to shoot up his back. Looking around in a darkness illuminated by the distant target area, he could see that he had landed in open heathland with little cover. He managed to hide his parachute in the bank of a small stream and, with the aid of his pocket compass, began to take some tentative steps south-west towards the distant Dutch border.

He made slow progress on the first day, with pain in his legs and back, passing small streams, farms and livestock. The next two days were much the same, and he ate sparingly from his escape pack. After the third night, he awoke to see sheep around him and a German shepherd. The German disappeared in one direction and Hayes sped in the other, then tried to hide. But a truck with armed youths and a Gefreiter (lance-corporal) in charge pulled up and he was quickly captured.

The Germans took him to a local cell, from where he was taken to a room for interrogation by a Hauptmann (captain) of the Wehrmacht, a local village leader and a Gestapo officer who accused him of spying and threatened incarceration in a concentration camp. But the captain confirmed that he was a genuine RAAF officer. From here, he was made to walk about eight miles to a railway station, under the guard of armed cyclists who protected him from infuriated civilians, and was placed on a train with his escorts to Dulag Luft, the interrogation centre at Oberursel near Frankfurt-am-Main.

On the second day of his capture, David Jennings was led out under armed guard and put in a truck with two airmen from another crew. The truck set off and other RAF personnel were picked up. Then someone with a badly burnt face was ushered in. 'Who are you?' said Jennings. 'I'm Billy,' said Bill Hughes, who was almost completely unrecognizable. Phil George was the next to be picked up, and the truck arrived at a large airfield. David Jennings and Bill Hughes were locked in the same cell and a request for a doctor was met solely with a roll of toilet paper, which David used to bind up Bill's wounds as best he could. The party was then transported to a train and off it went. During a stop at Kassel, the guards had to protect the prisoners from an angry mob. Eventually the train took them to the interrogation centre of Dulag Luft, where Bill Hughes was at last admitted to hospital.

The most detailed account of experiences as a PoW was provided by Brian Hayes. He arrived at Dulag Luft with his escorts, unpleasantly dirty as well as exhausted and hungry, but was immediately placed in solitary confinement. He dropped off to sleep on a low wooden bed with a paper mattress but was soon roused in his cell and led off for interrogation. He received the usual method employed by the Germans, the presentation of a bogus 'Red Cross' form requiring details of his squadron, base, name of commanding officer and other crew members, and so on. All Bomber Command aircrew had been advised about this German ruse, and Hayes merely filled in his name, number and rank, leaving the other sections blank. This was met with a mixture of threats and friendly cajoling, a return to his cell and then further bouts of interrogation.

The cell was alternately overheated and then switched to freezing cold, until after several days he was led to the chief interrogator, in the middle of the night. This officer produced a looseleaf book headed 'No 83 Squadron' and was able to describe precise details of the circumstances at Coningsby. Hayes was then asked about the methods of radio control, radar and combating German warning systems, as well as details of engines, guns and turrets. Although shaken by the extent of German knowledge, Hayes stated that he knew nothing about such matters. Eventually he was taken to the shower block, and later told that all the remainder of his crew were imprisoned except his friend Mathews. The knowledge that Albert had probably been killed was a great sadness to Hayes.

The main subject of further interrogation concerned what was called 'Village Inn', a new radar device in some rear turrets which contained an infra-red sensor for detecting night-fighters which had 'locked on' to a bomber. Of course, he denied all knowledge of this equipment and was eventually told that he would be sent to a PoW camp. He also received a warning that, if it subsequently turned out that he knew about this instrument, he would be returned to Dulag Luft and placed in solitary confinement.

Brian Hayes was then taken by train to the PoW camp, which turned out to be Stalag Luft III in Lower Silesia, now Zagan in Poland. This was the camp from which seventy-six Allied officers had escaped in the previous March, of whom fifty were murdered on Hitler's orders after recapture. To his delight, his pilot David Jennings and navigator Phil George turned up among a batch of prisoners some time later.

In his own account, David Jennings remembers that in Dulag Luft he was interrogated in a large room with a huge map of Europe on the wall. There were five German officers and two guards, and he was made to sit on a chair facing a table on which there were Luger pistols, microphones and a radio. He remained in this centre for a fortnight and was interrogated on about eight occasions. On the last day, he was allowed to visit his wireless operator Bill Hughes in hospital, before he was taken by train to Stalag Luft III.

Phil George's recollections mirror those of his pilot, except that he believes he was at Dulag Luft for about ten days and was interrogated on three or four occasions. His interrogator was a captain who stated that he had been shot down over the UK in a Heinkel III and then transported as a PoW to Canada. On the grounds of poor health, he had been repatriated to Germany, where he had been given non-combat duties. His questions mostly related to Pathfinder Force techniques, but Phil George was a recent recruit to No 83 Squadron and was able to say with some justification that he knew nothing about these matters. George and Jennings were on the train together when somewhere south of Bremen one of the guards pointed excitedly to a vertical vapour trail, which evidently was that of a V-2 rocket.

The target for No 5 Group on the night of 11/12 November 1944 was the Rhenania-Ossag oil refinery at Harburg in Germany. Lancaster A of No 83 Squadron was shot down before reaching this objective. *Author's collection*

Brian Hayes found Stalag Luft III to be a well-organized camp. Red Cross facilities were available, such as provision for studying on a wide variety of subjects. Parades for counting purposes took place twice a day and the men were locked in their huts before dark. There were about twelve rooms to a hut and his was about 12 feet by 10 feet, containing eight double-tiered beds with paper mattresses. Static and roving searchlights illuminated the whole area at night. Sentries with dogs patrolled every night, their duties even including crawling under the huts. Medical facilities in the compound were almost non-existent, although an Army medical officer from New Zealand did his best with aspirin and laxatives. More serious cases had to be moved to a small hospital named the Lazaret within the camp. Very serious or urgent cases had to be taken to the nearest city, Breslau.

The three prisoners from No 83 Squadron remained in this camp for several weeks, in the depths of winter. However, during January 1945 the Russians began another campaign and made rapid progress through western Poland until they reached the River Oder. By 29 January, the Allied prisoners were told to prepare themselves for a march further west, there being no transport available. The men in Brian Hayes's hut hastily fashioned a sledge, using bed boards as runners, and placed their packs on them. All the PoWs set off on the last day of the month, those in his hut taking turns with two pulling the sledge with harnesses, two pushing at the rear, two more on either side and two taking a rest by just marching.

The weather was freezing, well below zero, and there was heavy snow. There were constant delays and progress on the first day was slow. Nevertheless, they covered about twenty kilometres and reached the village of Kunau in the early evening. Brian Hayes remembers a touching incident while they were standing and waiting for accommodation to be found. He was leaning against the wall of a house when the door opened and an aged hand thrust a tin mug containing a hot drink at him. He will never forget this unexpected and compassionate gesture.

They were billetted in a church that night and were able to thaw out to some extent. The march resumed on the following day, passing through Wesau to Gross Selten, where they were acommodated in barns overnight. Hayes lay down on some straw but made the mistake of not removing his boots, which froze hard. These would have made marching extremely painful, but fortunately there was a day of rest. It began to thaw in the afternoon, turning the snow into ankle-deep mud. The sledge became useless and the men had to remove the essential items such as Red Cross rations and carry them in their improvised backpacks made out of scraps of blankets. They struggled on through Shon Heide to Muskau on the River Helase. Here they were housed in a glassworks where the furnaces were lit, providing a wonderful warmth.

On the next day they marched to the large town of Spremberg, which was also a rail centre. Here they were entrained in large French wagons of the 'Huit Chevaux Quarante Hommes' variety. There were sixty or seventy men in each wagon, so crowded that they had to take turns to sit down. There were no toilet facilities, so some ingenious prisoners cut holes in the wooden floors.

They remained in the wagons overnight but were allowed out for a brief spell the next morning. At last the train began to move and the prisoners were told that thcy were destined for Stalag III near Luckenwalde, to the south of Berlin. There were many delays and stops and they did not arrive until the evening of the following day. They were counted several times, searched and deloused, and entered their new huts early the next day.

David Jennings recollects that life in this camp was boring until the German guards were ordered by their high command to 'eliminate' all PoWs. The men were assembled on the parade ground, where machine guns were trained on them, but fortunately the English commander of the prisoners managed to persuade the German Camp Commandant not to carry out this order.

During this period the Russians continued their remorseless advances and by early April the Red Army had overrun the immediate area of Stalag III. This did not seem like a liberation to the Allied prisoners, for the Russians merely put their own guards on the camp and the situation became somewhat frightening, with the prisoners wondering if they were about to be shipped off to Siberia. Phil George and a Kittyhawk pilot who had been shot down over the Western Desert managed to 'escape' from this new situation and made their way to the east bank of the Elbe, where they crossed to the west via the 'Harry Truman' pontoon bridge which the US Ninth Army had constructed after a patrol of their First Army had made the memorable contact with the Russians at Torgau on 25 April.

Back in Stalag III, the Russians opened the camp to 'displaced persons', so that crowding became severe and food extremely scarce. After the German surrender, which became effective on 4 May, negotiations for the release of the PoWs were held up. On three occasions the men were loaded into trucks and then ordered out again. With thoughts of Siberia still in their minds, the PoWs were extremely relieved when on the fourth occasion they were driven to Gutterborg and crossed the floating bridge into American hands. From there they were taken to Leipzig and then flown to Brussels in DC-3 Dakotas. The next leg was by Lancaster transports back to England.

Bill Hughes died some years ago and did not leave any further record of his experience as a PoW except to say that he was moved from camp to camp and that his treatment was cruel. No information is available concerning the other two members of the crew, Stanley Burleigh and Bert Turton, except that they also became prisoners and survived the war. Burleigh's long overdue DFM was not gazetted until 1946.

As regards Albert Mathews, David Jennings was told at Dulag Luft that he had been killed in a gunfight. No details are available but it was known that he carried a revolver, which he may have used to protect himself from an angry mob. The raid on Harburg caused considerable destruction, with 119 killed and 5,205 people bombed out. He had been commissioned from warrant officer and awarded a DFC only a few days before. His body was never found: he is registered as having 'no known grave'.

Chapter 6

Act of Reconciliation

At 0310 hours on Thursday 15 March 1945, a Boeing Fortress III of RAF Bomber Command on return from an operation over Germany made a forced landing at Bassingbourn in Cambridgeshire, an airfield which was in use by the 91st Bomb Group of the US Eighth Air Force. Of course, forced landings by RAF aircraft were common in the Second World War, but this episode was exceptional since the pilot was alone at the controls, the other nine crew members being no longer on board. They were all 'reported missing'. The fates of some of them were soon made known by the Germans, but fuller circumstances did not become available to the British public until September 1992.

The Boeing Fortress III was employed by the RAF solely for radio countermeasures, being fitted with special equipment and aerials for that purpose. Only two squadrons were equipped with these machines, No 214 from February 1944 and No 223 from April 1945. *Mark Postlethwaite collection www.ww2images.com*

The Boeing B-17 Flying Fortress in Britain was one of the two major bombers employed by the USAAF on daylight raids over enemy territory, the other being the Consolidated B-24 Liberator. RAF Bomber Command employed only a few of the early B-17Ds in its night bomber role, those that survived being transferred to RAF Coastal Command for VLR (very long range) maritime work in mid-Atlantic. However, the later B-17G version was designated Fortress III by RAF Bomber Command and carried out a very useful role from February 1944 on radio countermeasures, being fitted with electronic equipment to jam enemy radar.

In a bombing role, these Fortress IIIs were capable of carrying up to 6,000 lb in their bomb-bays. In both the bomber and countermeasures roles, they were heavily armed with defensive fire against enemy fighters. There were twin 0.50 inch machine guns in the nose turret, chin turret, dorsal turret and tail turret, plus two more guns in waist positions and one in the radio compartment.

The Fortress that landed at Bassingbourn was one of these special machines, serial HB799 letter K of No 214 Squadron, based at Sculthorpe in Norfolk and forming part of Bomber Command's No 100 Group. The target for the night was the Wintershall synthetic oil refinery in the town of Lützendorf, near Leipzig in south-east Germany. The main bombing force for this operation consisted of 244 Lancasters, eighteen of which did not return. The raid resulted in what was later described from interpretation of reconnaissance photographs as 'moderate damage' to the target.

The Operations Record Book of No 214 Squadron in The National Archives provides a detailed account of the events that occurred within this machine during the sortie. At 1730 hours on the night of 14 March 1945, it took off from RAF Sculthorpe. The captain was Flight Lieutenant John C. Wynne DFC, who headed a crew of ten.

This crew completed their radar countermeasures mission and were on the way back to Sculthorpe when, at 2320 hours, their aircraft was attacked from below by a nightfighter which scored hits on the port inner engine. The enemy aircraft may have been a Junkers Ju88, armed with upward-firing 20 mm cannons. At the time, the Fortress was flying at 3,000 feet and about forty miles east of Pforzheim in west Germany. Wynne took violent evasive action and managed to shake off the attacker. About eight minutes later, the engine began to burn badly. It had lost oil pressure and Wynne ordered it to be shut down, but this proved impossible because the controls to it had been severed.

Wynne altered course on to 280° for the airfield at Reims in north-east France, which was in Allied hands, but warned the crew to stand by for baling out. He held this course for about five minutes, but then the engine began to burn furiously and also vibrate the whole aircraft. There was a serious danger of the port wing catching fire, which would have been disastrous. Wynne had no alternative but to order the crew to jump: this was accomplished within a few minutes, from a height of 5,000 feet. It later transpired that by this time they were flying near the German town of Bühl.

After the crew left, Wynne became entangled with his oxygen tube and could not free himself quickly. At this point the fire began to die down unexpectedly and he managed to control the aircraft by standing with one foot in each seat position. The fire did not get worse and he decided to continue in this attitude, hoping to reach Reims. After about another thirty minutes, the fire seemed to die out almost completely and he thought he could bring the aircraft all the way back to England. His 'George' automatic pilot had become unserviceable but he managed to trim the aircraft sufficiently to go forward on three occasions to the navigator's position, where he eventually found the log and the relevant maps.

Wynne then set course on 300° for England, intending to land at the first airfield he saw. The engine began to burn again after thirty more minutes but died down once more, apart from glowing and emitting sparks. He crossed the north coast of France at about 0240 hours and before long spotted the white cliffs of Beachy Head. He saw an airfield and circled it, firing the colours of the day, but there was no response and he continued on a course of 300° for another fifteen minutes. He then saw a searchlight and fired a red signal, while circling and flashing landing lights. The searchlight gave a homing which took him straight over London, which was partly lit up at this very late stage of the war.

He then headed due north and eventually found an airfield with its landing lights on. He made two circuits and fired another cartridge, receiving a green in return, which thus gave permission to land. The port tyre burst on touchdown, but the aircraft ran along the runway for about 1,000 yards before going down on the rim of the wheel. The propeller on the damaged engine flew off and made a hole in the nose, but otherwise the pilot and the Fortress were safe. The aircraft stopped, another cartridge was fired, and the crash waggon arrived. Wynne collected his kit, put a guard on the aircraft and reported to Flying Control. After learning that he was at the USAAF base of Bassingbourn, he made a telephone call to base.

I first researched this matter after receiving a letter dated 1 March 1991 from the Reverend Curt-Jürgen Heinemann-Grüder, a retired pastor living in a village near Pforzheim. He had written to the Public Record Office (as The National Archives was then named) asking for information about the

The British War Cemetery at Dürnbach, set in the mountains of Bavaria, is considered the most beautiful of all the war cemeteries in Germany. Nine of every ten men in the graves were killed while flying with RAF Bomber Command. *Courtesy of Reverend Curt-Jürgen Heinemann-Grüder*

nine men who had baled out, but required some research on behalf of his 'Cross of Nails' group, formed as the local representation of Coventry Cathedral's international symbol of reconciliation. These parishioners had learnt from a local article by an anonymous author that five of the nine RAF men had been murdered, and they wished to arrange a plaque to their memory. It was particularly necessary to know the precise names of those men who had not survived.

Memorials to commemorate RAF men who lost their lives in the Second World War are frequently erected, but it is a very unusual state of affairs when German citizens decide to put up a bronze tablet to the memory of those who were killed after participating in a bombing attack on their country. Yet this decision was taken after the Queen Mother and the German President, Dr Richard von Weizsäcker, had attended a service of reconciliation at Coventry on 14 November 1990, to mark the 50th anniversary of the destruction of the cathedral and the deaths of 580 civilians in the bombing.

I found the full names of these five men from the Commonwealth War Graves Commission, as well as the above details from the Public Record

A photograph taken on the night of 23/24 February 1945 over Pforzheim by a Lancaster of No 156 Squadron from the Pathfinder Force at Wyton in Cambridgeshire. The attacking force consisted of 367 Lancasters and thirteen Mosquitos, and the Pathfinders marked the city accurately as a target for 'area bombing'. The raid lasted for only twenty-two minutes and caused immense devastation. It was estimated that 83 per cent of the buildings were destroyed and 17,600 people killed from a population which in 1939 had numbered about 79,000. *Courtesy of Squadron Leader Howard W. Lees*

Office. It was also recorded that the five men were buried in Dürnbach War Cemetery, a village south-east of Munich in Bavaria. This information was passed on to the Reverend Heinemann-Grüder, who promptly sent a cheque via myself to the Royal Air Force Benevolent Fund.

Another photograph from the same sequence taken on the night of 23/24 February 1945 over Pforzheim, showing more clearly a Lancaster top right as well as the terrible firestorm which swept through the centre of the city. Such night photographs were taken with the aid of a flashbomb dropped to explode above the ground at the same time as a negative in the F24 camera carried by the aircraft was exposed. Most of this bombing took place from about 8,000 feet. Ten Lancasters were shot down over the target and two more crashed in France during their return flight. *Author's collection*

The events that took place after the nine men baled out could then be reconstructed from official sources, personal recollections of those who survived, and from subsequent newspaper reports. All landed by parachute and began to walk westwards in the direction of the Rhine. Eight of them were soon captured and taken to the town of Bühl. The navigator, Flying

IM GEDENKEN

AN DIE AM 17./18. MÄRZ 1945 AUF NS. BEFEHL
UMGEBRACHTEN BRITISCHEN FLIEGER

FO. HAROLD FROST
FO. GORDON HALL
FLT. LT. SIDNEY MATTHEWS
FLT. SGT. EDWARD PERCIVAL
FO. JAMES VINALL

VATER VERGIB LK 23.34.

DEN LEBENDEN ZUR MAHNUNG
1992

The bronze plaque on an outside wall of Huchenfeld church, near Pforzheim in Germany. It was unveiled on 18 November 1992 and is dedicated to five men from the crew of Fortress III serial HB799 of the RAF's No 214 Squadron based at Sculthorpe in Norfolk. An English translation reads:

IN MEMORY

On the days of 17/18 March 1945 on Nazi orders
British airmen were killed

FO. Harold Frost
FO. Gordon Hall
Flt.Lt. Sidney Matthews
Flt.Sgt. Edward Percival
FO. James Vinall

FATHER FORGIVE

Let the living be warned
1992

Courtesy of Reverend Curt-Jürgen Heinemann-Grüder

Officer George Pow DFC, had injured his ankle and was sent to hospital at Strasbourg, very fortunately for him in the light of future events. The Germans thought that they had captured the entire crew, but the first navigator, Flying Officer Dudley P. Heal, was found later. Both he and Pow were eventually liberated by the Allies.

The remaining seven men were taken in stages to the village of Huchenfeld, about two miles from Pforzheim on the foot of the Black Forest. Here they were locked up for the night of 17 March in the boiler room of a kindergarten, guarded by two members of the Luftwaffe. Up to this time their treatment from their guards had been fair, although they had spent three nights without sleep and felt uncomfortable and grimy. They were given a sparse meal and then settled down on logs of wood and piles of coke to go to sleep.

During that evening, fanatical Nazis of the SA 'terror' militia (Sturmabteilung) in the vicinity learnt of the presence of the RAF men. Feelings against the RAF were running very high since, only a few nights before, on 23/24 February, 367 Lancasters and thirteen Mosquitos had been despatched for the area bombing of the city of Pforzheim. The Pathfinders had marked the target very accurately and immense devastation had been caused in bombing with high explosives and incendiaries, concentrated into only twenty-two minutes. The only possible justification for this raid was that the city had been a centre for watchmaking before the war, and some of these specialists were probably employed on making precision instruments for the Wehrmacht.

It was estimated that 83 per cent of Pforzheim's buildings were destroyed while over 17,600 people were killed from a population which in 1939 had numbered about 79,000, less than half the population of Coventry. The destruction of Pforzheim and the resulting civilian deaths were *proportionally* even worse than the notorious raids on Dresden by the RAF and the USAAF on 13–15 February 1945. It was believed that the normal population of Dresden of 630,000 had swollen to over a million by refugees fleeing from the advancing Red Army, and the highest official estimate of deaths was 60,000.

Many of those sheltering in the village of Huchenfeld were refugees from the destruction of Pforzheim. Led by several of the fanatical Nazis, a group of the Hitler Jugend (Hitler Youth) and some middle-aged and elderly men of the Volkssturm (Home Guard) burst into the kindergarten and dragged out the seven RAF men, forcing them towards the graveyard of the village church. Three of the RAF men managed to struggle free and escape across fields in the confusion and darkness. These were the flight engineer Flying

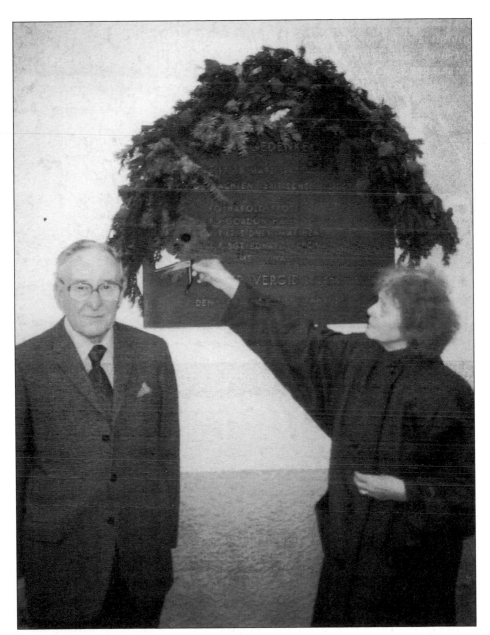

Thomas Henry Tate from Chalfont St Giles, the second wireless operator in Fortress III serial HB799 of the RAF's No 214 Squadron, photographed on 2 April 1995 with Gertrüd Heinemann-Grüder in front of the bronze plaque at Huchenfeld church, near Pforzheim in Germany. Tate baled out of the aircraft on the night of 14/15 March 1945 and then managed to escape from the executioners intent on killing the crew members, before becoming a PoW for the remaining few weeks of the war. *Courtesy of Reverend Curt-Jürgen Heinemann-Grüder*

The statue of Air Chief Marshal Sir Arthur Harris, Commander-in-Chief of RAF Bomber Command, unveiled in 1992 outside the RAF church of St Clements Dane in Aldwych. *Author's collection*

Officer James W. Vinall, the second wireless operator Flying Officer Thomas H. Tate and the air gunner Flight Sergeant Norman J. Bradley DFM.

The remaining four men were taken to the graveyard and shot by the German youths, who were given automatic guns and ordered to carry out the executions. Those killed were air gunner Flying Officer Harold Frost DFM, air gunner Flight Sergeant Edward A. Percival DFM, first wireless operator Flying Officer Gordon A. Hall and air gunner Flight Lieutenant Sidney C. Matthews DFC. Vinall was recaptured the following day at Dillstein, a suburb of Pforzheim, and also shot. The other two men were recaptured separately but were fortunate enough to be sent to a PoW camp.

Of the two men who escaped murder by the Hitler Youth, Thomas Tate was able to give an account of his experiences, in the course of the investigation that began in 1991. He related that, after parachuting safely, he and Bradley were picked up quickly and taken to an interrogation centre. By Friday 16 March they were locked up in the civil jail in Bühl, together with Frost, Vinall, Hall, Percival and Matthews. On the following day the seven RAF men were taken by lorry, with five guards, to Pforzheim. They were then escorted on foot through the appalling destruction of the city, during which they were pelted with rubble by onlookers. Following this, they climbed up the long path to Huchenfeld.

On arrival at the kindergarten, they were sent down an iron staircase into the cellar and given a bucket of water, in which they washed their socks. Tate then went to sleep on a pile of coke but was awakened in a dazed condition to find himself being dragged by several men out into the street. Someone beat him over the head with his fists and he saw a crowd of hostile people while being forced along the street towards the churchyard. He was stopped by the open door of a barn, with ropes hanging from solid beams, and he thought he was about to be hanged. He somehow managed to break free and ran back up the street in his bare feet, dodging people and hearing a shot fired at him from behind. He turned right and raced between houses which fortunately led him into the thick Black Forest. He covered himself with leaves and awaited the dawn.

As soon as it was light, he worked his way down a steep hillside to a winding path in a valley and then climbed another hill to a flat area of dense forest, in which there were many deer. After about three hours some twenty soldiers appeared, by which time his bare feet were so sore that he had no alternative but to surrender. The officer in charge was an older and kindly man, who lent him a pair of soft shoes when they moved on to a local barracks. During the afternoon, he was taken with two Luftwaffe guards to

Three visitors to the British War Cemetery at Dürnbach in Bavaria, photographed on 22 June 1994. Left to right: Gilbert Taylor from Birkdale; his wife Marjorie Taylor; the retired Pastor Curt-Jürgen Heinemann-Grüder. Marjorie Taylor's first husband was the air gunner Flying Officer Harold Frost DFM, who baled out of Fortress III serial HB799 of the RAF's No 214 Squadron on the night of 14/15 March 1945 and was one of those murdered by the Hitler Youth under the orders of the SA. They are standing behind his headstone. *Courtesy of Reverend Curt-Jürgen Heinemann-Grüder*

the local railway station. While in the waiting room, another hostile crowd gathered, but was kept away by the armed guards.

Eventually the train arrived and he was put on it with the two guards. It was destined for Ludwigsburg, a city in south-west Germany. The guards were friendly, speaking to him in imperfect English, assuring him that his comrades were safe, and sharing their bread and schnapps with him. One even took off his coat to shelter him against the cold. He was placed in a cell at Ludwigsburg and his borrowed shoes were returned. Thereafter, he was treated with decency, and eventually liberated by the Allies.

The SA men who were responsible for the atrocity at Huchenfeld seem to have believed that by forcing the youths to fire on the PoWs, they would escape justice themselves. If so, they were stupid as well as vicious. It must have been obvious that Germany had already lost the war. A week later, on 24 March 1945, French troops from the advancing Allied forces occupied Huchenfeld. Evidence of the five deaths was plain to see, for a line of five

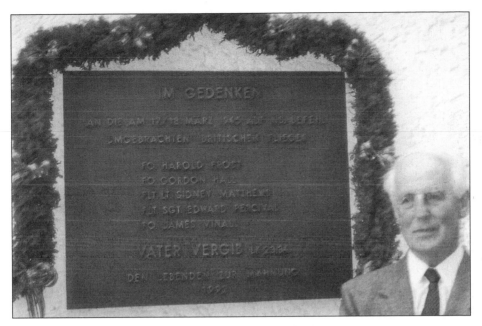

The pilot of Fortress III serial HB799 of the RAF's No 214 Squadron, John G. Wynne from North Wales, photographed on 19 November 1994 alongside the bronze plaque at Huchenfeld church, near Pforzheim in Germany. *Courtesy of Reverend Curt-Jürgen Heinemann-Grüder*

new crosses in the churchyard marked their graves. Officials of the War Crimes Commission arrived in the village, gathering evidence and making arrests. The bodies were exhumed and examined forensically.

Following my initial researches at the Public Record Office in 1991, I found a large file which included details of trials at the British Military Court for War Criminals relating to Huchenfeld. These began at Steele in Essen on 5 August 1946, when twenty-two Germans who were present at the murders of the five RAF men were tried. One of the Nazi leaders had committed suicide shortly beforehand. The RAF survivors Tate and Bradley gave evidence at the trials. It is not desirable to reopen old wounds by recording the names of the Germans, but five were acquitted, fourteen were sentenced to various terms of imprisonment and three were hanged. The court passed lenient sentences of three years on the convicted members of the Hitler Youth, some of whom were only 15 or 16 years old at the time. Their remaining terms of imprisonment were commuted by the military governor after about two years.

During this later investigation in 1991/2, very few of the parishioners in Huchenfeld – or indeed the citizens of Pforzheim – had any knowledge of the murder of the five RAF men. Most of them had been deeply shocked by the revelations in their local newspaper during the spring. A fund was set up by the local Protestant pastor, the Reverend Horst Zorn, and his presbyters for a bronze plaque to the memory of the five RAF men. There was opposition from some quarters, which was intensified when the statue of Air Chief Marshal Sir Arthur T. Harris was unveiled in May 1992 outside the RAF Church of St Clements Dane in Aldwych. He was known in Germany to have been the man who, after his appointment as Air Officer Commander-in-Chief of Bomber Command on 22 February 1942, did his utmost to intensify the area bombing of German cities to bring the country to its knees, instead of carrying out the selective bombing of military targets such as oil installations advocated by other strategists.

However, the original intention of most of the people at Huchenfeld prevailed, for they were supported by local principals and given extra impetus when the widow of Flying Officer Harold 'Jack' Frost, Mrs Marjorie Taylor, was traced and agreed to attend a service with her second husband, Gilbert Taylor. Their travelling expenses were paid by Horst Zorn.

On Wednesday 18 November 1992, the service was held at Huchenfeld church, with Mrs Taylor, her husband Gilbert and the Reverend Paul Oestreicher from Coventry Cathedral among the congregation, as was the mayor of Pforzheim, Joachim Becker. The British press had learnt of the event and several reporters of national newspapers were present at the ceremony. At the close of the service, the Reverend Paul Oestreicher presented Huchenfeld with a Cross of Nails.

The plaque on an outside wall of the church was then unveiled in the presence of a large crowd. It proved to be a very emotional occasion. One elderly man was shaking badly, supported by his daughter. He clasped the Reverend Heinemann-Grüder and sobbed while saying he had been one of the Hitler Youth who had shot the RAF men; he then left without giving his name. Marjorie Taylor had been apprehensive about attending, but said she had met nothing but warmth and kindness, with some people begging forgiveness.

This was not quite the end of the matter. The former RAF pilot John Wynne, farming in Wales, felt that some token from Britain should be given to the children in the new kindergarten at Huchenfeld. He contacted the Reverend Horst Zorn, who said that, if he insisted, a rocking-horse would be appreciated.

Thus, on the clear summer's day of 19 June 1994, a hand-carved rocking-horse from South Wales stood in a verandah outside the kindergarten, following a service in Huchenfeld church. A large crowd of excited children with their parents attended the ceremony, together with a band. The reins were given to the little head girl of the kindergarten, Maximiliana, who climbed on the horse and rode it with delight; it had been named 'Hoffnung' (Hope). The band played the resounding tune known in the English-speaking world as 'Roll out the Barrel' or 'Beer Barrel Polka'; this had always been named 'Rosamunde' in Germany but had been composed in 1927 by Jaromir Vejvoda in Czechoslovakia with the title of 'Polka of Modrany'.

The wishes of the Queen Mother and Dr Richard von Weizsäcker had become a reality in Huchenfeld.

Bibliography

Chapter One: The Enemy Within
Books
Foot, M.R.D. *SOE in France*. London: HMSO, 1966.
Henshaw, Alex. *Sigh for a Merlin*. London: John Murray, 1979.

Newspapers
The Times, 16 April 1947.
The Daily Mirror, 18 April 1947, 29 April 1947.

The National Archives
AIR 27/441   No 43 Squadron, Operations Record Book.
AIR 27/2088   No 605 Squadron, Operations Record Book.
AIR 27/2089   No 605 Squadron, Operations Record Book.
AIR 28/173   RAF Cosford, Operations Record Book.
AIR 29/962   RAF Kemble, Operations Record Book.
AIR 29/682   No 55 Operational Training Unit, Operations Record Book.
AIR 29/968   RAF Hullavington, Operations Record Book.
AIR 29/978   RAF Dumfries, Operations Record Book.
AIR 29/996   RAF Lyneham, Operations Record Book.

Chapter Two: The First Skyjack
Books
Barker, Ralph. *Down in the Drink*. London: Chatto & Windus, 1969.
Ufficio Storico Della Marina Militare. Roma, 1942–1959:
Vol. 3. *Navi Perdute – Navi Militare*.
Vol. 7. *La Difesa della Traffico con l'Africa Settentriole*.

The National Archives
AIR 27/1341   No 217 Squadron, Operations Record Book.

Chapter Three: Death of a Maverick
Books and Reports
Chorley, W.R. *RAF Bomber Command Losses of the Second World War, Vol. 4.* Hinckley: Midland Counties, 1996.
Emanovsky, Paul D. *Anthropological Summary: Remains of Wg Cdr Adrian Warburton.* US Army Central Indentification Laboratory, 22 November 2002.
Hinsley, F.H. *et al. British Intelligence in the Second World War, Volume 3, Part 1.* London: HMSO, 1984.
Spooner, Tony. *Warburton's War.* London: William Kimber, 1987.
Staerck, Christopher & Sinnott, Paul. *Luftwaffe: The Allied Intelligence Files.* Washington, DC: Brassey's Inc., 2002.

Newspaper
Ratcliffe, Christina. 'The Merry Month of May.' *Sunday Times*, 18 May 1980.

The National Archives
AIR 2/111   Combined Operational Planning Committee, 3 April 1944.
AIR 27/2007   No 540 Squadron, Operations Record Book.
AIR 28/61   RAF Benson, Operations Record Book.
AIR 40/201   Interpretation Report, 8.2.1945. Jet-Propelled Aircraft.
HO 30/608   Interpretation Report on Landsbeg A Lech Airfield, 24.4.1944.

Chapter Four: The Last Months of St-Ex
Books and Articles
Armitage, Sir Michael *et al. Chronicle of the Second World War.* Harlow: Longmans, 1990.
Cate, Curtis. *Antoine de Saint-Exupéry.* New York: Putnam, 1970.
Décot, Daniel. *Cette Journée de 31 Juillet.* Paris: Icare, Spring 1991.
Laage, Hermann. *Luftlangdung im Vercors.* Spandau: Der Landser, Nr 2451.
Lucas, James. *The Last Year of the German Army. May 1944–May 1945.* London: Arms & Armour Press, 1944.
Molony, C. F. & Flynn, C. *History of the Second World War: The Mediterranean and Middle East, Volume 5.* London: HMSO, 1975.

Phillips, John. *Adieu, Saint-Exupéry!* Freiburg im Breislau: Eulen Verlag, 1994.

Schiff, Stacey. *Saint-Exupéry: A Biography*. London: Chatto & Windus, 1994.

Smith, Maxwell A. *Knight of the Air*. London: Cassell, 1959.

Chapter Five: Lancaster Overdue
Books
Halley, James J. *The Squadrons of the Royal Air Force & Commonwealth 1918–1988*. Tonbridge: Air-Britain, 1988.

Middlebrook, Martin & Everitt, Chris. *The Bomber Command War Diaries 1939–1945*. London: Penguin, 1990.

Thetford, Owen. *Aircraft of the Royal Air Force since 1918*. London: Putnam, 1988.

The National Archives
AIR 27/699   No 83 Squadron, Operations Record Book.

Chapter Six: Act of Reconciliation
Newspaper and Magazine
The Independent, 24 November 1992.
Saga Magazine, September 1994.

The National Archives
AIR 27/1324   No 214 Squadron, Operations Record Book.
WO 235/235   British Military Court for the Trial of War Criminals.

Index